BEYOND THE PAGE

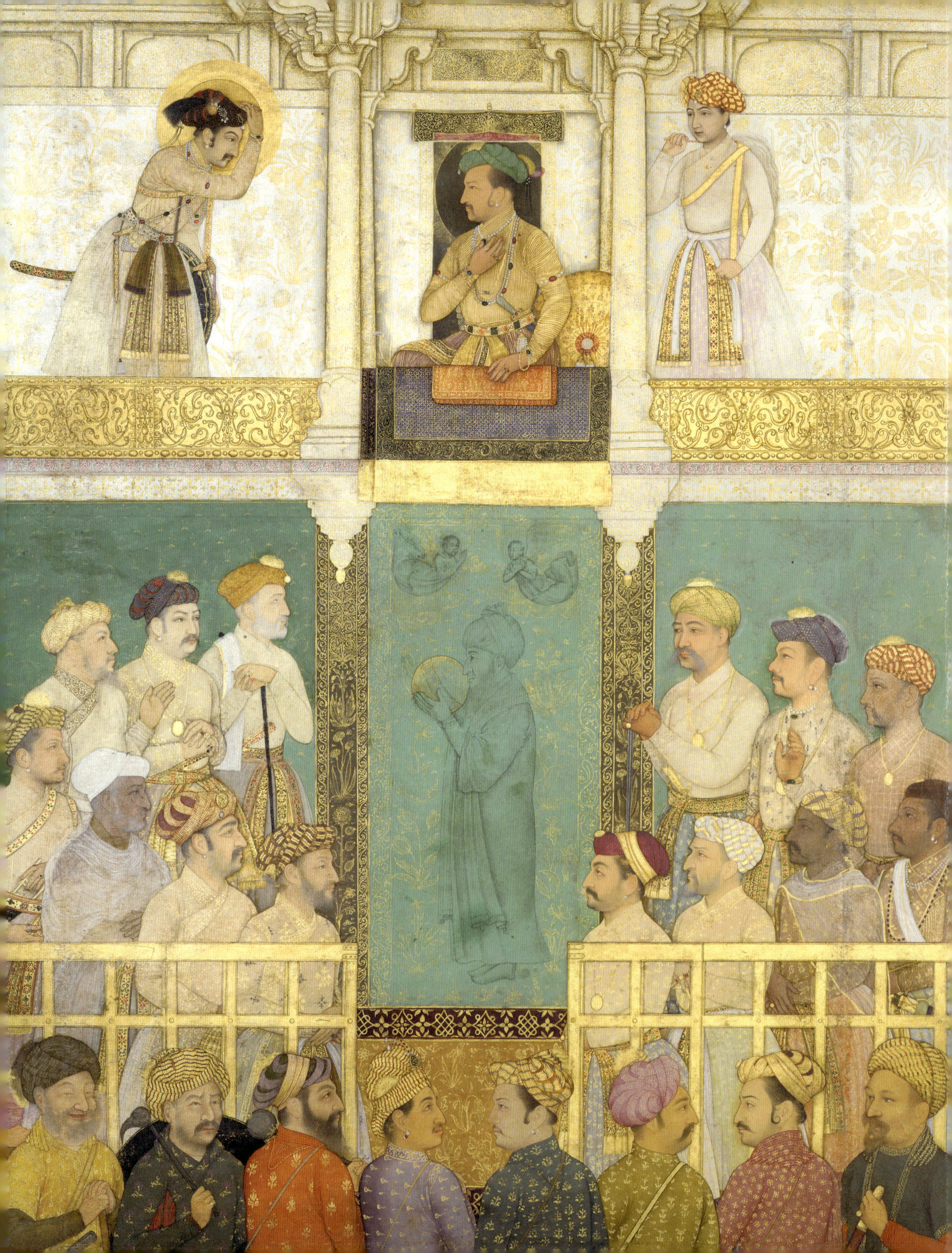

BEYOND THE PAGE

South Asian Miniatures and Britain, 1600 to now

EDITED BY
FAY BLANCHARD
& ANTHONY SPIRA

PWP Gallery

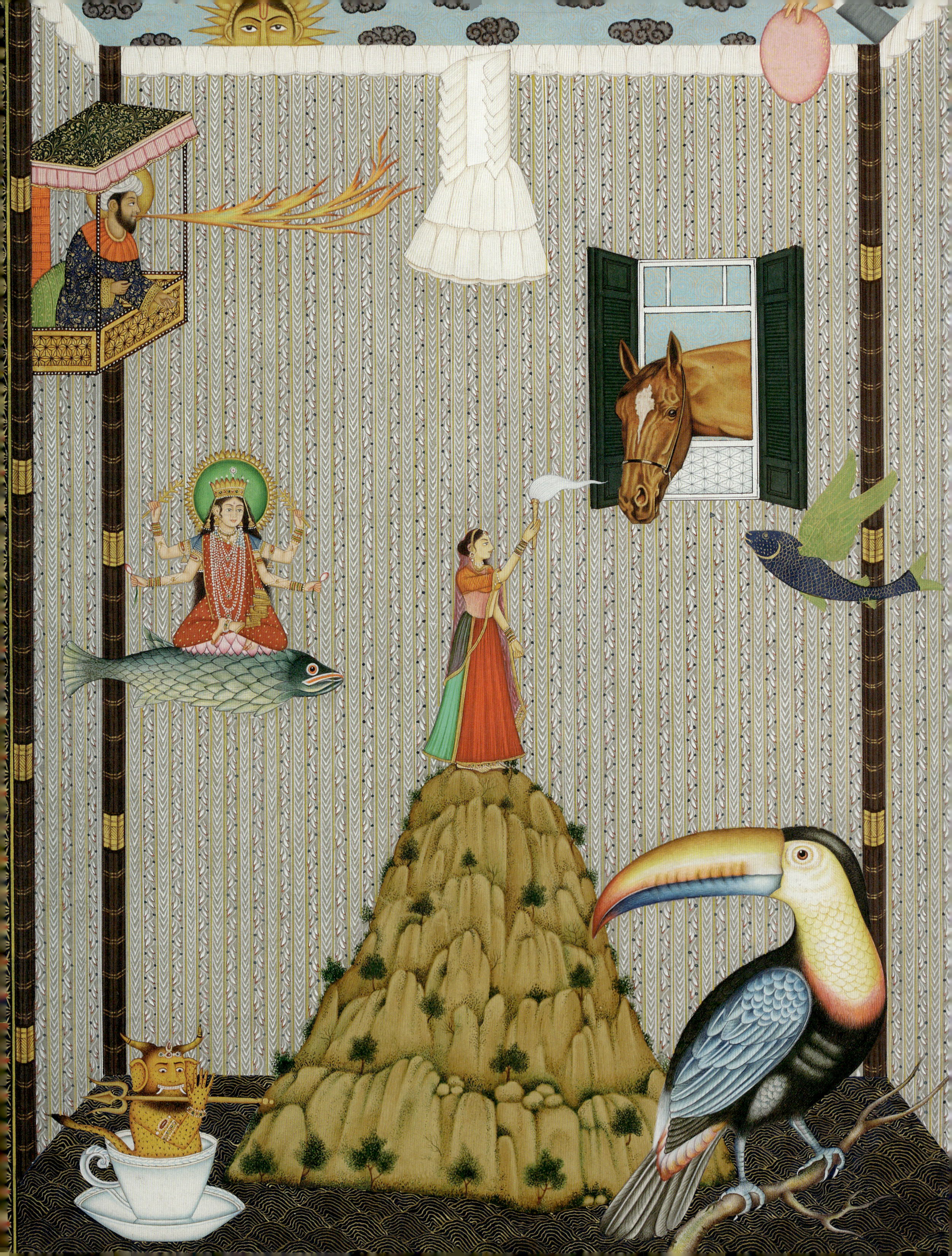

CONTENTS

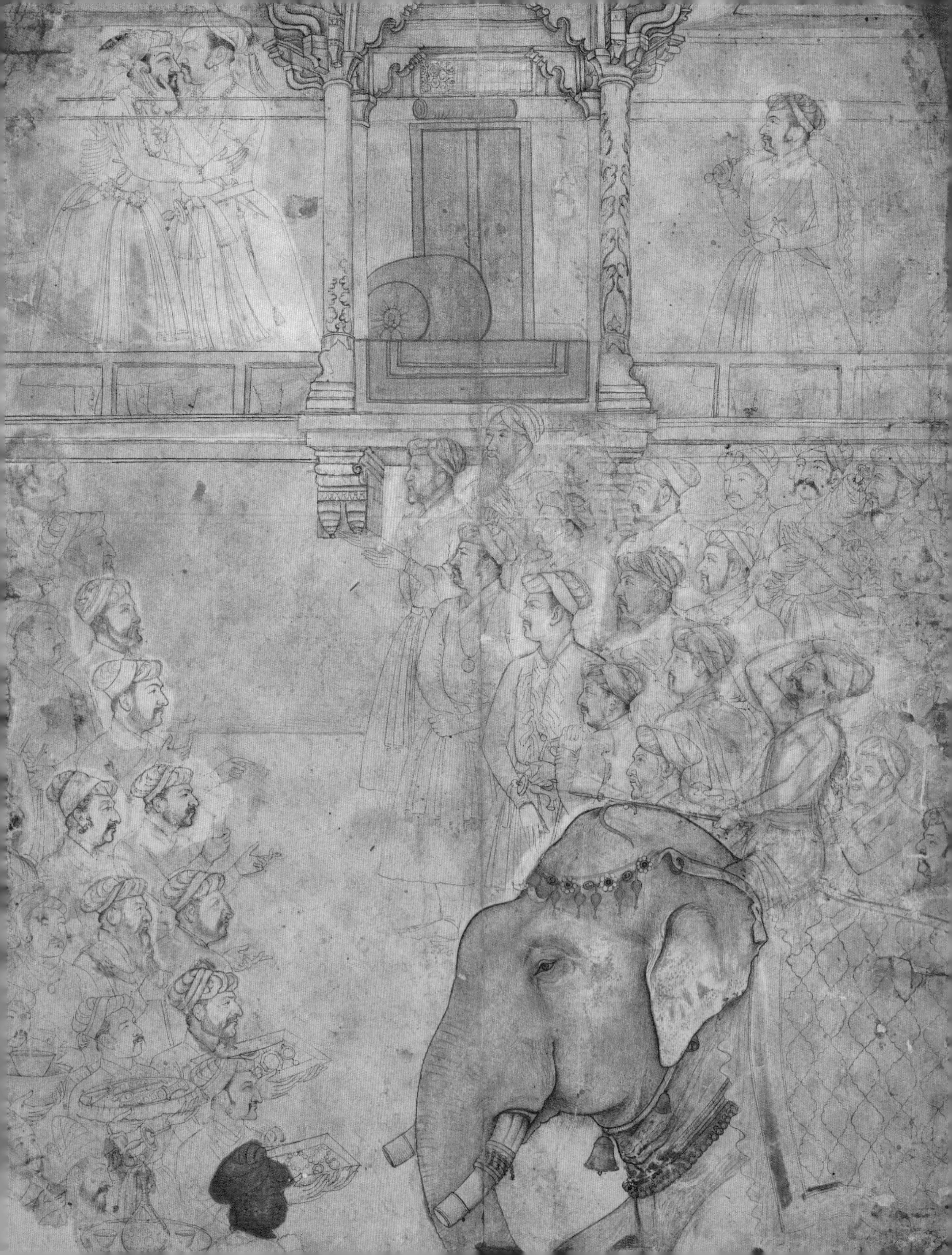

INTRODUCTION

This book, together with the exhibition it accompanies, addresses an important but overlooked area of British art history. It explores the role that Britain's incursions into South Asia played in the evolution of the miniature painting tradition, and its revival as an aesthetic and critical force in the twentieth and twenty-first centuries.

This subject covers a vast time frame and geographical area. So-called miniature painting itself is almost a catch-all term that contains multiple styles, approaches and subjects for paintings produced in the Indian subcontinent. The earliest dated Indian miniature paintings are illustrations of Buddhist and Jain texts from around 1200. By the 1500s, interactions between different artistic communities within South Asia and beyond led to new techniques and attitudes, some of which consolidated into regional styles. Miniature painting flourished in the ateliers of the Mughal, Rajput and Deccani royal courts up to the 1700s. Smaller family workshops catered for increased patronage from then onwards, including British patrons who introduced new media and themes to Indian miniature painting. Our story focuses on a handful of key encounters, in both directions, between South Asia and Britain. It is driven by the legacies that continue to hold a fascination for contemporary artists today and presents dialogues across generations and continents.

The term 'miniature' itself was first used in India by colonialists drawing connections to European illuminated manuscripts popular in the Middle Ages. Both forms shared a number of features such as intimacy of scale, bright colours and intricate application, all bound up in a book format, often illustrating religious iconography. Their portable nature also meant it was easy to acquire them. Ever since James I's envoy to the Mughal court was presented with Mughal royal portraits around 1617, South Asian miniature paintings have been amassed in public collections in Britain. In her essay for this publication, Emily Hannam charts the various processes of acquisition, whether gifts, exchanges, straight purchases or loot; and, later, direct commissioning of South Asian artists by officials from the East India Company. These include some of the finest depictions of royal portraits, court ceremonies and military victories commissioned by the Mughal emperors Akbar, Jahangir and Shah Jahan. They also include beautiful illustrations of popular literary and religious texts, such as the works of Persian classical poets and the Hindu *Ramayana*.

To produce these extraordinary paintings, the emperors employed large workshops, often comprising dozens of painters, many of whom had specialist skills in depicting flora, fauna, battle scenes, courtly proceedings or portraits. Some artists learned the trade as apprentices, usually in family workshops, making pigments from vegetable, insect or animal substances, and minerals such as precious stones and pure gold and silver, ground into a fine dust. Brushes were made from animal hair, most notably from squirrels. The many stages of colouring, built up layer by layer to enamel-like thickness, were applied to wasli, or handmade paper, before being polished with stone.

Produced as book illustrations or single works to be kept in an album or protected by a paper or cloth wrapper, the paintings were frequently framed within richly decorated borders and, in the case of some Mughal albums, accompanied by elaborate calligraphy. In terms of composition, individual paintings might use multiple perspectives, and bodies are often presented frontally with heads in profile, in order to present a whole story within a single scene.

This small-scale, portable quality also provided an ease of exchange and influence that could cross borders and continents. Since the sixteenth century, Jesuits visiting the Mughal courts had brought examples of works from Europe, introducing Western subjects, ideas of perspective and sense of modelling; James I was also using British paintings as diplomatic currency. At the same time, European artists began to be inspired by the systems of representation found in South Asian miniature paintings. Rembrandt is known to have been one of the earliest admirers of Mughal art, having copied a number of miniatures in the 1650s. His contemporary Willem Schellinks further integrated Mughal qualities into his paintings, and was clearly influenced by a visit to the Bodleian Library, Oxford, in the 1660s.

After the decline of the Mughal empire in the eighteenth century, European officers employed by the East India Company became a new source of patronage for court artists. This gave birth to the 'Company School' of painting as colonial patrons imposed European standards on South Asian pictorial conventions. This hybrid style of the miniaturists' remarkable skills and the European drive to create visual documentation of their new empire resulted in incredible records of architecture, street scenes and flora and fauna.

In the early twentieth century, in reaction against the British Raj and academic styles promoted in India and in British art schools, a new approach emerged. The Bengal School was a nationalist and avant-garde movement that rejected Western materialism and embraced Indian spiritual ideas. A revival of interest in miniature painting saw its potential as a means of cultural resistance to colonialism. This new direction was fuelled by the British art teacher E.B. Havell at the Calcutta School of Art, alongside the artist Abanindranath Tagore, a close friend of London-based artist and president of the Royal College of Art, William Rothenstein. A new Indian modernism was launched, with figures, including Samuel Fyzee-Rahamin and Abdur Rahman Chughtai, both of whom studied in London for short periods, the former at the Royal Academy, under John Singer Sargent. Chughtai, in Lahore, created an Islamic visual identity by combining Mughal tradition, art nouveau and graphic influences from Aubrey Beardsley, for example. Most importantly, these cross-cultural exchanges led to the adoption of the miniature tradition as an anti-colonial gesture, an attitude which endures to this day, resonating powerfully as we navigate the complex legacies of empire.

After independence and Partition, in 1947, the revival of interest in the miniature tradition evolved along different lines on each side of the border, but London played a central role, as Hammad Nasar explains in his essay. Artists Gulammohammed Sheikh from Baroda and Zahoor ul Akhlaq from Lahore came to London in the 1960s in thrall to the excitement of contemporary Western art. While in London, they both discovered the depth of holdings of miniature paintings at the Victoria and Albert Museum (V&A), seeing many iconic works in the flesh, rather than in reproduction, for the first time. While Sheikh enjoyed the multiple focal points and what he called the 'temperature' of the colours in miniatures, Akhlaq exploited their formal properties – the borders, framing devices and application of paint. The work of their British contemporary, the painter Howard Hodgkin, a frequent visitor to the subcontinent, who collected large numbers of miniature paintings himself, also reprises elements from his Indian interests, most notably, perhaps, his use of horizontal bands of colour. Sheikh's and Akhlaq's experiences in London, totally independent of one another, radically changed the course of their practices, as Nasar explains, and they both returned to their respective homes determined to set up miniature painting workshops and to share their developments with a growing community of artists.

In Baroda, Sheikh was a key figure in the Baroda Group and the National Figurative Movement, both of which identified historical Indian traditions as the bedrock of their approaches. Vivid storytelling was also central to the practices of Bhupen Khakhar and Nilima Sheikh, both of whom also studied in Baroda, as did the younger artist N.S. Harsha. Nilima Sheikh was also an important contributor to the rise of the women's movement in Indian art in the 1980s, alongside Arpita Singh, whose formative years were in New Delhi. Their subjects would often reflect feminist themes such as injustice and inequality, and signal their interests in crafts such as weaving, as they and a growing number of female artists were to raid the traditionally patriarchal workshops of the royal courts in their work.

In Pakistan, miniature workshops at the National College of Arts (NCA) in Lahore – originally led by Rudyard Kipling's father, Lockwood Kipling, and where Chughtai had studied in the 1930s – became a full-fledged department founded by Akhlaq in 1985. Here, many of the most famous names in South Asian contemporary art today learned their trade and studied Mughal miniature painting from British and American catalogues and collections published online. The writer Virginia Whiles, who was a lecturer at the NCA from 2000 to 2002, suggests that 'collective action has permeated the consequences of Pakistan's traumatic birth as a nation'[1] but, despite sometimes being grouped under the term 'neo-miniature', these artists all developed strong independent practices. Their work is invariably immersed in the technical rigours of the South Asian miniature tradition but intent on reflecting contemporary politics and socioeconomic realities.

Shahzia Sikander's breakthrough work *The Scroll* (1989–90, cat. 96) is an epic panorama that reimagines a miniature-inspired setting from a feminist perspective; Imran Qureshi's trademark 'blood splats' recall various traditional rituals alongside brutal current affairs, including bombings in Lahore; Nusra Latif Qureshi layers imagery from East and West, from the past and the present, to fuse global cultural and historical imagery; Ali Kazim reinterprets the art of the past through carefully crafted portraits of humans and animals. Others offer pointed critiques of the miniature tradition and its legacies: Hamra Abbas questions the power structures behind ownership of the paintings; Muhammad Zeeshan confounds its principles by working on a monumental scale, swapping squirrel hair for graphite and wasli for industrial sandpaper; and Rashid Rana inserts commercial advertising into Mughal form, to undermine the reverence ascribed to the miniature tradition. While at times providing a critique, these artists also extend the possibilities of miniature painting, ensuring its continued relevance. Despite this wide variety of distinct approaches, these artists are all rooted in a common appreciation of the foundations of miniature painting, in a shared affinity and attitude.[2] Their paintings, sculptures, installations and films – which burst out 'beyond the page' – are all underpinned by a certain intimacy, rigour of application, structural play, political critique and utopian spirit.

The idea of the workshop, which was central to how South Asian miniatures were produced, also retains a striking relevance today. By valuing collaboration and collective means of production, *Karkhana* (2003, cat. 117), meaning 'workshop', is a key work in this project. It was produced by six artists – Imran Qureshi, Aisha Khalid, Hasnat Mahmood, Nusra Latif Qureshi, Talha Rathore and Saira Wasim – each of whom started two paintings before mailing them to the next artist, who would then intervene before sending them on. The result is twelve playful layered paintings, produced by all six artists, reinventing the Mughal workshop in the age of FedEx.

A number of British artists also realize work through collaborations in South Asia. David Alesworth works with Lahore-based miniature painter Shakila Haider to produce a series of paintings showing indigenous South Asian plants flourishing in British suburbia; Alexander Gorlizki established a studio in Jaipur in 1996, with miniature painter Riyaz Uddin, to create dreamscapes that quote freely from imagery found in miniature painting; and the Singh Twins – British artists of Sikh heritage, who live and work near Liverpool – have been producing miniature-inspired work together since the 1980s to address themes of contemporary culture and politics.

Other artists, from Britain and elsewhere, have found resonance in Indian spirituality and philosophy. From the 1950s, the Scottish painter Alan Davie included enigmatic symbols in his paintings, from sources as varied as American Indian pottery, ancient rock carvings, Aboriginal art and Jain manuscripts. More recently, Nicola Durvasula, who taught art history in Hyderabad in the 1990s, has produced small-scale monochromes by soaking paper in water from the sacred Ganges river, which is also the setting for Jess MacNeil's short, mesmerizing film of floating boats. Matthew Krishanu's paintings allude to the historical Christian Mission in India and Bangladesh, while Raqib Shaw grew up in the Kashmir valley in a Muslim family, but went to a Christian school where he was taught by Hindu scholars. This mix of cultures feeds into the fantastical, intricate worlds of his

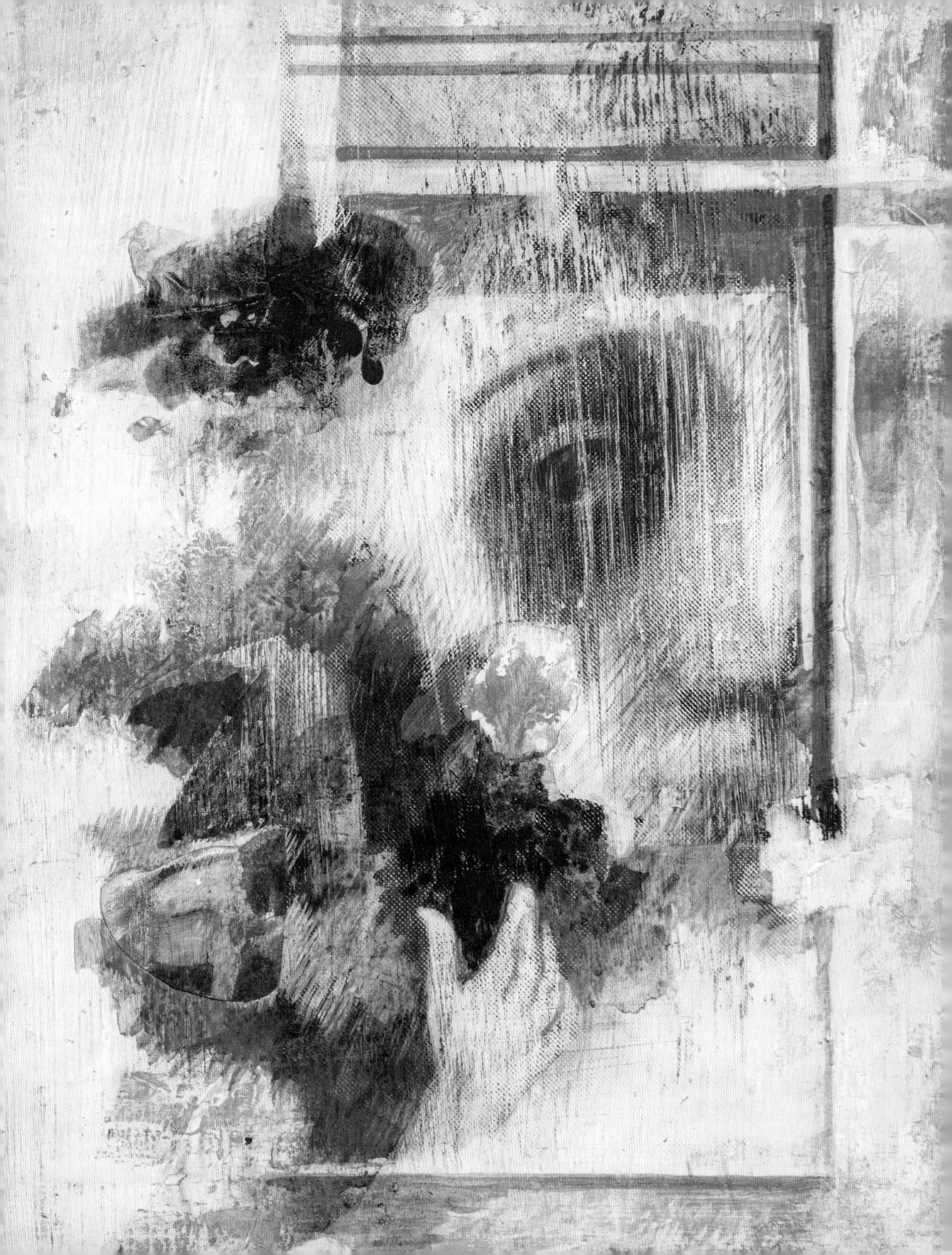

paintings, fashioned using a porcupine quill and embossed gold.

Correspondences and dialogues across the continents – and across time – are of course frequent and take many forms. There is a sense of a search for innovation through tradition, often in a slow, meticulous, hand-crafted process that is deeply rooted in history but also in the private space of a studio. Olivia Fraser moved to India in 1989, following in the footsteps of an ancestor who commissioned the 'Fraser Album', one of the most significant collections of Company School paintings. She studied traditional miniature painting techniques and uses them in her own work, often representing archetypal Indian iconography. Lubna Chowdhary's enigmatic wooden sculptures emerged from her investigations into colonial-period furniture in the V&A. Produced using state-of-the-art computerized numerical control (CNC) and traditional manual craft, these items appear functional albeit removed from their usual environment. Noor Ali Chagani trained at the NCA in Lahore but lives in Luton, near Milton Keynes. His hand-made miniature terracotta bricks reimagine, in three dimensions, some of the architectural spaces seen in miniatures. These spaces – which include utopian palaces or dream-like fortresses found in miniatures – are also evoked in the large sculpture, permanently sited outside MK Gallery, by Dhruva Mistry, an Indian artist who studied and taught in Baroda and spent many years in Britain in the 1980s and 1990s. The Box, Plymouth, with whom this project is co-produced, have their own direct connection to the subject in a group of eighteenth-century Indian miniature paintings held in their collection.

The small number of examples cited here provide an indication of the many directions in which miniatures have been taken, and demonstrate their ongoing resonance. The South Asian miniature tradition continues to flourish as a potent source of knowledge, understanding and inspiration. The artists involved often engage in highly promiscuous acts of borrowing that simultaneously extend, subvert and reimagine its tropes. The conversations between multiple generations of artists, at the heart of this exhibition, are based on artworks in British collections, originally acquired through imperial imperative and, since, reclaimed by contemporary South Asian artists. Miniature painting has always been an art of dynamic adaptation, exemplifying migrations of form in its evolution, in a way that also reflects the movement of people. Contemporary migrations

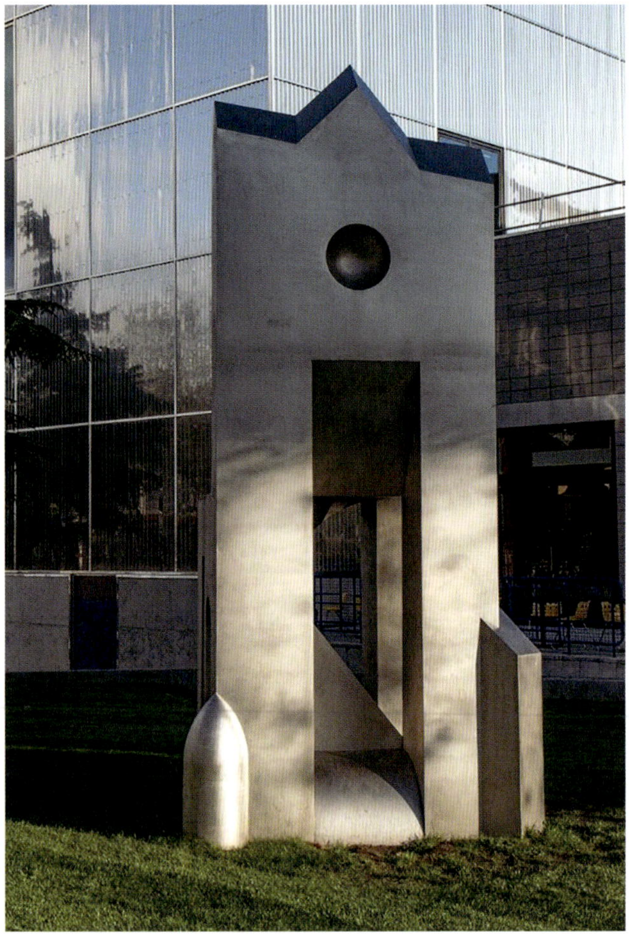

Dhruva Mistry, *The Object*, 1995–97.

from the subcontinent to Britain, and elsewhere, have caused a radical transformation of cultural experience and a rethinking of ideas around identity, belonging, home and nationalism. At its heart, this exhibition addresses the circulation of knowledge, culture and power in the entangled histories of empire and globalization. It explores an enduring preoccupation with the inescapable legacies of the colonial past, how an 'indigenous' tradition became adopted as an explicitly postcolonial expression. This book and the exhibition it accompanies chart a journey from a time when many artworks were known by the name of the owner or commissioner and not the maker. Now South Asian artists are amongst our most celebrated, with major commissions and exhibitions worldwide. Bringing together these dialogues across generations and continents, the ambition of this project is to encourage further thought, research and investment into this often overlooked area of British, and global, art history in order to address what these issues mean for museum collections and artistic practice in Britain today.

There are many people whose enthusiasm and generosity have made this project possible. We are of course extremely grateful to all the artists, especially to those who have produced new work, and to all those who shared their influences and interests in historical works.

The many lenders to the exhibition, all listed at the back of this book, have gone to extraordinary lengths to accommodate our requests. We appreciate the vulnerability of the historical pieces – some of which, for conservation reasons, can only be displayed once every ten years – and are grateful to the museum curators who shared their expertise and facilitated the process, especially Divia Patel, Senior Curator at the Asian Department at the V&A, who has long nurtured the relevance of historic miniatures to fuel contemporary practice. Private collectors, too, have been incredibly supportive and enabled us to build this complex exhibition to share with large new audiences. We are extremely grateful to Bolton & Quinn for helping us to increase our reach and impact on our audiences.

We could not have embarked on such an ambitious project without the very generous support of many people, especially the Bagri Foundation and the Exhibition Circle of Friends, wonderfully chaired by Tarana Sawhney, who are listed, alongside all supporters, at the back of the book.

It has been a privilege to be guided on this journey by Emily Hannam and Hammad Nasar, whose combined knowledge of the historic and contemporary fields have been so instructive and insightful. We are grateful to Cleo Roberts-Komireddi and Elizabeth Brown for providing additional entries for the section of works.
It has been a pleasure to work with designer Lucy Morton and Clare Martelli and Natasha Collin at PWP.

The team at MK Gallery have been exemplary, as ever, in their management of this complex operation, brilliantly led by Head of Exhibitions Fay Blanchard, with assistance from Madeleine Jordan and our team of technicians who have made the exhibition a reality. At The Box, Steve Conway, Nicoletta Lambertucci and Terah Walkup from the Collections team have worked closely with colleagues at MK Gallery and have been ably supported by Kate Johnson, Exhibitions Officer, and Nicki Thomas, Registrar.

ANTHONY SPIRA DIRECTOR, MK GALLERY
VICTORIA POMERY CEO, THE BOX

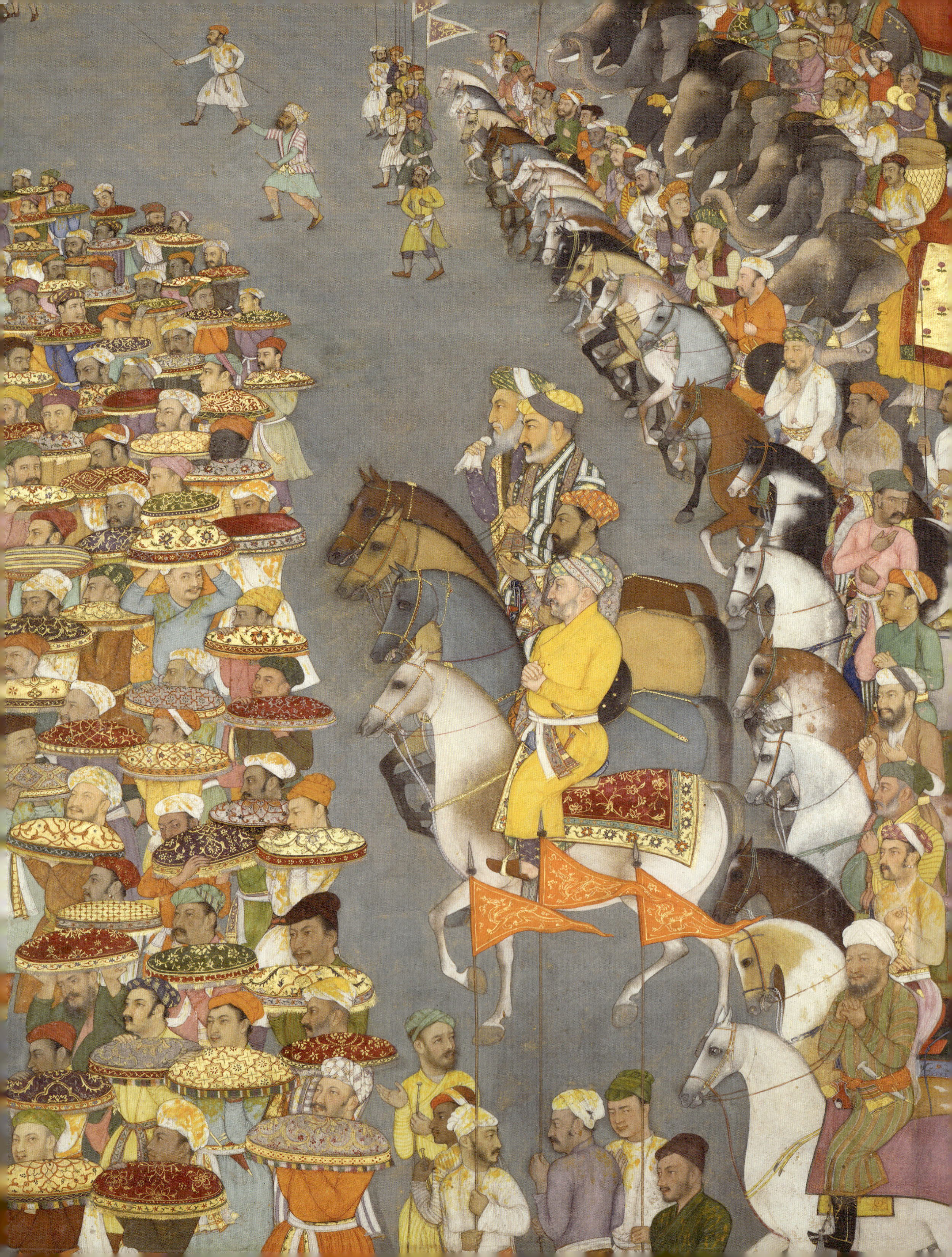

HISTORIC WORKS

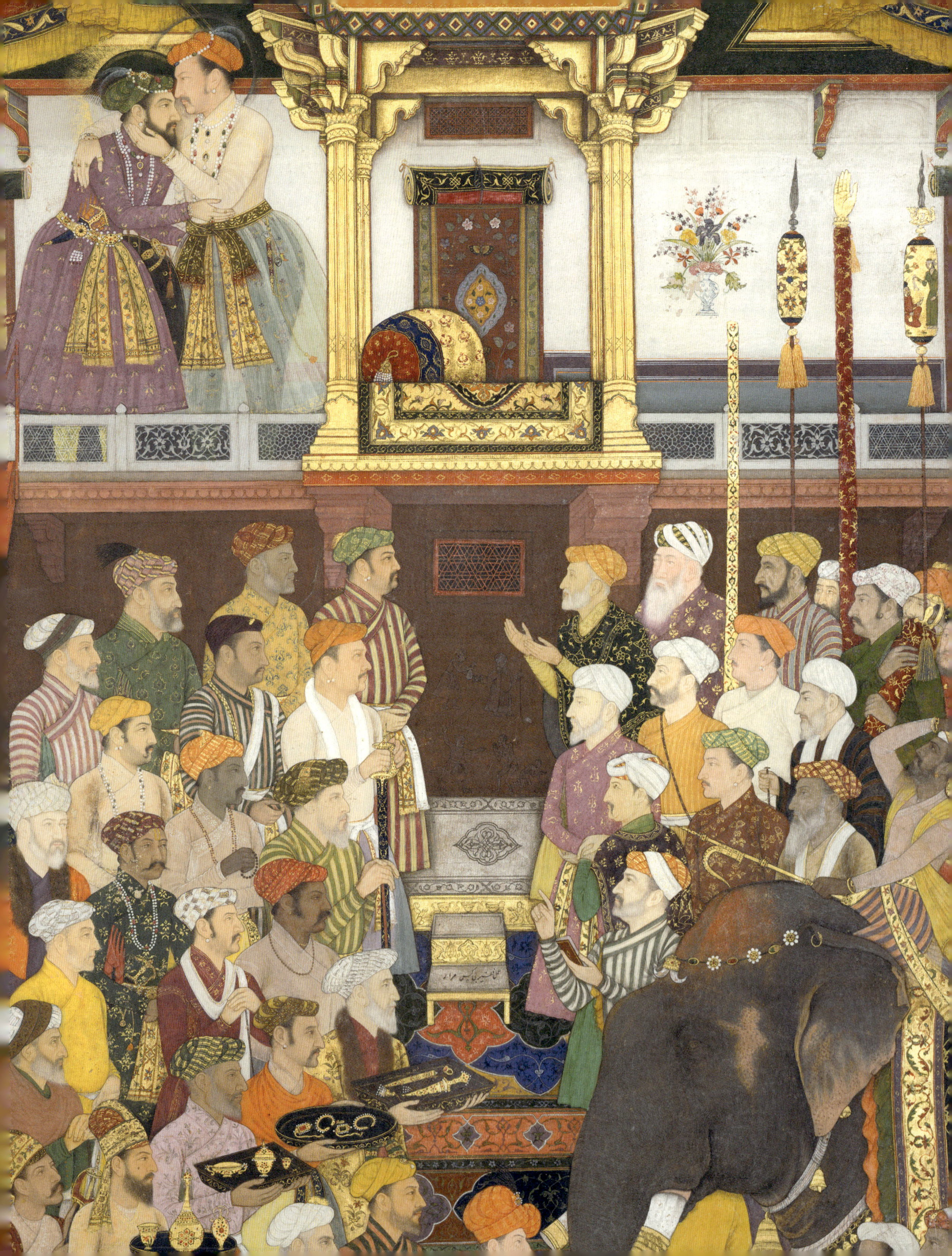

Emily Hannam

MINIATURE PAINTINGS IN BRITISH COLLECTIONS

Exactly how many South Asian miniatures are held in British collections? (Has anyone counted? Should someone have counted? How would one even go about counting?) The answer is surely tens of thousands (over a hundred thousand?), mostly in the collections of public museums and libraries. Are they all catalogued? What about the private collections?

South Asian miniatures have been arriving in Britain for more than four hundred years. Collected by passionate connoisseurs, ignored and maligned by others – perhaps their exact number is irrelevant. What is more important is the fact that so many of these are very good paintings, and by named artists, famous in their time – the equivalent of European 'old masters'. Among them are some of the most historically and culturally significant South Asian paintings in the world, particularly in the case of Mughal imperial paintings. A great number of those in European and North American collections spent much of their former lives in Britain too. And, unlike other South Asian artforms, miniatures tell their own histories quite well. Notes and seals of previous owners are found on their reverse sides, below the margins and inside the covers. They are listed in library catalogues and inventories and often it is possible to reconstruct at least part of their life stories. Yet, despite the thousands of important examples held on this island, South Asian miniature painting remains absent from the mainstream art-history courses taught in British schools and universities.[1] British scholars of South Asian art are few and far between, and it is thanks only to a small handful of devoted curators that South Asian paintings are exhibited in Britain at all. How did we come to this? And why is it that miniatures are so marginalized in the story of British art history?

MINIATURES IN PRECOLONIAL BRITAIN

Easily portable, labour-intensive and often imbued with overt symbolism or meaning, miniature paintings were among the luxury gifts traditionally presented to and by rulers as part of established gift-giving rituals. Among the earliest South Asian miniatures to arrive in Britain were royal portraits presented to Sir Thomas Roe (1551–1644), envoy of King

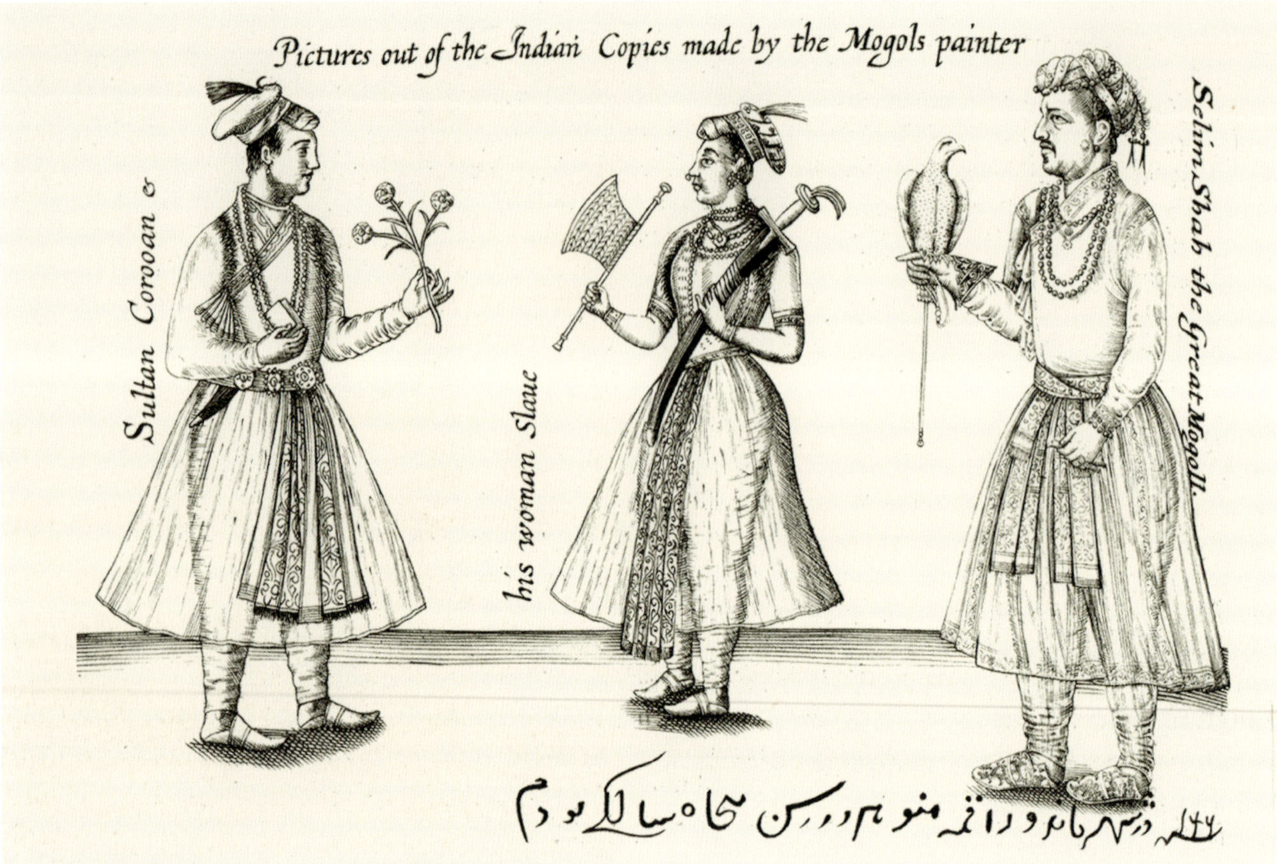

FIG. 1 Unknown artist, 'Pictures out of the Indian Copies made by the Mogols painter'. From Samuel Purchas, *Hakluytus Posthumus, or Purchas his Pilgrimes*, London, 1625.

James I (r.1603–25) during his sojourn at the Mughal court. Emperor Jahangir (1569–1627) may have given these portraits to Roe during the New Year celebrations in 1617 when the English ambassador presented gifts of several oil paintings to the emperor, including portraits of King James and Queen Anne.[2]

Although Roe's miniatures no longer survive, engravings based on them do. Some of the Mughal portraits brought back to England in 1619 by Sir Thomas Roe are depicted in fig. 1. They show Emperor Jahangir, his son Prince Khurram, and a woman wearing a turban and carrying a sword. She is possibly Jahangir's wife Nur Jahan, although identified in the print as 'his woman slave'. The London engraver copied a Persian inscription in the hand of Jahangir specifying that his portrait was 'painted by Manohar in the town of Mandu in 1026 Hijri [1616] when I was in my fiftieth year'. Very few Indian miniatures arrived in Britain in the seventeenth century but prints based on them increased public awareness of the art form (see cat. 1).

A later 'small book with East Indies drawings'[3] appears in the 1655 inventory of Alethea Howard, Countess of Arundel (1585–1654), one of the greatest English art collectors of the seventeenth century. The book is listed among the prints and drawings of her estate in Amsterdam, where she had fled with her collection to escape the English Civil War, and is thought to be the same exquisite Mughal album with portraits of Jahangir's successor Emperor Shah Jahan (1592–1666), his wife and young children that the artists Rembrandt and Willem Schellinks copied in 1656 (see cat. 3 & 4).[4] The album had probably been brought to England two decades earlier after another English nobleman, William Feilding, Earl of Denbigh (1587–1643), 'returned from ye great Mogor full of jewells'.[5] Denbigh had visited Shah Jahan at Burhanpur in 1632 and introduced himself with a splendidly illuminated letter from King Charles I.[6]

As a response to the beautiful volumes brought back as diplomatic gifts, Charles I (r.1625–49) issued an explicit royal command to British merchants that they deliberately seek out 'oriental' books when journeying eastwards and send them on to the Archbishop of Canterbury:

> As the King has considered that there is a great deal of learning fit to be known written in Arabic, and great scarcity of Arabic and Persian books in this country ... every ship ... at every voyage shall bring home one Arabic or Persian manuscript book, to be delivered to ... the Archbishop of Canterbury, who shall dispose of them as the King shall think fit.[7]

The Archbishop of Canterbury, William Laud (1573–1645), was vice chancellor of the University of Oxford and amassed more than 250 Arabic, Persian, Turkish and other Asian volumes from merchants of the East India and Levant companies. He later deposited them in the Bodleian Library, including the first Mughal album to enter a British public collection (see cat. 2). By the end of the seventeenth century, the vast numbers of European merchants operating

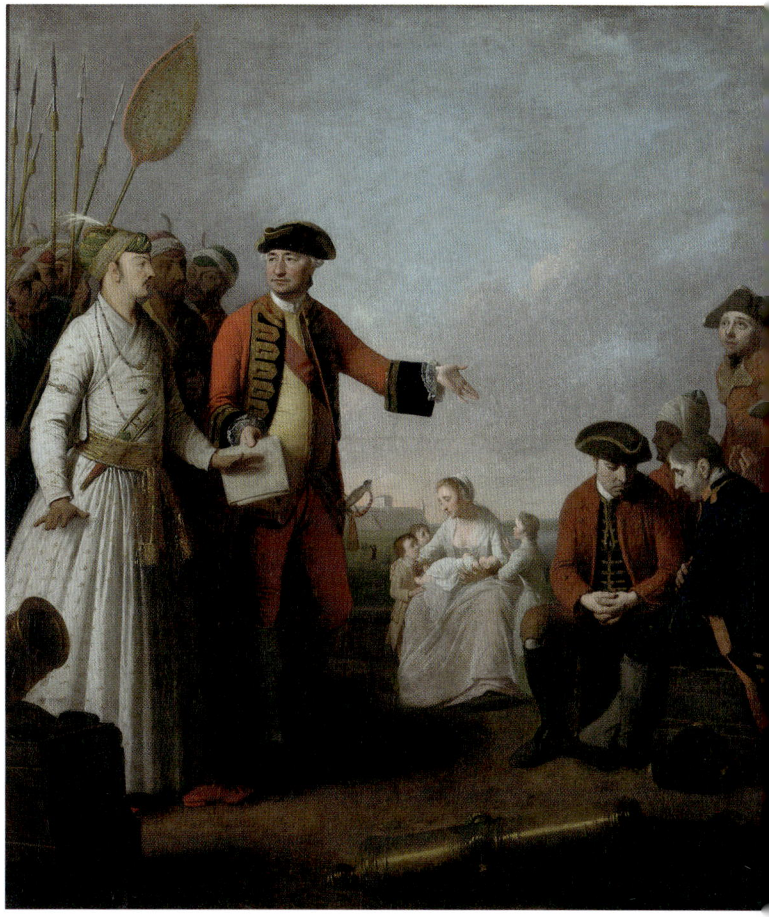

FIG. 2 Edward Penny, *Lord Clive Receiving from the Nawab of Bengal the grant of a sum of Money which was later to be used to establish the charity known as Lord Clive's Fund*, 1772.

in the major South Asian trading centres had created a new market for Indian artists who established workshops creating likenesses of Indian royal figures to be sold to foreigners as luxury souvenirs (see cat. 4, fig. 13). One such album painted in Hyderabad was among Sir Hans Sloane's 1753 bequest to the nation, the founding collection of the British Museum.[8]

MINIATURES AND THE EAST INDIA COMPANY

Miniatures continued to be bought and used as high-level gifts into the second half of the eighteenth century, as the East India Company's power and ambition grew. Major-General

Robert Clive (1725–1774), whose victory over the Nawab of Bengal in 1757 laid the foundations for British rule in northern India, amassed a sizable collection of Indian paintings through his diplomatic exchanges: a list of his belongings sent back to England in 1766 included '4 Books of Pictures containing 135 Pictures received'.[9] At a time when Robert Clive was being investigated by Parliament on charges of corruption, the East India Company Court of Directors commissioned Edward Penny (1714–1791), the first Professor of Painting at the Royal Academy, to paint Clive (fig. 2) as a righteous and benevolent victor presenting disabled Company soldiers and widows to Najm ud-Dawla (1750–1766), the Nawab of Bengal.[10] Penny's depiction of the 15-year-old Nawab may have been based on a miniature portrait given to Clive in India.

Captain Archibald Swinton (1731–1804), Clive's Persian interpreter in India, also returned to his native Scotland with a great collection of paintings and manuscripts, some of which he received as gifts, whereas others he had actively collected (see cat. 7). By this point the Mughal imperial library was already being broken up. Many fine paintings and manuscripts were taken to Iran after Nadir Shah (1688–1747) looted the city of Delhi in 1739, and less than fifty years later the palace was again sacked by the Afghan Ghulam Qadir (d.1789). Impoverished members of the royal family and nobility offered their collections of books and paintings to dealers, who sold them on to collectors in the more prosperous cities of Lucknow, Patna and Calcutta. The most prolific collector of the period was Asaf ud-Dawla, the Nawab of Awadh (1748–1797), who brandished his books and albums to East India officers 'boasting that they were the "king's"'[11] – the implication being that they came from the Mughal imperial

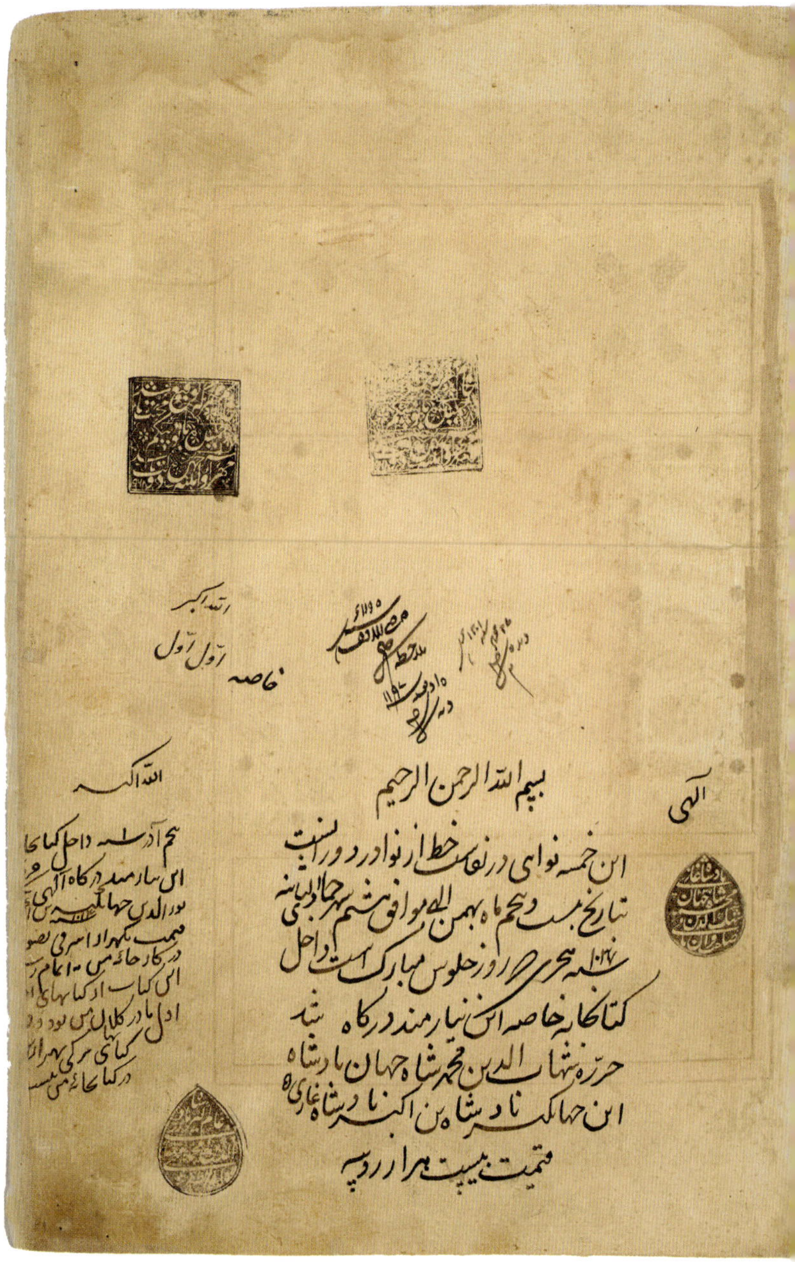

FIG. 3 Folio 1a from a manuscript of the *Khamsa* (Quintet) of Mir Ali Shir Navai.

library. After the Nawab's death, the East India Company's governor general of Bengal, Sir John Shore (later Lord Teignmouth, 1751–1834) was offered the famous *Padshahnama* manuscript (see cat. 11–13, 15) from the Nawab's library. He politely declined but suggested that it and other volumes of similar calibre (see cat. 10 & 18) might be sent as gifts to the great bibliophile George III (1738–1820).

Figure 3 shows the first page of a manuscript sent to George III from the ruler of Awadh, Saadat Ali Khan (1752–1814), with seal impressions and inscriptions showing its history in the Mughal imperial libraries. The square seal impression is that of Hamida Banu Begum, wife of the second Mughal emperor Humayun, dated 1560–61. The inscriptions in the hands of Mughal emperors Jahangir and Shah Jahan state that they inherited the book on their respective accessions. Jahangir gives a value of 1,000 ashrafis, a valuation which Shah Jahan almost doubled to 20,000 rupees. The teardrop-shaped seal impressions are those of Shah Jahan and Alamgir. Later inspection notes were written by Lucknow royal librarians in 1781, 1782 and 1786.

One of George III's sons, Prince Augustus Frederick, Duke of Sussex (1773–1843), also amassed a famous library, which by 1823 included hundreds of paintings illustrating scenes of the Hindu epic text the *Ramayana* (see cat. 21). The Duke of Sussex acquired the series as a gift from Colonel James Tod (1782–1835), who had himself received the paintings as a present from Maharana Bhim Singh of Mewar (1768–1828) on his departure from Udaipur in 1820. These were just a small selection of the 40 crates of Rajasthani manuscripts, paintings and antiquities that Tod had brought back from India.[12]

Tod was among the second generation of British officers to develop a keen interest in the art and culture of South Asia. Motivated by Enlightenment curiosity, these men learnt local languages, forged local connections, and created unprecedented opportunities to buy Indian art, thanks in part to supplementing their salaries through private commerce (see cat. 8–9). British employees of the East India Company also commissioned new paintings directly from local artists, many of whom had moved from Delhi to Bengal and Awadh in search of patronage (see cat. 25–26). As Indian artists began to work freelance for British patrons, many adapted their traditional working methods to suit British tastes: painting in thin layers of soft watercolour wash on British paper and using illustrations from English books as models. To distinguish this way of painting from the *Dilhi qalam* (Delhi style),[13] which involved detailed underdrawings, hard layers of colour and meticulous dotting and shading, the term *kampani qalam* (Company style) came into use.[14] Examples of the *kamapani qalam* include the many thousands of natural-history paintings made for British patrons in India in the late eighteenth and early nineteenth centuries (see cat. 30–36), among them the 326 bird and animal studies made for Lady Mary Impey (1749–1818), wife of Sir Elijah Impey, then Justice of the Supreme Court at Calcutta (see cat. 28–29).

As well as natural-history and landscape paintings, ethnography was a favourite subject of British patrons in India who commissioned local painters to depict the 'costumes, castes and trades' of the subcontinent. The most famous of these is the so-called Fraser Album, a group of more than 90 watercolour portraits of real, named people of all levels of Indian society commissioned by William Fraser (1784–1835),

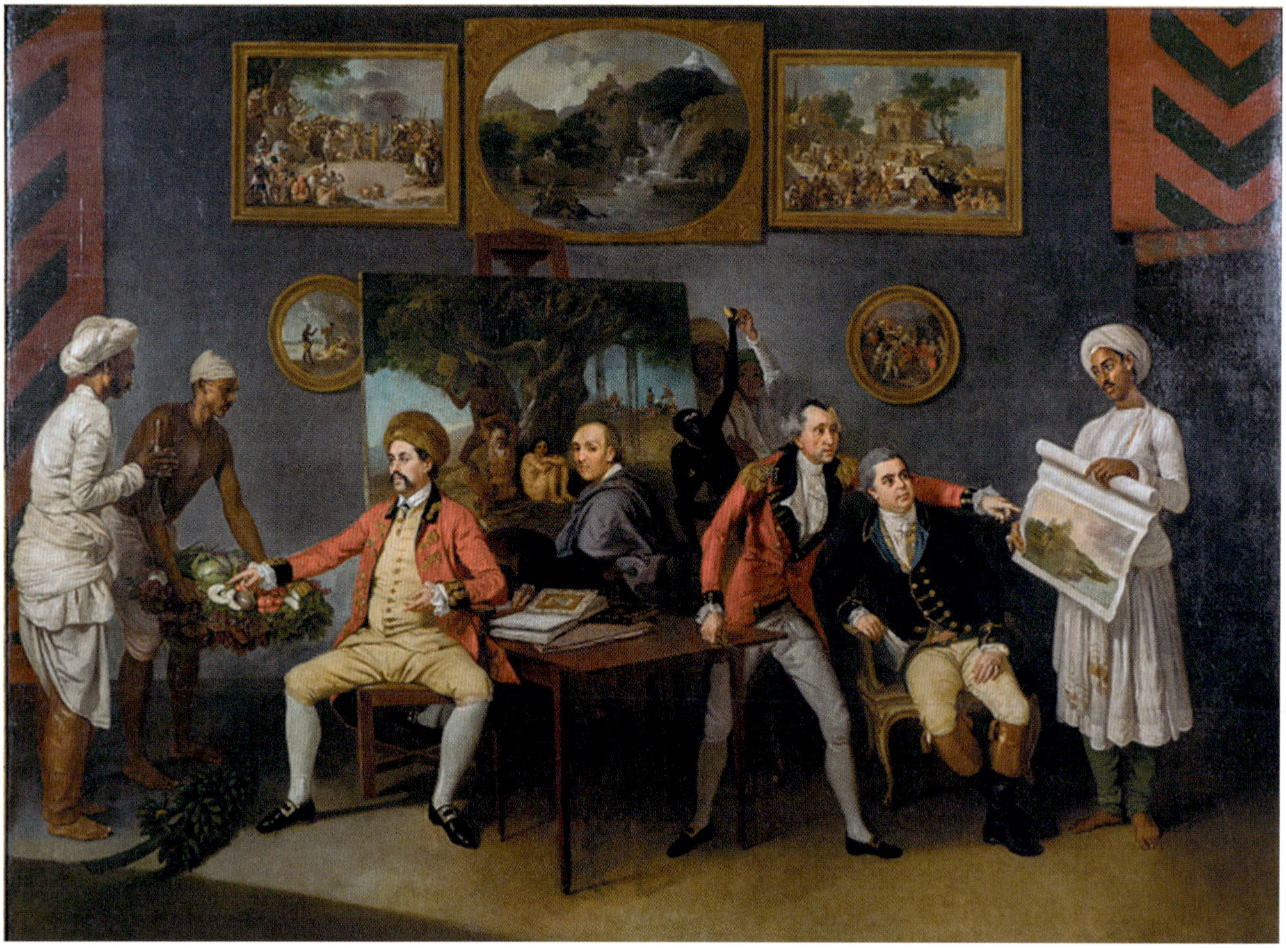

FIG. 4 Johann Zoffany, *Colonel Antoine Polier, Colonel Claude Martin and John Wombwell with the Artist, an Indian Painter and Assistants*, 1786–7.

when secretary to the Resident at Delhi, and his brother James Baillie Fraser (1783–1856) (see cat. 37–39). The Fraser brothers' close friend Colonel James Skinner (1778–1841) also patronized Delhi artists, probably many of the same ones.[15] His artistic commissions included illustrated histories of the princely families of north-western India (see cat. 40) and the so-called *Skinner Album*: a volume of portraits of his soldiers and employees.[16]

By the end of the eighteenth century, thousands of volumes of Indian paintings were already in Britain, some of which remained with the descendants of those who had brought them, while others entered the art market and were bought by enthusiasts with no obvious connection to India (see cat. 22–24).

One such collector was William Beckford (1769–1844), famous in his time for his passionate collecting of luxury art and furniture from across Europe and Asia. Beckford owned more than 25 albums of Indian paintings and calligraphy: eight of these were from the collection of Archibald Swinton (see p. 14);[17] the others he bought from Antoine Polier (1741–1795), a Swiss-French engineer based in Lucknow in the 1770s and 1780s (see cat. 1 & 6).[18] Johann Zoffany painted an album of miniatures lying open on the table between Colonel Antoine Polier and himself, at the centre of the painting shown here (fig. 4). Before leaving India in 1788, Polier arranged the sale of 17 of his albums of Indian paintings and calligraphy to William Beckford.

By the end of the eighteenth century, thousands of Indian paintings and manuscripts were in Britain, most of them collected by East India Company officers and their wives. The fact that so many paintings and manuscripts were ending up in private hands or on the open market compelled the East India Company to establish its own library in London to specifically house incoming Asian collections. The Court of Directors announced its interest in creating this 'public Repository' in 1798 in light of the

> frequent practice among our Servants, especially in Bengal, to make Collections of Oriental manuscripts, many of which have afterwards been brought into this country. These remaining in private hands, and being likely in a course of time to pass into others, in which probably no use can be made of them, they are in danger of being neglected, and at length in a great measure lost to Europe as well as India.[19]

The library was founded three years later at East India House, the Company's headquarters on Leadenhall Street. Early acquisitions included 197 volumes from the library of Tipu Sultan (1751–1799), 'captured at Seringapatam',[20] and in 1807 Richard Johnson (cat. 14) sold his vast collection of paintings and manuscripts to the library for 3,000 guineas (some £250,000 today).[21] But by the 1820s, attitudes towards Indian miniatures had already begun to change. This was true both in Britain, where India was increasingly viewed as backward and decadent, and in those parts of India under British rule, where English language, arts and literature were increasingly promoted at the expense of local cultures. Certain iconographies of Indian miniatures were considered so embarrassing that a clerk annotating the 'List of Oriental Drawings' (Johnson's collection) in Leadenhall Street noted that Album 42 contained '*Raga Mala*, 35 drawings of which some are excessively obscene and should be destroyed'.[22]

To counteract the growing intellectual apathy towards India, the Sanskrit scholar and former president of the Asiatic Society of Bengal Henry Thomas Colebrooke (1765–1837) arranged a meeting at his house in London in January 1823, the purpose of which was to 'consider the expediency of instituting a Society for the encouragement of science, literature and the arts in connection with India, and other countries eastward of the Cape of Good Hope'.[23] He and a group of 25 scholars and former colonial officers founded what soon became the Royal Asiatic Society under the patronage of King George IV, with James Tod as its first librarian. While Tod developed and catalogued the collection at their headquarters off Bond Street, those in charge of the East India Company's library 3 miles away largely disregarded its collection of Indian paintings and manuscripts and discouraged any interested visitors. In March 1841 a former Company servant, Peter Gordon, published an anonymous article in which he declared East India House 'filthier than a tavern' and that the library

> continues virtually sealed up; it is the most valuable oriental collection in the world; but it is unvisited ... [and] it is lodged in improper hands ... the property is not even secured by

the most common and necessary precautions ... It may be remarked that the Company is everywhere present in the character of an exactor, but nowhere to be found for the purposes of justice and of reparation.[24]

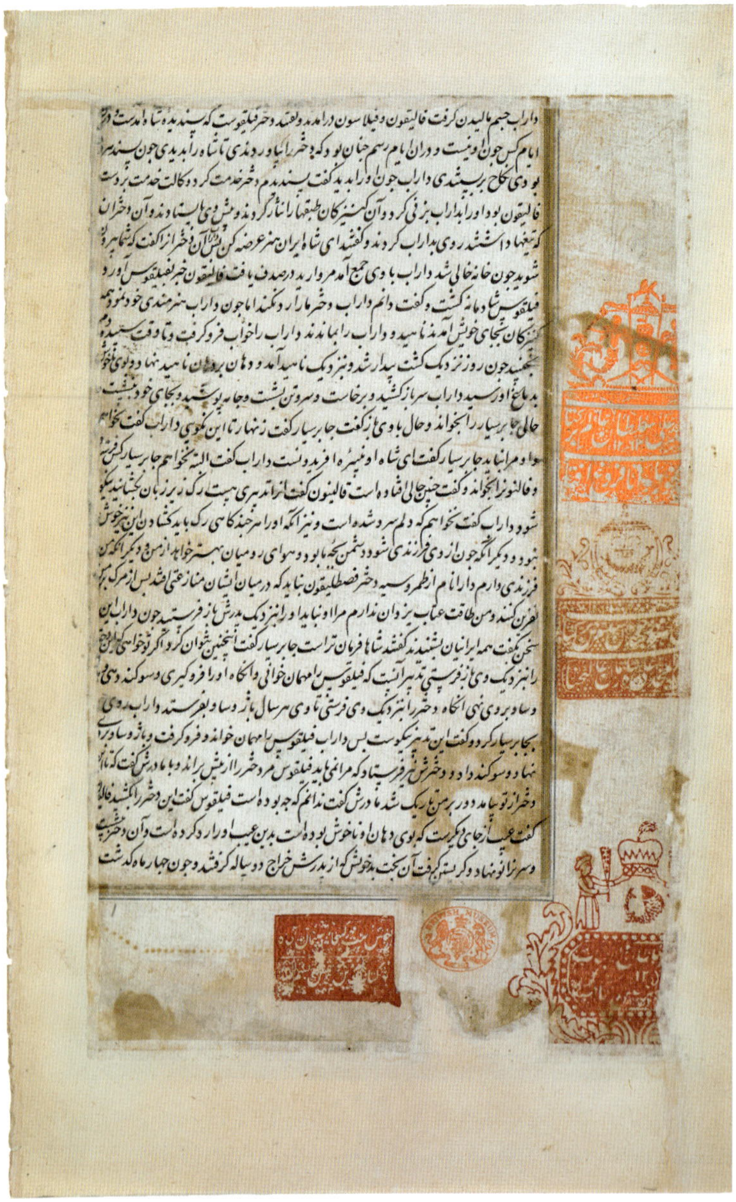

FIG. 5 Folio 129v from a manuscript of the *Darabnama*.

MINIATURES DURING THE RAJ

Following the Indian Rebellion (India's First War of Independence) of 1857–58, the East India Company was dissolved and the administration of British India passed to the British Crown, to be administered by Her Majesty's Government. The old East India Company library moved to Fife House in Whitehall, home to the India Office. Its largest subsequent acquisition consisted of over 3,500 manuscripts that had been looted from Delhi and bought in 1859 at public auctions by the Government of India.[25]

As well as the plundering of Delhi, in March 1858 East India Company troops ransacked the libraries of the Qaiserbagh Palace in Lucknow. Thousands of books from the Lucknow royal library were destroyed and only a few hundred survived (see cat. 42). In 1868 Colonel George William Hamilton (1807–1868), who had served in India from 1823 to 1867, presented 352 volumes to the British Museum from his collection of more than a thousand manuscripts, 'very many [of which] were rescued by him from destruction during the Indian Mutiny, especially at Lucknow, several bearing the vermilion stamp of the library of the Kings of Oude [Awadh]'.[26] Soon after this large acquisition, the trustees of the British Museum created a special Department of Oriental Manuscripts within its library and went on to acquire other manuscripts of the same provenance.[27]

Figure 5 depicts a folio from a sixteenth-century illustrated copy of the *Darabnama* (*Tales of Darab*) written and illustrated at the Mughal court in Fatehpur-Sikri and purchased

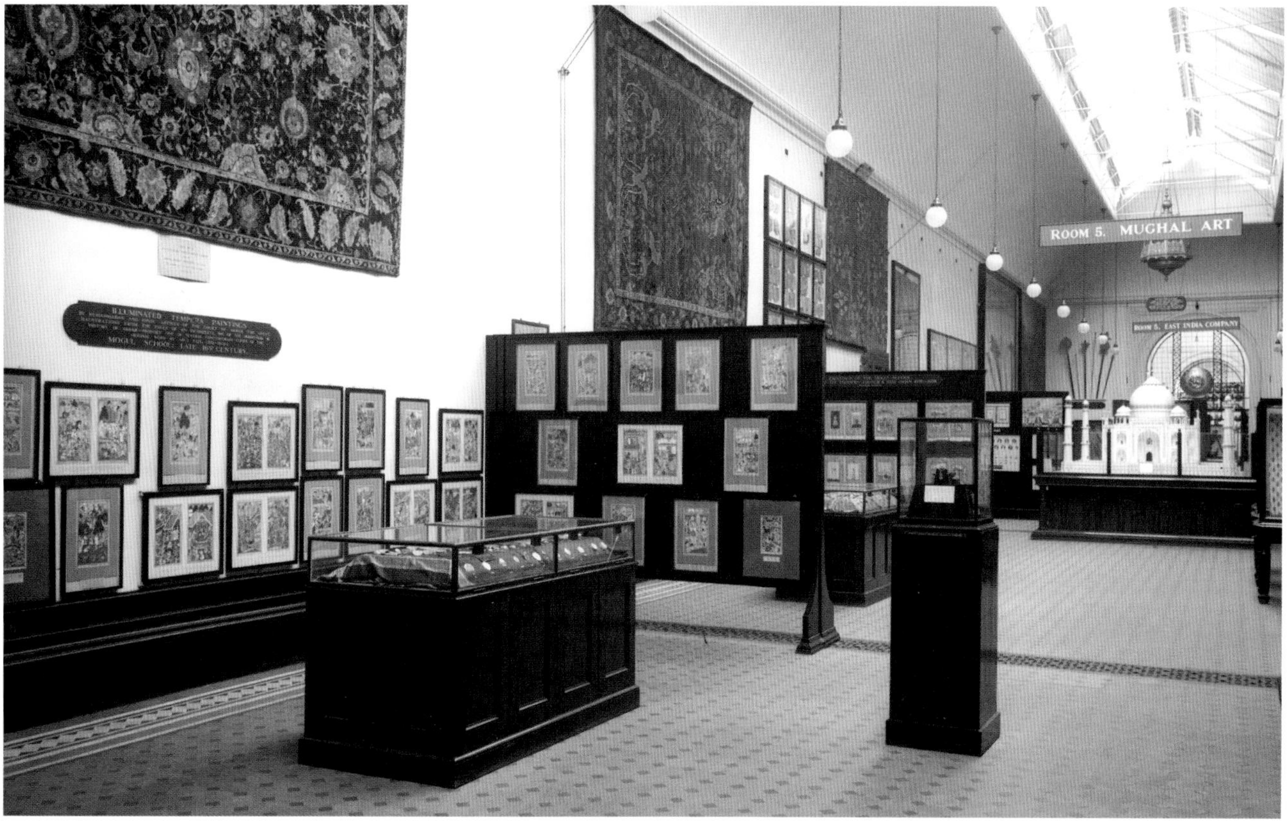

FIG. 6 Unknown photographer, *Pages from the 'Akbarnama' on display in the Mughal Room of the India Museum, South Kensington, 1934.*

by the British Museum in February 1893 from London bookseller Bernard Quaritch. The bright-red stamp impressions made by the Lucknow royal librarians state that the book was in Awadh by 1828 and inspected every ten years. The latest stamp dates to 1847, suggesting the manuscript was among the books looted from the Qaiserbagh Palace in 1857, many of which are now in British collections.

It was around this time that the term Indian 'miniature' first came into use in Britain, as more examples of Indian painting as a book art, similar to that found in medieval Western manuscripts, entered public collections. Up to this time, 'miniatures' were mostly commonly referred to as either Indian or Hindustani 'drawings', 'pictures' or 'paintings'. The South Kensington Museum, known after 1899 as the Victoria and Albert Museum (V&A), also made significant acquisitions of Indian miniatures and manuscripts, including the famous *Akbarnama* and *Hamzanama* folios (see cat. 44–45). But not all institutions were interested, and by the early twentieth century Indian collections in Britain started to find their way to America. Colonel Henry Hanna (1839–1914) exhibited his collection of 130 Indian paintings in London and lent them to the Laing Art Gallery in Newcastle, but after repeatedly trying to sell them to a British institution for £7,500 he eventually agreed an offer of £3,100 from the Detroit collector Charles Freer.[28] Charles Hercules Read (1857–1929), Keeper of British and Medieval Antiquities at the British Museum, sold his Mughal and Persian paintings not to his own institution but to private individuals, including the American collector J.P. Morgan (1837–1913).[29]

In 1895 the V&A bought 273 folios of an *Akbarnama* manuscript dating to the 1590s (fig. 6) for the total cost of £100. The museum staff mounted and framed the 116 illustrated folios as individual works and from 1932 until 1955 displayed them in the Mughal galleries of the Indian section (then known as the India Museum).[30]

In India, collecting and connoisseurship of historic paintings also suffered a widespread lack of interest from British subjects during the late eighteenth and early nineteenth centuries. In 1872 Henry Baden-Powell (1841–1901) wrote disparagingly from Lahore that

> all native pictures have the skies painted exactly alike; ... if trees are introduced, their colour and treatment is always the same ... always is stiff, intractable and regular.... No native has any idea of using his eyes.[31]

Art societies across India organized exhibitions of European art, seeking to instil 'good taste' among the middle and upper classes. Indian patrons began to demand that 'traditional' miniature artists work in a European photo-realistic style, copying likeness from photographs (see cat. 47) or painting over prints and photographs. In the Government Art Schools of Madras, Calcutta and Bombay[32] drawing from European sculpture casts and studying the work of European old masters were fundamental elements of the curricula, intended to encourage Western 'ways of seeing'. John Lockwood Kipling (1837–1911), principal of Mayo School of Arts in Lahore (est. 1875), was unique in that he encouraged his students to draw what they saw in the city around them, and the South Kensington Museum bought several examples of his students' drawings.[33]

The man who played the most influential role in combating the dominance of Western art and reviving interest in Indian miniature painting in both India and Britain was another art educator, Ernest Binfield Havell (1861–1931). During his decade as principal of the Calcutta School of Art from 1896 until 1906, Havell reorganized the curriculum with the specific objective of 'making Indian art the basis of all instruction'.[34] He sold most of the European paintings in Calcutta's Government Art Gallery and used the proceeds to buy 'fine old specimens of oriental art industries', including seventeenth-century Mughal paintings, which he planned to use as teaching models for his students.[35] Even before Havell arrived in Calcutta, the Bengali artist Abanindranath Tagore (1871–1951), nephew of the poet and painter Rabindranath Tagore, was experimenting with miniature painting, but it was his relationship with Havell at the turn of the century that proved crucial in shaping a new, miniature-inspired movement in Indian art (see cat. 48 & 54).[36] In 1905 Havell appointed Tagore vice principal of the Art School, to teach alongside the 'traditional' painter, Ishwari Prasad (cat. 47). After Havell returned to England in 1906, Tagore founded the 'Indian Society of Oriental Art' to promote the new movement, soon known as the 'Bengal School'. A review of its inaugural exhibition hailed him as 'the greatest of Indian living artists' and credited his art as being at once 'national', 'individual' and 'distinctly Indian'.[37] Tagore's students included Samarendranath Gupta

(1887–1964), who later joined the Mayo School of Art where he taught the young Abdur Rahman Chughtai (1899–1975; see cat. 55–56), who would become one of Pakistan's most prominent modern artists. Another great supporter of the Indian Society of Oriental Art was Percy Brown, who published the first groundbreaking study of Mughal painting in English during his term as principal of the Calcutta Art School from 1909 to 1927.[38]

Back in Britain, Havell set about increasing awareness and mobilizing support for Indian art, both historical and contemporary. In January 1910 he gave a lecture to the Royal Society of Arts[39] to which the chairman, George Birdwood (1832–1917), a former curator of the Government Art Museum in Bombay and a 'special Referee' for the Indian Section of the South Kensington Museum, responded by comparing one of the Buddhist sculptures Havell had described to a 'boiled suet pudding'. The ensuing debate around the existence of what could be termed Indian 'fine art' was steered by the British artist William Rothenstein (1872–1945) (see cat. 50) and was the catalyst for Rothenstein and Havell to found a new India Society in London. Like its counterpart in Bengal, the Society's aim was to organize exhibitions, lectures and publications to promote understanding and appreciation of Indian art and culture. A proposal was made early on to 'keep out the undesirables'.[40]

Another great proponent of the India Society was the British-Ceylonese art historian Ananda Coomaraswamy (1877–1947), a pioneering collector of Indian miniature paintings from the old Rajput courts of the Punjab Hills (known as *pahari*, 'from the hills'). By the early twentieth century, Mughal miniatures had become scarce among Indian dealers as their sources dried up and instead they turned to the minor royal families of Punjab and Rajasthan, whom they persuaded to sell off their ancestral collections.[41] Writing to Rothenstein from Allahabad in October 1910, Coomaraswamy wrote:

> I have got hold of a magnificent lot of old Rajput cartoons and tracings of miniatures – I can't tell you how beautiful some of them are … I have been spending more than all my possessions on pictures.[42]

He encouraged Rothenstein, who was also in India at the time, to buy Rajput paintings and drawings (see cat. 65), and back in England they championed the art form. In 1912 Coomaraswamy presented Rajput miniatures to the British art world in an article in the *Burlington Magazine* and four years later published his two-volume *Rajput Painting* (1916), illustrated mainly with examples from his and Rothenstein's collections. He also sold miniatures to the British Museum, including the first Pahari paintings to enter its collection.[43]

In parallel to the India Society's promotion of Indian miniatures, the 1911 Delhi Durbar rekindled interest in Mughal painting both in India, where the Durbar exhibition had a whole section dedicated to painting, and in Britain, where the *Festival of Empire* exhibition at Crystal Palace included Mughal paintings from the India Office collection and many private donors.[44] Despite Havell's concerns about the exhibition's overtly imperial messaging, the India Society organized the display in the hope it would inspire enthusiasm and 'lead to better things afterwards'.[45] An exhibition of Bengal School painters took place at the V&A in 1914. Ten years later, 96 Mughal and Rajput paintings, including loans from the India Office and William Rothenstein, were displayed in the 1924 *British Empire Exhibition* at Wembley, an event

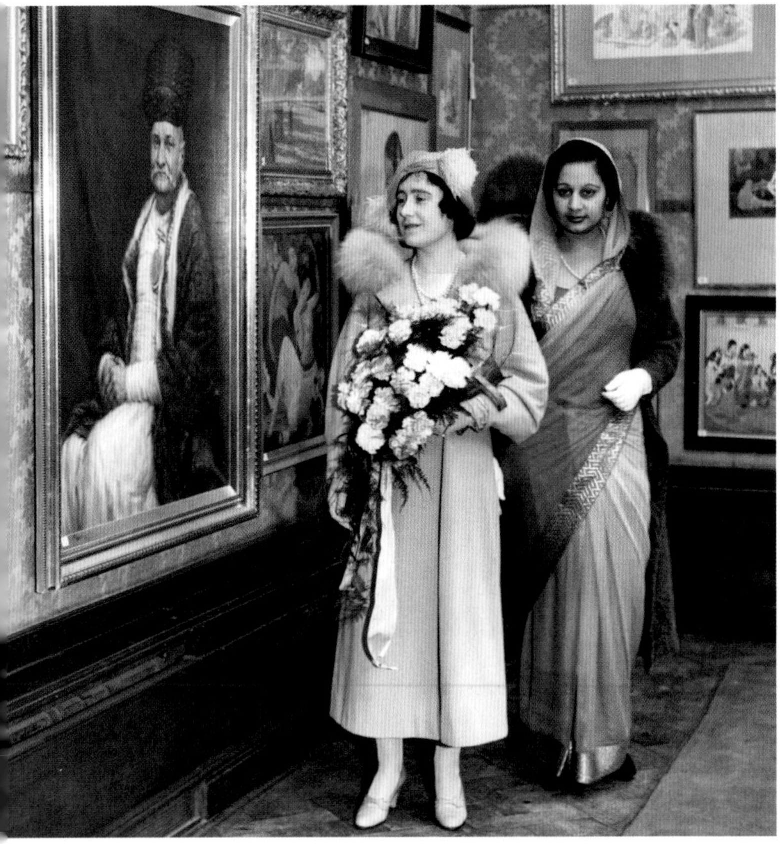

FIG. 7 Unknown photographer, *Elizabeth, Duchess of York, and Maharaj Kumari Devi of Burdwan at the opening of the 'All-India Exhibition of Modern Indian Art' organized by the India Society at the New Burlington Galleries on 10 December 1934.*

which received 27 million visitors over its long run. Works by many contemporary artists were also shown, including Abanindranath Tagore and Abdur Rahman Chughtai.[46] In his review of the 1924 exhibition, O.C. Gangoly, vice president of the India Society in Calcutta, specifically praised the imperial patrons for the emergence of 'new' Indian painting:

> It is said that the supreme significance of the British connection in India is to help modern India to recover the glories of her ancient culture. In the sphere of art, the sleeping princess is opening her eyes to the golden touch of British sympathy. She appears to have sent precious jewels to add to the lustre of the Imperial crown.[47]

In 1925, the Bombay painter Samuel Fyzee-Rahamin, who had also exhibited in the Wembley exhibition, became the first Indian artist to have works acquired by the Tate, where Rothenstein was on the board of trustees (see cat. 51–52). Rothenstein and other members of the India Society were also heavily involved in the *Art of India* exhibition held at London's Burlington Fine Arts Club in 1931.[48]

Soon afterwards the Society organized the largest exhibition of modern Indian painting ever staged, with illustrations to the *Arabian Nights* by Abanindranath Tagore and three watercolours by Abdur Rahman Chughtai (see fig. 7).[49] Also on display were works by Ranada Ukil and Samuel Fyzee-Rahamin lent by Queen Mary.

Throughout the first half of the twentieth century, royal patronage boosted the efforts of the India Society to promote greater public understanding of Indian painting in Britain.

Elizabeth, Duchess of York opened the 1934 exhibition, declaring 'I am sure that many people will be most grateful to the India Society for assembling in London such an interesting collection of modern Indian art, and in declaring the Exhibition open, I hope that it will meet with the encouragement and the admiration that it so fully deserves.'[50]

In 1944 the Dowager Queen Mary (1867–1953) became the official patron of the India Society and was a major donor to their next venture, *Art from India and Pakistan 2400 B.C. to 1947 A.D.*, a landmark exhibition that opened at the Royal Academy of Arts just three months after India gained independence and was partitioned. The enormous display included 500 historic paintings and manuscripts from British collections and loans from the old British Government museums in Calcutta and Lahore.[51] In a review (drolly headlined 'Anon was India's greatest artist')[52] the critic Bernard Denvir suggested,

> Although they [the English] had no direct influence on Indian art, it is to the enthusiasm and scholarship of a few Britons that the world owes the preservation of many ancient treasures.[53]

MINIATURES IN POSTCOLONIAL BRITAIN

Prior to Independence, several British collectors employed in the Indian Army or Civil Service amassed considerable miniature collections, particularly of Rajput paintings, which they subsequently bequeathed or sold to British public institutions.[54] The National Art Collections Fund (NCAF, now the Art Fund – the UK's largest art charity), supported many of these acquisitions, including more than 400 paintings from the estate of Patna barrister Percival Chater Manuk (1873–1946) and his companion, Gertrude Mary Coles (1884–1946) (see cat. 59–61).[55] Manuk originally intended to bequeath his Indian paintings to the National Gallery, and the then director, Sir Charles John Holmes (1868–1936), who had travelled to Asia, was keen to expand the collection. It was the trustees, however, who rejected the offer, which they considered at odds with the institution's remit.[56]

New acquisitions, particularly of Rajput paintings, were led most notably at the British Museum and the V&A by curators Basil Grey (1904–1989)[57] and William Archer (1907–1979).[58] Archer initially derided miniatures:

> I was excited by Cézanne, Picasso and Negro art, by the modern and primitive as against the classical and refined, I tended to scoff at what was exquisite or figurative.... To miniatures I believed I was firmly allergic.[59]

His feelings changed when his friends Manuk and Coles introduced him to their collection:

> As 'P.C' brought out his pictures, hinged on great sheets of card in albums with scarlet leather covers, I marvelled at what I saw and gasped at the stupid arrogance that had prevented me from going to see him previously ... I saw it as a type of art to which even the hardened adherent of the modern movement could respond.[60]

Following his appointment at the V&A, Archer catalogued the many hundreds of new acquisitions and reorganized the museum's displays into a panorama of Indian paintings arranged by period and style: from copies of Ajanta frescoes to Mughal, Deccani, Rajput and Pahari paintings (all divided into schools), to Company and bazaar paintings, ending with modern and contemporary works.[61] He made huge strides in the study of Pahari painting in particular[62] and championed Indian modern art, supporting the many South Asian artists who travelled to Britain on Commonwealth scholarships.[63]

In parallel, Archer's wife Mildred (1911–2005) researched and published the collections of the India Office at Whitehall. There she recalled initially having to make do with 'a small room with a sink and gas-ring where the staff made their tea', cataloguing the paintings as best she could on the draining board.[64] She discovered several dusty bundles of Indian natural-history paintings that had never been inventoried and even found a parcel of architectural drawings stuffed up a chimney.[65] Mildred Archer worked on the India Office collections for a total of 25 years and published them extensively, including the first books on Company paintings.[66]

In 1972 the Antiquities and Art Treasures Act expressly prohibited the export of artefacts and antiquities (defined as artefacts that were more than one hundred years old), which hindered subsequent acquisitions of paintings by British institutions since it required verifiable evidence of their being in the country before this date. Private collections continued to be formed by British connoisseurs, including the artist Howard Hodgkin (see cat. 67) and film-maker James Ivory,[67] although by this point really important paintings were few and far between. Hodgkin recalled the daunting piles of pictures and auction catalogues full of 'copies or copies of copies' and the 'bottomless pit of Indian painting' because so much was third-, fourth- or fifth-hand.[68] Many of the best examples offered in the last 50 or 60 years came from families with historic links to India – the Fraser Album for instance, and paintings from the Clive and Swinton collections, some of which were assigned to British public collections having been accepted by HM government in lieu of millions of pounds' worth of inheritance tax.[69]

The year 1972 also saw the creation of the British Library in St Pancras, to which the 'oriental' books from the library of the British Museum were transferred, joined in 1982 by the India Office Library and Records. Around the same time, St George's Hospital on Hyde Park Corner (now the Lanesborough Hotel) closed down and Robert Skelton (1929–2022), keeper at the V&A, lobbied to convert the building into a national museum of Asian art, one that would unite the South Asian collections of the V&A, British Museum and British Library and give them greater prominence. Although the proposal came to nothing, Skelton left a great many other legacies through his wide research on South Asian art and enthusiastic support of fellow curators, academics, collectors, dealers and artists. Long after the India Society had disbanded, its spirit was resurrected when Skelton became the founding president of a new Indian Art Circle, a monthly lecture series on all aspects of South Asian art held at the School of Oriental and African Studies (SOAS), which continues to this day.

Robert Skelton's counterpart at the British Museum initially, and later the British Library, was Jeremiah (Jerry) P. Losty (1945–2021). For the 1982 Festival of India, Skelton curated *The Indian Heritage* exhibition at the V&A[70] in parallel to Losty's enormous *Art of the Book in India* at the British Museum.[71] The two scholars were involved in or influenced in some part most of the major exhibitions of Indian miniatures in Britain since.[72] As well as exhibitions, books and catalogues, a perhaps even wider-reaching contribution has been the efforts of museum and library staff in uploading information and high-resolution images to their online databases, allowing British collections to be viewed digitally and studied across the world.

Nevertheless, the overwhelming lack of curiosity surrounding South Asian miniatures in Britain today is concerning. In his review of the British Museum's 2007 exhibition *Faith, Narrative and Desire: Masterpieces of Indian Painting*, Andrew Graham Dixon wrote that the museum 'has a collection of around 6,000 Indian paintings, which remains something of a well-kept secret' – despite the museum's displays of miniatures almost every year for the preceding half-century.[73] A better-kept secret is the enormous discomfort surrounding Indian miniatures within the wider British art establishment, severely hampering their study and public enjoyment. Miniatures have never aligned with British perceptions of what constitutes 'fine art' (i.e. paintings and sculpture), and instead were traditionally considered on a par with drawings and illustrated books. The fact that South Asian art raises uncomfortable questions about Britain's colonial past equally undercuts the entire field, to the point where any miniature posted on social media today receives a torrent of claims to 'give back' supposedly stolen goods.

Now, more than four centuries after the first Indian paintings arrived in Britain, it is worth reflecting on the role of miniatures not just in South Asian art history, but in the narrative of British art – an integral component of what is a diverse and globally entangled story.

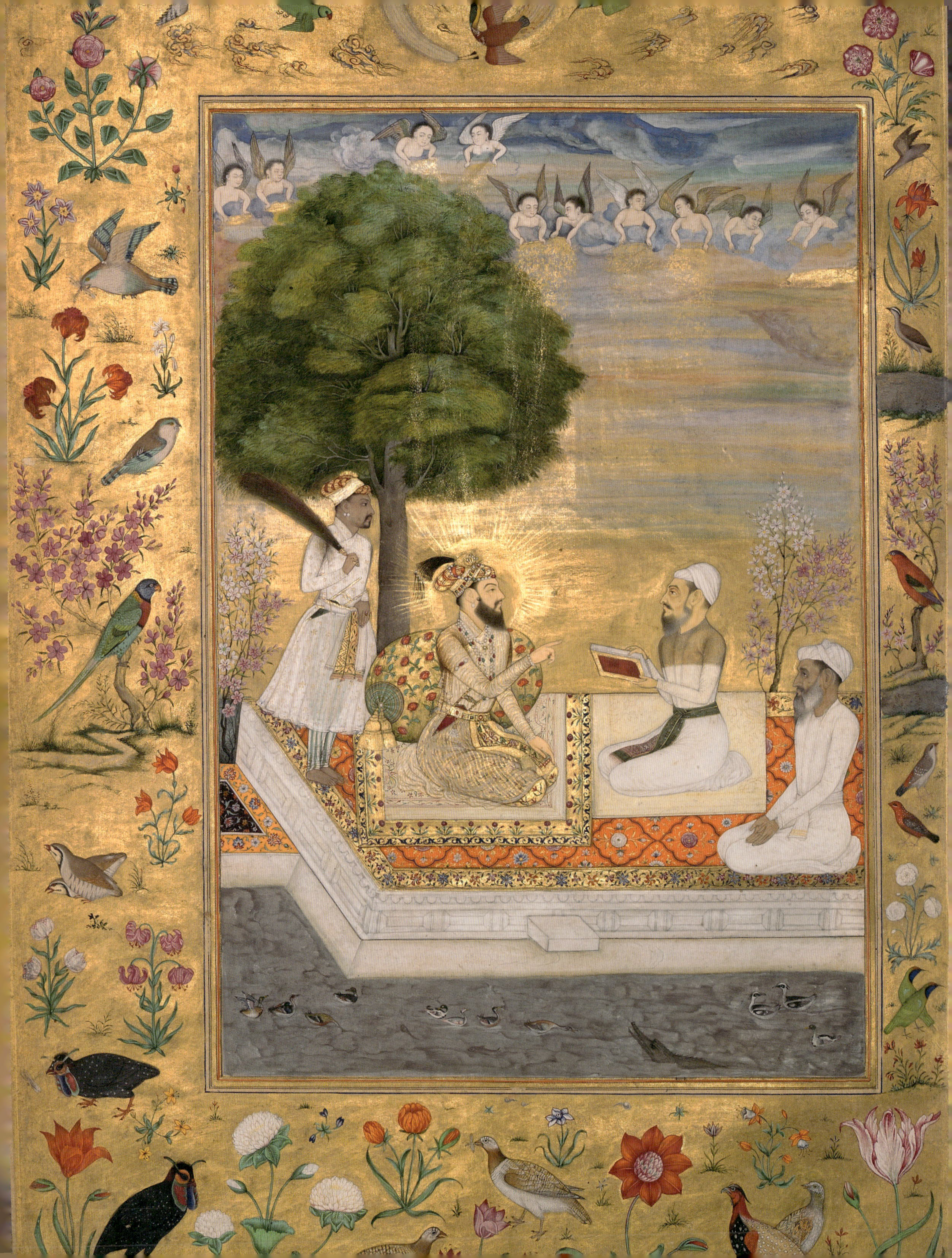

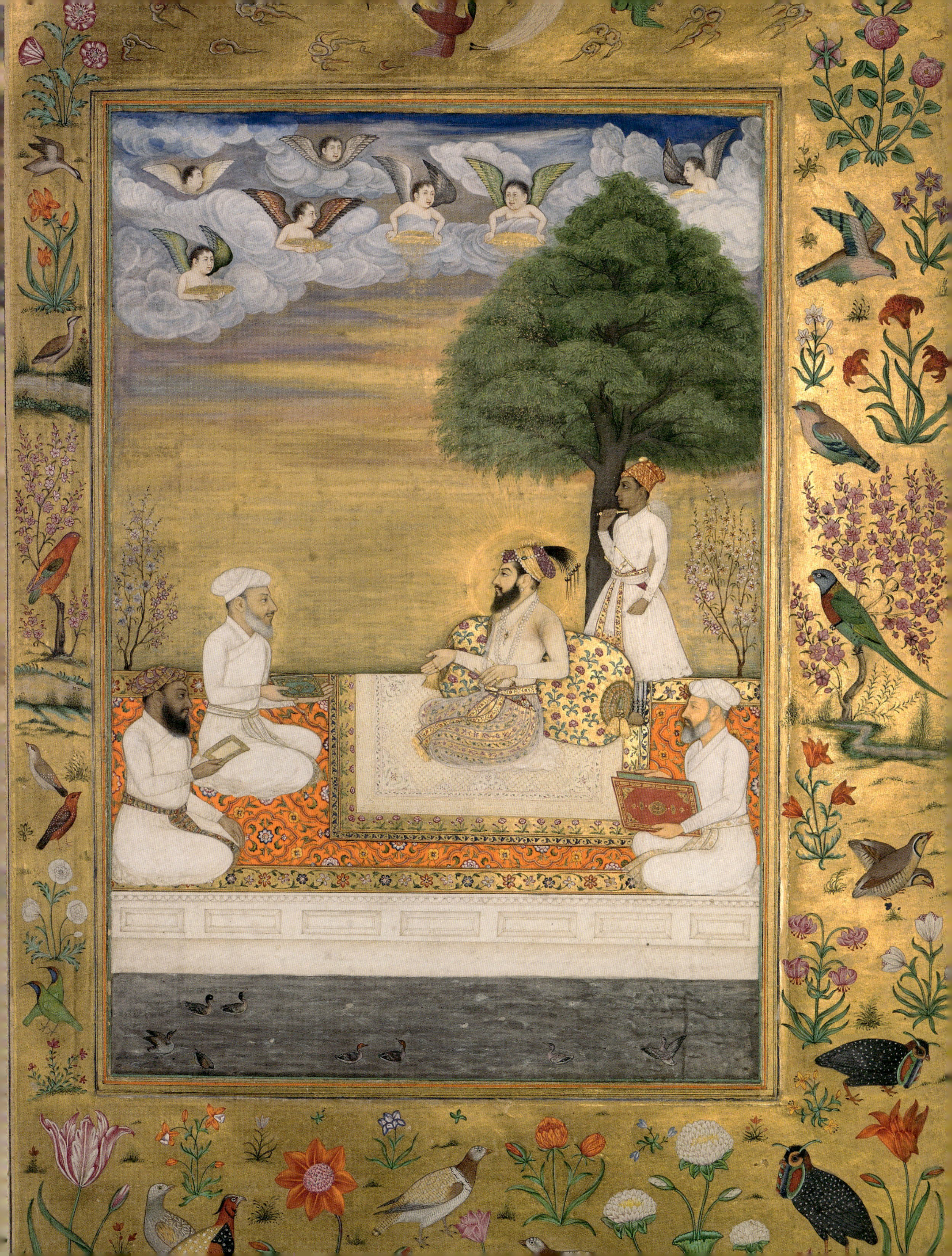

UNKNOWN ARTIST

1 Emperor Jahangir

c.1615 | watercolour and metallic paints on paper | 8.6 × 4.4 cm | British Museum

One of the first South Asian miniatures to arrive in Britain was a small portrait of the Mughal emperor Jahangir holding a falcon on his outstretched hand, painted by his artist Manohar. It was among the paintings brought back from India by Sir Thomas Roe in 1619 (see pp. 11–12), and within a year Compton Holland (d.1622), one of the leading print publishers in London, launched a print made after it onto the open market (fig. 8). Engraved by Renold Elstrack, this is the earliest example of an English artist copying and adapting the work of a Mughal painter.

Manohar's portrait of Jahangir is now lost. The painting shown here is from an album that arrived in Britain in 1790, sold by Colonel Antoine Polier to William Beckford (see pp. 16–17).[74] Its similarity to the painting given to Sir Thomas Roe suggests it may have been traced from the same original, a practice common in the Mughal workshops.

FIG. 8 Renold Elstrack, *The true Portraicture of the Great and Most Potent Monarch, Padesha Shalsallam, caled the Great Mogoll of the Easterne India. King of forty 5 Kingdoms*, c.1620.

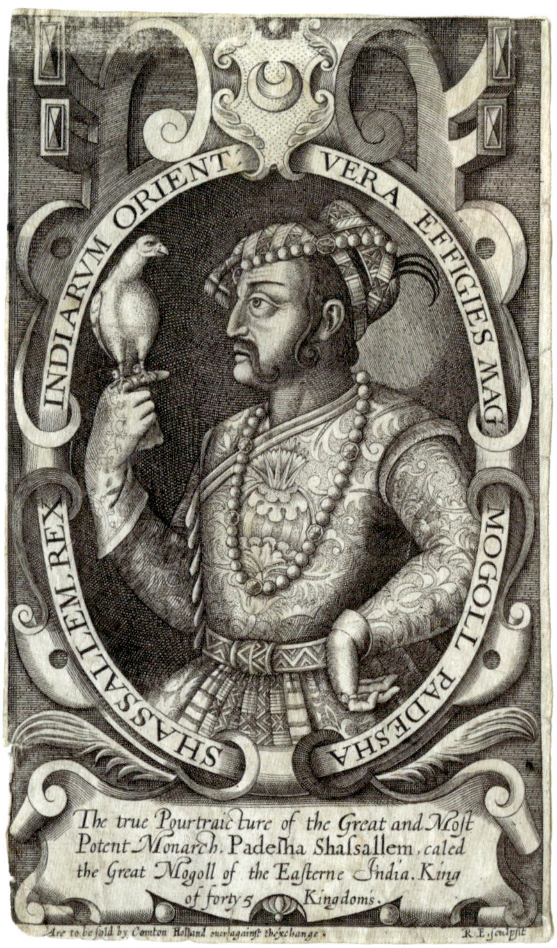

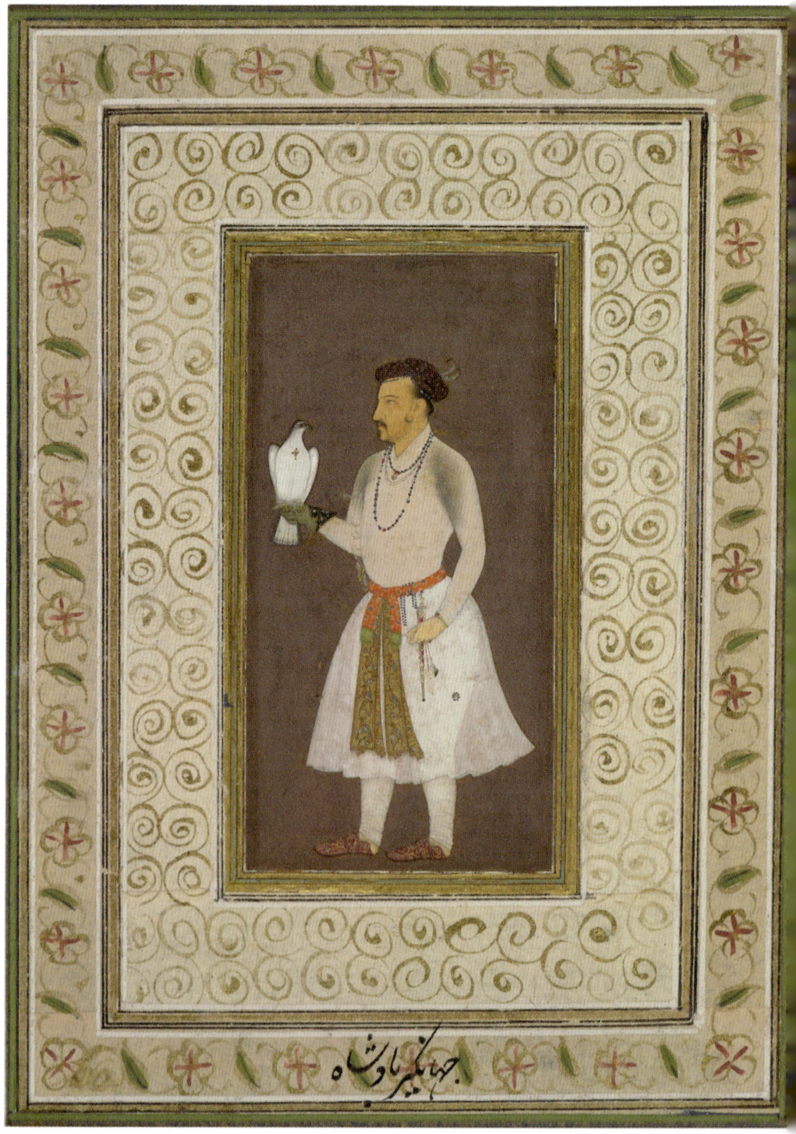

UNKNOWN ARTIST

2 A Mughal prince drinking wine carried in a palanquin formed of six women

c. 1610 | watercolour and metallic paints on paper | page 38 × 24.6 cm | Bodleian Library

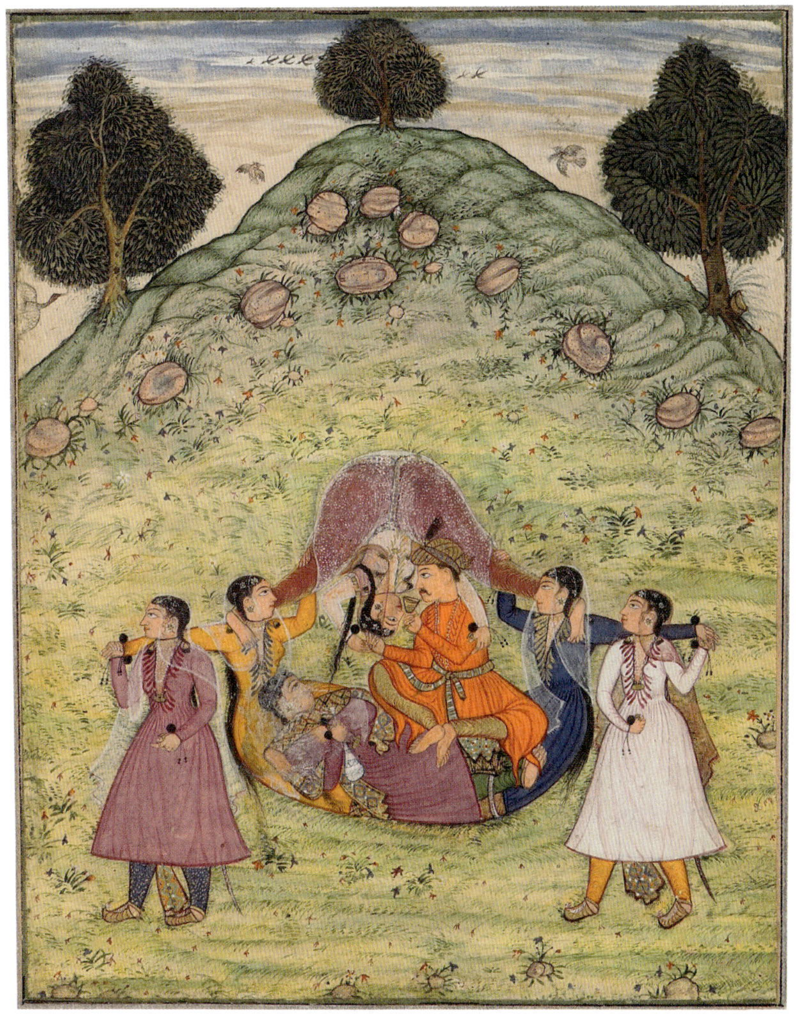

This curious painting is from the so-called Laud Ragamala, a *muraqqa* (album) of 30 paintings and 99 specimens of Arabic and Persian calligraphy donated to the University of Oxford in 1640 by its then chancellor, the Archbishop of Canterbury, William Laud (see p. 13). It was assembled twenty or thirty years earlier in the workshop of the Mughal nobleman Abdur Rahim (1556–1627), the commander-in-chief of the Mughal armies and a great patron of the arts.[75]

This painting is a variation of the *Nava Nari Kunjara* (nine women elephant), a motif originating in medieval Hindu art in which nine women, representing the nine *Rasas* (emotional states), form an elephant ridden by Lord Krishna, who represents mastery over the senses.[76] In this Mughal adaption of the motif, six women form a palanquin carrying a Mughal prince. He drinks wine poured by the woman underneath him and accepts the caresses of the woman above him.

Assembling a *muraqqa* was an act of connoisseurship in which paintings and poetry were juxtaposed to create new meanings and inspire dialogue when viewed in company. The Quranic verse on the opposite page asks 'Consider then whatever idols you invoke besides Allah: if Allah willed some affliction for you, could they undo His affliction?'[77]

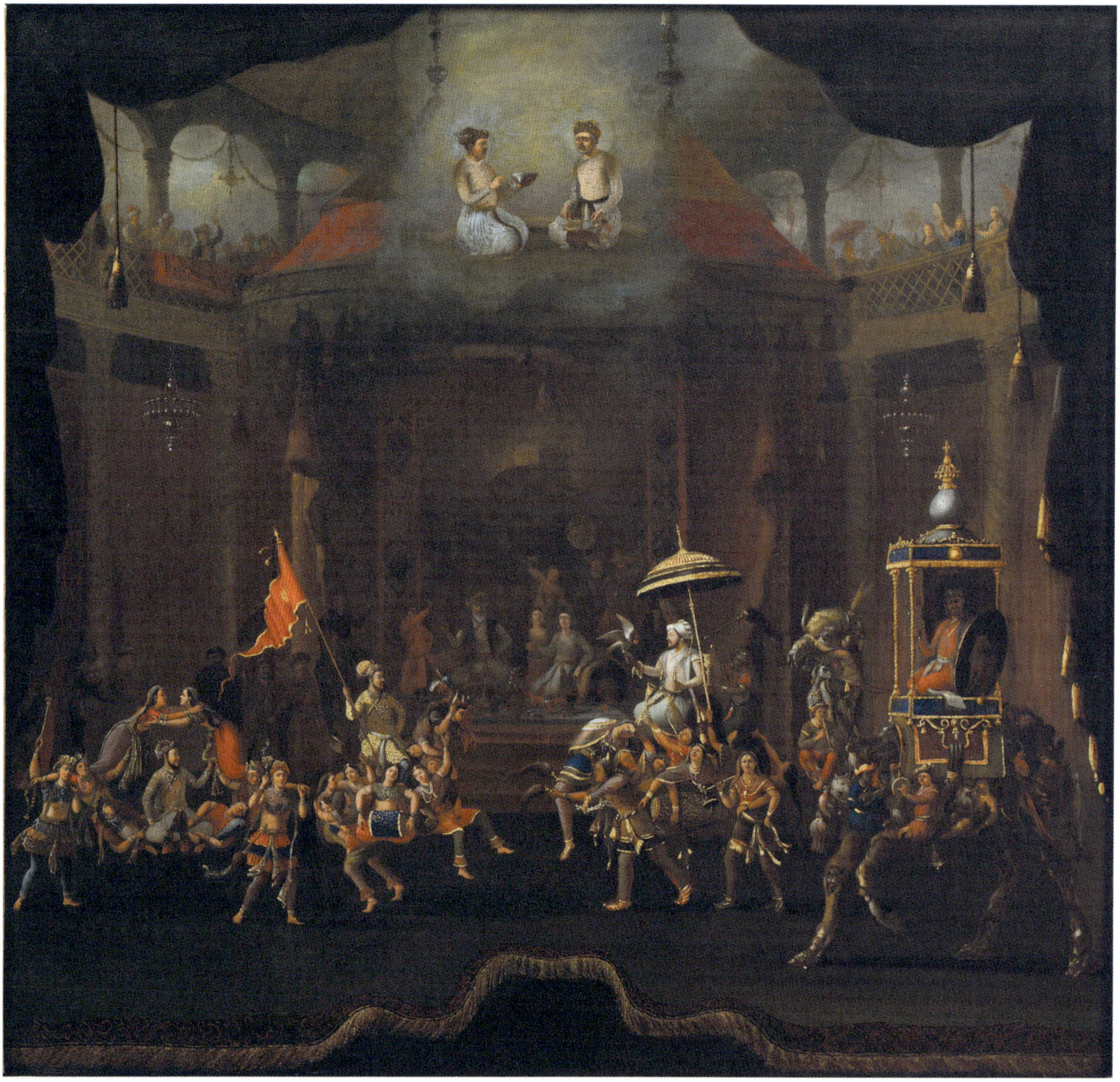

WILLEM SCHELLINKS

3 Parade of the sons of Shah Jahan

c.1660 | oil on canvas | painting 78 × 83.8 cm | Victoria and Albert Museum

The Dutch painter and poet Willem Schellinks (1623–1678) was the first European artist to show a deep appreciation of South Asian painting. In 1657 he wrote a poem praising the art of India above that of Europe[78] and in the following years painted at least six oil paintings incorporating Indian imagery.[79] One of the Indian albums Schellinks studied was the same royal Mughal album copied by Rembrandt (fig. 9),[80] thought to have been owned by the English art collector Alethea Howard, Countess of Arundel, who lived in Amsterdam from 1641 until her death in 1654 (see pp. 12–13).

The subject of this extraordinary painting is the war of succession fought between the sons of Emperor Shah Jahan in 1658–9. The four princes ride composite mounts similar to that in cat. 2 (a palanquin, a horse, an elephant and a camel) while their father and sister seated at the centre look on. Their ancestors, emperors Akbar and Jahangir, appear in the heavens. On the right, Prince Awrangzeb, the war's villainous victor, looks outwards towards the viewer holding a large and bloodied dagger. The painting's stage-like setting is based on the interiors of Amsterdam's city theatre, where a play about the Mughal's famous forebear, *Den Grooten Tamerlan* (The Great Timur), opened to wide acclaim in 1657.[81]

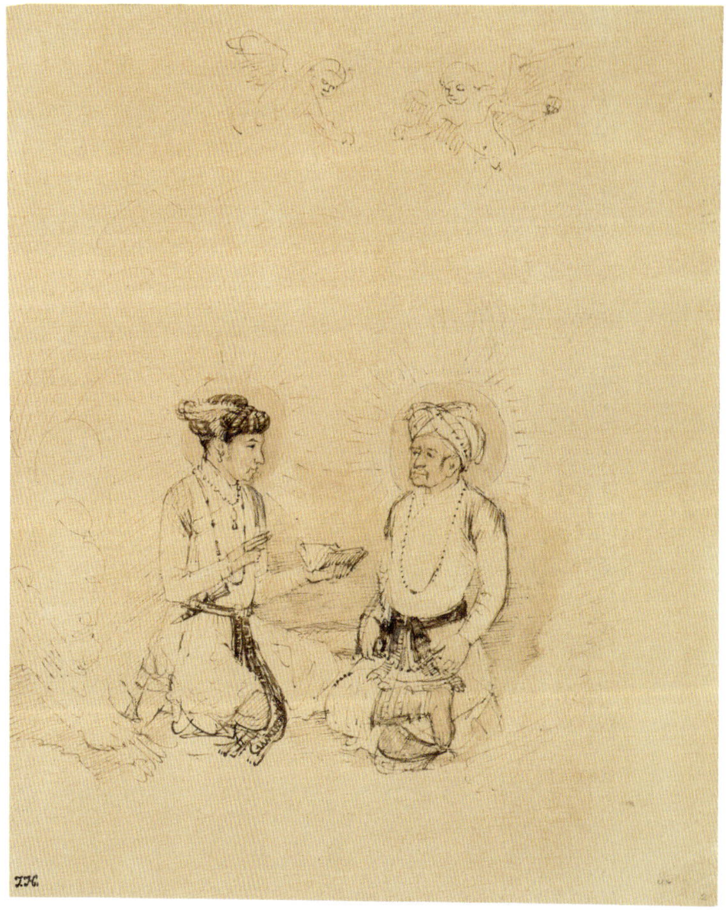

FIG. 9 Attributed to Rembrandt, *Emperors Akbar and Jahangir in Apotheosis*, c.1656.

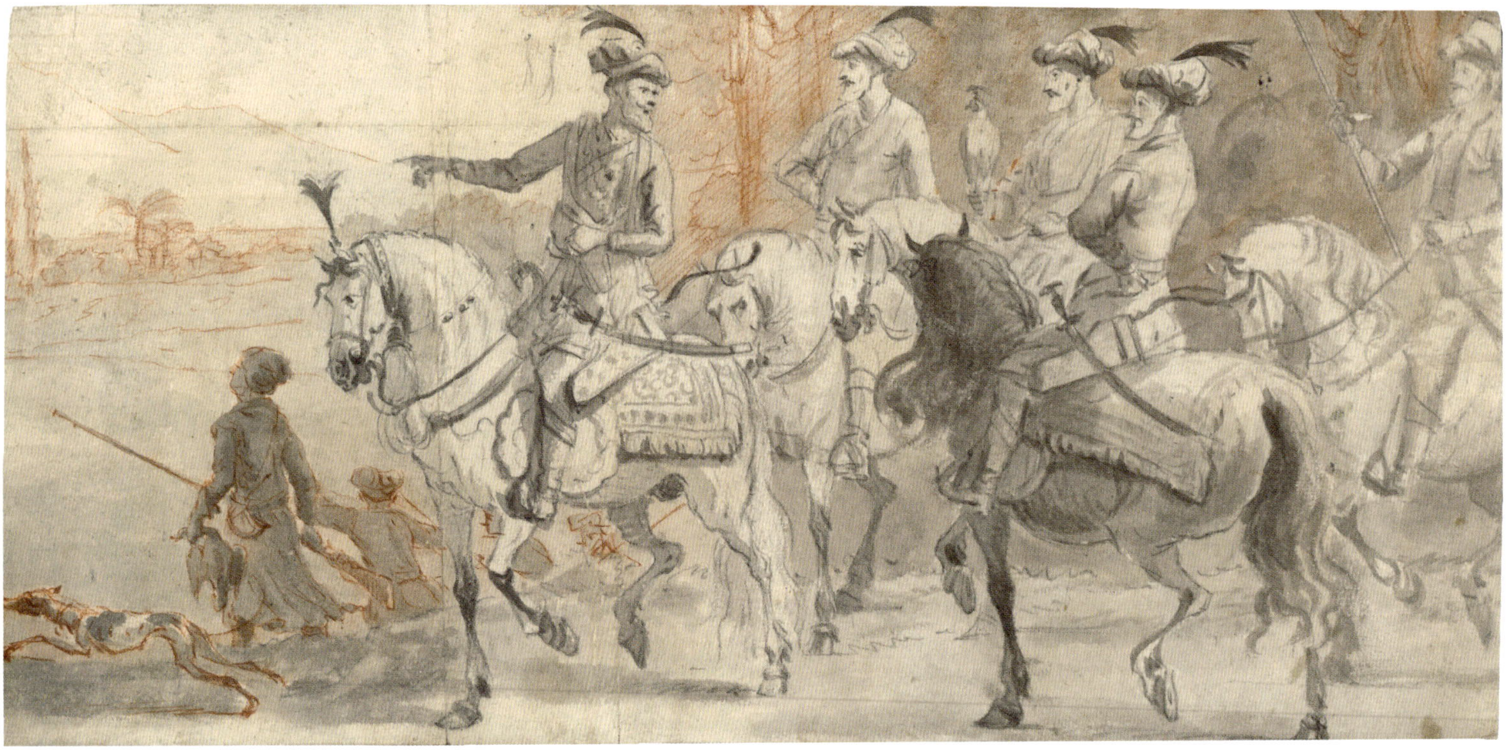

ATTRIBUTED TO WILLEM SCHELLINKS

4 Shah Jahan hawking

c.1657–60 | graphite and red chalk with grey wash on paper | 24.3 × 50.5 cm | British Museum

The artist of this drawing copied the figure of Shah Jahan from a painting in the same royal Mughal album that Rembrandt studied, thought to have been owned by the English art collector Alethea Howard, Countess of Arundel (see pp. 12–13). The original painting from her album survives today in Vienna (fig. 12).[82] Whereas the Mughal artist depicted Shah Jahan hawking with his sons in the lush landscape of Burhanpur, the Dutch artist placed him in a European-style hunting scene with 'exotic' palm trees in the background.

The attribution to Schellinks is based on the drawing's similarity to a signed painting by the artist in the Orientalist Museum in Doha (fig. 10), but there are significant differences between the two works. In the sketch the artist reproduced the head of Shah Jahan repeatedly for each of the figures. In the painting, however, Schellinks copied portraits of Shah Jahan and his four sons made by Gujarati artists in Surat in the late 1640s, some of which are also now in Vienna.[83] In his 1657 poem in praise of Indian art, Schellinks commended the work of both Gujarati and Mughal artists, suggesting his awareness of the differences between them. Schellinks, Rembrandt and at least one other European artist are known to have made sketches from these portraits by Gujarati painters (see figs 11–13).[84]

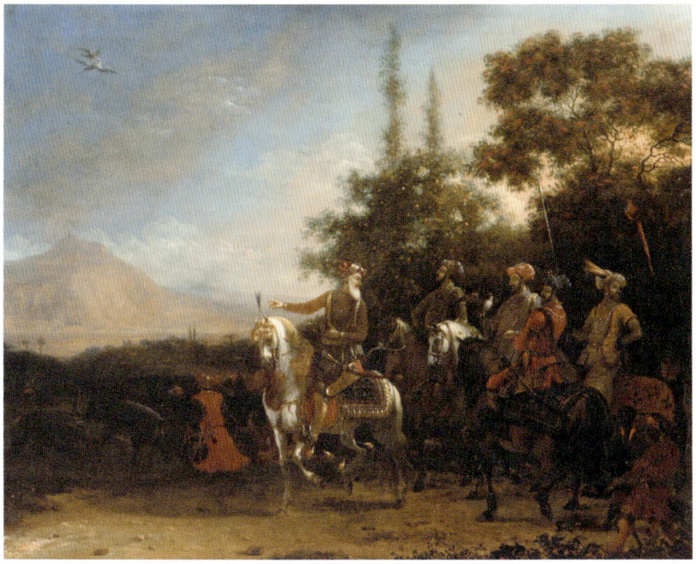

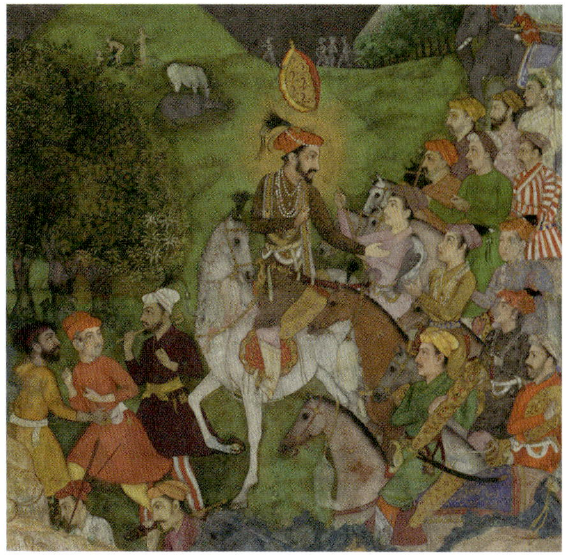

FIG. 10 *(& detail, left, below)* Willem Schellinks, *Hunting Scene with Shah Jahan and his Sons*, c.1665.

FIG. 11 Rembrandt, *Dara Shikoh (detail, centre, below)*, c.1655–60.

FIG. 12 Mughal artist, *Shah Jahan and his Sons Hawking (detail, above)*, c.1630.

FIG. 13 Gujarati artist, *Dara Shikoh (detail, below)*, c.1645–50.

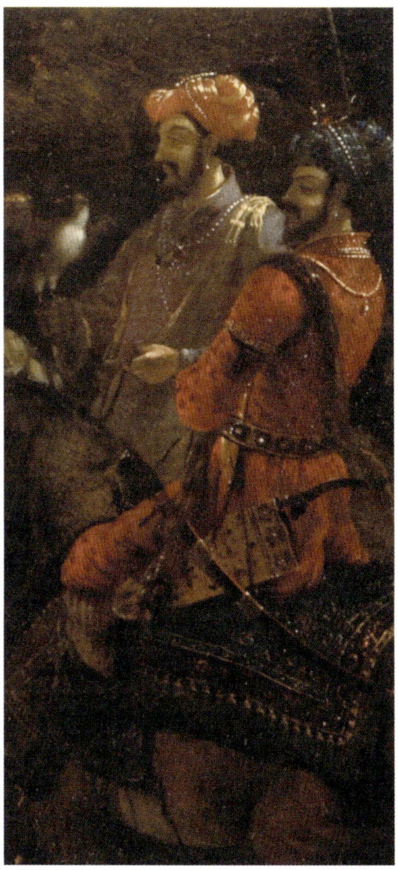

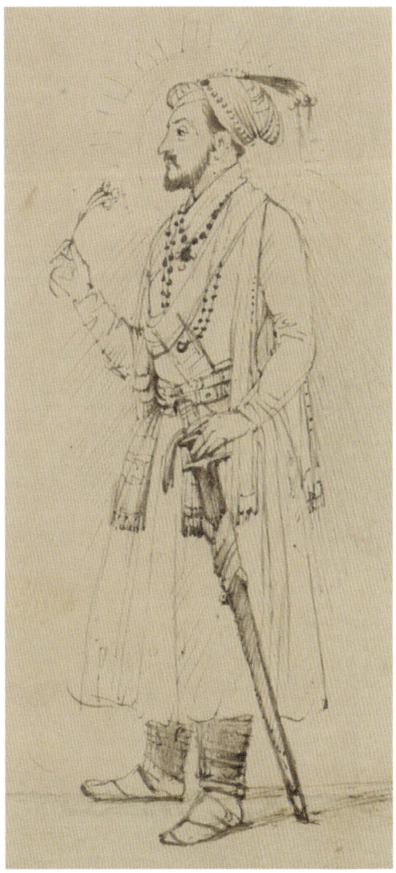

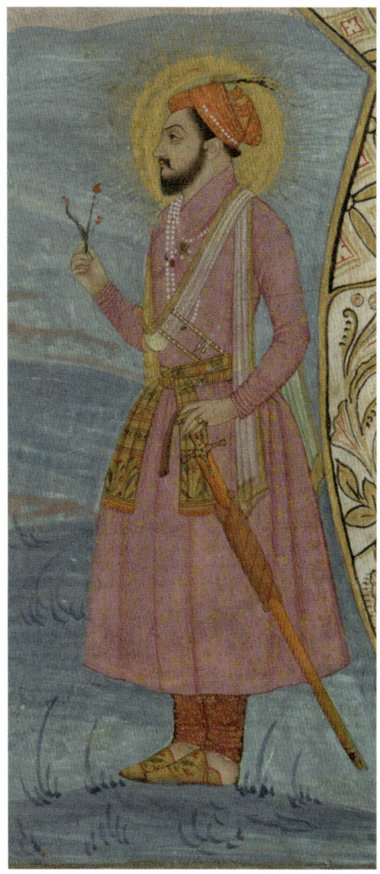

MUHAMMAD HUSAYN KASHMIRI

5 Verses of Persian poetry

*c.*1600 | ink and metallic paints on paper | page 37.1 × 23.9 cm | Royal Collection/HM King Charles III

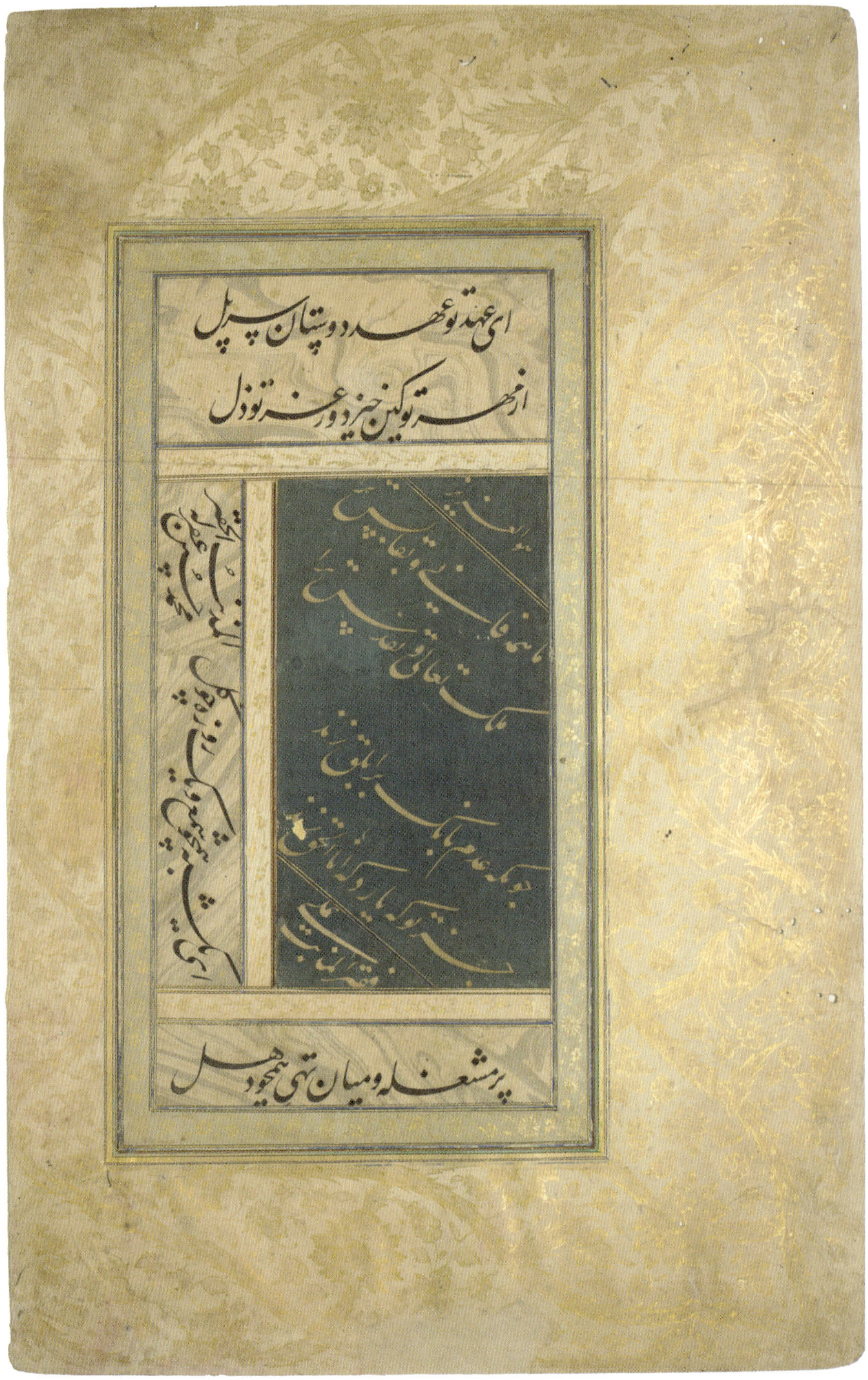

Twenty-three loose pages from this Mughal *muraqqa* (album) with exquisite gold-painted borders assembled around 1600[85] arrived in Britain in the 1720s. They were apparently salvaged from the bound volume after it suffered water damage, evidence of which is still visible along the page edges. A small inscription on one of the pages states *malik-i thomas sahib* (the property of Mister Thomas).[86]

The Persian verse on the green tinted paper is by Nizami,[87] with the words cut out of the paper rather than written. The Mughal master calligrapher Muhammad Husayn Kashmiri (see cat. 8) wrote the verse by Abu-Said Abul-Khayr[88] on the marbled paper sprinkled with gold flecks beside and above the verse of Nizami. The complex structure of these album pages would have been planned well before any of the individual pieces of paper were adhered. The assembler would have worked from the outside inwards, starting with the outer borders. They would have laid out the calligraphy, then prepared the narrow pieces of paper to fill the gaps between them. Thin rulings in gold and coloured paint were then carefully drawn to cover the edges between the separate pieces of paper.[89]

CHITARMAN

6 Shah Jahan

1627–8 | ink on paper | 17.1 × 8.9 cm | British Museum

This preparatory drawing is from an album of 74 sketches owned by William Beckford, formerly in the collection of Antoine Polier (see pp. 16–17). The drawings in this album all date from the seventeenth and eighteenth centuries, but this small half-length portrait of Emperor Shah Jahan is the only sketch attributed to a named artist. An inscription in Persian reads 'exercise by Chitarman, first regnal year'. Chitarman was a leading painter in Shah Jahan's workshop and the sketch may have been a preparatory drawing for a painting made to commemorate the emperor's accession (see fig. 14).[90]

The Persian numeral 2 above the sketch denotes a grading used by collectors and dealers in northern India. In March 1775 Polier sent 96 paintings to his artist Mihr Chand with instructions for having them mounted, and noted that 'Forty-two of them are of the first order (*aval*) and forty-one of the second category (*duvum*) while thirteen are useless (*nakara*).'[91] After Polier and Beckford, the album passed through the hands of several collectors before the British Museum bought it in 1935 from Luzac & Co.

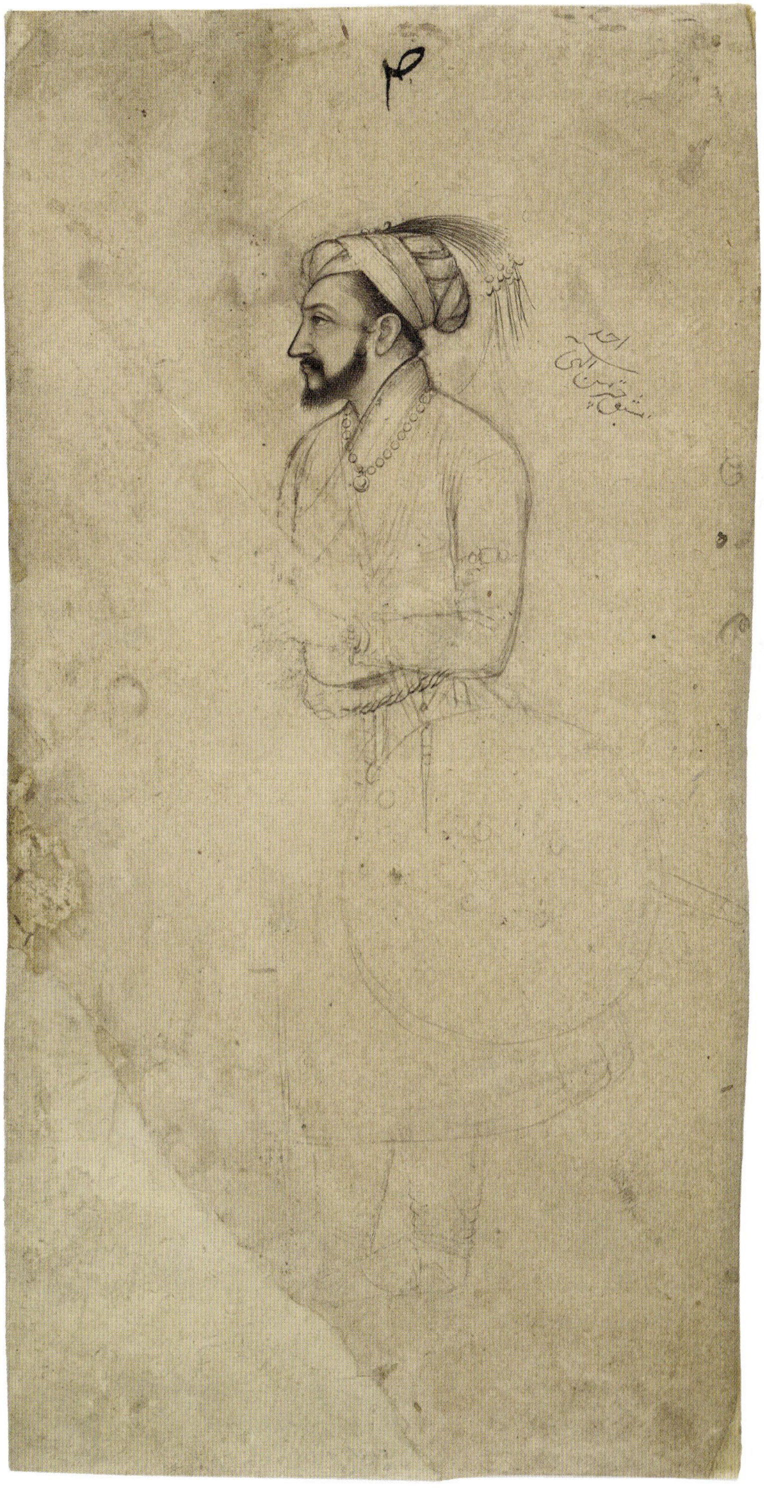

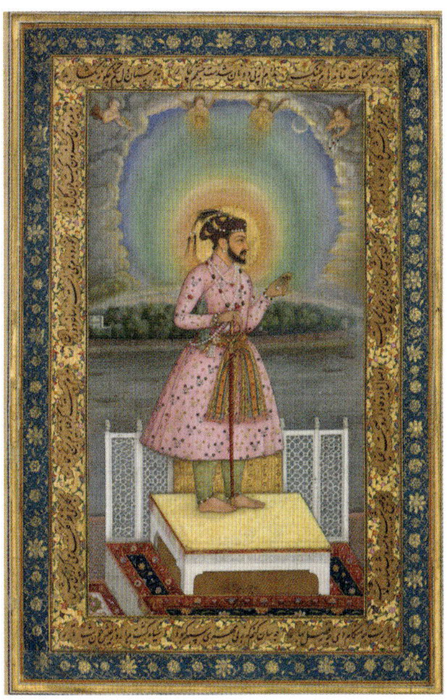

FIG. 14 Chitarman, *Shah Jahan on a Terrace, Holding a Pendant Set with His Portrait*, 1627–8.

UNKNOWN ARTISTS

7 Miniature Mughal portraits set in wooden panels

17th and 18th centuries | each panel 45.3 × 32 cm | National Museum of Scotland

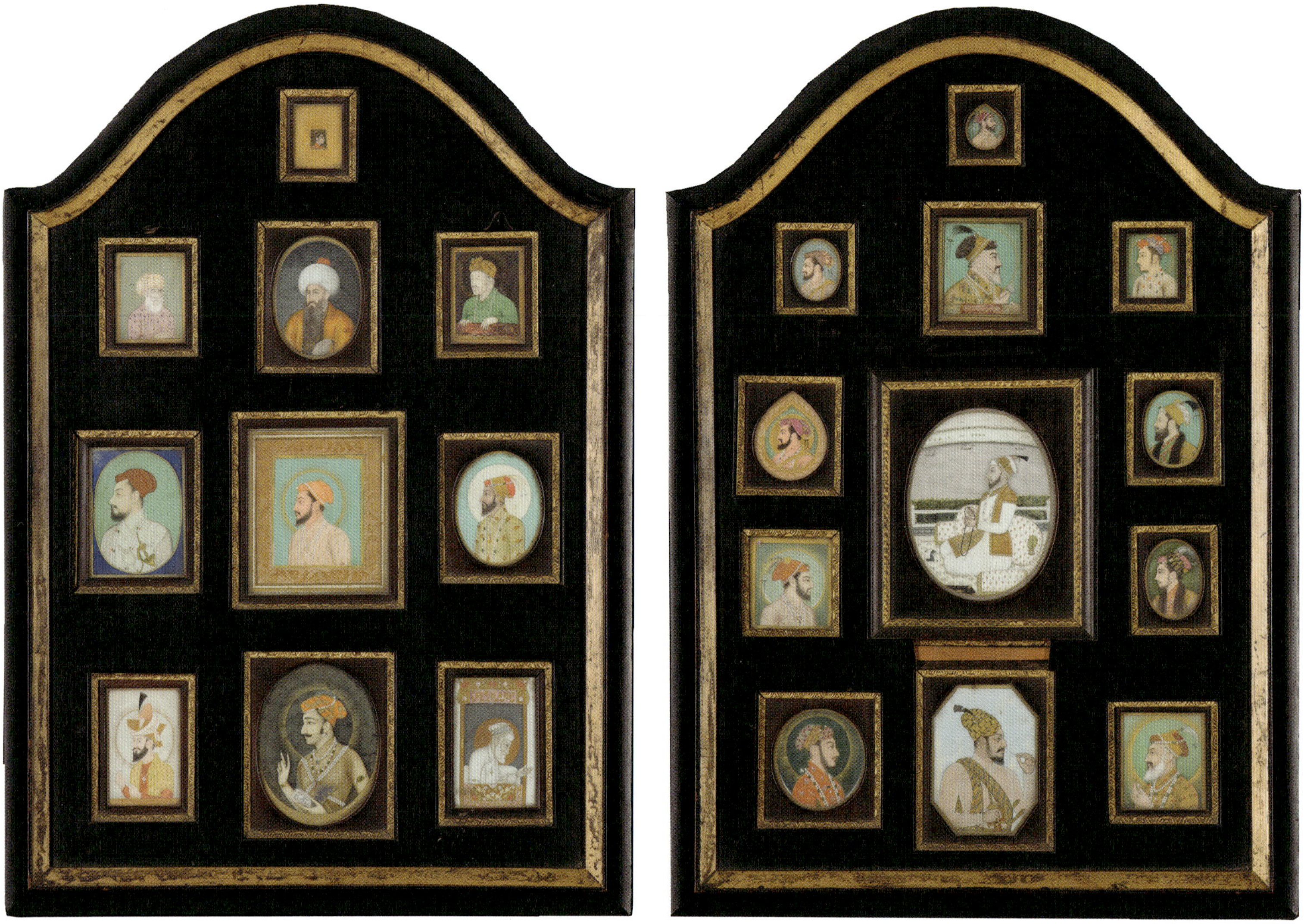

Captain Archibald Swinton, Robert Clive's Persian interpreter, collected these miniature portraits in Bengal in the mid-eighteenth century.[92] The largest is a likeness of the Mughal emperor Shah Alam II, whom Swinton met when negotiating the Treaty of Allahabad in 1765, and may have been a gift from the emperor to commemorate that occasion. The others may have been collected with the help of his friend Ghulam Husayn Khan, a cousin of the Nawab of Bengal.[93] More than a decade after Swinton returned to Scotland, he had the miniatures framed in a European style.[94]

Apart from the painting of Shah Alam II, the portraits in these frames mostly depict

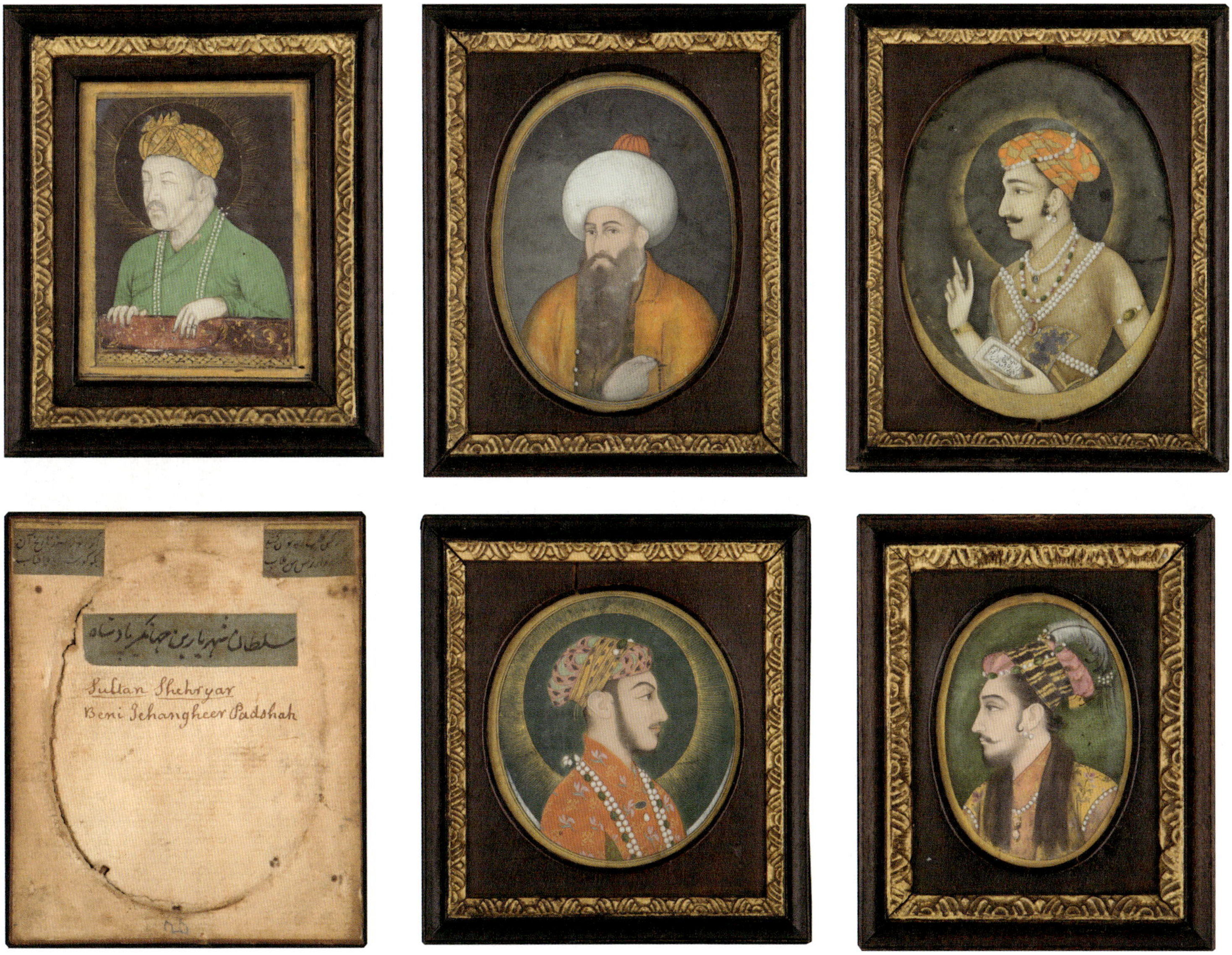

sixteenth- and seventeenth-century members of the Mughal imperial family, and may originally have been intended to be worn as jewellery on chains.[95] By the time Swinton acquired them, the portraits were mounted into an album with Persian inscriptions identifying each of the figures in the margins below. When Swinton had the miniatures framed, he kept these labels and had them stuck to the backs of the paintings. Most of Swinton's South Asian paintings were sold off in 1810; of those that stayed with the family, many were accepted by the government in lieu of inheritance tax from the estate of Sir John Swinton in 2021 and allocated to the National Museum of Scotland.[96]

MADHU

8 The singer on the balcony

1595 | watercolour and metallic paints on paper | painting 22 × 13 cm | Bodleian Library

Sir Gore Ouseley (1770–1844) purchased this Mughal illustrated manuscript of the *Baharitsan* (Garden of Spring) by the Perisan poet Jami in 1800 during his posting as major-commandant and later aide-de-camp to Nawab Saadat Ali Khan of Awadh. Gore Ouseley taught himself Persian, Arabic and Sanskrit, and during his ten years in Lucknow bought hundreds of manuscripts and paintings, many of which originated in the Mughal imperial library.

The master calligrapher Muhammad Husayn Kashmiri (see cat. 5) transcribed this copy of the *Baharistan* in Lahore for the Mughal emperor Akbar in 1595. The text was commonly used as a textbook for children and Akbar may have commissioned it specifically for the education of his three grandsons: princes Khusraw, Parvez and Khurram (later Emperor Shah Jahan).[97]

In the story depicted here, the author tells that one day a celebrated young singer was performing on a balcony under the gaze of her master while a youth, enraptured by her, stood listening. The master of the house noticed her watching the young man and invited him in to dine. While they conversed, the youth's eyes remained fixed upon the singer and the host left the two alone. They declared their love for each other, but the youth professed 'on the day of resurrection, friendship will become enmity, except the friendship of the chaste, which will ever increase in attachment. I do not wish for our love to diminish and our friendship turn to hatred', and so he departed.[98]

Gore Ouseley disbound the *Baharistan* volume after he returned to England; he then added a lengthy introduction to the text and a note on its author, and rebound its pages in red velvet covers.[99] After Gore Ouseley's death in 1844, James Bardoe Elliott (1785–1863), formerly a judge in Patna, purchased hundreds of his Persian manuscripts, and in 1859 donated them to the Bodleian Library.[100]

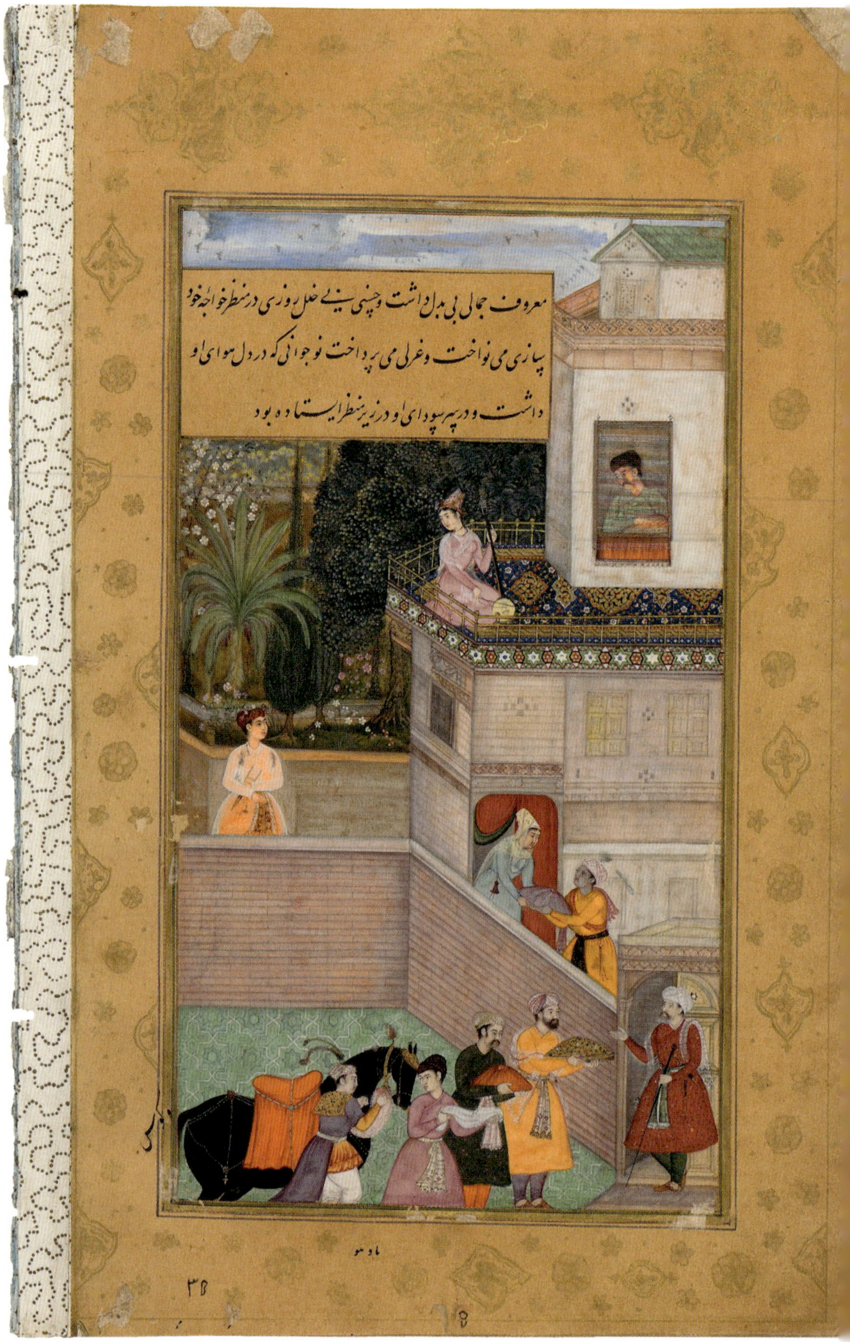

UNKNOWN ARTIST

9 # Jesus as Salvator Mundi

*c.*1600 with later additions | ink on paper | page 36.5 × 26.5 cm | Bodleian Library

This brush drawing is from an album assembled by Gore Ouseley of various paintings and pages of calligraphy that he purchased in Lucknow between 1795 and 1805. His son, the English composer Sir Frederick Ouseley (1825–1889), sold this with other volumes that he had inherited from his father to the Bodleian Library in 1858.

Labelled 'The Holy Family' in Gore Ouseley's hand, this painting is not a copy or tracing of a specific European print but an adaption of different figures from sixteenth-century engravings: Christ holding an orb and palm, possibly from a depiction of the Trinity in which he sits on a cloud; Mary with clasped hands from a lamentation scene; and winged angels in adoration. The Spanish Fathers of the Third Jesuit Mission to the Mughal court presented European printed books with Christian imagery to Akbar in Lahore in 1595 and remained attached to the court for many years. Many Mughal painters of the time imitated and adapted the figures and modelling techniques seen in these engravings brought by the Jesuits and others. The Iranian emigré artist Aqa Riza, head of Jahangir's workshop when he was a prince, encouraged his students to study European prints and copy them as part of their artistic training.[101]

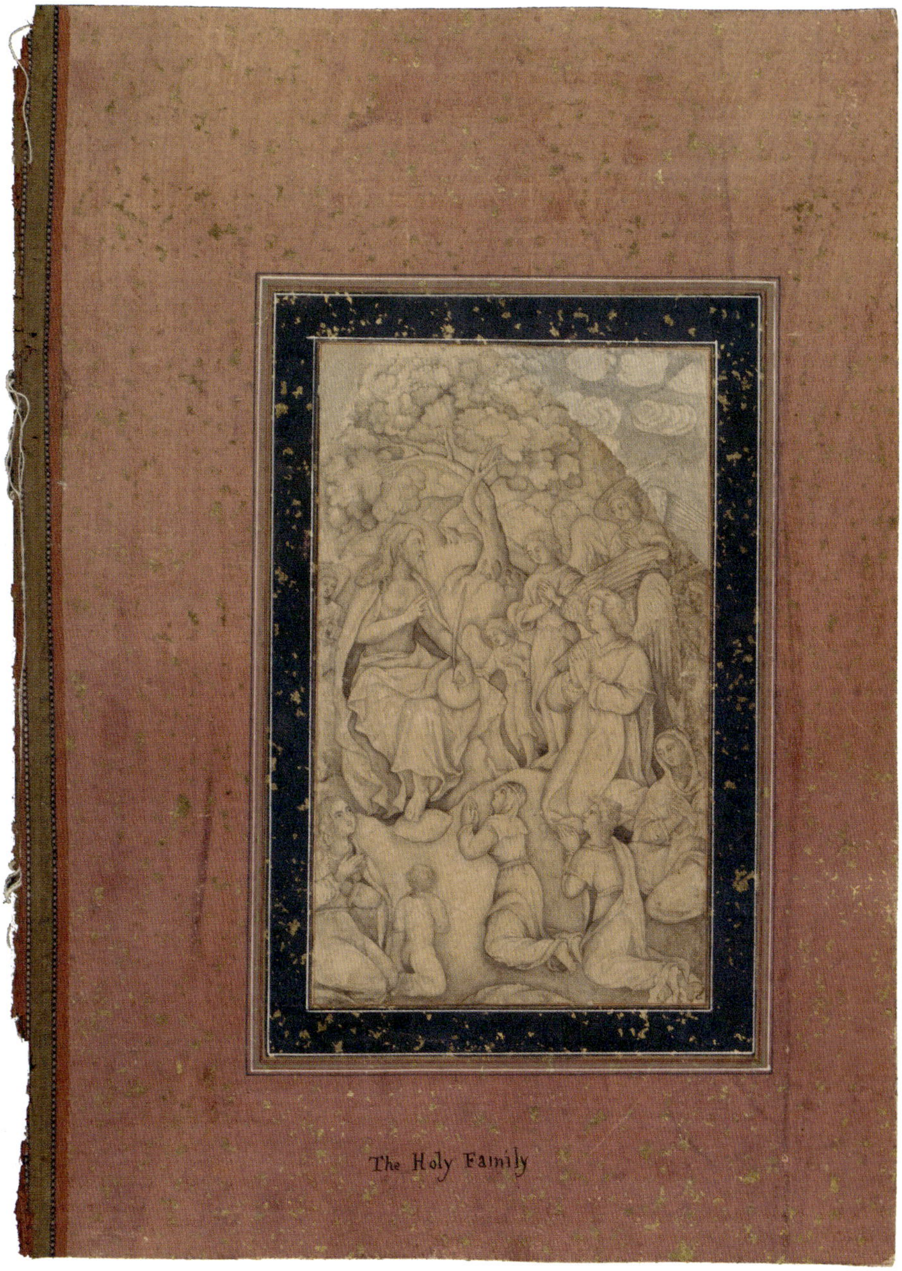

GOVARDHAN

10 The Kaaba moves for Saint Rabia al-Adawiyya

c.1605–10 | watercolour and metallic paints on paper | page 34.4 × 23 cm | Royal Collection/HM King Charles III

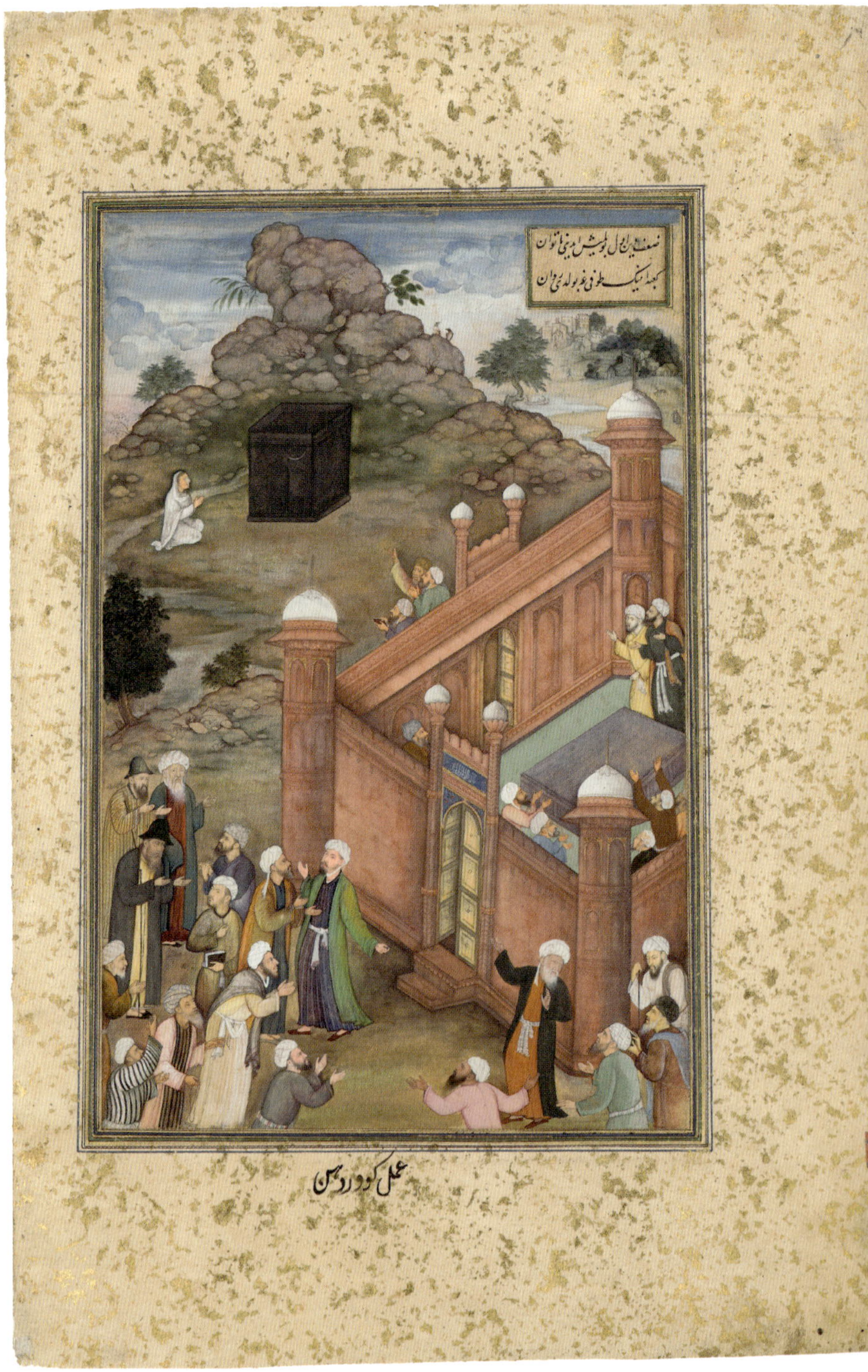

Saint Rabia al-Adawiyya of Basra (d. 801), shown in the background of this painting, was the first female Sufi saint in Islam, renowned for her poverty and piety. The artist Govardhan depicts her pilgrimage to Mecca when God moved the Kaaba to meet her halfway.[102] Saint Rabia's face has suffered paint loss to such an extent that the underdrawing is visible, possibly a result of this part of the page being repeatedly touched to impart blessing. In the foreground is another Muslim saint, Ibrahim bin Adham of Balkh (d. 770). Having given up his kingdom and wealth to become a wandering dervish, he arrives at the Masjid al-Haram after a 14-year journey crossing the desert in prayer, only to discover the Kaaba is no longer there.

This painting is from a fifteenth-century manuscript of the *Khamsa* (Quintet) of Mir Ali Shir Navai, one of the six volumes presented as gifts from Nawab Saadat Ali Khan to George III in 1798 via the East India Company governor general, Lord Teignmouth (see p. 15). The first page (fig. 3) bears the seal of Hamida Banu Begum (d. 1604), grandmother of the Mughal emperor Jahangir, who inherited it after her death. Jahangir wrote a note on the same page, calling it 'one of my most treasured books'. He had all but one of the original fifteenth-century illustrations removed (probably to mount in an album) and commissioned new paintings, including this one, to be added in their place.[103]

BALCHAND

11 Prince Khurram attacking a lion in December 1610

c.1640–50 | watercolour and metallic paints | painting 34.1 × 23.5 cm | Royal Collection/HM King Charles III

The large illustrated manuscript of the *Padshahnama* (Book of Emperors), is the most famous of the six volumes presented as gifts from Nawab Saadat Ali Khan to George III in 1798 via Lord Teignmouth (see p. 15). In a memo to the king, Teignmouth described it as 'the most splendid Persian manuscript I ever saw ... This was the Book which was shown to me at Lucknow, & I was then informed that the deceased Nabob Asoph uddoulah [Asaf ud-Dawla] purchased it for 12000 Rupees – about £1500.'[104]

Shah Jahan commissioned the *Padshahnama* as a celebratory record of his life and the Mughal dynasty. This painting by his senior artist Balchand[105] illustrates an episode which took place when Shah Jahan (then Prince Khurram) was 18. Towards the end of a day's hunting, after nightfall, Jahangir shot several times at a large lion before it turned and ran towards the emperor, prompting Anup Ray, Jahangir's chief steward, to tackle it. The steward was on the ground with one of his arms inside the lion's mouth when Khurram struck the lion with his sword. Rajah Ramdas Kachhvaha and Hayat Khan joined him in attacking the lion and together they rescued Anup Ray.[106]

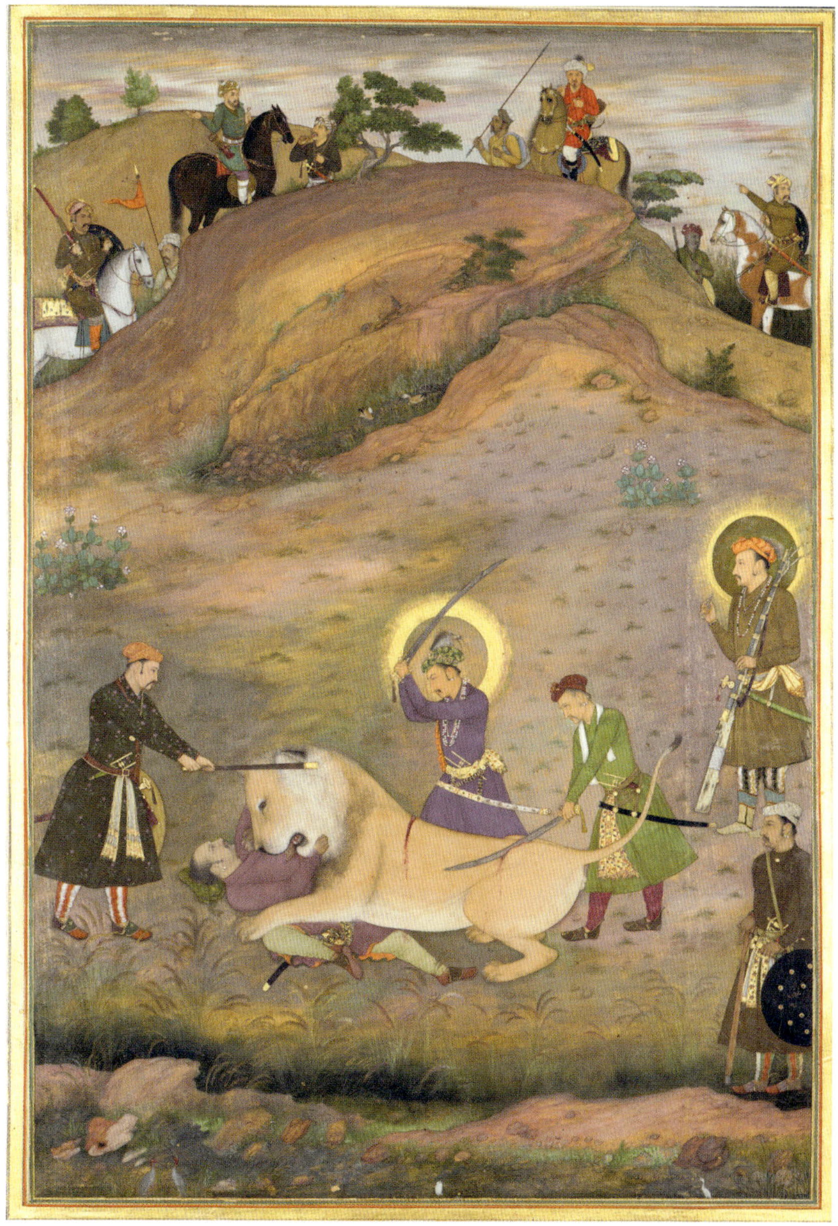

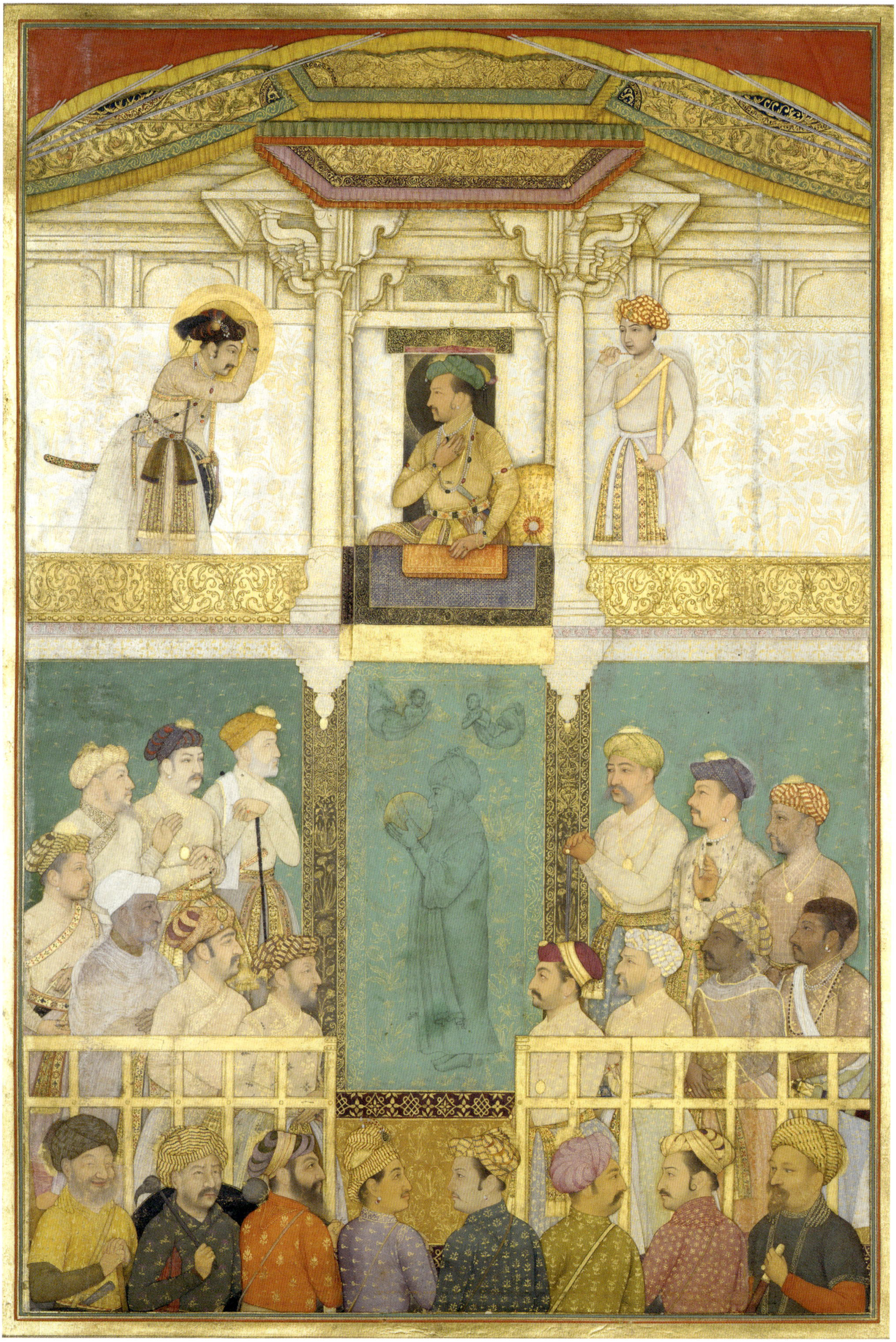

ATTRIBUTED TO ABID

12 Prince Khurram departs from Ajmer for his first Deccan campaign on 30 October 1616

c.1640–50 | watercolour and metallic paints on paper | painting 35.6 × 24.2 cm | Royal Collection/HM King Charles III

Abid, a master artist of Shah Jahan's atelier to whom this painting is attributed, was one of the sons of the Iranian artist Aqa Riza, who encouraged his students to copy European prints as part of their artistic training (see cat. 9).[107] Abid's modelling of soft, rounded faces, often in three-quarter view, suggests he may also have studied miniature paintings brought to the Mughal court by European diplomats or missionaries (see fig. 15). This scene depicts Shah Jahan taking leave of his father as he sets off on his first Deccan campaign, an early milestone in his military career.

The *Padshahnama* illustrations are now among the most famous Mughal paintings in the world, but for the first 150 years after the manuscript arrived in Britain it was known only to scholars and visitors to the royal libraries. During a visit to Windsor Castle in the summer of 1873, Nasir ud-Din Shah, the king of Iran (r.1848–96), recorded in his diary that 'I was shown some Persian manuscripts, in particular a history of India written like a diary and very beautifully illuminated in the Indian style – a magnificent book.'[108]

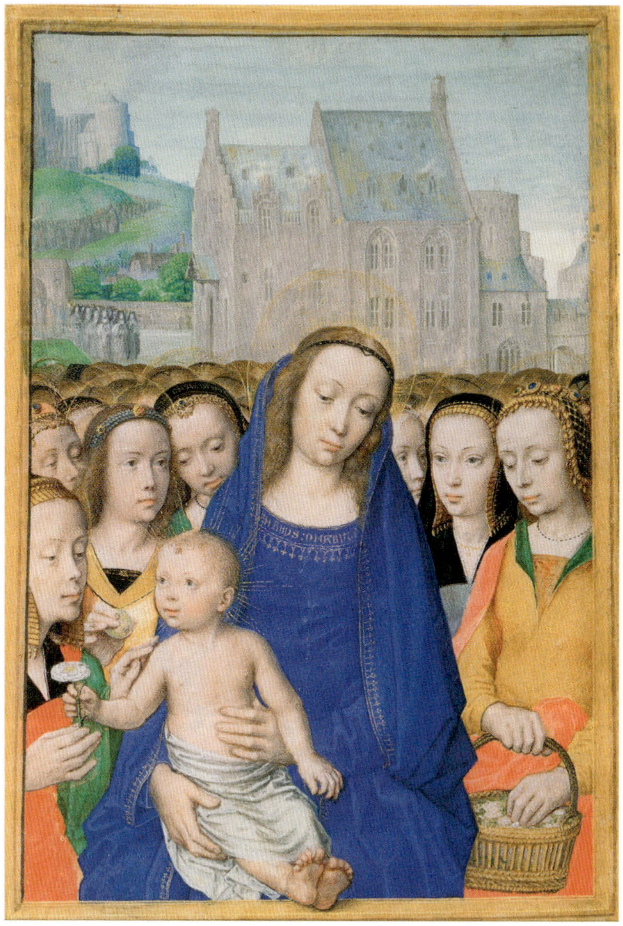

FIG. 15 (*above*) Gérard David, *Virgin and Child with Female Saints*, 1500.

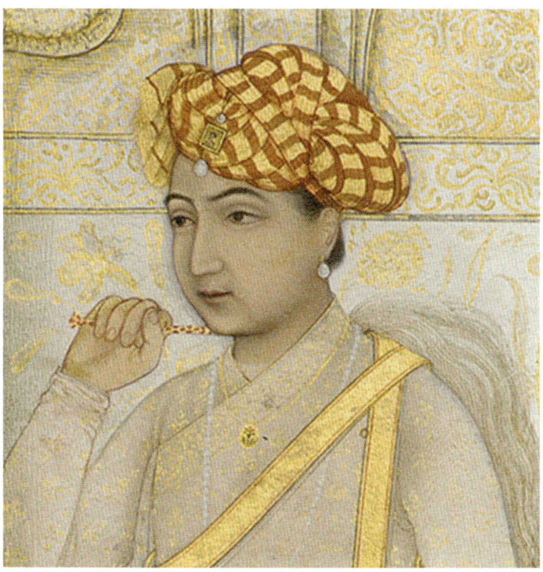

Detail of cat. 12 (*left*) showing Abid's sculptural approach to modelling faces. As a contemporary visual trick, the artist depicts Jahangir's attendant wearing a turban ornament with a miniature portrait of Shah Jahan in his 50s – the emperor's age at the time Abid made the painting.

MURAR

13 Jahangir receives Prince Khurram on his return from the Deccan on 10 October 1617

c.1640–50 | watercolour and metallic paints on paper | painting 30.8 × 20.9 cm | Royal Collection/HM King Charles III

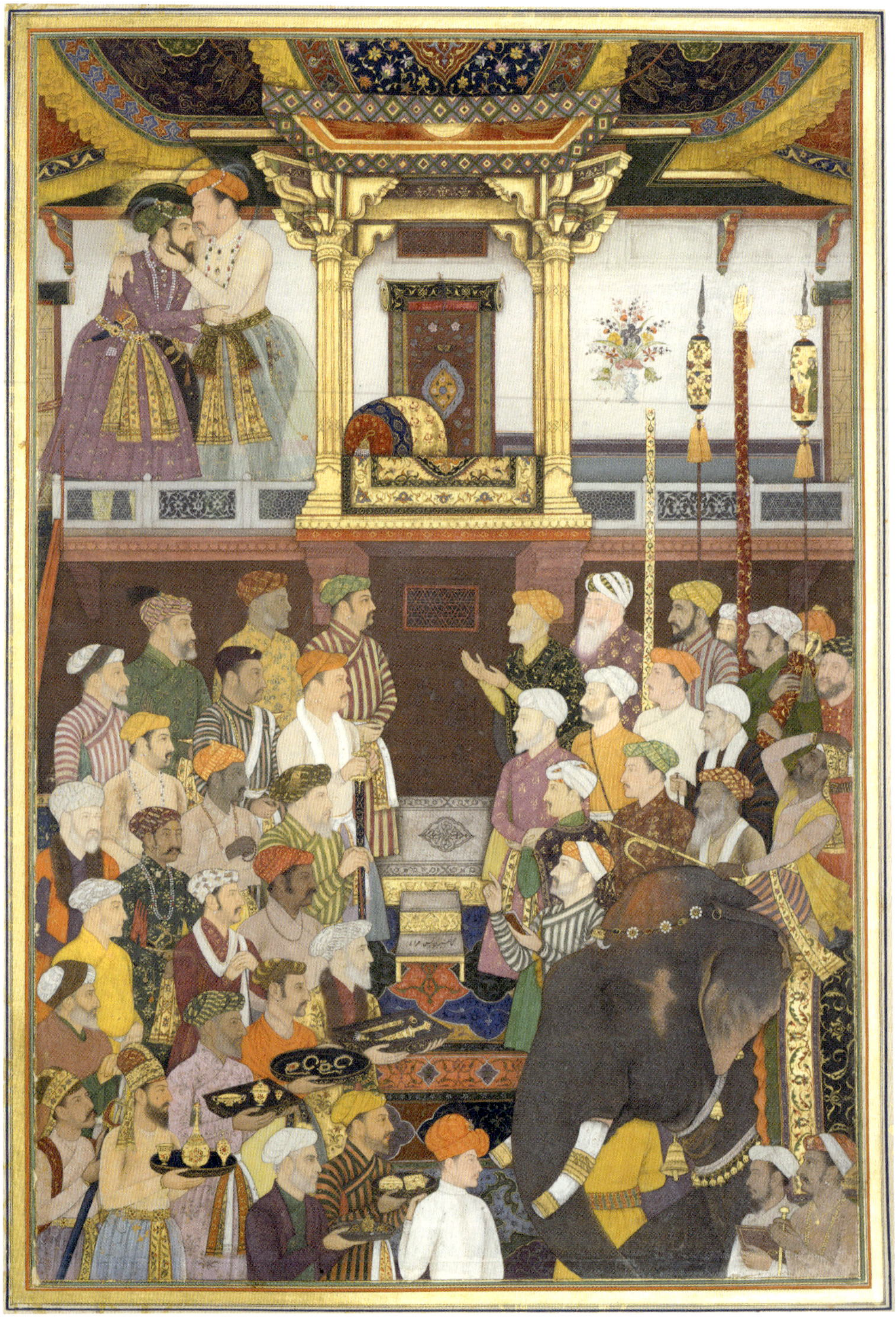

The figure holding a paintings folder at the lower right of this painting is a self-portrait of the artist Murar, even though the event depicted took place more than twenty years before he painted it. Diagonally opposite Murar, Jahangir embraces Prince Khurram following his triumphant return to the court at Mandu from the Deccan campaign. In the foreground, two Deccani nobles and the Mughal officers who negotiated their treaty of surrender carry gifts from Adil Shah of Bijapur.

The *Padshahnama* manuscript was first exhibited in public in 1947 at the Royal Academy exhibition of art from India and Pakistan, on loan from King George VI (see p. 23). It then appeared in three exhibitions at the British Museum in 1960, 1976 and 1982,[109] before the manuscript was disbound for conservation in 1993. While disbound, the opportunity was taken to display all 46 of the book's illustrations together, and in 1997 they went on an international tour taking in New Delhi, London and five museums in America.[110] The intended rebinding of the manuscript never occurred and the paintings have remained individually mounted, separated from the text, allowing them to be more easily (and safely) studied and displayed.

UNKNOWN ARTIST

14 Jahangir receives Prince Khurram on his return from the Deccan on 10 October 1617

c.1640–1760 | ink and watercolour with metallic paints | 29.6 × 20.8 cm | British Library

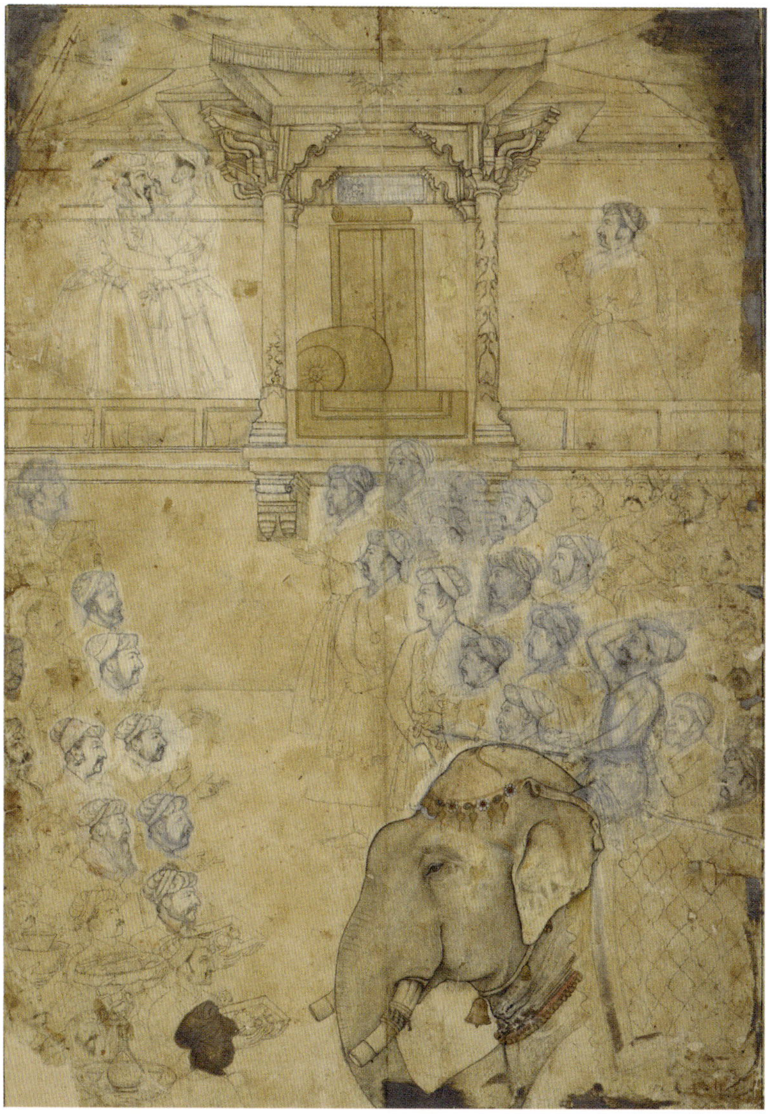

This unfinished painting was bought in Lucknow by the East India Company officer Richard Johnson (see p. 17). It depicts the same scene as Murar's painting (cat. 13) but the composition and details differ, including the courtiers lined up on either side of the emperor and his son.[111] Many of the figures (identified by name in tiny inscriptions) are historically incorrect for this episode and the painting is possibly an exercise made by another later artist.[112] The work is significant in that it shows the typical working process of a Mughal painter when creating a finished painting from a drawing. The heads were drawn using *charbas*, thin pieces of transparent deerskin frequently used to trace and duplicate the outlines of portraits from one painting to another. The artist then applied a thin white wash over specific areas where they redrew and modelled the underdrawings before they began to apply the layers of coloured paint.

UNKNOWN ARTIST

15 The delivery of presents for Prince Dara Shikoh's wedding in December 1632

c. 1640 | watercolour and metallic paints on paper | painting 33 × 23 cm | Royal Collection/HM King Charles III

This is on one half of a double-page illustration from the *Padshahnama* manuscript depicting the delivery of the *sachiq* (presents sent from the bridegroom's family to the bride) in anticipation of the marriage of Shah Jahan's son, Dara Shikoh, to his cousin, Nadira Banu. Their wedding was the first major celebration in Agra after the Mughal court spent over a year in mourning for Shah Jahan's wife, Mumtaz Mahal, who had died in 1631.

The *Padshahnama* text recorded that 'two lacs of rupees, one lac in cash and one in goods, half of which were precious gems and the other half fine textiles, were taken from the royal treasury ... to the domicile of the chaste Jahan Banu Begum.'[113] Several of the figures are splattered in turmeric, a reference to the often messy pre-wedding *haldi* ceremony whereby the bride and groom are slathered in turmeric powder mixed with oil and rosewater.

The *Padshahnama* paintings were fully published for the first time in 1997 in a book to accompany its international touring exhibition.[114] The Royal Collection Trust has since digitized the paintings, publishing them in high resolution on the Royal Collection's website, and they are among the historic paintings most frequently referenced in the work of contemporary South Asian artists (see cat. 119).

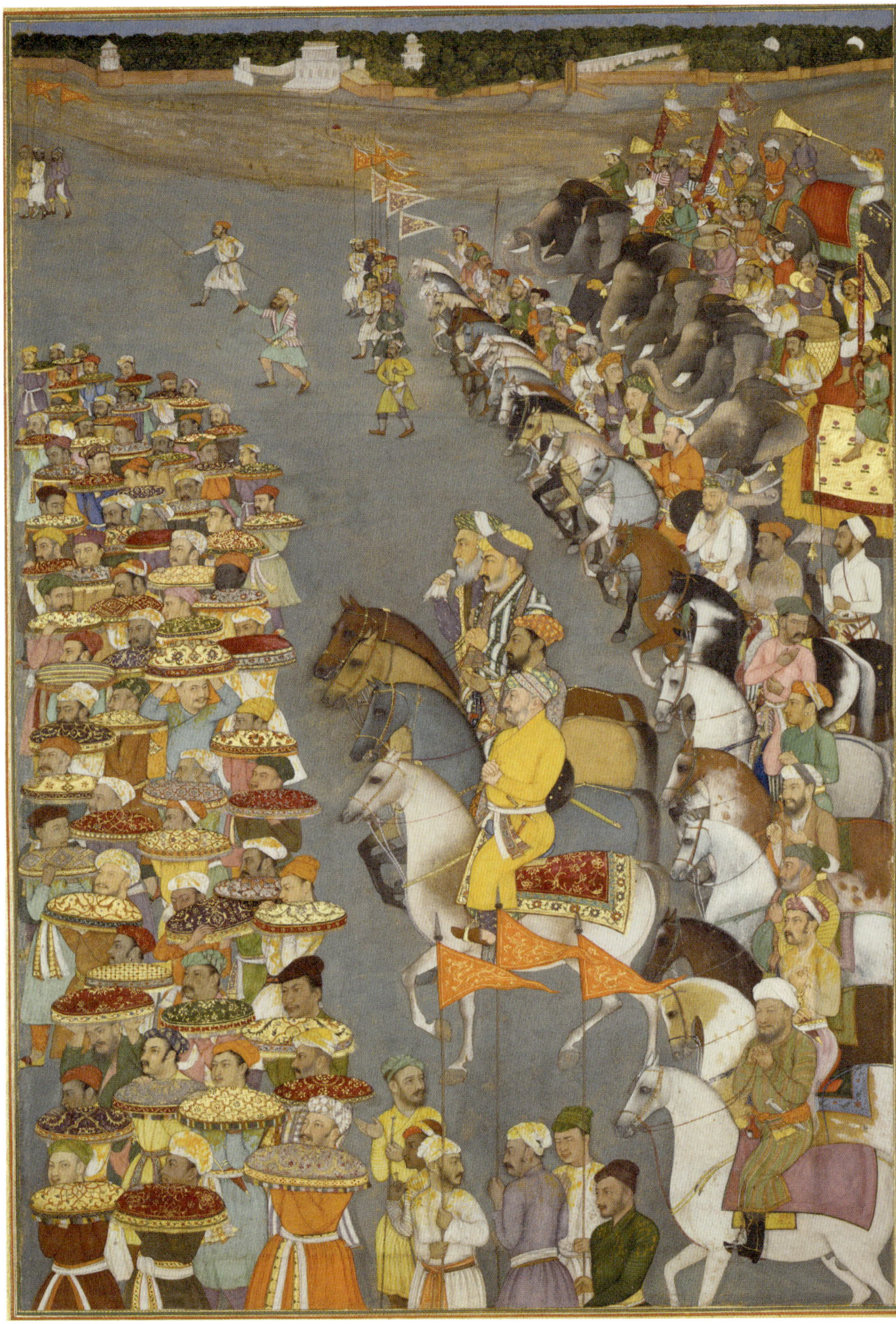

UNKNOWN ARTIST

16 A dervish from the Dara Shikoh album

c. 1635–45 | watercolour and metallic pigments on paper | 32 × 22 cm | British Library

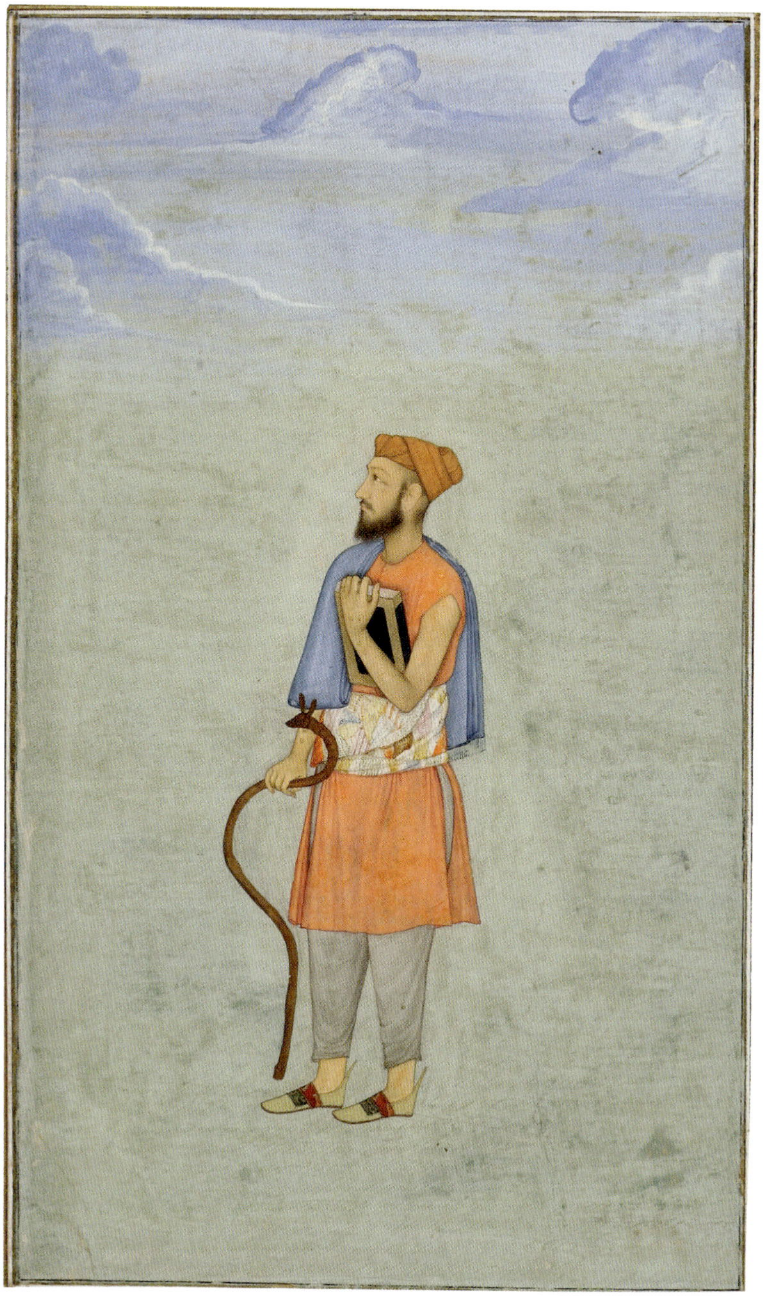

In June 1908 the India Office Library purchased an exquisite Mughal album for £66 from the London book auctioneers Hodgson & Co.[115] The catalogue listed 'A seventeenth century Oriental album ... containing 69 highly finished coloured drawings, comprising 42 portraits of Persian Celebrities, Indian officials &c, 24 very beautiful drawings of flowers and birds ... and 64 specimens of Calligraphy, with a dedication inscription to an Indian Princess, dated 1646.'[116] The Indian princess cited was Nadira Banu Begum (1618–1659), wife of Mughal Prince Dara Shikoh (1615–1659) (see p. 46), whose dedication describes her as 'his dearest intimate friend'.[117] Both husband and wife died during the war of succession (see p. 31) and a later note records that by 1661 the volume was in the care of the lady Pariwash, librarian to Dara Shikoh's sister, Princess Jahanara (1614–1681).[118]

Copies of some of the paintings in the Dara Shikoh album are found in later Mughal albums, now in the V&A and the Royal Collection, suggesting it remained in northern India until at least the second half of the eighteenth century.[119] In the summer of 1823 a *munshi* (clerk) in Madras sent the volume to one Lieutenant Charles Forn of the 6th Regiment at Vellore, and it was later owned by a Christopher Abbot Jr.[120] When the India Office acquired the album, the (numbered) pages had been rebound in a muddled order. Five of them had been removed and are still missing.

UNKNOWN ARTIST

17 Prince Shah Shuja receiving artists and scholars

c.1650 | watercolour and metallic paints on paper | page 38.2 × 22.5 cm | Bodleian Library

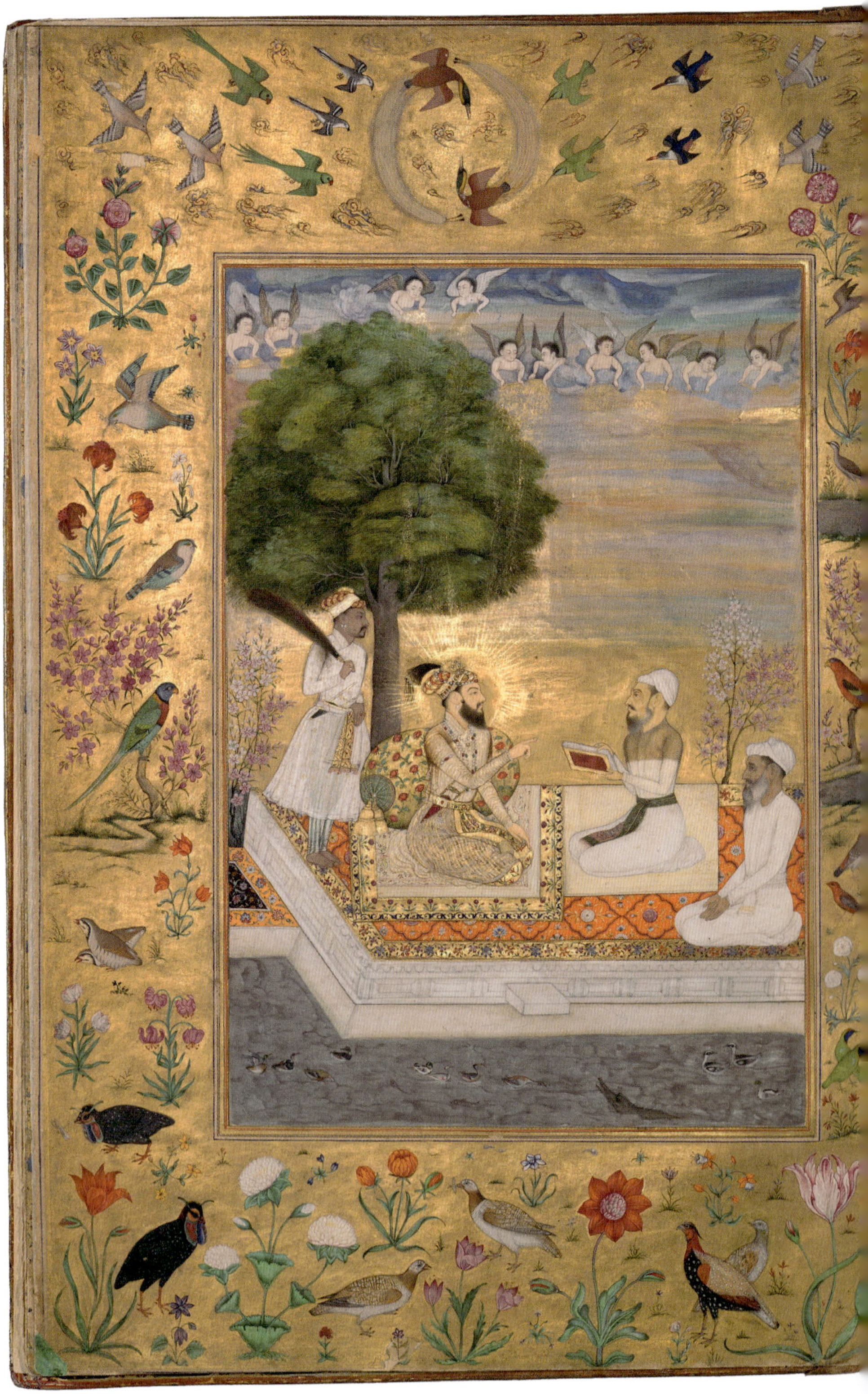

The exceptionally high quality of this royal Mughal *muraqqa* suggests it was presented to an East India Company official as a high-level diplomatic gift from an Indian ruler. The volume contains 41 paintings and 37 calligraphic specimens and is thought to have been assembled for Shah Shuja (1616–1660), the second son of Shah Jahan, when he was governor of Bengal.[121] This double-page composition is the conclusion of the *muraqqa* showing the prince in conversation with scholars and artists, probably some of the individuals who were involved in the album's creation. The man kneeling holding the large volume on the far right may be a self-portrait of the artist of these pages, and sitting

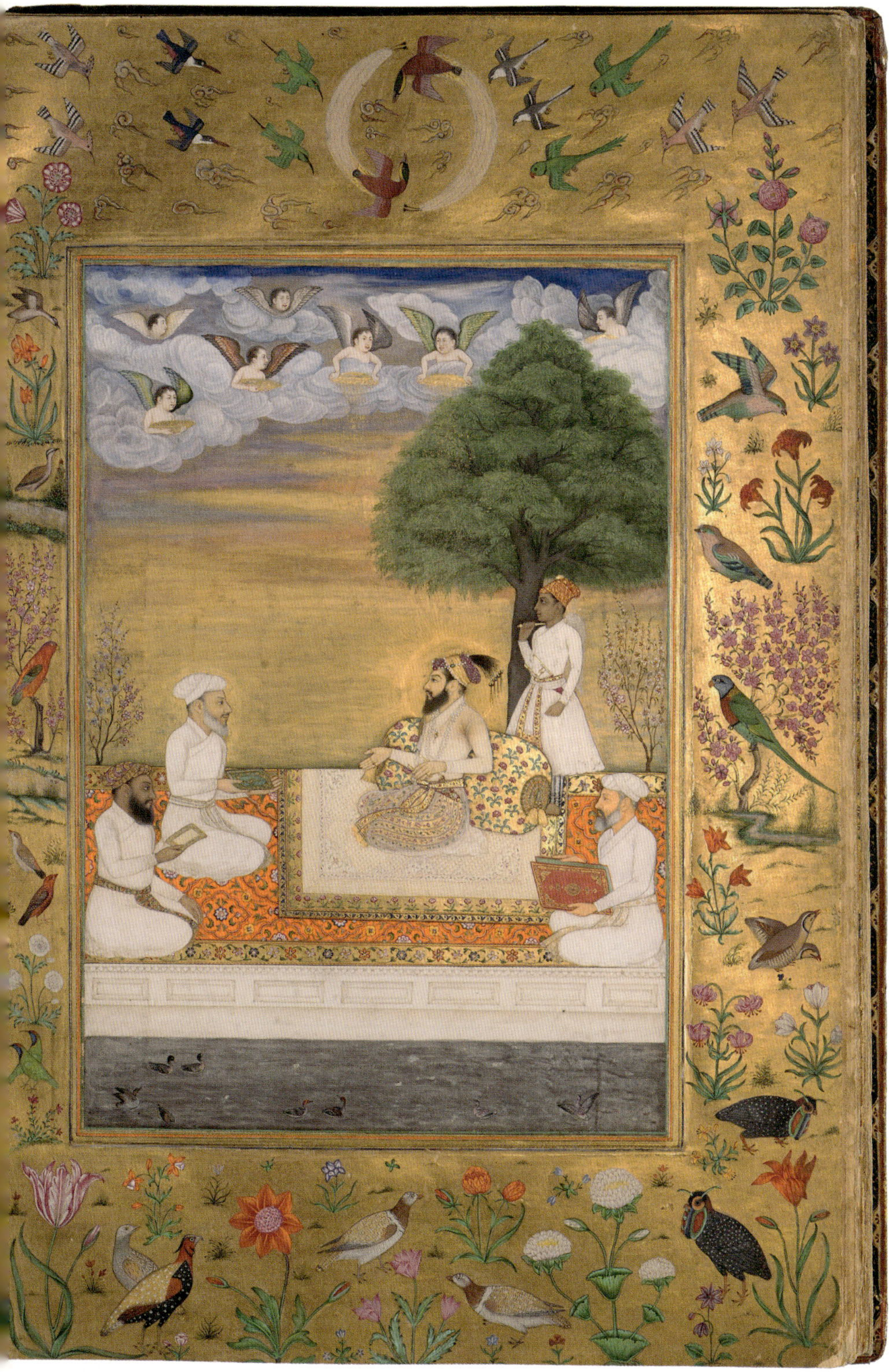

opposite Shah Shuja may be the illuminator of the fine margins and bookbinder, both holding examples of their work.

The album was already in England in the collection of physician Charles Chauncy (1706–1777) by his death, when it was inherited by his brother Nathaniel (d.1790), both described two decades later as 'very able scholars and able bibliomaniacs'.[122] When the brothers' combined library was sold at auction in 1790[123] the English antiquary Francis Douce (1757–1834) bought the album and later bequeathed his collection of books and manuscripts to the Bodleian Library.

UNKNOWN ARTIST & MUHAMMAD PANAH

18 Women in outdoor cloaks

c. 1720–40 | watercolour and metallic paints on paper | page 42 × 28 cm | Royal Collection/HM King Charles III

A signature at the top of the painting on the right gives the name of the Mughal artist Muhammad Panah, who worked for Emperor Muhammad Shah (r. 1719–48).[124] It is a copy in reverse of the seventeenth-century painting it faces in an eighteenth-century Mughal album, a phenomenon seen in many openings in the album and one which reflects the training practices of Mughal artists whereby they traced and copied the works of older masters.

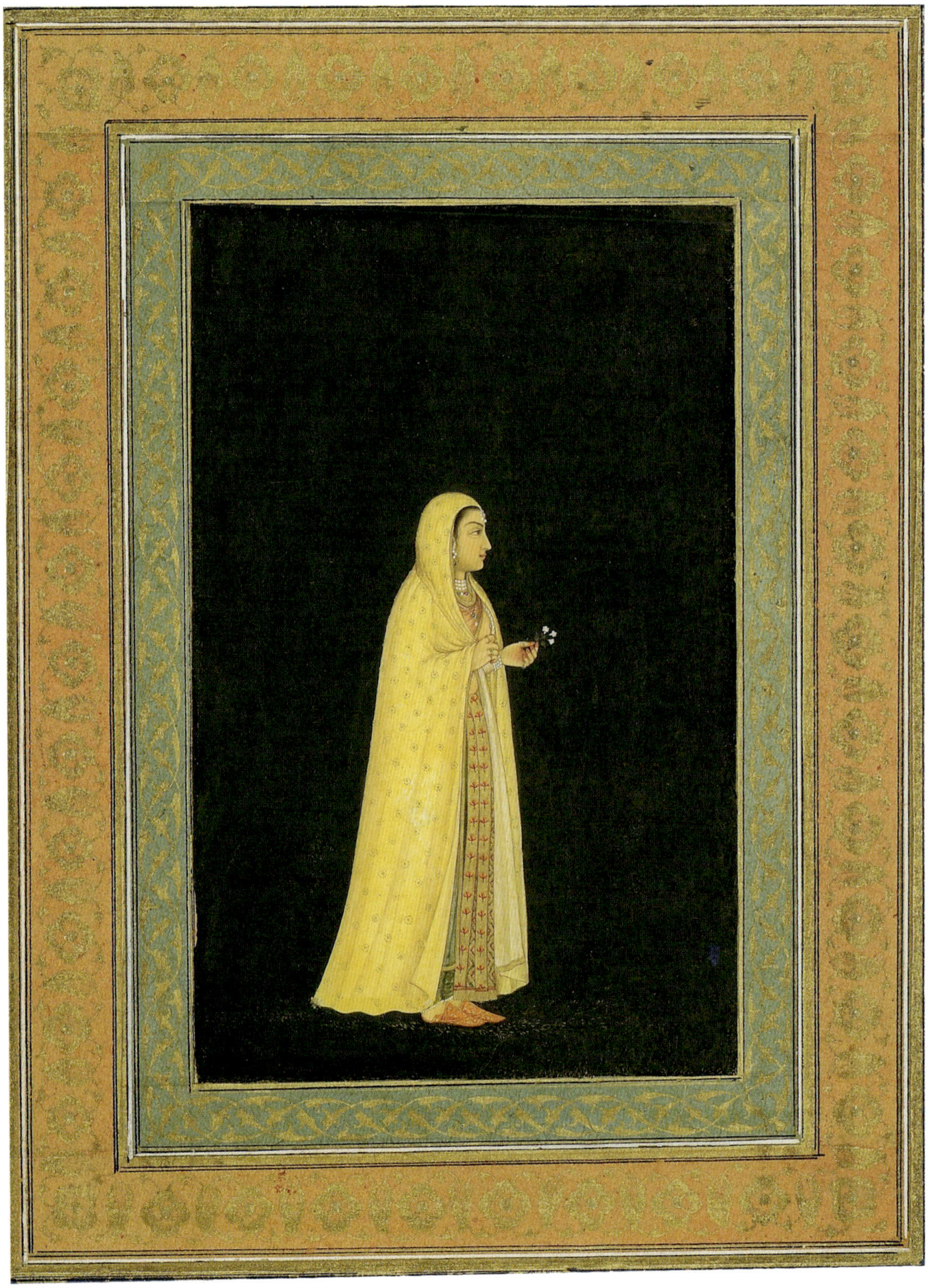

The figure in the earlier portrait originally stood against a green background (as in cat. 16); Muhammad Panah overpainted this with a heavy black wash so that the two paintings appear as a pair. Other interventions to earlier paintings in this album, probably also made by Muhammad Panah, covered areas of paint loss or infilled holes caused by insect damage, a widespread problem in South Asian libraries.

Assembled at the Mughal court *c.*1720–40, this *muraqqa* was later bought by Asaf ud-Daula, ruler of Awadh and arguably the greatest collector of Mughal art of the eighteenth century. It was among the six volumes presented as gifts from his successor, Nawab Saadat Ali Khan, to George III in 1798 via the East India Company governor general Lord Teignmouth (see p. 14).[125]

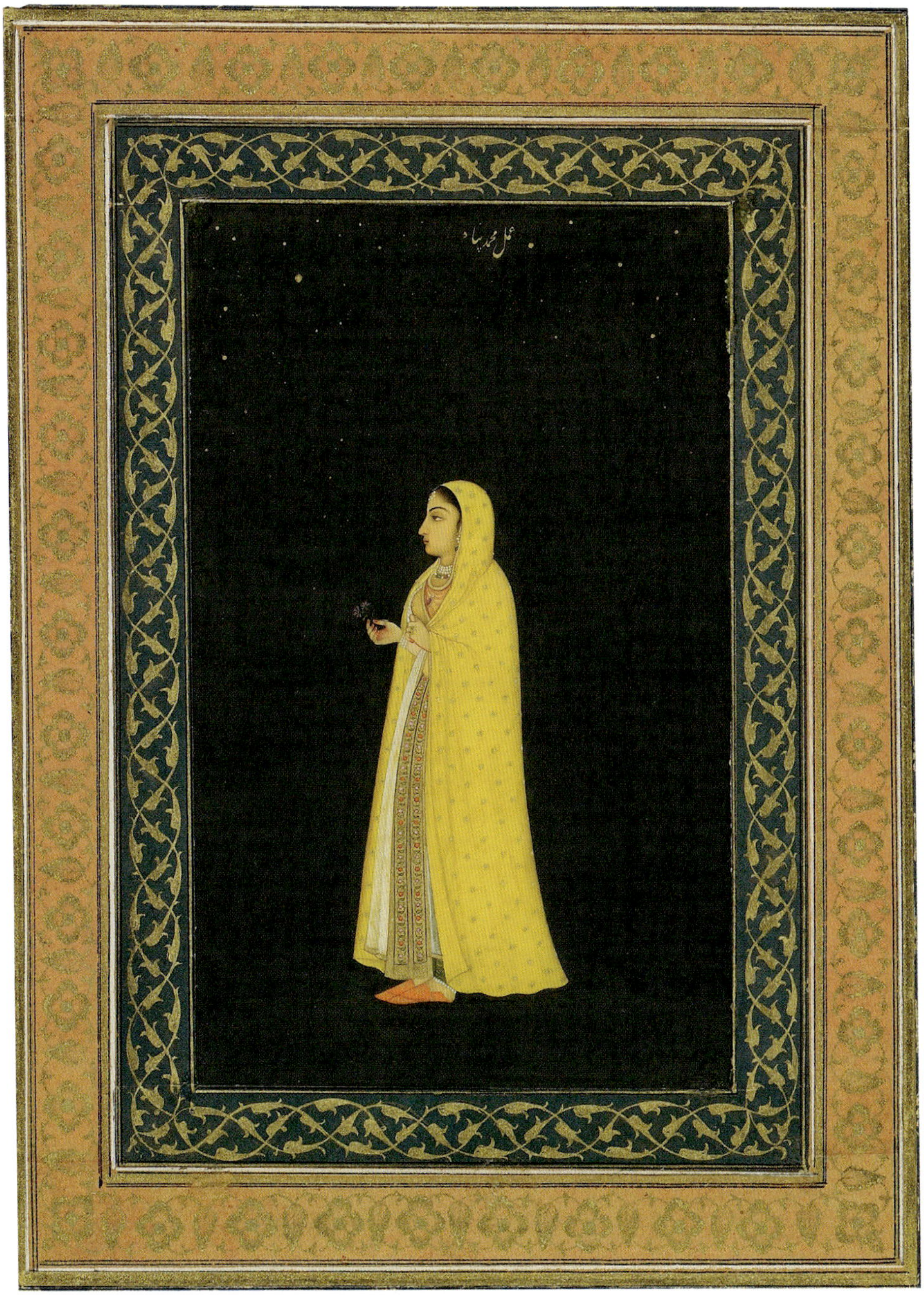

UNKNOWN ARTIST

19 # Composite elephant fight

c. 1630 | ink, watercolour and metallic paints on paper | 13.7 × 20.6 cm | Victoria and Albert Museum

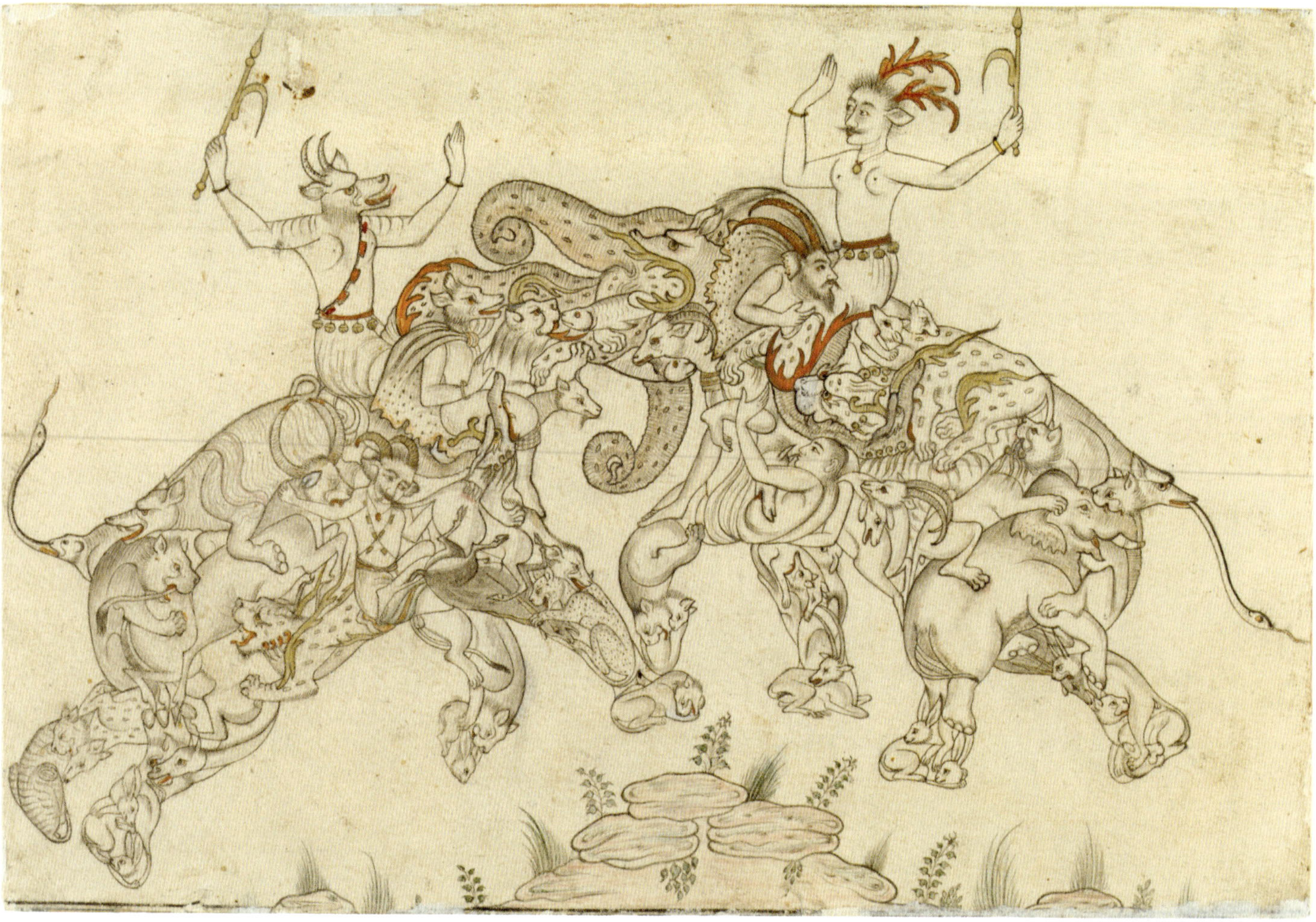

The composition of this Deccani painting is fundamentally two fighting elephants ridden by a mahout, a familiar courtly sight, but the artist transformed the forms into composite and demonic creatures.

The V&A purchased this painting in 1903 from the Dutch bookselling firm Martinus Nijhoff with a group of South Asian works which included paintings commissioned by William Fullteron (see cat. 25–26).

The diabolic, part-animal, part-human figures with horns and jangling bells and the flaming mythical creatures (*qilin*) are ultimately inspired by Iranian iconography. Demons (*divs*) abound in

HAJJI GHULAM HASSAN

20 Composite elephant

c.1600–1700 | ink, watercolour and metallic paints on paper | 12.5 × 19.2 cm | Bodleian Library

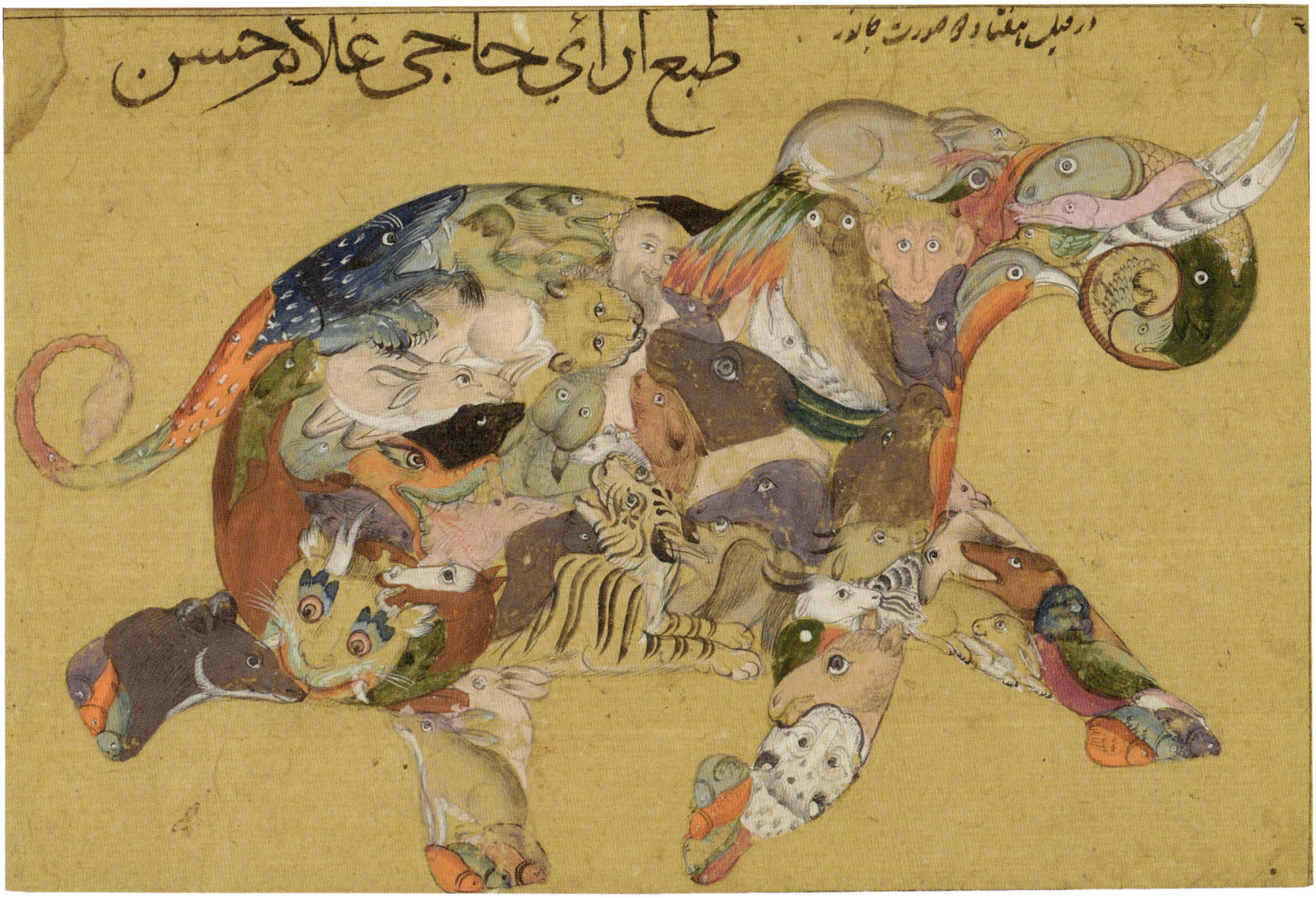

Persian literature, such as the composite creatures who carry flames in Nizami's Tale of the Turquoise Pavilion:

> each devil's snout was a trunk! And each sported heavy horns as well: so that each showed like and bull and an elephant in one! And each one gripped his firebrand; each one as fowl as a drunkard's tongue; flames darted from their gullets in demonic tongues that chanted ditties as they snapped their castanets of shoulder-bones – and such a jingle-jangle in a moment that it takes to breathe a breath, all the world alike they ceased to dance.[126]

ATTRIBUTED TO MANOHAR

21 Rama and Sita united in marital happiness

c.1649–52 | watercolour and metallic paints on paper | 22.9 × 39 cm | British Library

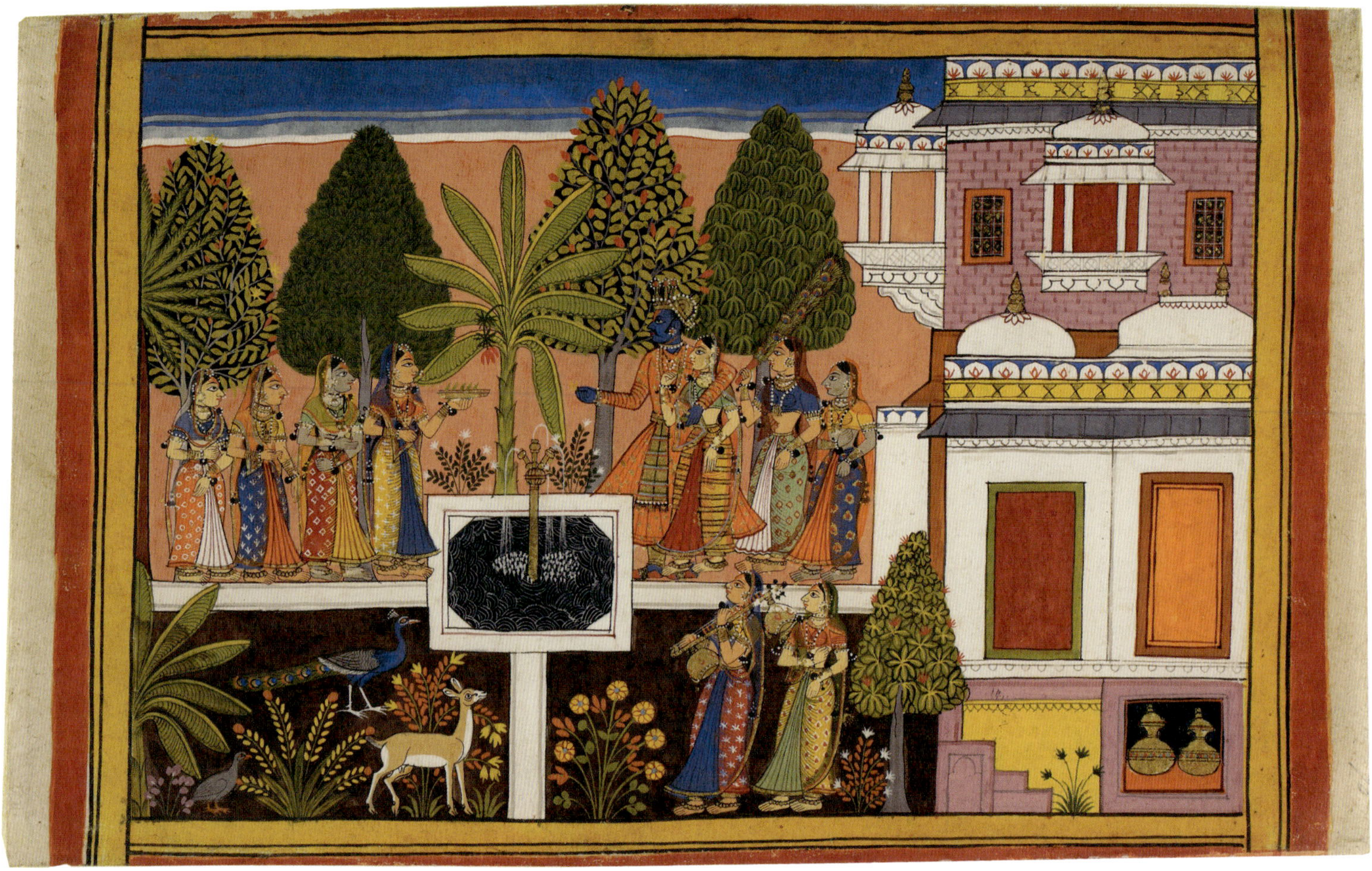

When Colonel James Tod, the East India Company's agent to the western Rajput states, left Udaipur in 1820, his parting gifts from Maharana Bhim Singh (1778–1828) included five bundles of loose pages from an illustrated copy of the Hindu epic poem *Ramayana* (Rama's Journey). This series is now commonly known as the Mewar *Ramayana*, after the Rajput kingdom in Rajasthan where it was made for Maharana Jagat Singh I (r.1628–52) and completed in 1653 under his son Raj Singh I (r.1652–80). Both claimed to be direct descendants of Rama. The scribe and artists spent more than five years completing the work, which originally included as many as 450 paintings. Here, Rama and Sita are reunited after she was rescued from a year of captivity in the garden of the demon king Ravana.

On his return to Britain in 1823, Tod presented the paintings to the Duke of Sussex, one of George III's sons, who, like his father, was a well-known bibliophile and later became a prominent member of the Royal Asiatic Society. He had them bound into two volumes, which the British Museum later purchased in the 1844 sale of the duke's library. The pages were disbound again after they became part of the British Library's collection in 1972.[127]

UNKNOWN ARTIST

22 Deccani noblemen

c. 1700 | watercolour on paper | 35.6 × 25 cm | Cottonian Collection

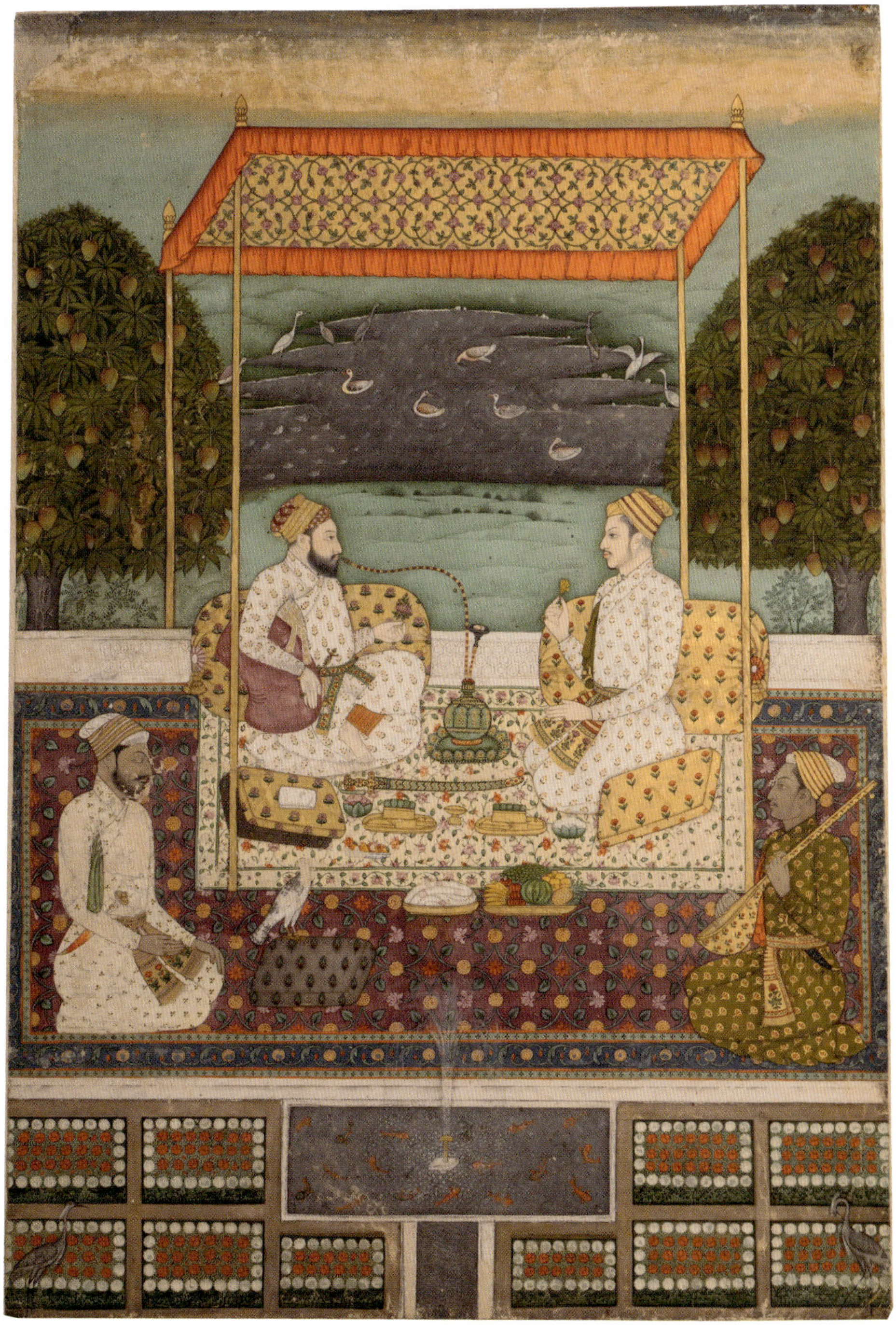

The Cottonian Collection in Plymouth holds a diverse group of more than twenty South Asian paintings and album folios originally purchased in London by the customs official Charles Rogers (1711–1784), an antiquarian and avid collector of prints and drawings. This portrait of Deccani noblemen during a moment of leisure was probably Rogers's finest Indian purchase. A note on the back suggests that one of the sitters is Mubariz Khan, whom the Mughal emperor Alamgir appointed governor of Bijapur in 1704.[128] Many Mughal-trained artists travelled south with the Deccan campaigns of the late seventeenth and early eighteenth centuries, bringing with them the realism of Mughal portraiture. Local artists adopted certain Mughal compositions and approaches while retaining the brighter Deccani colour palette of violets and oranges and local motifs, including the mango tree laden with fruit.

Rogers bequeathed his collection to his brother-in-law, William Cotton (d. 1791), and it passed through two further generations of the Cotton Family until 1853, when William Cotton III (1794–1863) donated it to the proprietors of the Plymouth Public Library. In 1915, ownership of the Cottonian collection transferred to the Plymouth Corporation and the works moved to the Plymouth City Museum and Art Gallery, now known as The Box.

UNKNOWN ARTIST

23 A pleasure garden in Hyderabad

c.1760 | watercolour on paper | 23.6 × 33 cm | Bodleian Library

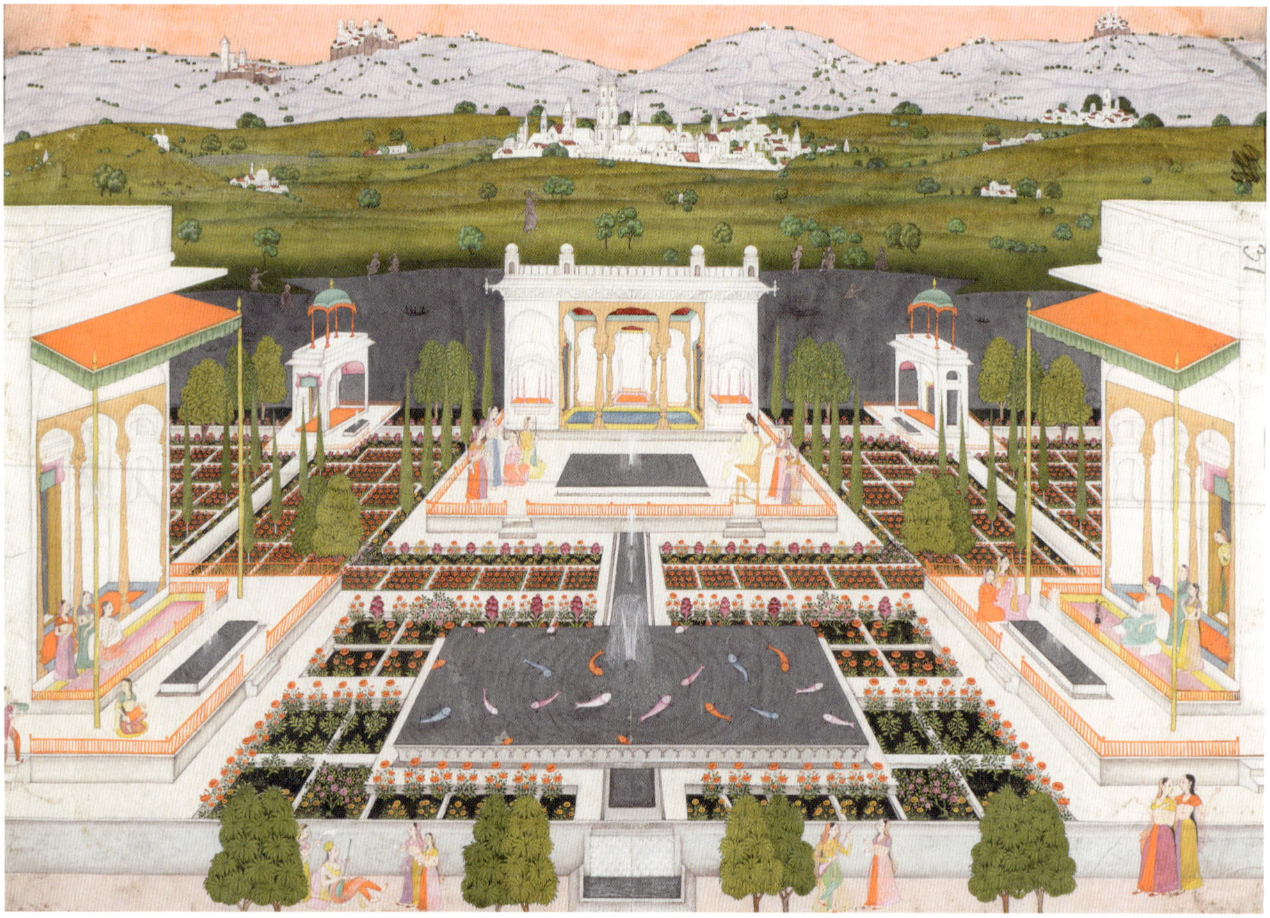

The artist of these Deccani paintings is thought to have worked for Salabat Jang, Nizam of Hyderabad (r.1751–62) and probably his successor, Nizam Ali Khan (r.1762–1803), in the second half of the eighteenth century.[129] Richard Johnson (see p. 17) acquired a set of 36 *Ragamala* paintings by the same artist while he was posted to the Nizam's court, 1784–5.[130] The artist's experiments with scale and dramatic perspective suggest an awareness of European topographical prints, known to have circulated in India since the late sixteenth century and among the works of art highly desired as gifts by eighteenth-century Indian rulers (see figs 16 & 17).[131]

The depiction of the tiny distant figures as black silhouettes ('matchstick men'), a feature common in Mughal and Deccani paintings, may also derive from European engravings. *Firangi* (foreign) inspiration in the garden scene is also apparent in the lofty church towers and spires of the distant European townscapes which dot the background. The man at the centre appears to wear a European hat as he sits cross-legged on a tall European chair listening to a group of female musicians.[132] The beardless figure riding in the elephant howdah may be the same man, and the sepoys (foot soldiers) at the front of the procession are attired in the red uniform of the East India Company's Madras Army.

It is likely that a British official acquired these paintings in Hyderabad in the late eighteenth century. The English antiquary Francis Douce obtained them in London, and assembled the pictures into one of his 11 Indian albums.[133]

UNKNOWN ARTIST

24 A royal procession to Golconda

c.1760 | watercolour on paper | 27.5 × 33 cm | Bodleian Library

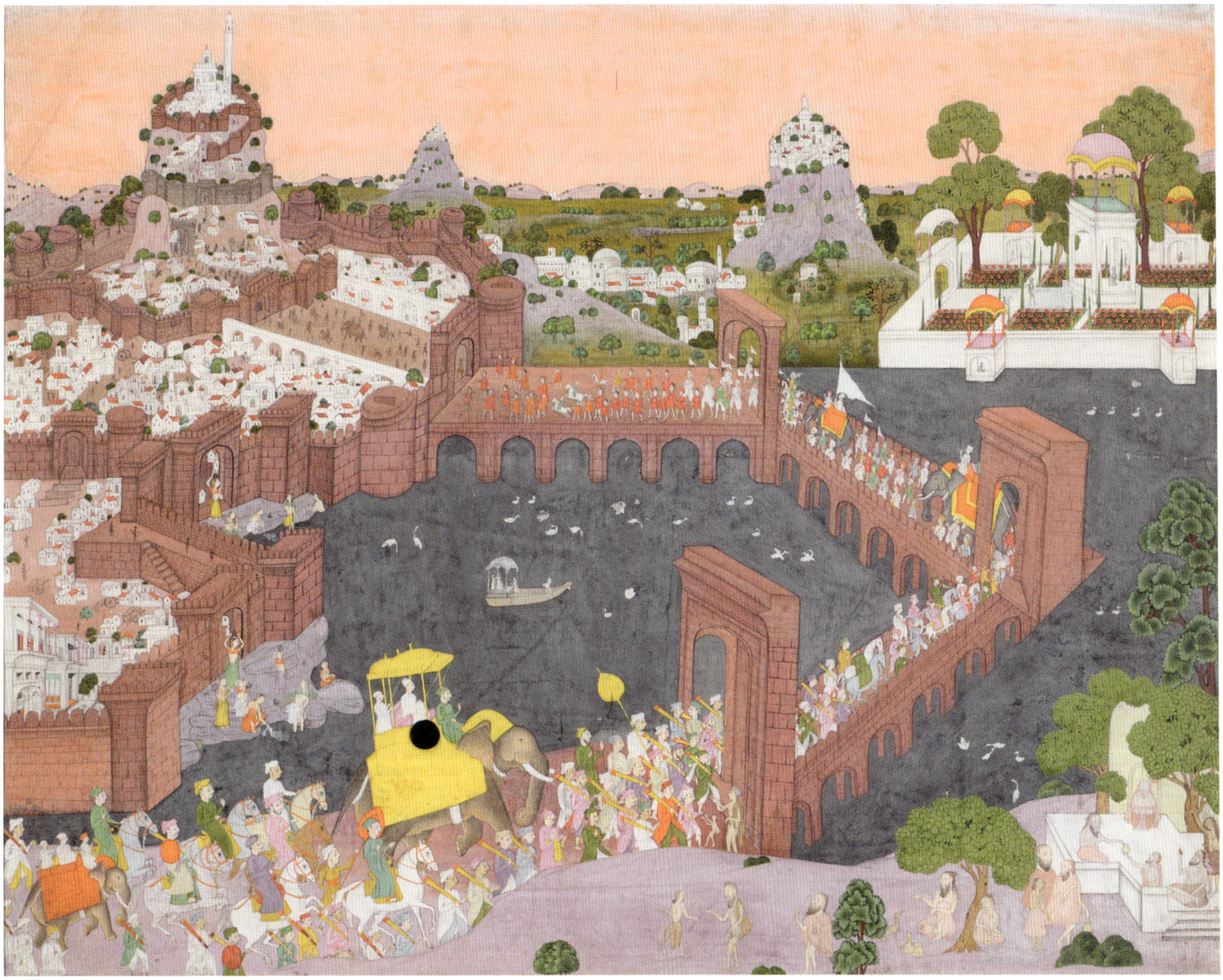

FIG. 16 Gabriel Perelle, *Veuë et perspective du château de Versailles*, 1661–95.

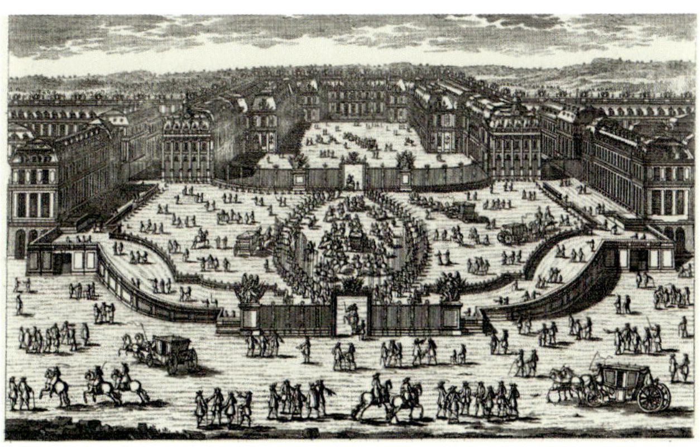

FIG. 17 William Henry Toms, *St James's Palace and Parts adjacent*, 1736.

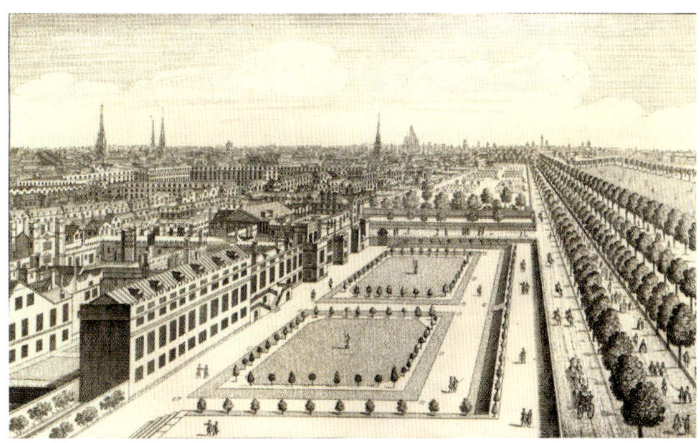

DIP CHAND

25 Portrait of William Fullerton

c.1764 | watercolour and metallic paints on paper | 26.2 × 22.6 cm | Victoria and Albert Museum

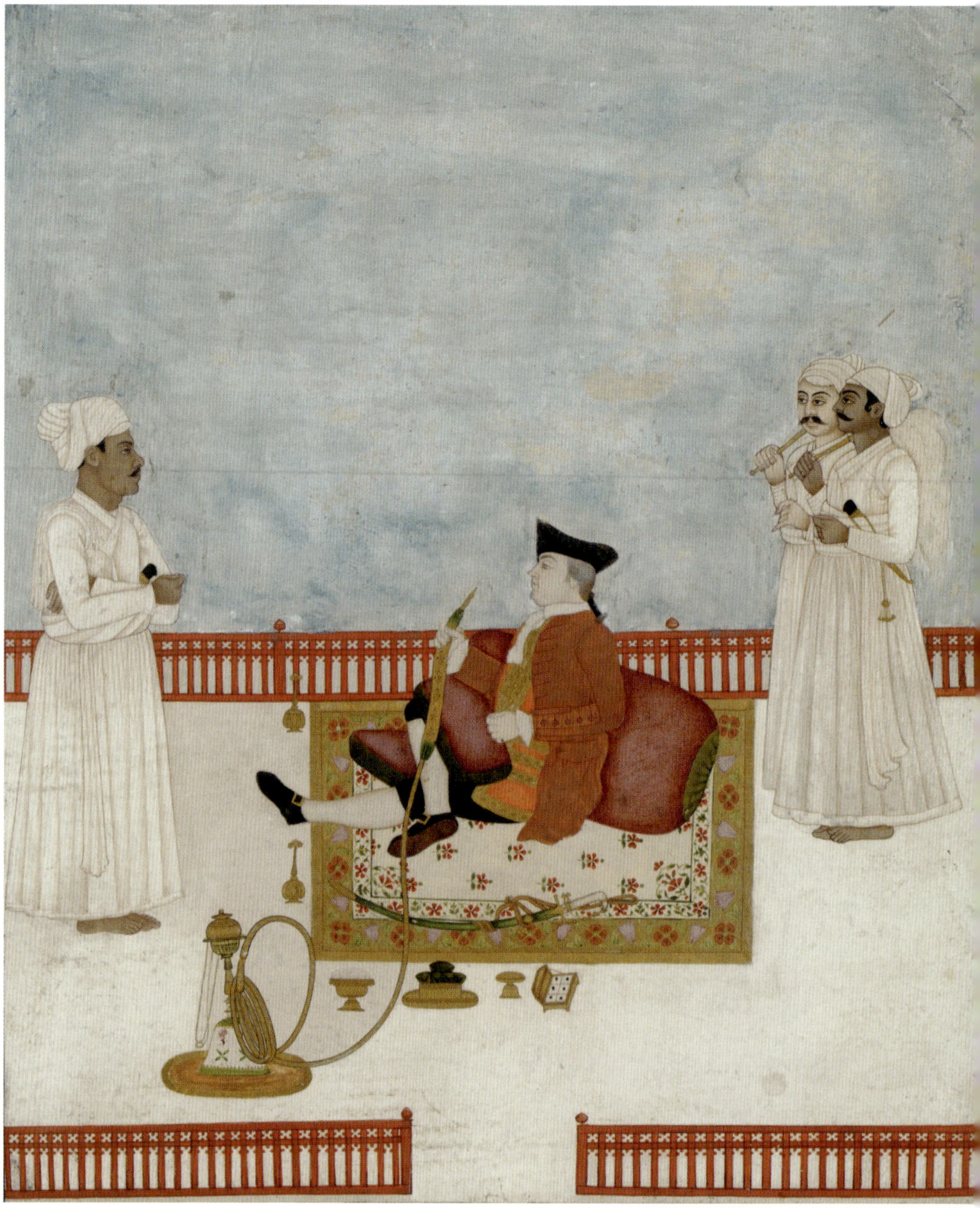

William Fullerton (d.1805) was an archetypal Scottish 'nabob'. A corruption of the Persian word *nawab* (meaning governor or viceroy), 'nabob' was a derogatory term used in eighteenth-century Britain to refer to any East India Company officer who had made presumedly ill-gotten wealth in Asia. Fullerton arrived in India in 1744 as a junior doctor and by virtue of his excellent linguistic skills and close relationships with the local nobility made a fortune in private trade. It was also through these friendships that Fullerton was able to commission a series of portraits from Dip Chand, an artist employed by the Nawab of Bengal and his circle (see fig. 18).

Fullerton's portrait shows him receiving a visitor while seated on the floor smoking a *huqqa*, a happy adopter of the Bengali aristocratic lifestyle (although he still wears British clothes). A note on the back of the painting ('W.F 1764') suggests it dates to when Fullerton was living in an affluent area of Patna while working on the famous inquiry into the conduct of Nanda Kumar, a minister of the Nawab of Bengal. The Calcutta Council charged him with misconduct the following year and Fullerton resigned in protest, leaving India in 1766.[134]

The Bengali nobleman Ghulam Husayn Khan wrote 16 years after his friend's departure that it was always Fullerton's intention to return 'on his being able to obtain certain conditions and stipulations for himself. [But] it appears that his intention did not tally with the decrees of Providence, for he has not yet appeared although there is intelligence of his being alive and in health.'[135]

The portrait is signed by the Murshidabad artist Dip Chand, one of the few named artists working in Bengal at the time.[136]

ATTRIBUTED TO DIP CHAND

26 Lady of William Fullerton's household smoking a *huqqa*

c.1764 | watercolour on paper | 24.5 × 16.5 cm | Victoria and Albert Museum

As well as commissioning his own portrait from the artist, Fullerton commissioned Dip Chand to paint portraits of members of his Indian household and other acquaintances in Patna. The woman shown here may be one of Fullerton's *bibis* (Indian wives). In an almost opposite version of his portrait, she perches on an English chair with her legs tucked up under her, smoking from a *huqqa* that rests on an English candle stand.

The V&A purchased a set of seven of these miniatures with pages of calligraphy owned by Fullerton from the Dutch rare book seller Martinus Nijhoff in 1903,[137] ten years before the acquisition of Fullerton's portrait in 1913 from a Mrs Emily Reet. The British Library acquired four more paintings from this set in 2010 and others remain in private collections.[138]

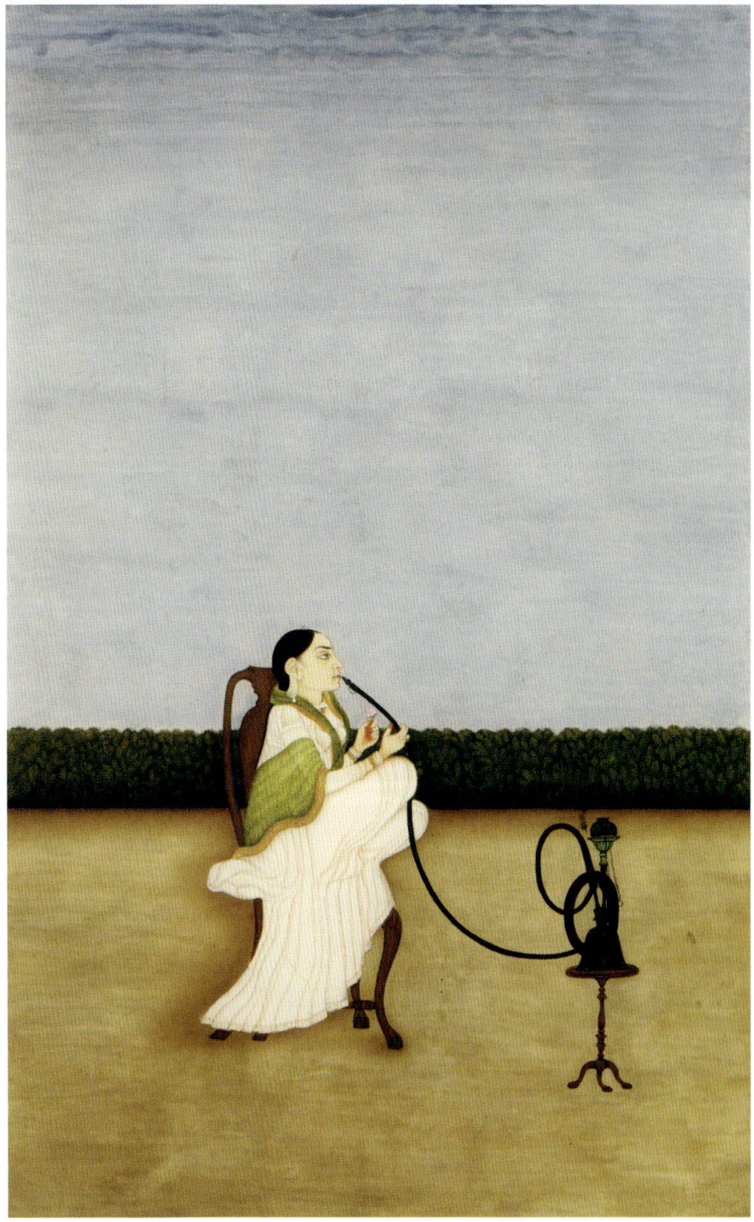

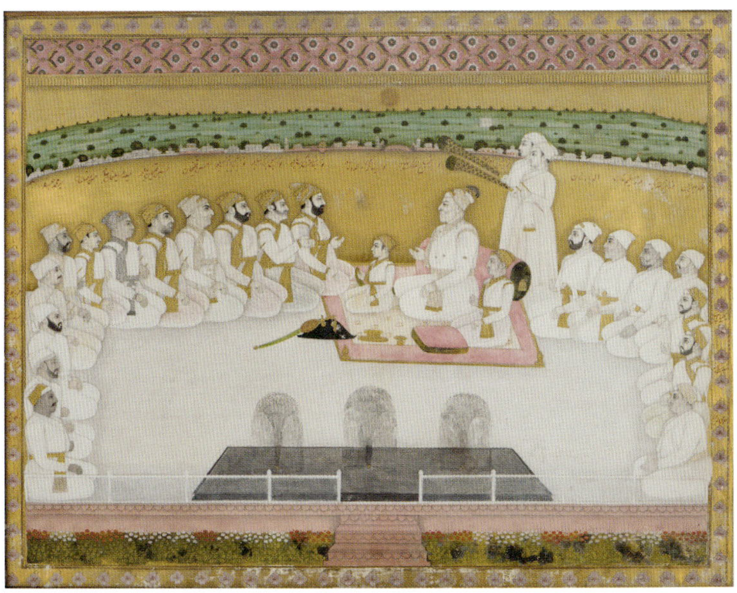

FIG. 18 Unknown artist, *Alivardi Khan, the Nawab of Bengal (1671–1756), presides over the adoption of Ikram ud-Dawla by Shahamat Jang*, c.1748.

UNKNOWN ARTIST

27 Forty-one portraits

c. 1780–1800 | watercolour and metallic paints on paper | 49 × 72 cm | Victoria and Albert Museum

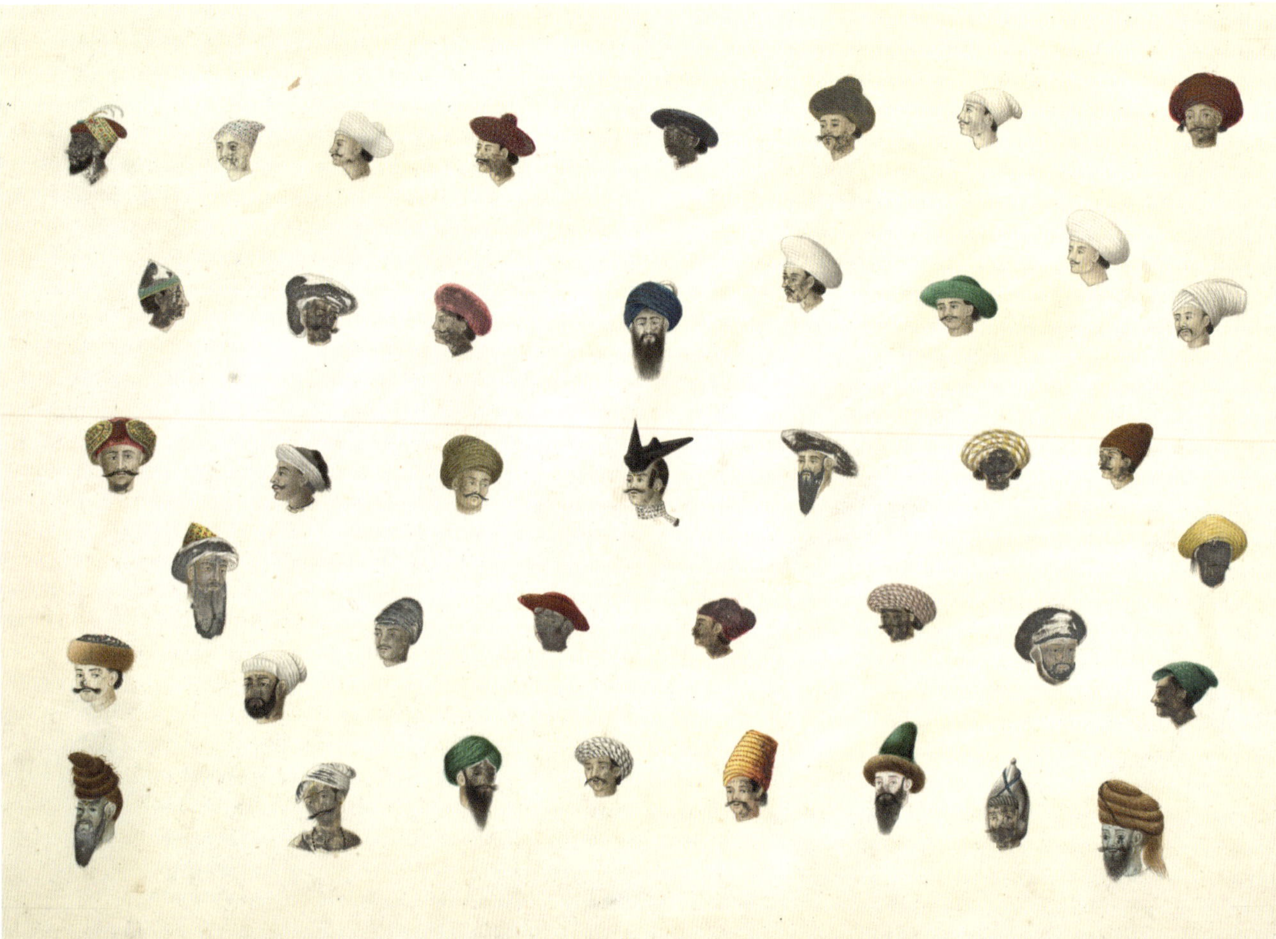

These floating heads belong to figures commonly depicted in late-eighteenth-century paintings by artists from Murshidabad in western Bengal. Such works showing grand court receptions and Hindu and Muslim festivals were typical of the paintings made for British Company officers stationed in Bengal as a record of 'oriental' life. This painting may have been used as a visual aid for the Murishidabad painters who reproduced such scenes, and as such is an unusual survival. The heads include some belonging to recognizable historical figures, including Mir Jafar, the Nawab of Bengal (1691–1765); Shuja ud-Daula, the Nawab of Awadh (1732–1775); and a soldier wearing the 'sundial' headdress of the Bengal native inventory, which was discontinued in 1800.[139]

The V&A bought this painting as part of a volume of 49 large watercolours entitled 'Views in India' in March 1887 from a Mr T. Toon of 38 Leicester Square. The price of the album was £50, a fairly high sum, most likely on account of its Indian landscape scenes by British artists William Orme and Samuel Davis dating to the 1780s and 1790s, rather than its inclusion of works by Indian artists of the same period.

SHAYKH ZAYN UD-DIN

28 A female Malabar trogon

1779 | watercolour on paper | 53.2 × 75.3 cm | private collection, London/Karachi

The Patna painter Shaykh Zayn ud-Din (active 1774–1783) made this meticulous life-size study of a Malabar trogan perched on a branch of Malabar melastome (Indian rhododendron) during his third year of working for Lady Mary Impey in Calcutta. Using English watercolours on English Whatman paper, with his own fine handmade brushes, the artist precisely documented the tiniest details of his subject, including the bristling tufts of hair-like feathers which cover the bird's nostrils. He recorded the local names of the species in Hindustani (Urdu) and his own name, to which Lady Impey added a note that the artist was 'a native of Patna' and that the subjects were from her own collection.[140] Following Sir Elijah Impey's death in 1809, his large collection of South Asian paintings was sold off at Phillips of New Bond Street. Archibald Impey (1766–1831), Elijah's illegitimate son born before his marriage to Mary, bought 64 of the natural-history paintings in the sale, and made them available to scholars for study. The ornithologist John Lathan referred to this particular specimen 'of Lady Impey' when describing the differences with the male and female Malobar trogan in his celebrated *General History of Birds* published in 1822.[141] Archibald's widow Sarah Impey later bequeathed the paintings to the Linnean Society of natural history, where they remained for more than a century before being sold at Sotheby's in 1963. They are now dispersed in public and private collections across the world.[142]

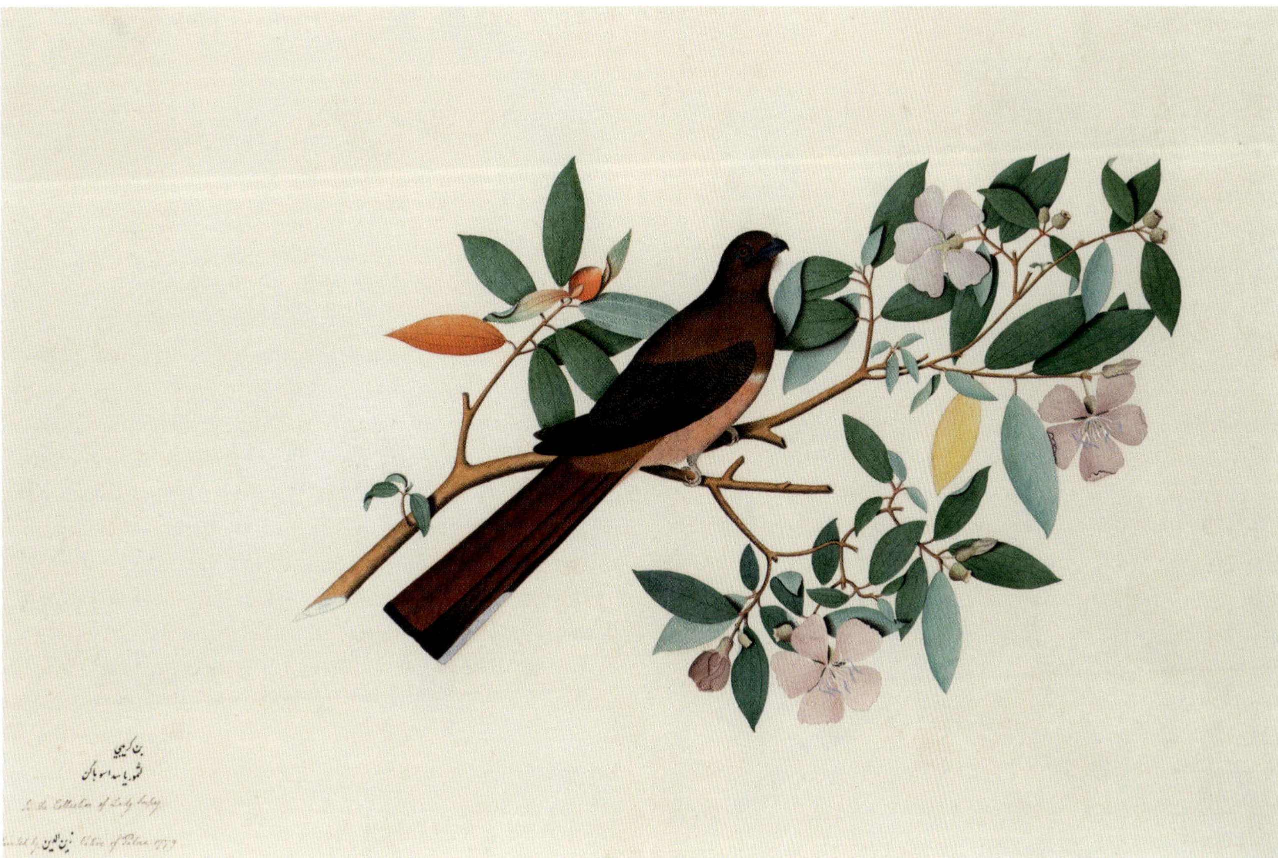

BHAWANI DAS

29 Banded krait

1782 | pencil and watercolour on paper | 76.5 × 48.4 cm | Wellcome Collection

The Patna artist Bhawani Das is thought to have worked for the Scottish botanist Dr James Kerr (1737–1782) in the early 1770s before being hired by Lady Impey around 1779.[143] It is possible that the paintings of reptiles and amphibious creatures he made for her may have been copies of earlier works created for Kerr rather than real animals living in her Calcutta menagerie.

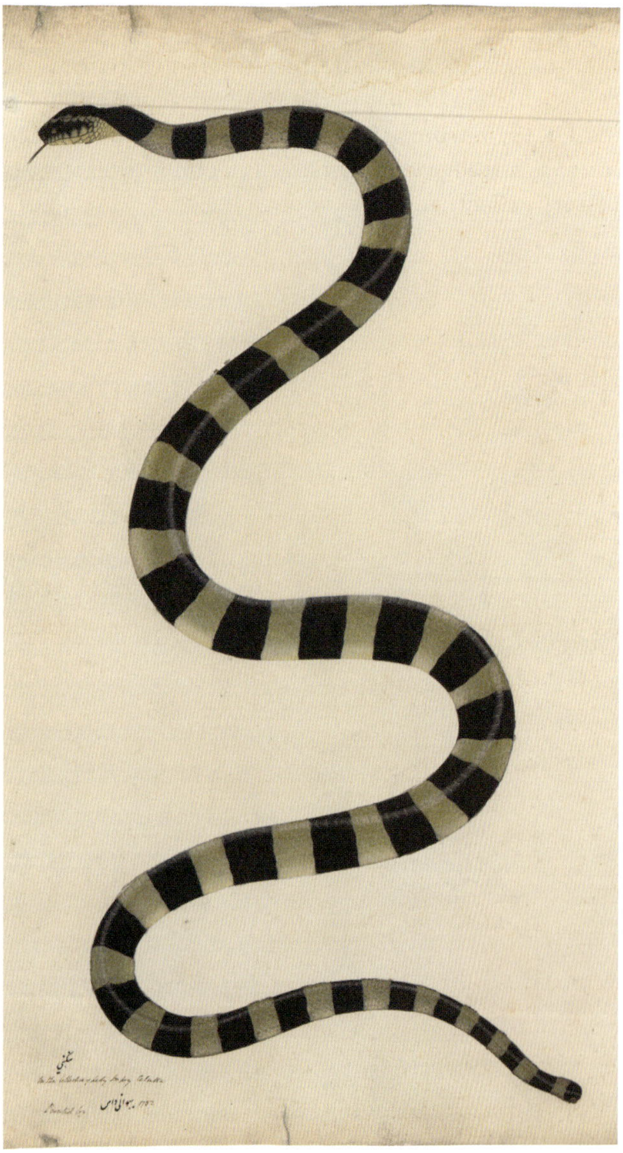

UNKNOWN ARTIST

30 Hoolock gibbon

c.1799–1806 | watercolour on paper | 25.1 × 20.8 cm | British Library

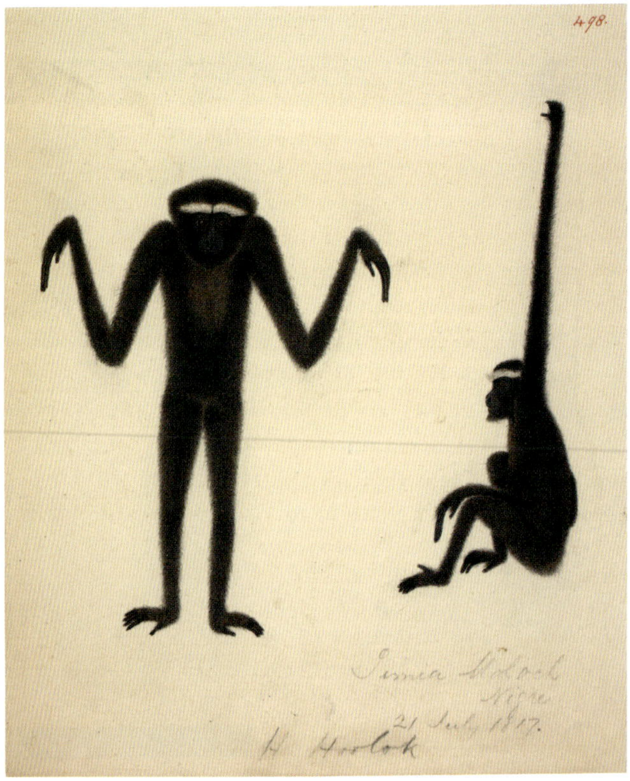

Before leaving India in 1805, Governor General Wellesley appointed Dr Francis Buchannan-Hamilton superintendent of his menagerie at Barrakpore. Wellesley gave him an allowance of 100 rupees a year to retain artists and a further 60 rupees for paints.[144] These two views of a male hoolock gibbon (*Hylobates hoolock*) were among the hundreds of drawings that Buchanan-Hamilton commissioned. His collections arrived at the Company's London library in six batches from 1808 to *c.*1818. This page was among a group of 135 botanical drawings and 14 drawings of mammals and birds sent to England in 1816 (the year after Buchanan had returned to England) by Nathaniel Wallich (1786–1854), superintendent of the Calcutta Botanic Garden. The name of the artist is not recorded, but they may have been one of a team of local artists trained in Calcutta by the botanist William Roxburgh (1751–1815).

UNKNOWN ARTIST

31 Cheetah from Seringapatam

c. 1800–1805 | watercolour and metallic paints on paper | 31.2 × 60.6 cm | British Library

The Marquess Richard Colley Wellesley (1760–1842) established a large botanic garden and menagerie at his summer residence in Barrackpore, just outside Calcutta, and commissioned a series of paintings (2,660 in total) of plants, birds, animals, insects and fish from his team of local painters.[145] The names of the artists employed by Wellesley were not recorded, but the painter of this work evidently trained in the Mughal style, placing the cheetah in a miniature-like landscape and using fine brushstrokes of metallic paint to give sheen to the cheetah's coat.

Many of the inhabitants of the governor general's menagerie at Calcutta were gifts sent to him by Indian rulers or senior Company officials. An inscription on the reverse of this drawing states that it was 'Drawn from life from a Cheeta that was found in the Palace of Tippoo Sultan at Seringapatam, 1799'. Contemporary records suggest that Tipu's cheetahs were initially intended as gifts for George III and Queen Charlotte but evidently Wellesley chose to spare them the long journey to London.[146] Notes pasted on the front give the animal's precise measurements, suggesting the drawing was intended as a scientific record.

Wellesley had his natural-history studies bound into 27 volumes, which were sold at auction in London in 1843, the year after his death. Thirteen years later, the library of the East India Company bought them from a J. Fletcher for £50 and they now form a sizeable part of the British Library's natural-history collection.[147]

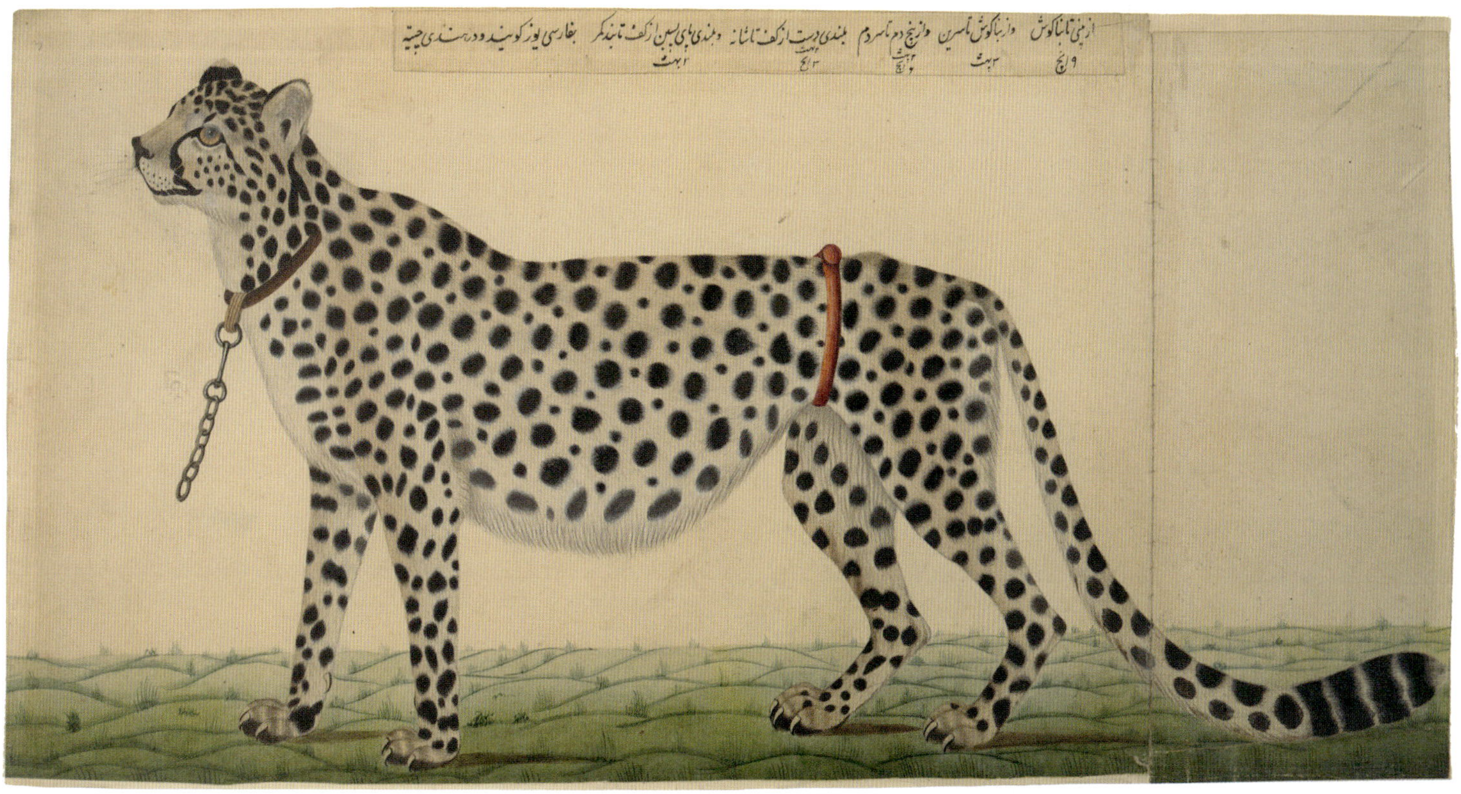

UNKNOWN ARTIST

32 Cassia fistula Willd

c.1795–1804 | watercolour, ink and pencil on paper | 54.4 × 38 cm | Royal Botanic Gardens, Kew

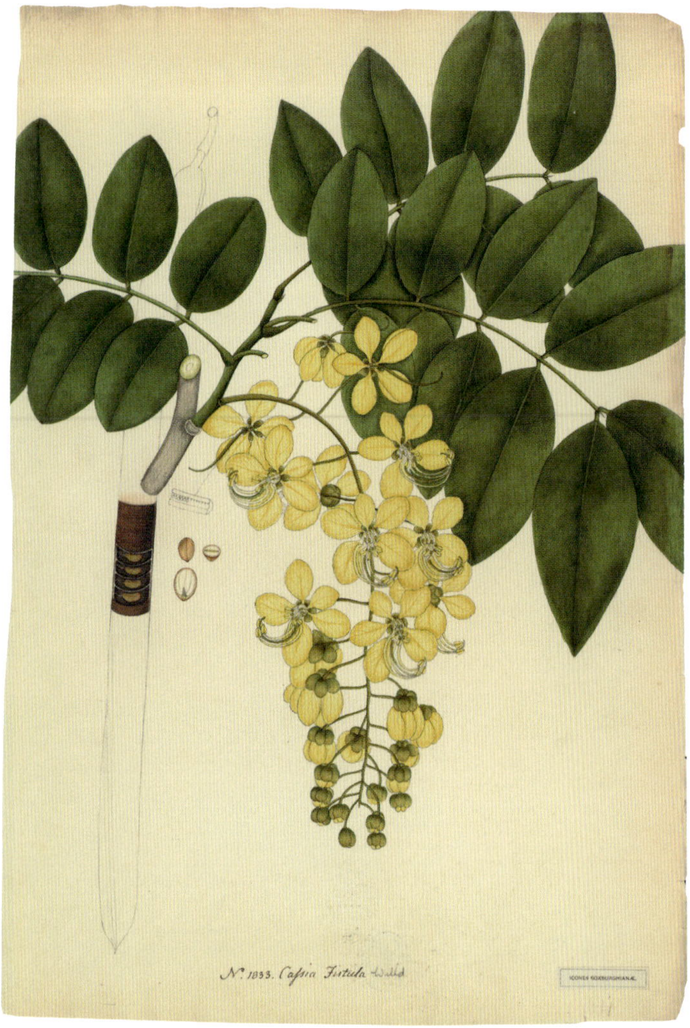

UNKNOWN ARTIST

33 Pinus longifolia Willd

c.1795–1804 | watercolour, ink and pencil on paper | 44.4 × 29.2 cm | Royal Botanic Gardens, Kew

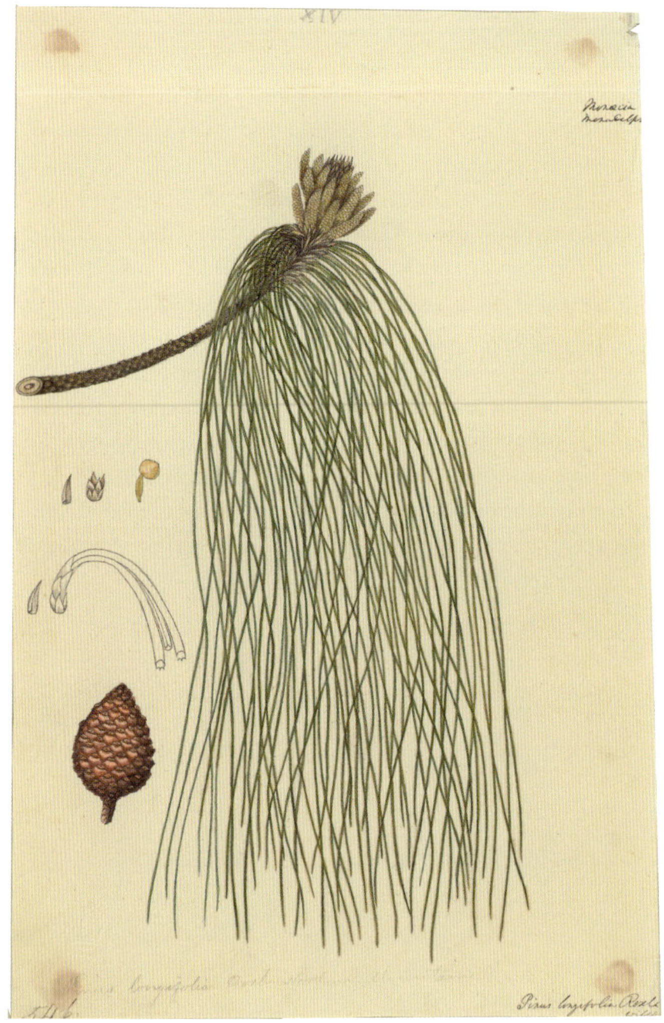

Colonel Robert Kyd founded the Calcutta Botanic Garden in 1786 and in 1793 Dr William Roxburgh became its first paid superintendent.[148] While Roxburgh studied the plants and made descriptions of them, he employed a small team of artists to make life-size illustrations to accompany his texts. During his 22 years as superintendent he commissioned more than 2,500 such drawings, which today remain in India,[149] as well as a duplicate set by the same artists as the originals, which he sent to the library of the East India Company in London. Roxburgh's friend the Rev. Dr William Carey (1761–1834) posthumously published Roxburgh's catalogue of Indian plants *Flora Indica; or Descriptions of Indian Plants* in three volumes between 1820 and 1832, but without illustrations to accompany the text. When the East India Company collections were divided up in 1879, the Roxburgh collection was sent to the Royal Botanic Gardens at Kew and was largely unknown until the 1950s.[150]

UNKNOWN ARTIST

34 Mangifera sylvatica R.

c. 1795–1804 | watercolour, ink and pencil on paper | 54.5 × 37 cm | Royal Botanic Gardens, Kew

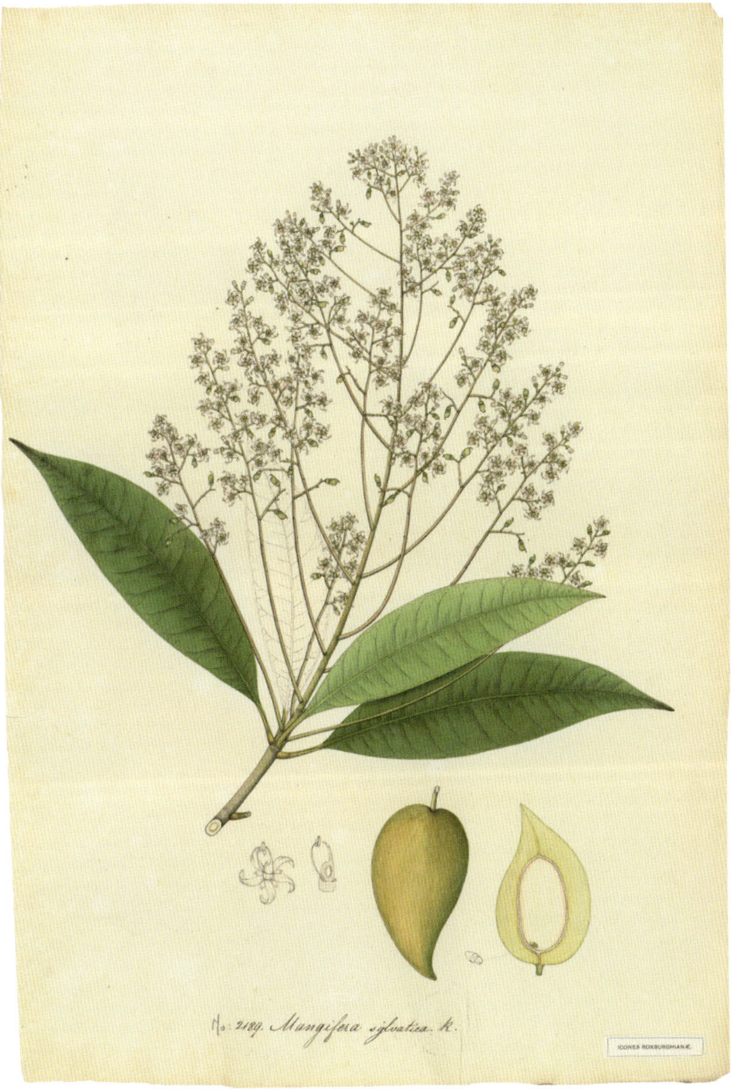

CHUNNI LAL

35 A cycad leaf

1809 | watercolour, ink and pencil on paper | 55.3 × 37.9 cm | Royal Botanic Gardens, Kew

The Patna painter Chunni Lal was one of at least seven artists to work for Scottish surgeon Adam Freer (1747–1811) and is known to have worked for at least two other East India Company patrons in Bengal.[151] Almost 400 drawings commissioned by Freer survive in the Royal Botanic Gardens, Kew. Like Lady Impey, Freer labelled and dated many of the drawings and recorded his artist's names on the bottom corners of the pages. This painting depicts the *Cycas revoluta*, native to Japan, a species then commonly cultivated in the gardens of Calcutta.[152]

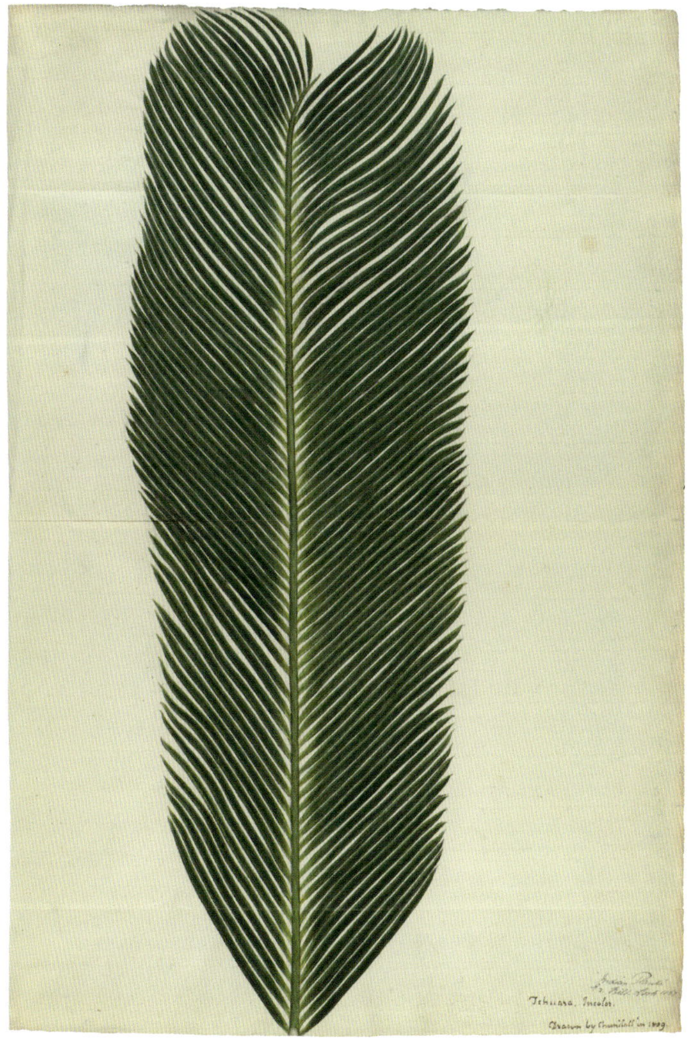

VISHNUPERSAUD

36 Cobra lily

c.1821 | watercolour and ink on paper | 53.8 × 35.7 cm | Royal Botanic Gardens, Kew

The Dutch surgeon Nathaniel Wallich (1786–1854) commissioned more than one thousand drawings during his time as superintendent of the Calcutta Botanic Garden, including a large number by the painters Vishnupersaud and Gorachand. When he travelled to London on leave in 1828 Wallich brought the Garden's enormous collection of botanical drawings with him. He commissioned the Maltese artist Maxim Gauci (1774–1854) to copy 300 of the most recent paintings of rare Asian plants, including this one by Vishnupersaud depicting a species of cobra lily (*Arisaema tortuosum*), which Wallich found during an expedition to Nepal in 1821. Gauci's lithograph copies were hand-coloured by John Clark to illustrate Wallich's three-volume publication *Plantae Asiaticae rariores*, which was published in 12 parts between 1829 and 1832.[153] Wallich returned to India in 1832 leaving his collection in London in the East India Company library; this is now housed in the Royal Botanic Gardens, Kew. In 1950, Wilfrid Blunt (1901–1987) included one of Vishnupersaud's watercolours in his now classic book on the subject, *The Art of Botanical Illustration*.

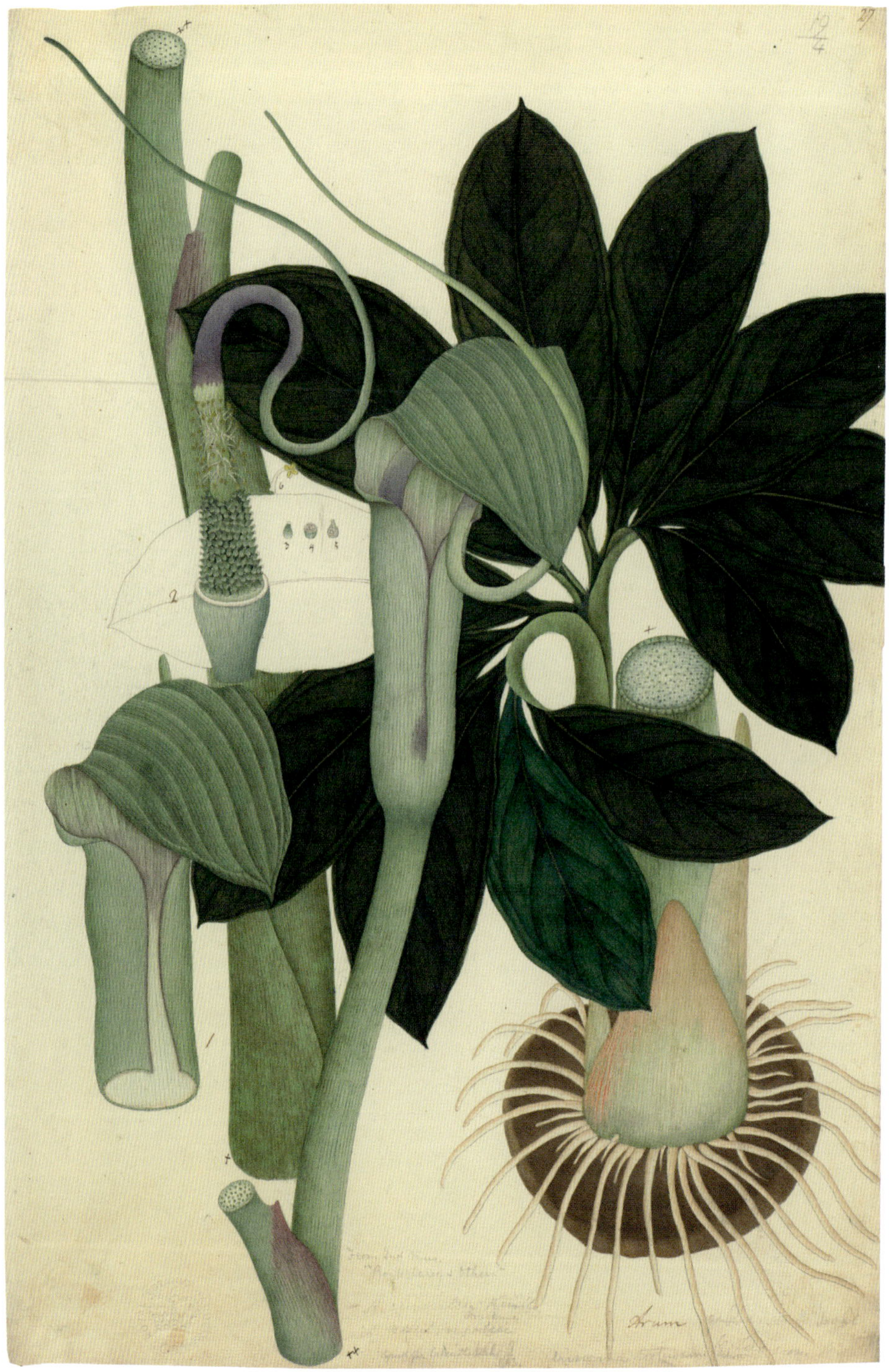

UNKNOWN ARTIST

37 Ghulam Husayn Khan, an Afghan inhabitant of the Fort of Ali Jan Khan in Kasur, with Munni Banu, the nurse, and a child

1817 | pencil and watercolour on paper | 31 × 41.8 cm | private collection, London/Karachi

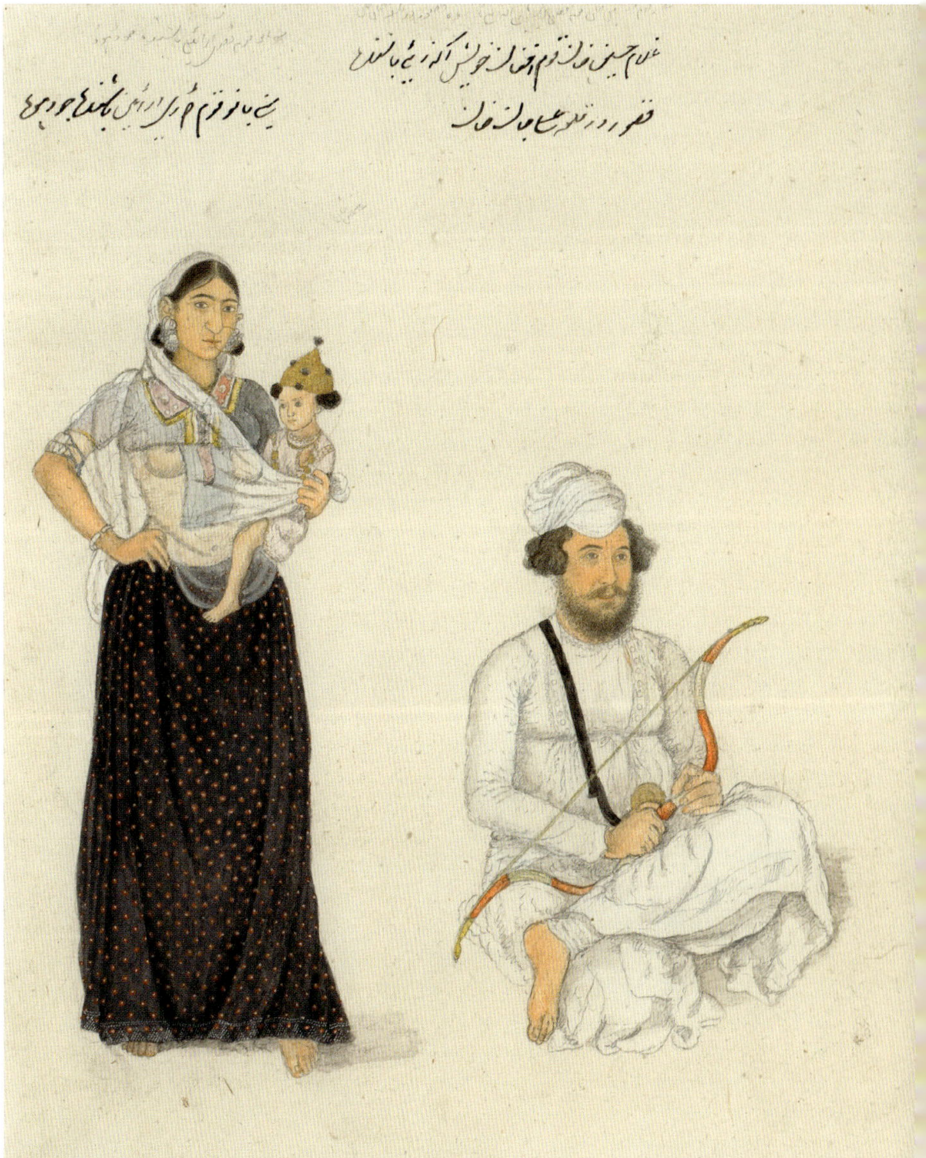

This double portrait belongs to a series of more than ninety watercolours by Delhi artists commissioned by William Fraser, then assistant to the East India Company Resident at Delhi, and his brother, James Baillie Fraser (see pp. 15–16). James was an artist and writer and planned to publish a book on the people and costumes of India using these paintings as the basis for its illustrations.

The names of the artists who worked for the Fraser brothers are unknown apart from Lalji, who James mentioned in a letter shortly after his arrival in Delhi in 1815:

> I have prevailed upon William to sit for his picture to Lalljee, a native who takes likenesses remarkably well – he was a pupil of Zofanies, and does not disgrace his teacher considering the usual want of idea of light & shade that the natives in general labour under – his son paints better than himself.[154]

In 1816 James left Delhi and gave his brother instructions for the portraits he wanted for his book, in a 'Memo of Native drawings wished for'.[155] William brought his artist with him when he travelled to Punjab, where this portrait was made in 1817.[156] It is thought that his artist wrote the inscriptions labelling the figures in pencil, which William then went over in ink. Here they name the sitters as Munni Banu and Ghulam Husayn Khan, inhabitants of Ali Jan Khan's fort in Kasur. Munni Bani was the wet nurse for the child she carries, identified in another portrait as the son of Osman Khan.[157]

After the rediscovery of the watercolours in 1979 at the Fraser family home in Scotland, the brothers' descendants sold them individually in sales at Sotheby's in London and New York.[158]

UNKNOWN ARTIST

38 Mawlavi Salamat Ullah with Ghafil Beg, a disciple, and Nur Muhammad, a sitar player

c. 1820 | pencil and watercolour on paper | 30.9 × 41.4 cm | private collection, London/Karachi

This portrait from the Fraser series depicts a Muslim scholar introduced to the Fraser brothers by their close friend, Colonel James Skinner (see p. 15). While staying at Skinner's estate in Hansi in October 1820, James Baillie Fraser wrote to his father describing his ambitious project:

> The native Drawings of Costume will form unquestionably the finest collection that ever visited England from hence & include the inhabitants of all the districts near Dilhee ... an immense variety of the nobles of Hindoostan ... and fuqeers & persons of singular character and appearance.[159]

The inscriptions on this page describe Mawlavi Salamat as 'inhabitant of Mathura',[160] a city south of Delhi, and his musician Nur Muhammad as a 'former inhabitant of Nizamgarh', north-east of Delhi.

Although Fraser's book never materialized, James Skinner did produce illustrated volumes of a similar type. Titled the *Tashrih al-aqvam* (Description of Castes) and completed in 1825, Skinner's books included paintings of some of the same figures who sat for the Fraser artists, clearly copied from the same original watercolours. These include the portrait of Ghulam Husayn Khan (see cat. 37), used to illustrate Skinner's section on the *Kasuri* – Muslim Afghans of Kasur.[161]

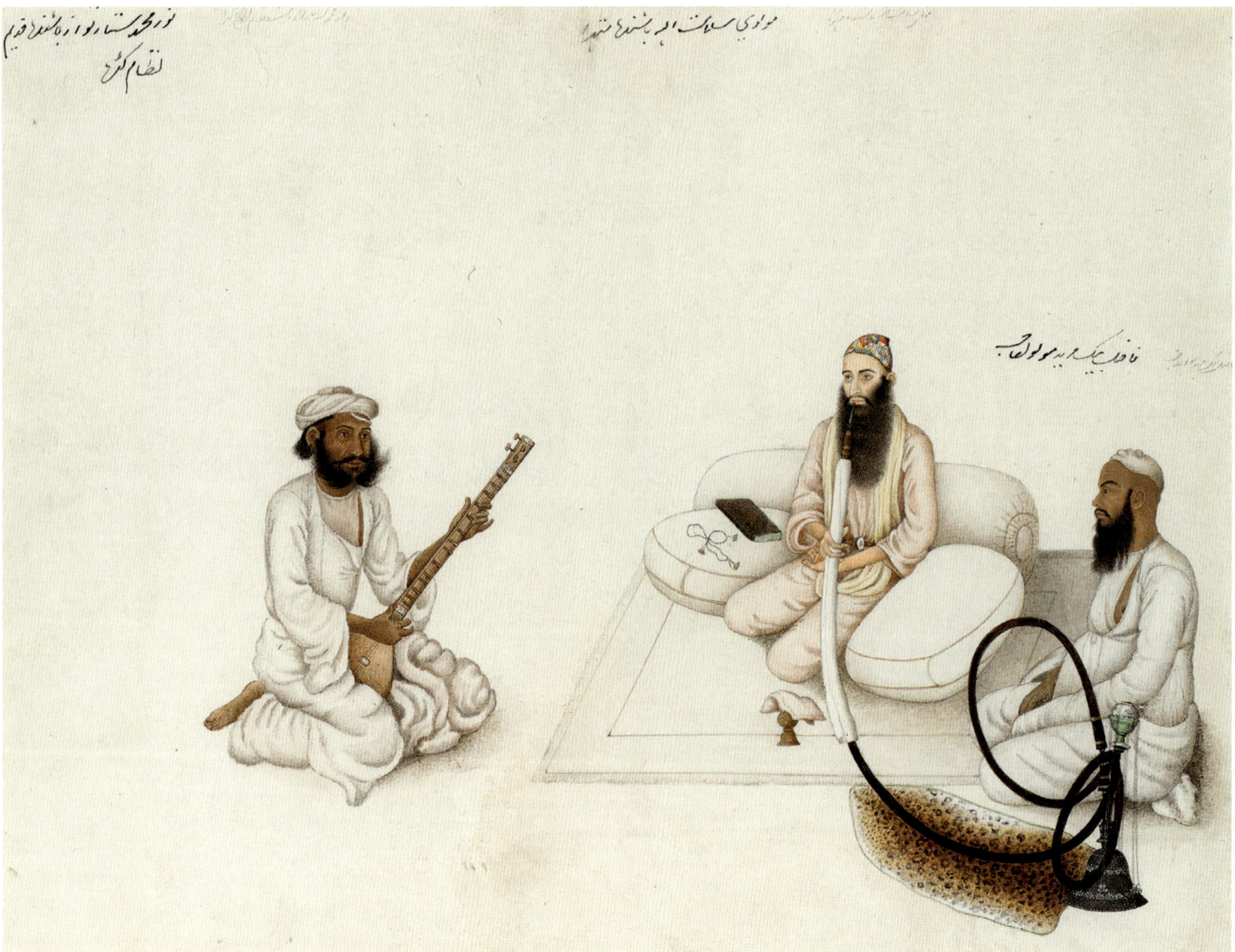

UNKNOWN ARTIST

39 A trooper of Skinner's Horse

c. 1821 | pencil and watercolour with metallic paints on paper | 29.2 × 20.3 cm | private collection, London/Karachi

The low-ranking soldier depicted here was in the service of the Fraser brothers' close friend, the half-Rajput, half-Scottish colonel, James Skinner. Skinner wrote to James Fraser in February 1821 that William had yet to send his painter 'to take the drawings of my men so you better write him again on this subject'.[162]

Skinner recruited hundreds of young men from villages around Delhi and Haryana to support his irregular cavalry regiment, popularly known as Skinner's Horse. He took a deep interest in the men who served under him and knew the names of the individual villages from which they came. Skinner's friend Sir John Malcolm (1769–1833) said of him and his relationship with the 'native irregulars':

> I do not mean to flatter when I say you are as good an Englishman as I know; but you are also a native irregular, half born and fully bred; you armed them, understand their characters, enter into their prejudices; can encourage them, without spoiling them; know what they can and, what is more important, what they *cannot* do. The superiority of your corps rests upon a foundation that no others have.[163]

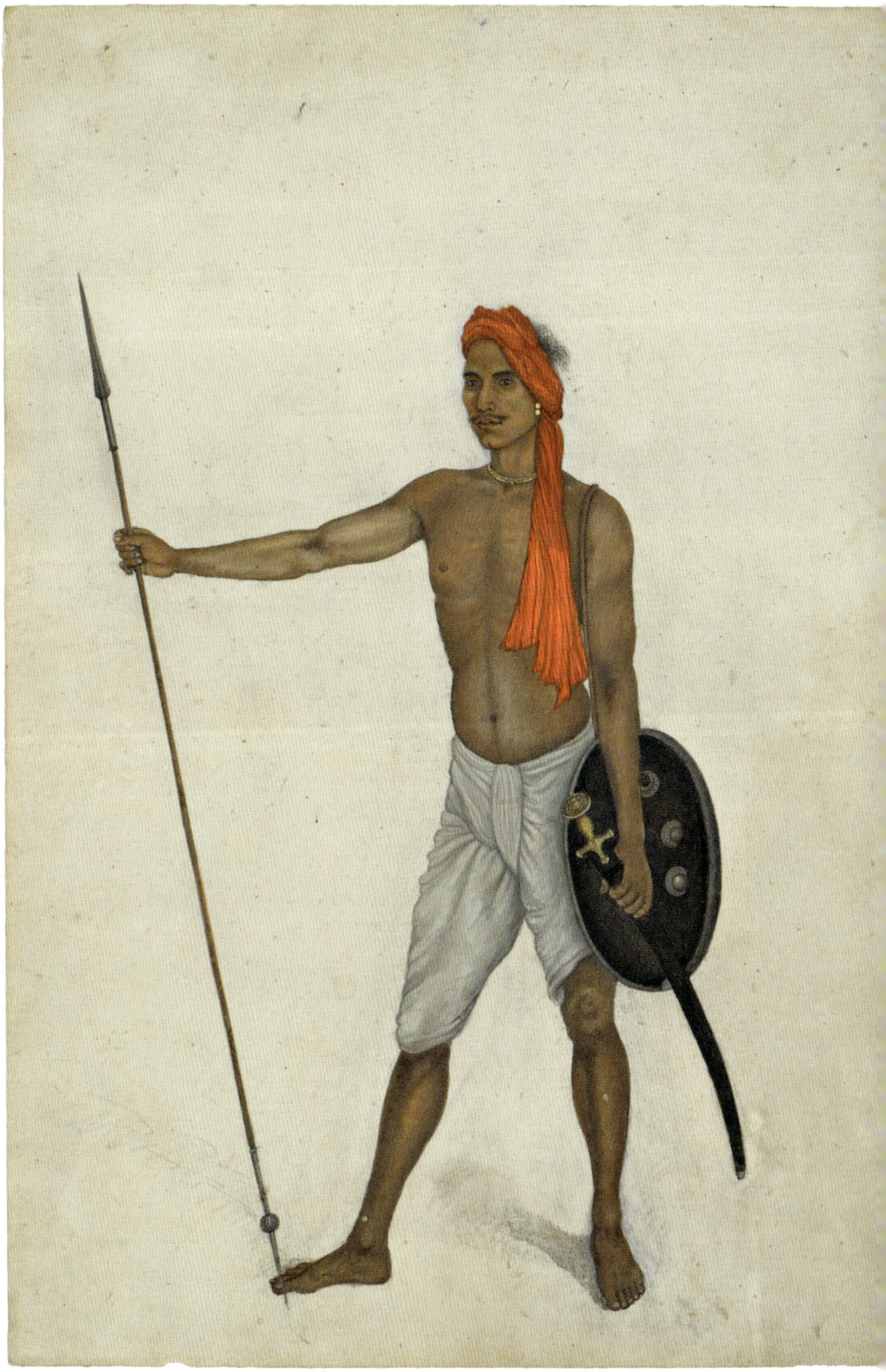

UNKNOWN ARTIST

40 The Rani of Radaur

1820s | watercolour with metallic paints on paper | page 30 × 21 cm | British Library

The *Tazkirat al-Umara* (Biography of the Nobles) is a history of the princely families of Rajasthan, Haryana and Punjab written in Persian by Colonel James Skinner. Skinner had met most of the people depicted in the book, this copy of which is illustrated with 38 portraits of the heads of the families described. It is unknown whether he ever encountered the one woman represented: described as the 'Rani of the late Rup Singh of Radaur', a Sikh state in northeastern Haryana bordering Punjab. The portrait is a generic likeness of an aristocratic Sikh woman, seated on the floor of a richly decorated palace in typical Punjabi dress. Her long, uncut hair is wound in a tall coil on the centre of her head, covered by a gold embroidered *chunni* (veil) and adorned with an ornate *mathapatti* (forehead band).

Skinner presented this copy of his book as a gift to his friend Sir John Malcolm, the recently retired governor of Bombay, in 1830. The British Museum purchased it from Malcolm's son, General George Malcolm, in 1865 and the manuscript is now part of the British Library's collection.[164]

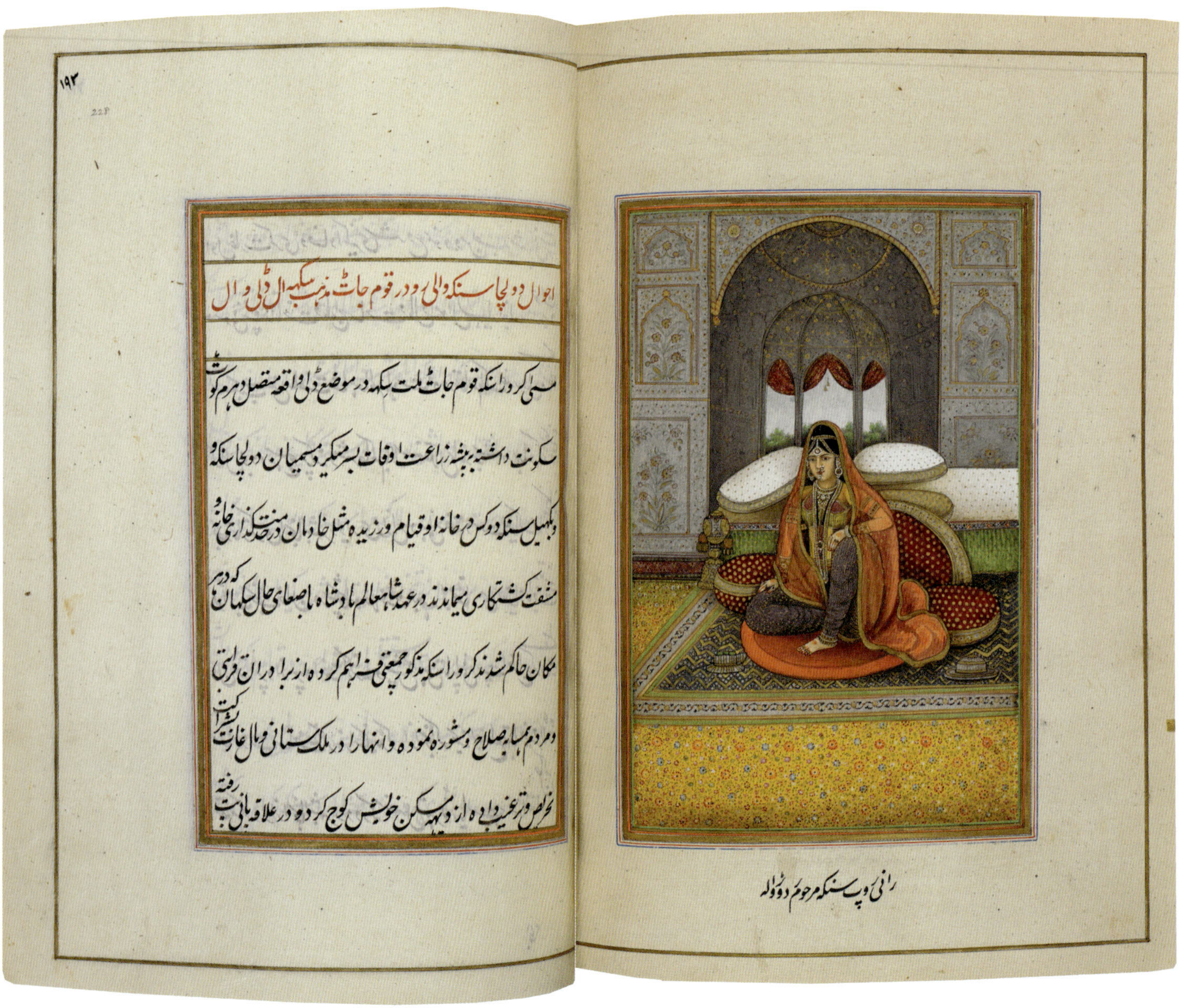

PRINCE DARA BAKHT

41 Calligram in the shape of a lion

c. 1845 | ink and watercolour on paper | 26.8 × 30.5 cm | British Library

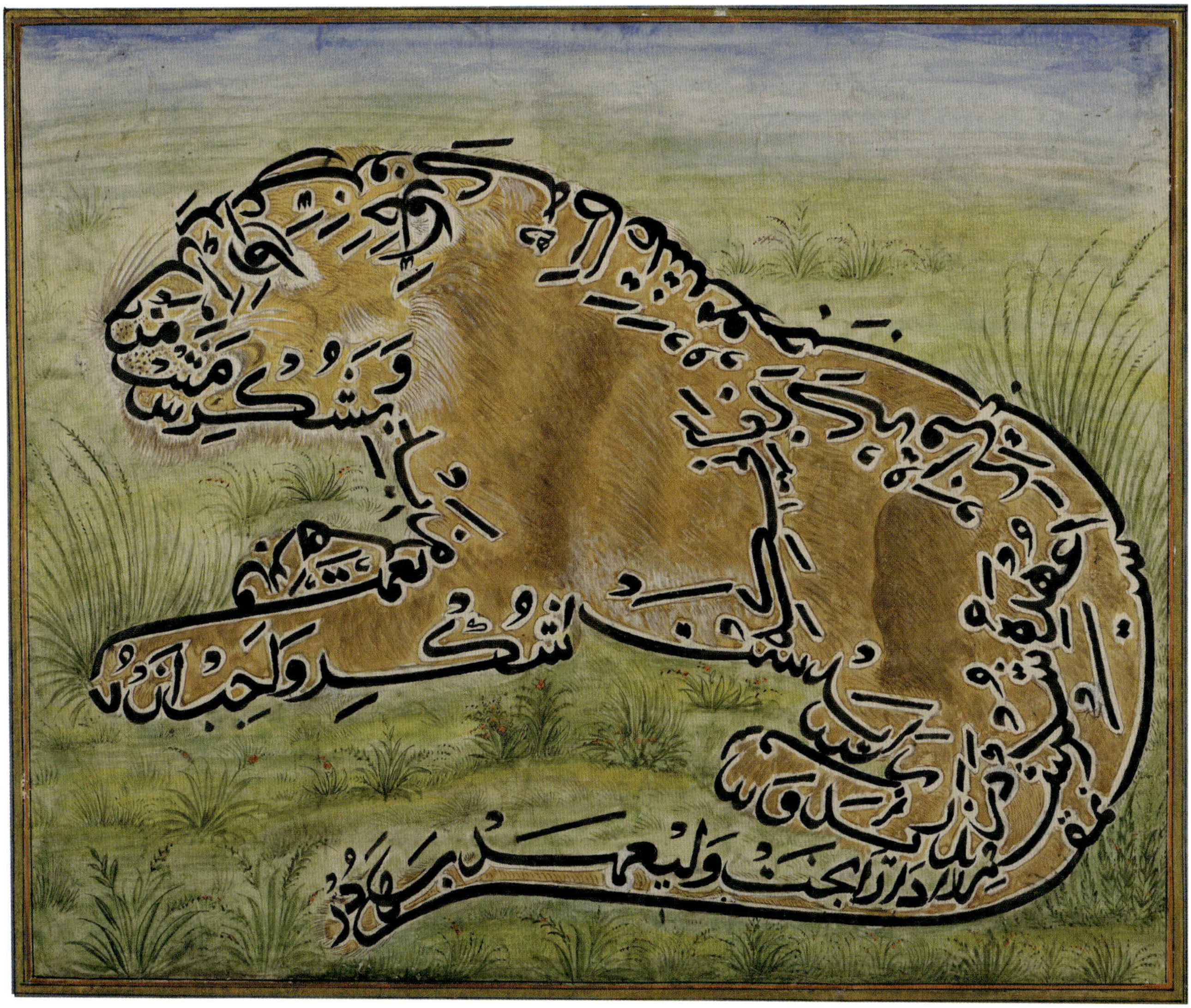

Compiled in 1854, this album contains specimens of calligraphy by the last Mughal ruler Bahadur Shah II (r. 1837–57), his sons and members of his court. Calligraphy was an art form practised by both male and female members of the Mughal royal family and nobility.[165] The lion's tail in this zoomorphic calligram is signed *Mirza Dara Bakht Vali Ahd Bahadur* (Prince Dara Bakht Heir Apparent), the eldest son of Bahadur Shah II and crown prince until his death (1790–1849).

The civil servant and linguist Lewin Bentham Bowring (1824–1910) acquired the album in Delhi in 1854, but how he obtained it is currently unknown.[166] Bowring presented the volume to the British Museum in the summer of 1856 while on leave in Britain, less than a year before the start of the Indian Rebellion, which ended in the demise of the Mughal dynasty and the emperor being exiled to Rangoon.

UNKNOWN ARTIST

42 Dildar Mahal enters royal presence in 1845

c. 1850 | watercolour and metallic paints on paper | page 46 × 29.5 cm | Royal Collection/HM King Charles III

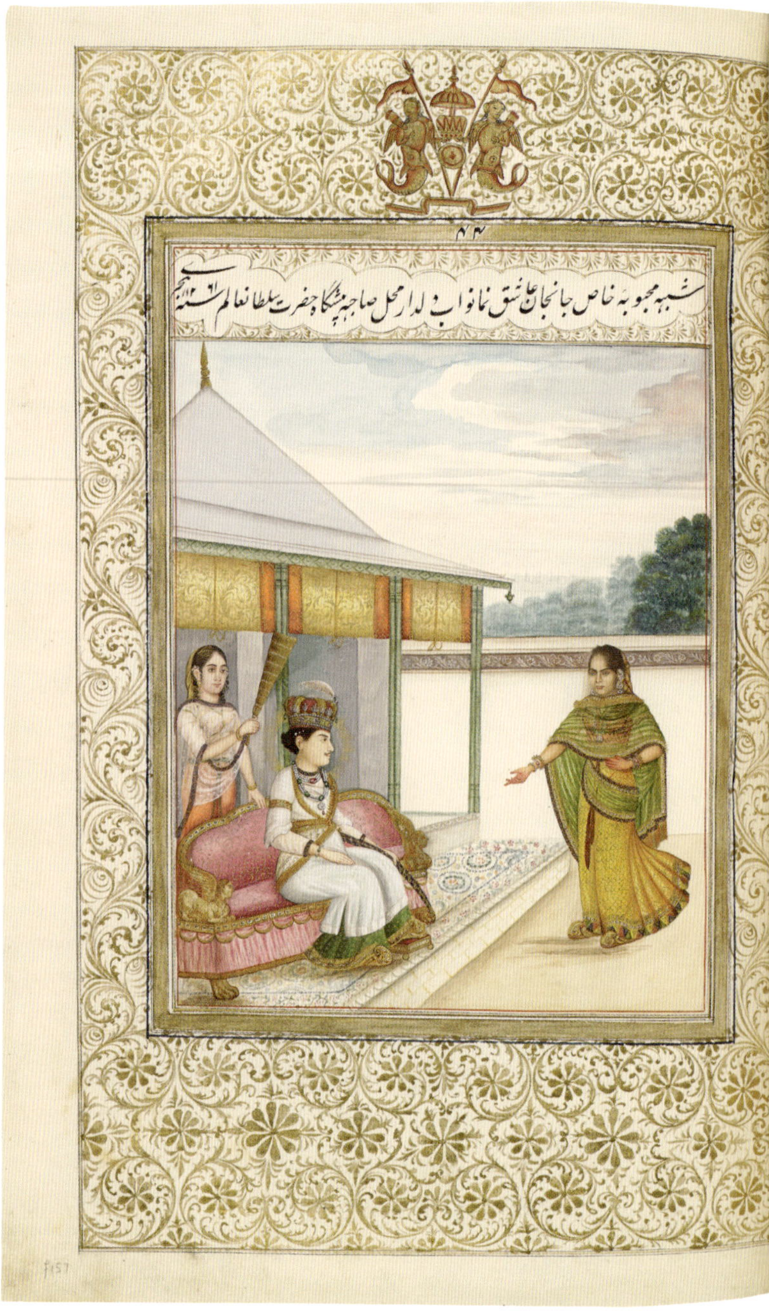

The most lavish manuscript surviving from mid-nineteenth-century Lucknow is this illustrated and illuminated copy of the *Ishqnamah* (Book of Love), commissioned during the reign of the last king of Awadh, Wajid Ali Shah (r. 1847–56), whose coat of arms decorates the borders above each of the illustrations. The text is a youthful autobiography written by Wajid Ali Shah in Urdu rhyming couplets. It revolves around the theme of *ishq* (love), and nearly all of the manuscript's 104 illustrations portray the two great loves of his life: music and women.[167] The paintings show the Lucknow court artists' training in the Mughal stippling technique and their study and adaption of English watercolour illustrations. For the depiction of the king's wives and concubines, his painters based their portraits on photographs taken by the Lucknow photographer Ahmad Ali Khan (see fig. 19).[168] The women's faces are detailed individually but frank and unsmiling, their eyes downcast as if avoiding the photographer's eye.

East India Company soldiers took the large book when they stormed the Qaiserbagh Palace in 1858 and Sir John Lawrence (later governor general and first viceroy of India) presented it to Queen Victoria.[169]

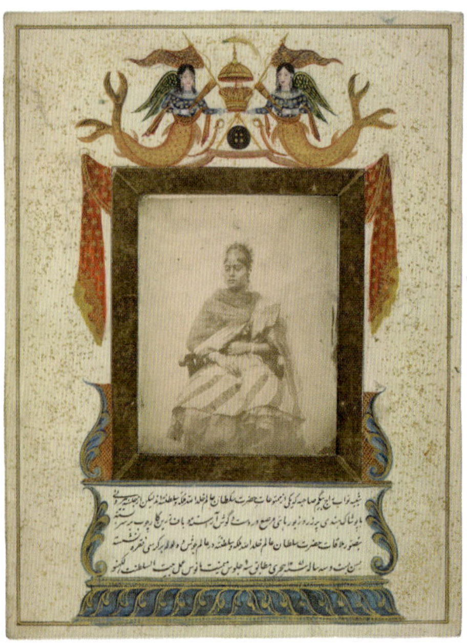

FIG. 19 Ahmad Ali Khan, *Picture of Nawab Raj Begum Sahibah one of the concubines of the Sultan … aged 23 years. Dated 1271 (1854/55) … of the kingdom of Lucknow*, c. 1855.

MUKHLIS

43 Tamrusiya and her brother Mihrasb under the Waqwaq tree

c.1580 | watercolour and metallic paints on paper | 35.5 × 23 cm | British Library

The *Darabnama* (Tales of Darab) is a medieval Persian romance based on the life of the legendary King Darab.[170] This folio is from a sixteenth-century copy of the story that was written and illustrated at the Mughal court in Fatehpur-Sikri. Mukhlis's painting illustrates an episode of the text that comes after Darab falls in love with the widowed Queen Tamrusiya, but they are separated by stormy seas. Tamrusiya finds her brother, Mihrasb, and together they have adventures in the Greek islands, one of which Mukhlis depicts as the mythical island of Waqwaq, inhabited by strange trees which grow human heads as fruit.

By 1828 the book was in the library of the rulers of Awadh in Lucknow, as indicated by the earliest of the bright red stamp impressions made by the Lucknow royal librarians, who inspected the volumes every ten years (see fig. 5). The latest stamp dates to 1847, suggesting the *Darabnama* was among the books looted from the Qaiserbagh Palace in 1857 (see pp. 18–19). The British Museum purchased the volume from London bookseller Bernard Quaritch on 15 February 1893. The manuscript is now part of the British Library's collection and its 157 pages with illustrations are individually mounted.

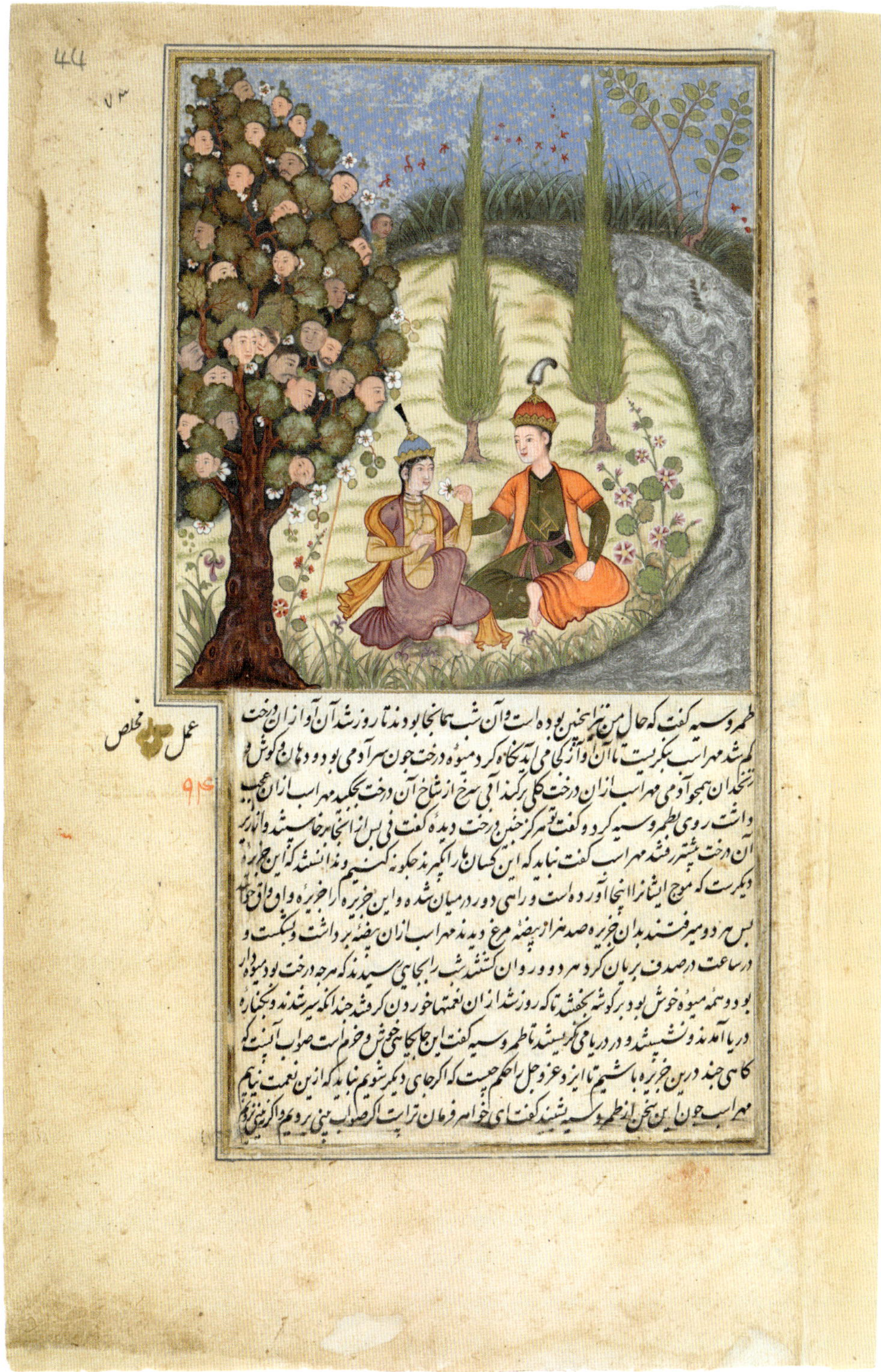

MISKIN & ASI

44 Battle scene

c. 1590–95 | watercolour and metallic paints on paper | 32 × 18.4 cm | Victoria and Albert Museum

This gruesome battle scene is from a manuscript thought to be the first illustrated copy of the *Akbarnama* (Book of Akbar), the official chronicle of the reign of the third Mughal emperor, prepared for him in Lahore in the 1590s. Inscriptions in red ink in the margin below this painting name the artist Miskin as responsible for the *tarh* (outline composition), with the colour and details painted by his brother Asi. Miskin was one of the master artists of Akbar's painting atelier and the subject of the first monographic article to discuss a Mughal artist, published in 1928.[171]

The manuscript remained in the library of Akbar's's son Jahangir, and grandson Shah Jahan, but by the second half of the eighteenth century it was in Lucknow and its pages disbound.[172] Major John Clarke, a British army officer stationed in Awadh between 1858 and 1862, acquired 273 of the manuscript's folios, then loosely held between lacquered boards. Thirty or so years later, Frances Clarke, the major's widow, offered them to the South Kensington Museum. She initially suggested a purchase price of £300 for the damaged pages and covers but in the end accepted the Museum's much lower valuation of £100.[173]

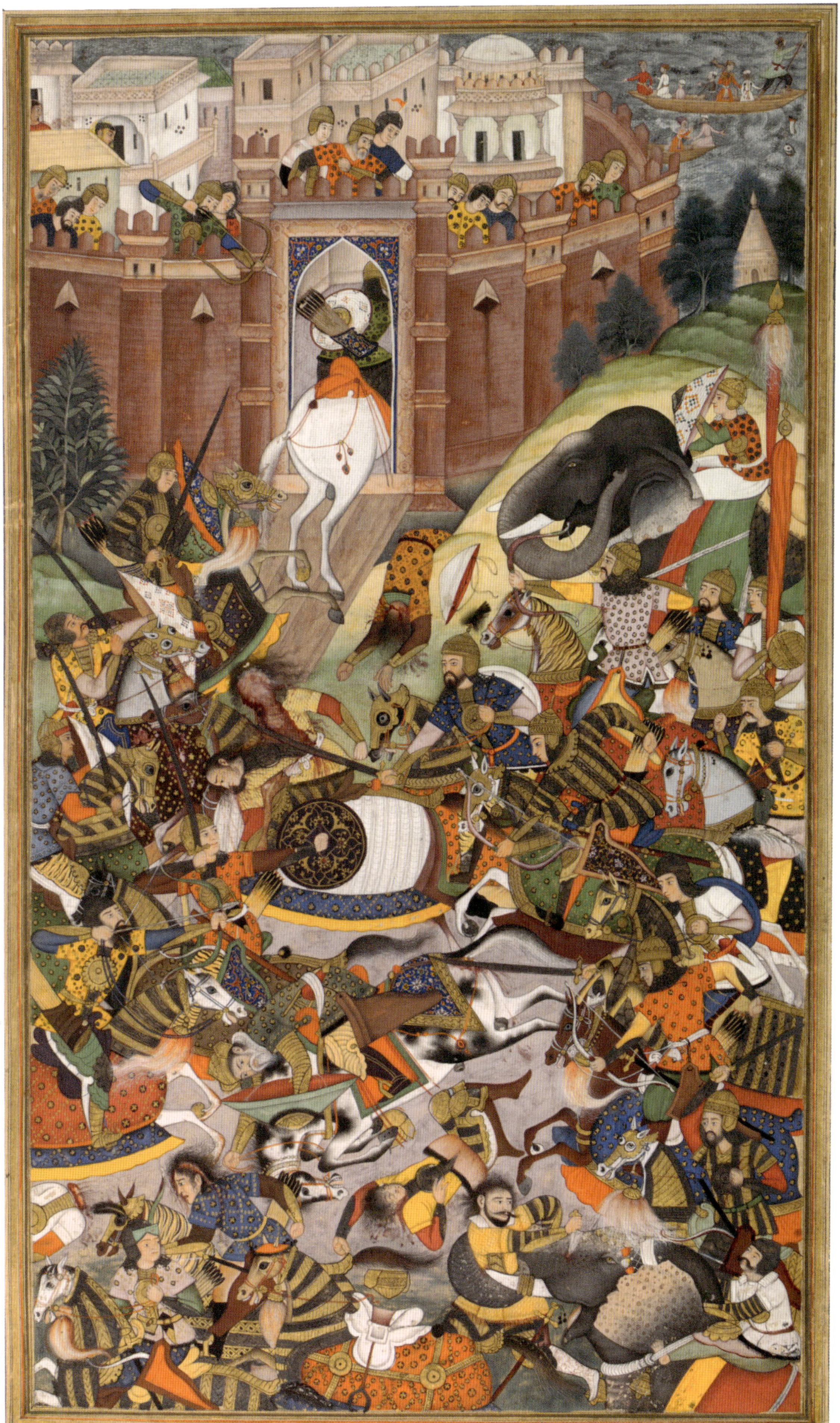

UNKNOWN ARTIST

45 Hamza arrives in Mecca

c. 1562–77 | gouache on prepared cotton backed with paper | 66.4 × 50.5 cm | Victoria and Albert Museum

The young Mughal emperor Akbar commissioned the *Hamzanama* (Tales of Hamza) in the 1560s. Akbar's court chronicler Abul Fazl described the popular Persian epic as 'represented in twelve volumes, and clever painters made the most astonishing illustrations for no less than one thousand and four hundred passages of the story',[174] of which fewer than two hundred survive today. Averaging around 68 × 52 cm each, these illustrations are more than double the size of most surviving Mughal paintings of the sixteenth century. Howard Hodgkin called them 'perhaps the greatest single achievement of Indian pictorial art apart from the Ajanta caves'.[175]

In 1881 Caspar Purdon Clarke bought 24 pages from the *Hamzanama* manuscript for the South Kensington Museum during a buying trip to India. He discovered them in 'one of the picturesque huts on the Hawa Kadal bridge spanning the River Jhelum' in Srinagar, Kashmir, where several of the large pictures painted on cotton were being used as draft excluders, plastered over the windows.[176] When William Morris saw them on display in London the following year he recommended their treatment of trees, foliage and flowering plants as admirable studies for tapestry and wallpaper design.[177] Many of the paintings had suffered at the hands of iconoclasts who smeared brown paint over the faces of all the living beings – even the elephant in this surreal scene of Hamza arriving with his entourage in Mecca.

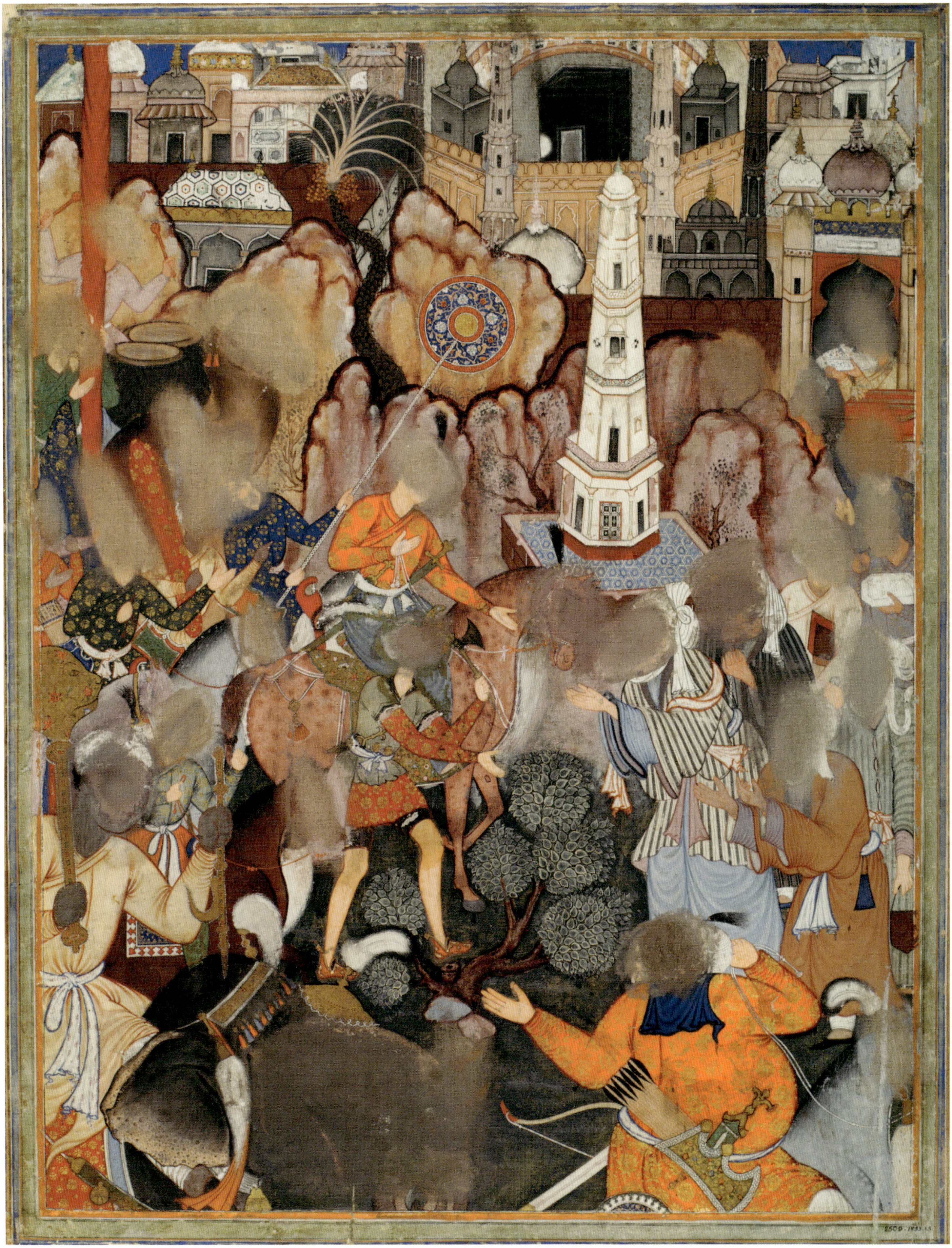

THE INDIAN PRESS ALLAHABAD, AFTER ABANINDRANATH TAGORE

46 The Last Moments of Shah Jahan

1903 | chromolithograph on paper | page 35.5 × 25.5 | Wellcome Collection

In late 1902 the Bengali artist Abanindranath Tagore presented *The Last Moments of Shah Jahan* with two other works at the Delhi Durbar Exhibition of Arts and Crafts.[178] The night scene shows the dying emperor imprisoned in the Agra Fort as he gazes wistfully at the Taj Mahal, the tomb of his wife, with their daughter Princess Jahanara sitting beside him, head in her hand. The *bhava* (emotion) and sentimentality echoed the nostalgia of art nouveau in *fin de siècle* Europe, and the painting won him a silver medal at the Delhi exhibition.[179]

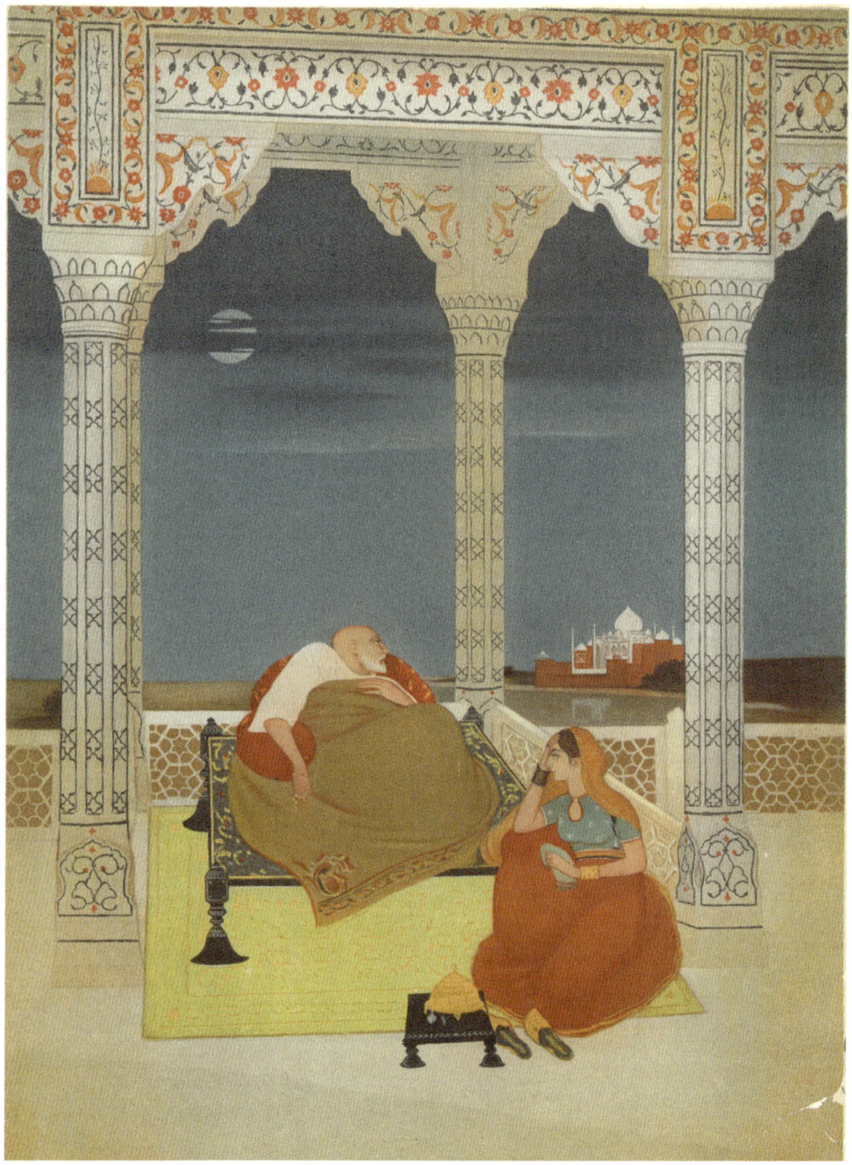

Tagore began his career as a writer and illustrator in Calcutta at the height of the Raj and did not encounter Mughal paintings until introduced to them by E.B. Havell in his mid-twenties. He recorded his reaction to his first encounter with a painting by the seventeenth-century artist Mansur:

> I was lost for words. I then noticed Havell standing silently behind me with a pleased expression as he had anticipated my reaction. I felt so dizzy. So! our old art too contains an embarrassment of riches. Why then did I agonise so long about finding proper indigenous material to emulate?[180]

ISHWARI PRASAD

47 Portrait of E.B. Havell

c. 1904 | watercolour on paper | 19.5 × 13 cm | British Library

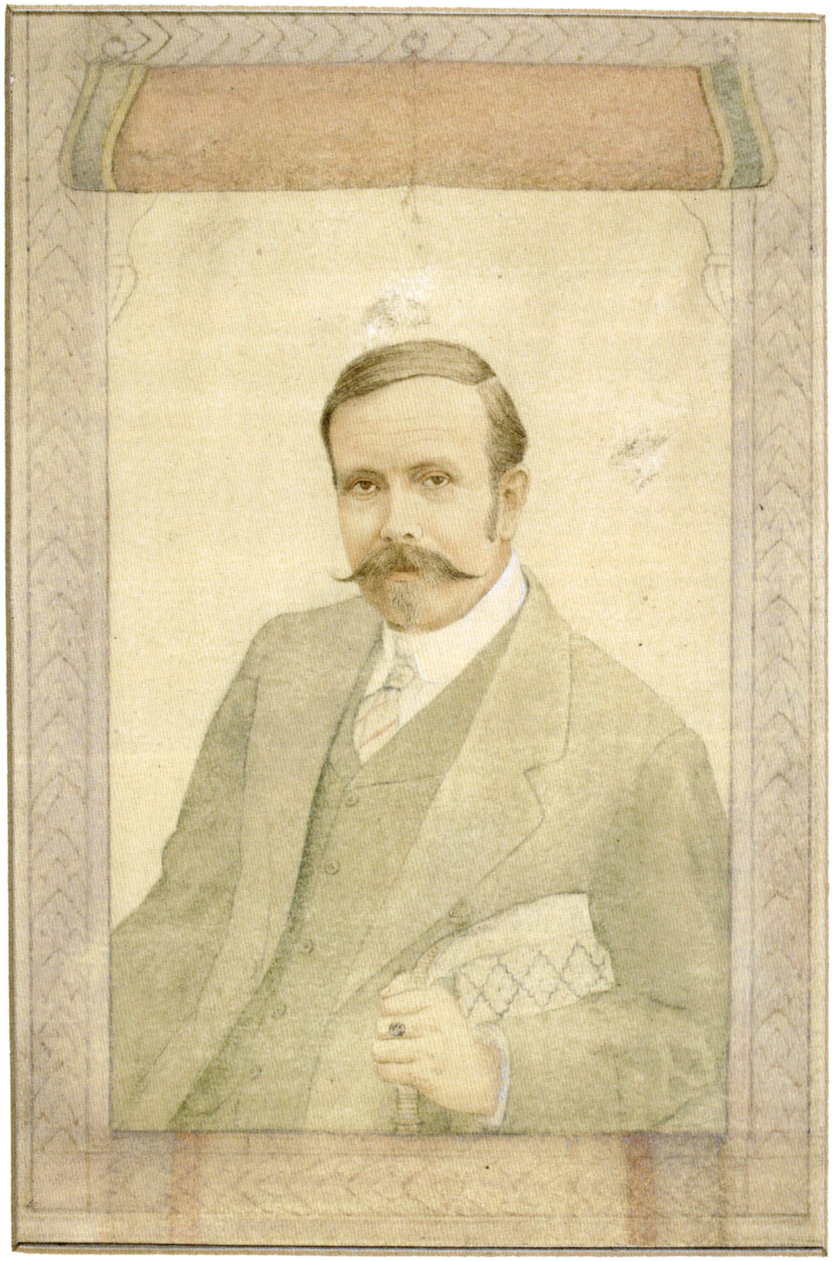

Ernest Binfield Havell (1861–1934) was principal of the Government School of Art and Keeper of the Government Art Gallery in Calcutta from 1896 until 1906 and authored some of the first books in English on South Asian painting (see p. 20). The painter Ishwari Prasad (1870–1950) was a hereditary artist, taught by his mother, Sona Kumari, and grandfather, Shiva Lal, a leading Company painter in nineteenth-century Patna who claimed descent from the great masters of the Mughal court.[181] For his first full-time job, Prasad worked as the retained artist of a wealthy businessman in Mathura, for whom he primarily painted miniature portraits from photographs according to the late-nineteenth-century trend. In 1904, as part of Havell's efforts to revive traditional arts at the Calcutta school, Prasad was appointed Professor of Fine Arts and Indian Painting to teach his inherited working methods. His likeness of Havell recalls the Mughal *jharokha* (balcony) portrait and its painted frame imitates the decorated paper borders of Mughal albums.

Havell's daughter, Lady Sonia Wilson, presented this portrait of her father to the British Library in 1968, along with a collection of printed photographs of staff and students at the Calcutta art school in the early 1900s.[182]

ABANINDRANATH TAGORE

48 A Music Party

c. 1905 | watercolour on paper | painting 12.2 × 7.7 cm | Victoria and Albert Museum

Lady Sonia Wilson, the daughter of E.B. Havell, donated this painting by her father's famous protégé to the V&A in 1951. Havell claimed Tagore's rejection of Western art and pioneering assimilation of Indian painting traditions were entirely thanks to his new displays of Mughal and Rajput paintings in the Calcutta Art Gallery.[183] The artist later wrote that he felt swept along in Havell's cultural revolution: 'As I felt the tug of the wind I tore out the ropes and flung myself in.... Getting rid of Western art, I now took up Indian art.'[184]

Tagore's new trademark wash technique is most often credited to the *morotai* painting method he saw practised by the Japanese painter Yokoyama Taikan (1868–1956),[185] and in 1908 *A Music Party* appeared in the influential Japanese art journal *Kokka*. Tagore's building up of colour in pale, muted tones as well as his Mughal arrangement of planes could also be attributed to his colleague Ishwari Prasad. Here Tagore uses the same motif of the rolled fabric blind seen in many of Prasad's works, including his portrait of Havell from around the same period (see cat. 47).

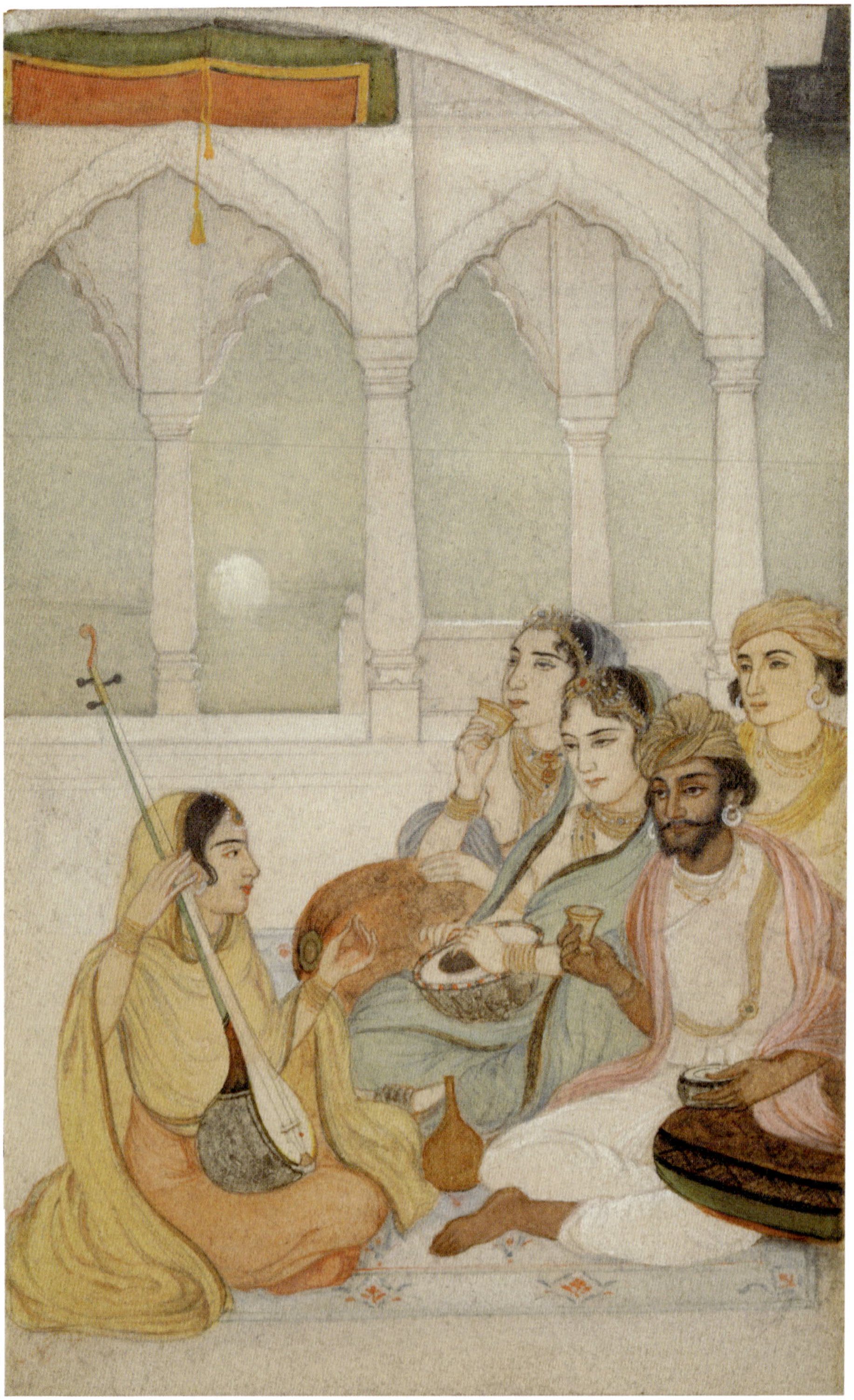

UNKNOWN ARTIST

49 A Mughal prince and princess on their wedding night

c.1640 | watercolour and metallic paints on paper | 33 × 44.5 cm | Victoria and Albert Museum

The V&A purchased this album page in 1911 from Luzac & Co., a bookseller specializing in 'Oriental and Foreign books' based on Great Russell Street. 1911 was the year of the Delhi Coronation Durbar, an event which rekindled British public interest in Mughal art and India's imperial history. The painting was originally registered as a portrait of Prince Salim (the future Emperor Jahangir), 'Mogul work; about 1580'.[186] This misidentification of what is now known to be a portrait of one of Shah Jahan's sons painted in a style of more than half a century later shows just how rudimentary knowledge of South Asian painting in Britain was at the start of the twentieth century before any books on the subject had been published.

The painting probably depicts Prince Murad Bakhsh, who, at the age of 14, married Sakina Banu, the daughter of a powerful Iranian nobleman at the Mughal court, in Agra. On the first night (*Suhag Raat*) of a Mughal marriage the female members of the groom's family would chaperone the bride to her husband's bed. One of the women attempts to coax the princess with a cup of wine, but etiquette dictated the bride should appear timid and she pulls her back.

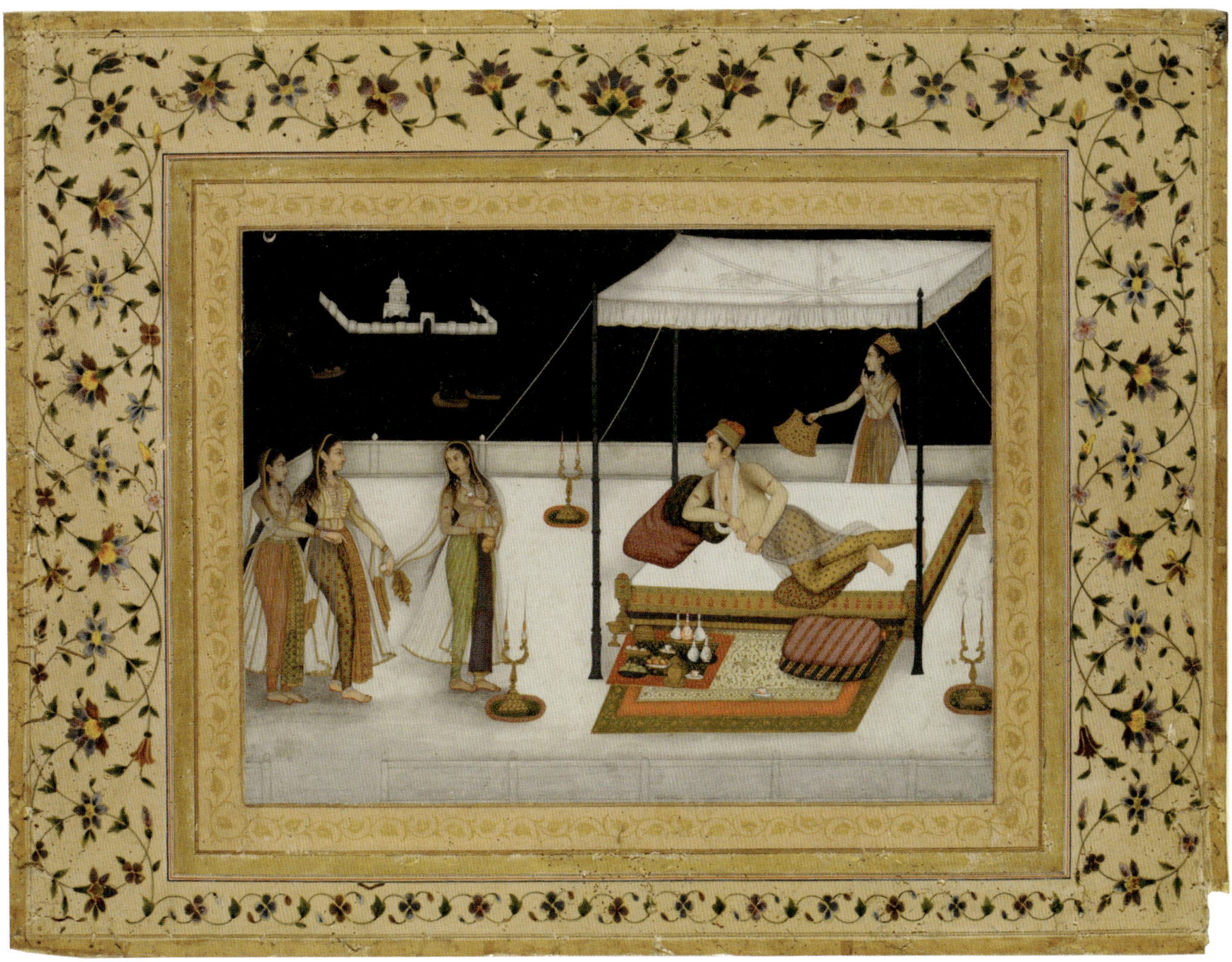

WILLIAM ROTHENSTEIN

50 Sir Thomas Roe's embassy to the court of Jahangir

1924 | oil and pencil on canvas | 52.5 × 110.5 cm | Bradford District Museums and Galleries

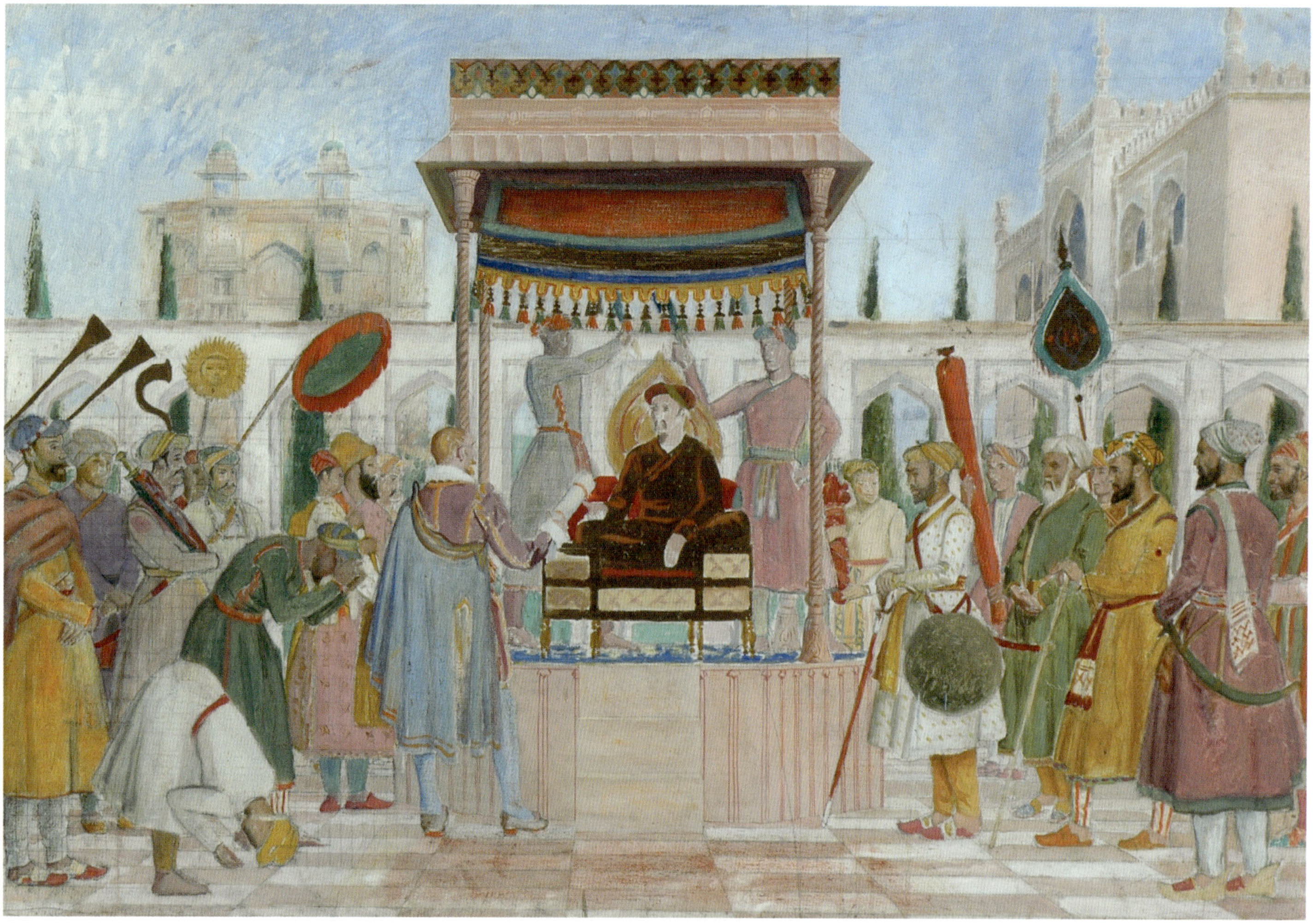

In 1924 the artist and founding member of the India Society, William Rothenstein (see p. 21) received the commission to paint the official reception of Sir Thomas Roe at the Mughal court in Ajmer, a late addition to the decorative scheme of St Stephen's Hall in the Palace of Westminster. The space served as the main public entrance to the House of Commons and its display of enormous narrative paintings intended to immerse visitors in a panorama of momentous events in the 'Building of Britain'.[187]

This scene of Jahangir receiving the English ambassador was live in the public imagination, having been staged repeatedly over four months as part of the Festival of Empire pageant in 1911.[188] Volunteers performed the 'historical' pageant alongside the *Festival of Empire* exhibition at Crystal Palace, where the Indian Court included a popular display of Indian art. Many of the paintings on show were loaned from the India Office, prompting the Earl of Crewe, then Secretary of State for India, to request Indian paintings be hung in his office in Whitehall.[189] Rothenstein may have drawn on figures from these and other Mughal works for his St Stephen's Hall commission (see figs 20 & 21).

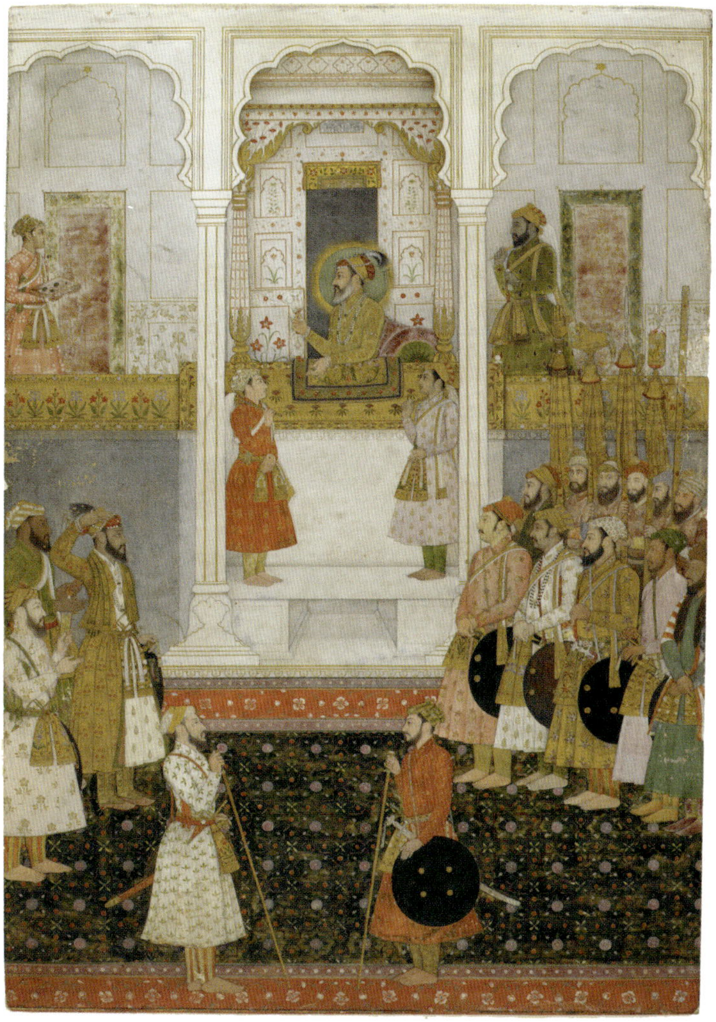

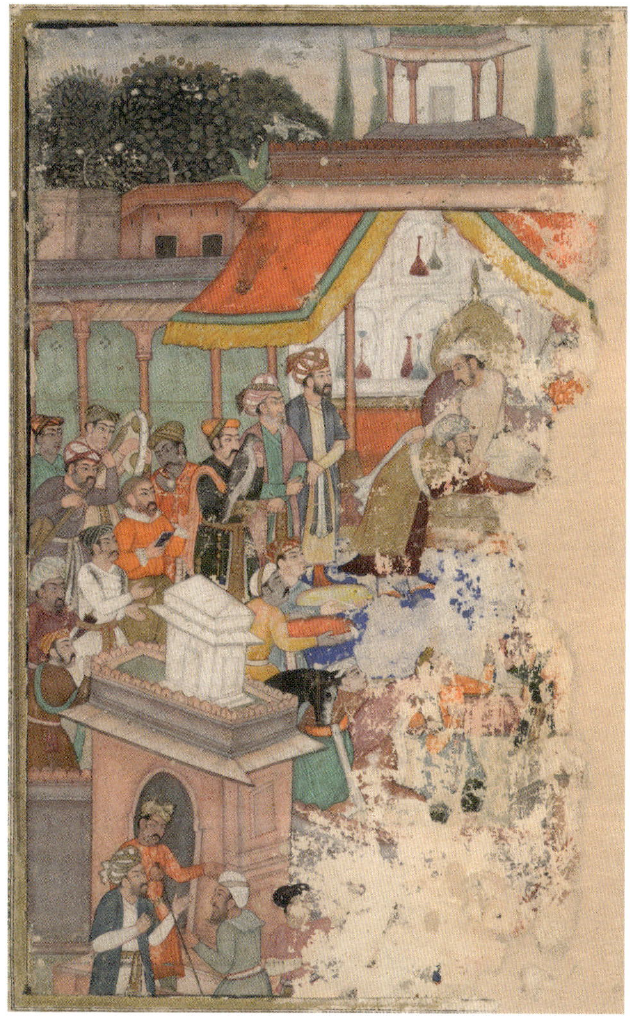

Figure 20 was one of many Mughal paintings from the India Office Collection that hung in the office in Whitehall from 1911 until curators suggested they be removed for conservation in the 1970s.

The National Art Collections Fund presented figure 21 to the British Museum on the retirement of Laurence Binyon, Keeper of the Sub-Department of Oriental Prints and Drawings, a member of the India Society and a close friend of William Rothenstein.

FIG. 20 Unknown artist, *Shah Jahan in Durbar*, c.1650.

FIG. 21 *Jahangir investing a courtier with a robe of honour*, c.1616–18.

SAMUEL FYZEE-RAHAMIN

51 Raagni Todi, Goddess Tune

1913 | watercolour and pen & ink on paper | 51.6 × 36 cm | Tate

Born into a Jewish family in Poona, Samuel Fyzee-Rahamin (1880–1964) studied first at the Sir J.J. School of Art in Mumbai before he won a scholarship to London, becoming one of the first two Indian students to study at the Royal Academy Schools. When he returned to India in 1908, Samuel Rahamin began a successful career as a portrait painter in the Western style, but he later made a spectacular conversion to the 'new school' of Indian painting. *Raagni Todi* is from a series based on traditional *ragamala* iconography, inspired by his wife, the well-known singer and writer Atiya Fyzee.[190] (When the couple married, they joined their family names and Samuel converted to Islam.)

Fyzee-Rahamin exhibited the *ragamala* paintings in his first exhibition held in February 1914 at the Galerie Georges Petit in Paris and again at Goupil Gallery in London later that summer. The Regent Street gallery published Atiya's book *Indian Music* (1914) to accompany the exhibition, using her husband's paintings as the illustrations. Atiya published a second edition of her book in 1925, the year Bombay industrialist Sir Victor Sassoon (1881–1961) bought *Raagni Todi* for the Tate.[191]

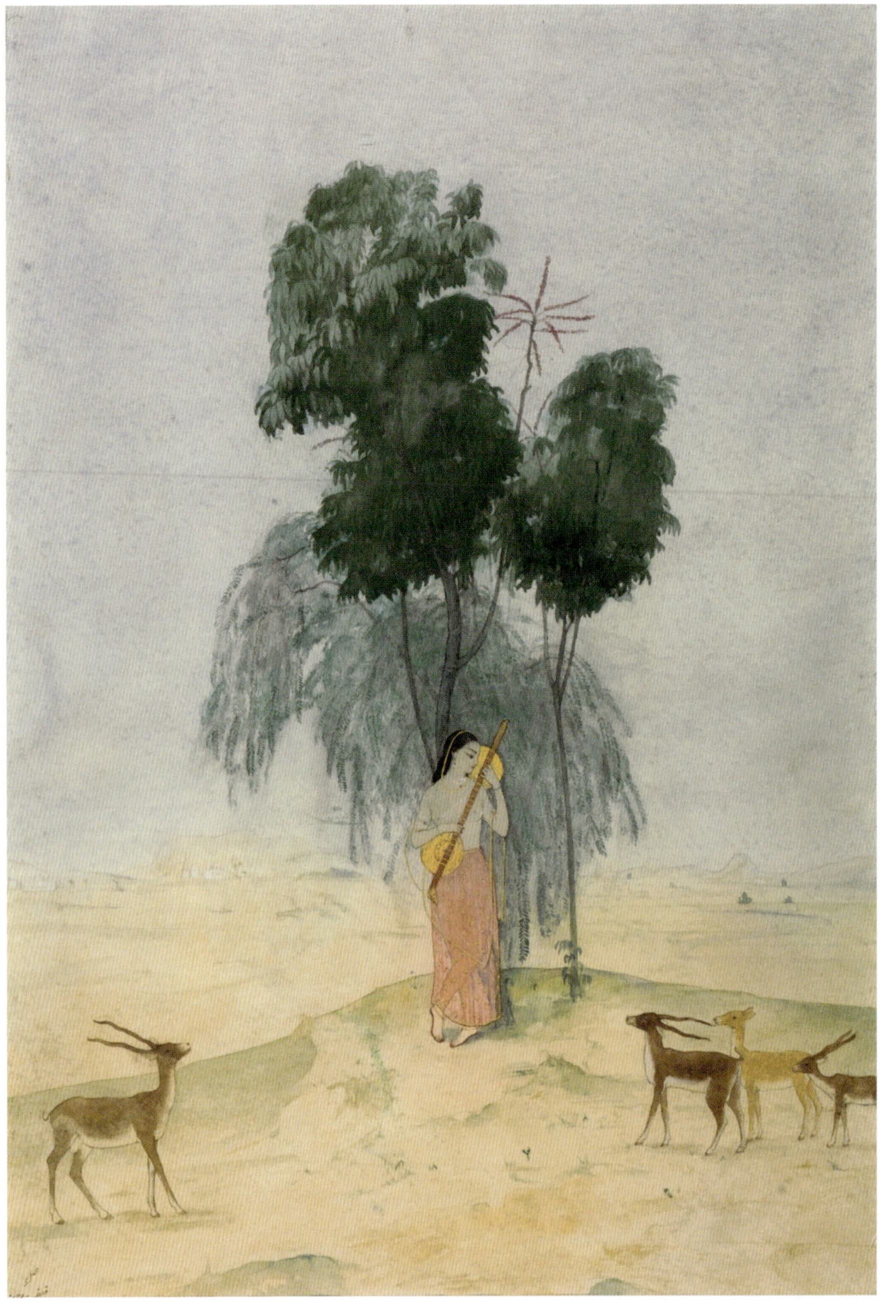

SAMUEL FYZEE-RAHAMIN

52 A Rajput Sirdar

c. 1914–15 | watercolour and pen & ink on paper | 53.1 × 32.3 cm | Tate

Samuel Fyzee-Rahamin first exhibited this watercolour as *Portrait of a Rajput Warrior of Rajputana* at his 1918 solo exhibition at the Knoedler Gallery in New York. It remained unsold until his 1925 exhibition *India: Vedic, Mythological and Contemporary Water-Colours* at Arthur Tooth & Sons in London, when the artist was at the height of his fame. Months earlier, Fyzee-Rahamin had lent works to the Indian section of the *British Empire Exhibition* in Wembley, where Lord Birkenhead, then Secretary of State for India, bought two of his paintings.[192] *The Rajput Warrior* illustrated an article in *Apollo* on 'Mr Fyzee-Rahamin's Paintings' and the *Burlington Magazine* posted an advert for his London solo show.[193] A representative of the Indian State of Bhavnagar purchased this work from Arthur Tooth and, as with the painting bought by Victor Sassoon (cat. 51), immediately donated it to the Tate. Queen Mary also bought one of Fyzee-Rahamin's paintings, a portrait of the famous Indian musician Veene Sheshanna, which she lent to the 1934 *All-India Exhibition of Modern Indian Art*, organized by the India Society at the Burlington Galleries (see fig. 7).

More than half a century after Fyzee-Rahamin painted the portrait, his wife Atiya recalled that 'The name of the Rajput Sirdar is Maharawal Udey Rana – a first class warrior *sirdar* (courtier) of the Court (*Durbar*) of Udeypoor, Rajputana – of *Chawan* clan descended from the Sun and the Moon – painted from life – when we were the guests of the Ruler.'[194]

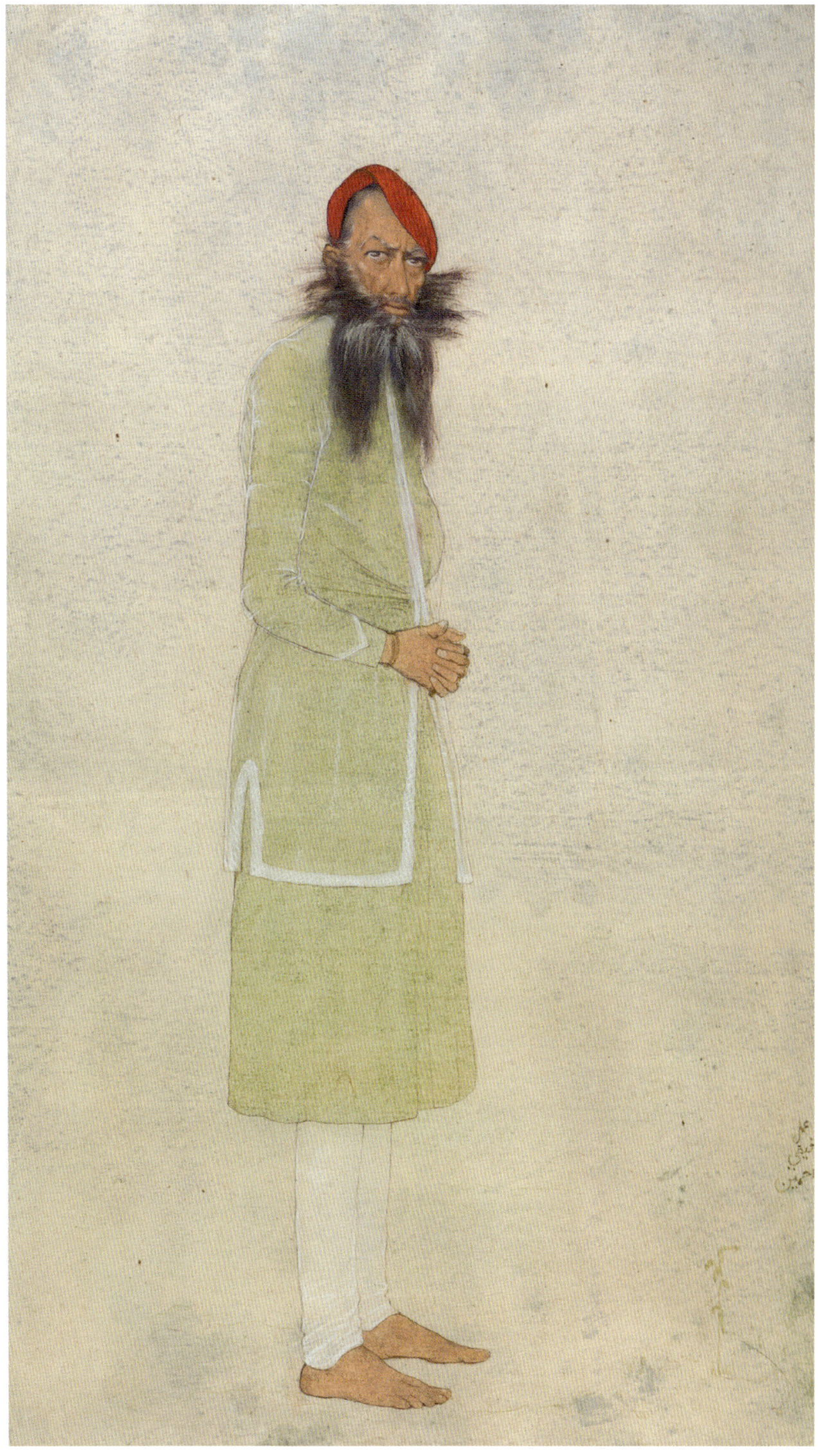

BALCHAND

53 Shah Shuja, Awrangzeb and Murad Bakhsh

*c.*1635 | watercolour and metallic paints on paper | painting 23.8 × 16.9 cm | Victoria and Albert Museum

When 'An Album of superb Indian miniatures and calligraphy' came up for auction in early 1925, the V&A made an agreement with the American collector Alfred Chester Beatty that they would purchase it between them.[195] Now known as the 'Minto Album', these 40 pages were sold anonymously at the time by the fifth Earl of Minto (1891–1975), whose father had been the viceroy of India, and whose great-great grandfather had been the governor general. Along with the 'Wantage Album' pages, acquired by the museum four years earlier[196] and those of the 'Kevorkian Album', sold to the New York dealer Hagop Kevorkian in 1929 (see fig. 14), they form a group of folios from seventeenth-century imperial Mughal albums that were reassembled *c.*1800 with copies of earlier Mughal paintings.

As identified in the inscription in the border below, this painting depicts three of Shah Jahan's sons: Shah Shuja, Awrangzeb and Murad Bakhsh on horseback, and was painted by the artist Balchand (see cat. 11), who also signed the painting on the tree trunk behind the three figures. A copy of this painting appears in cat. 17, an album thought to have been assembled for Shah Shuja in the 1640s.[197]

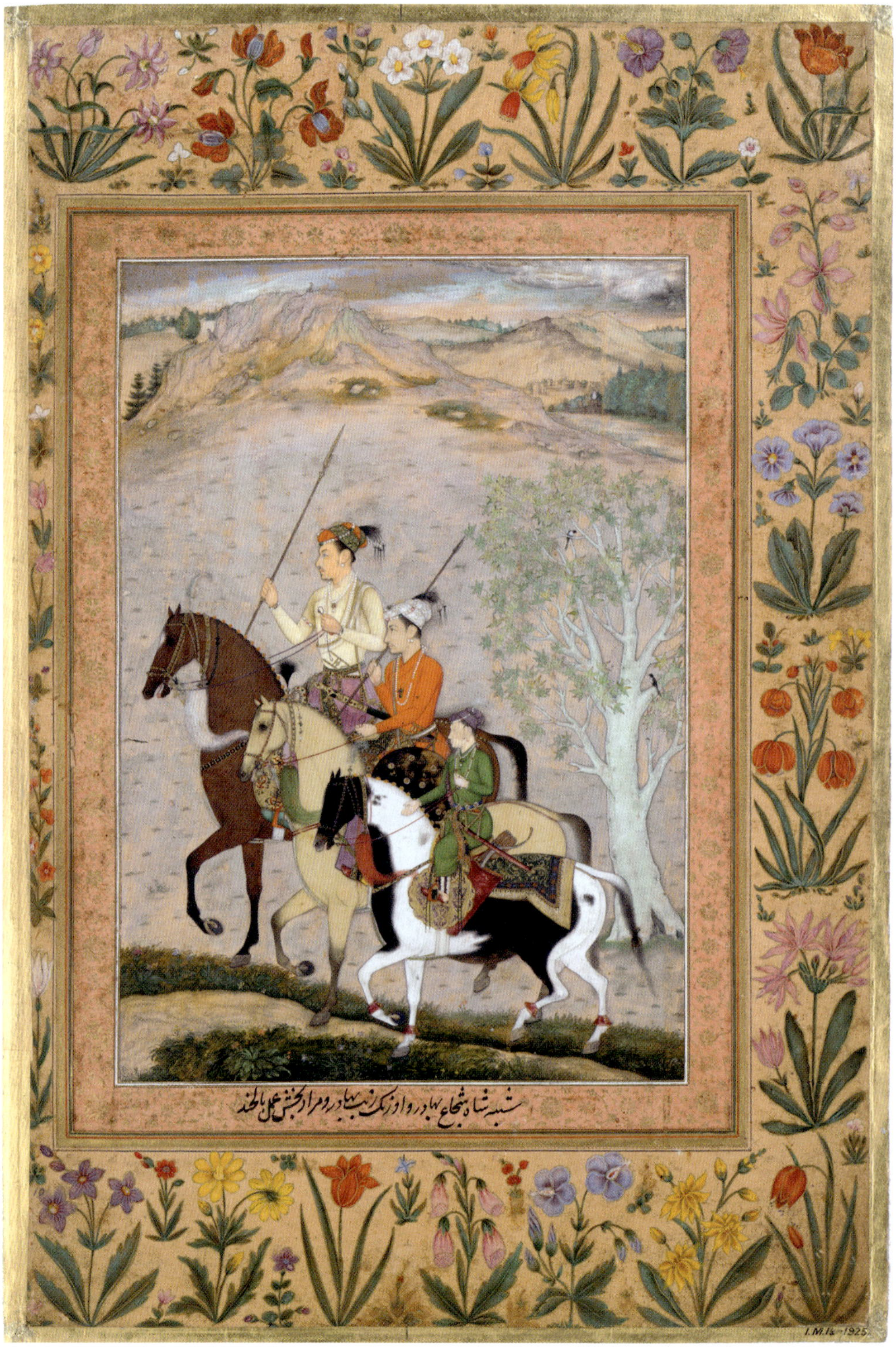

CIRCLE OF ABANINDRANATH TAGORE

54 Untitled

early 1920s | watercolour on paper | 30.5 × 15 cm | property of a collector

From 1905 to 1915, Abanindranath Tagore taught the new 'Indian style' of painting at the Calcutta School of Art. Combining certain qualities of Mughal painting with those of European art nouveau and subtle Japanese wash, his students depicted 'Indian' themes, particularly *nayikas* (heroines) and characters from history and Hindu epic texts. The idealized female figure was a recurring motif, symbolising Indian tradition and 'the motherland'.[198] Tagore's students went on to teach at art schools across India, bringing the main characteristics of the new art movement with them.

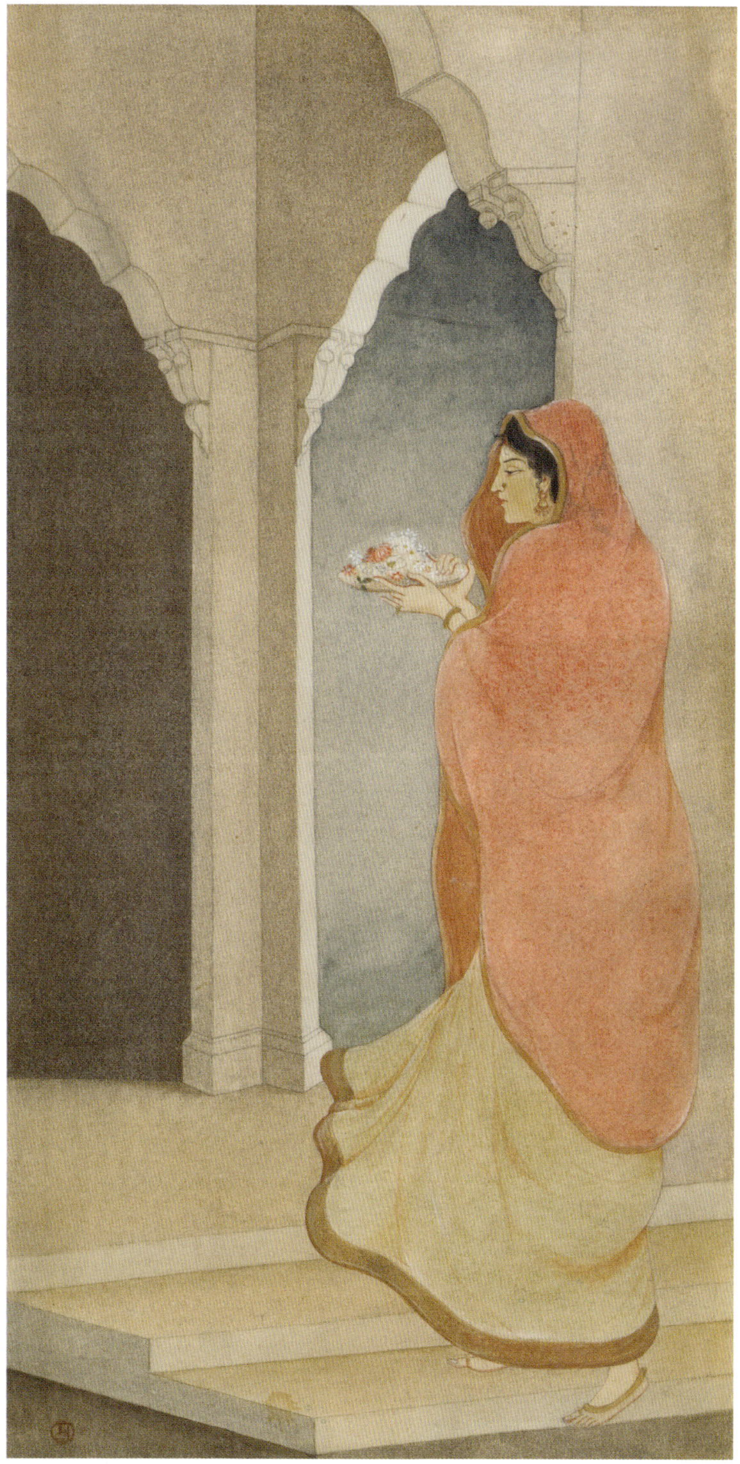

ABDUR RAHMAN CHUGHTAI

55 A Serenade

1938 | watercolour and wash on paper | 56 × 40 cm | Arif Chughtai and the Chughtai Museum

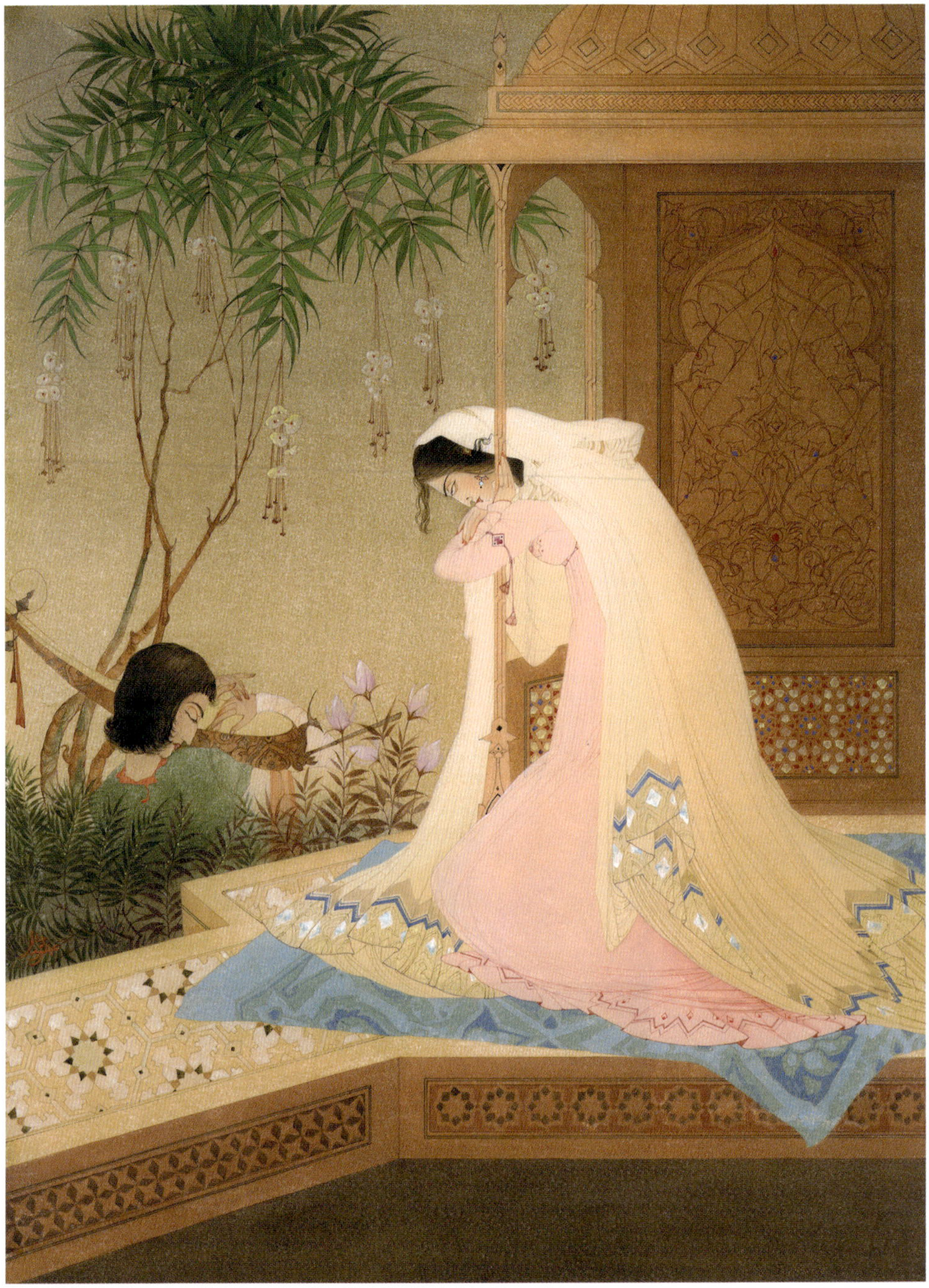

Abdur Rahman Chughtai (1894–1975) is considered by many Pakistan's first national artist. Born in Lahore, Chughtai studied at the Mayo School of Art in the 1910s when Samarendranath Gupta (1887–1964), one of Abanindranath Tagore's first students, was a teacher there. His early works show great indebtedness to the artists of the Bengal School as well as to European approaches to watercolour painting.

Chughtai began to paint at a time of increasing nostalgia for the 'golden age' of the Mughal Empire, inspired in part by the Delhi Durbars of the early twentieth century. An ambitious artist, he studied printmaking and in the late 1920s published a book of chromolithographs after his series of paintings inspired by the poetry of the late Mughal poet Mirza Ghalib (1797–1868). He titled the book *Muraqqa-i-Chughtai* and sent copies to well-known figures of the art worlds of both England and India.

ABDUR RAHMAN CHUGHTAI

56 The Wasted Vigil

1920s | watercolour on paper | 43.2 × 56.6 cm | property of a collector

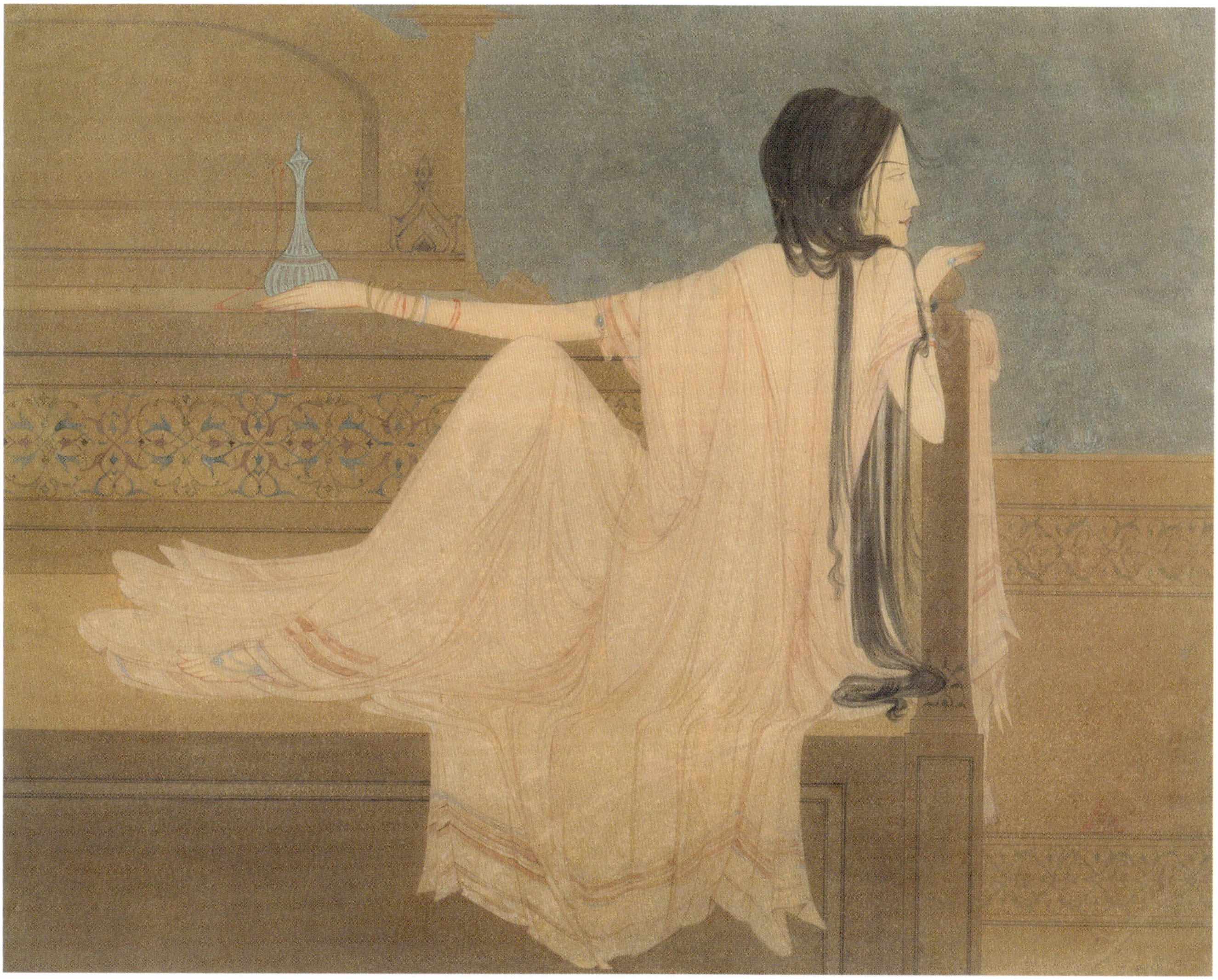

The Wasted Vigil and *A Serenade* were among the illustrations of the *Muraqqa-i-Chughtai* that the artist most frequently reproduced. British Pakistani author Nadeem Aslam referenced Chughtai's painting in the title of his 2008 novel *A Wasted Vigil*. 'The artist and God knows that it ain't gonna happen', he wrote. 'So once you look at the title, it's quite a chilling picture.'[199]

UNKNOWN ARTIST

57 Mahavira, founder of the Jain religion

1503 | watercolour and metallic pigments on paper| 15 × 31 cm | Wellcome Collection

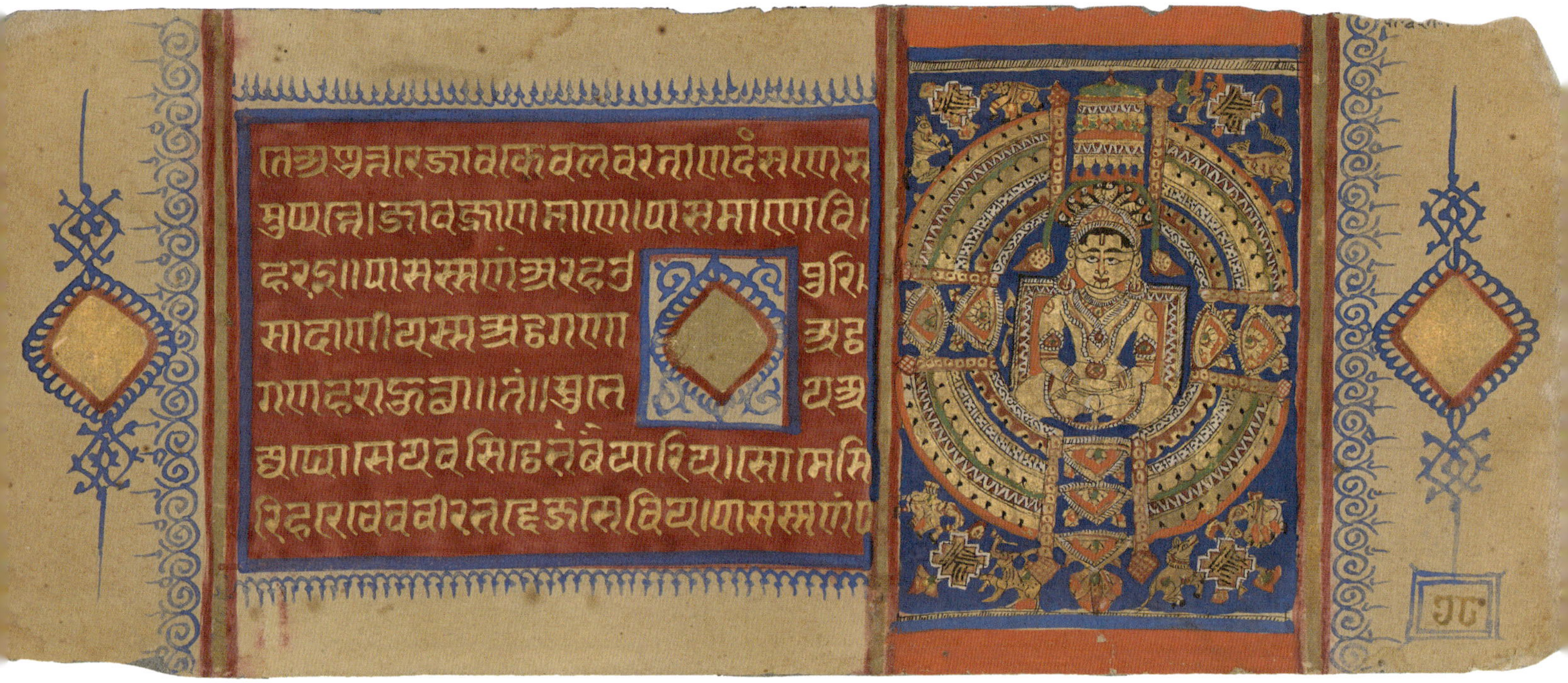

The majority of the Indian collections of the Wellcome Institute arrived in the early 1920s after Sir Henry Wellcome employed an agent, Dr Paira Mall (1874–1957), to gather material for him in India.[200] The millionaire collector paid Mall £5,000 a year for more than a decade and instructed him not to return until 'India is completely ransacked as far as we possibly can for literature and other objects of interest connected with ancient medicine'.[201]

Although not directly linked to medicine, one of Dr Mall's most valuable acquisitions for Wellcome was an early illustrated manuscript of the *Kalpasutra* (Book of Rituals), the canonical text of Jain literature, dated 1503. Such manuscripts were commissioned by wealthy Jain families of Western India and donated to local temples for the autumn festival of Paryushan, when monks traditionally recited the *Kalpasutra* text. The horizonal format of the book's pages derives from earlier palm-leaf manuscripts and the paintings are in a traditional style practised by artists in fifteenth- and sixteenth-century Gujarat. This image shows Mahavira, the founder of the Jain religion, surrounded by birds and beasts, preaching to all beings of the Universe.

ATTRIBUTED TO MANAKU

58 Radha and Krishna

c.1730–35 | watercolour and metallic paints on paper, with beetle-wing details | page 25.6cm × 30.7cm | Victoria and Albert Museum

This is one of three illustrations of the Sanskrit devotional poem *Gita Govinda* (Song of the Cowherd) sold to the V&A in 1930 by Maulvi Muhammad Hussain (b.1856), a retired judge in the Small Cause Court in Delhi.[202] Almost one hundred paintings from the same series have survived, first sold on the market in the 1920s by a dealer in Basohli, a small Rajput court in the Punjab Hills.[203] According to an inscription on one of the pages now in the Lahore Museum, a woman named Malini commissioned the paintings from the family workshop of the artist Manaku (1700–1760) in 1730.[204] The artists cut beetle-wing cases into different shapes and adhered them to the paper to suggest carved emeralds, a decorative device now typically associated with paintings from Basohli.

This painting illustrates song 11 of the poem, which describes Radha's feeling shy at the sight of Krishna waiting for her:

> So came she where he sat awaiting her
> At the bower's entry, like a god to see
> With marriage-gladness and the grace of heaven.
> The great pearl set upon his glorious head
> Shone like the moon among the leaves, and shone
> Like stars and gems that kept her gold gown close;
> But still a little while she paused – abashed
> At her delight, of her deep joy afraid.[205]

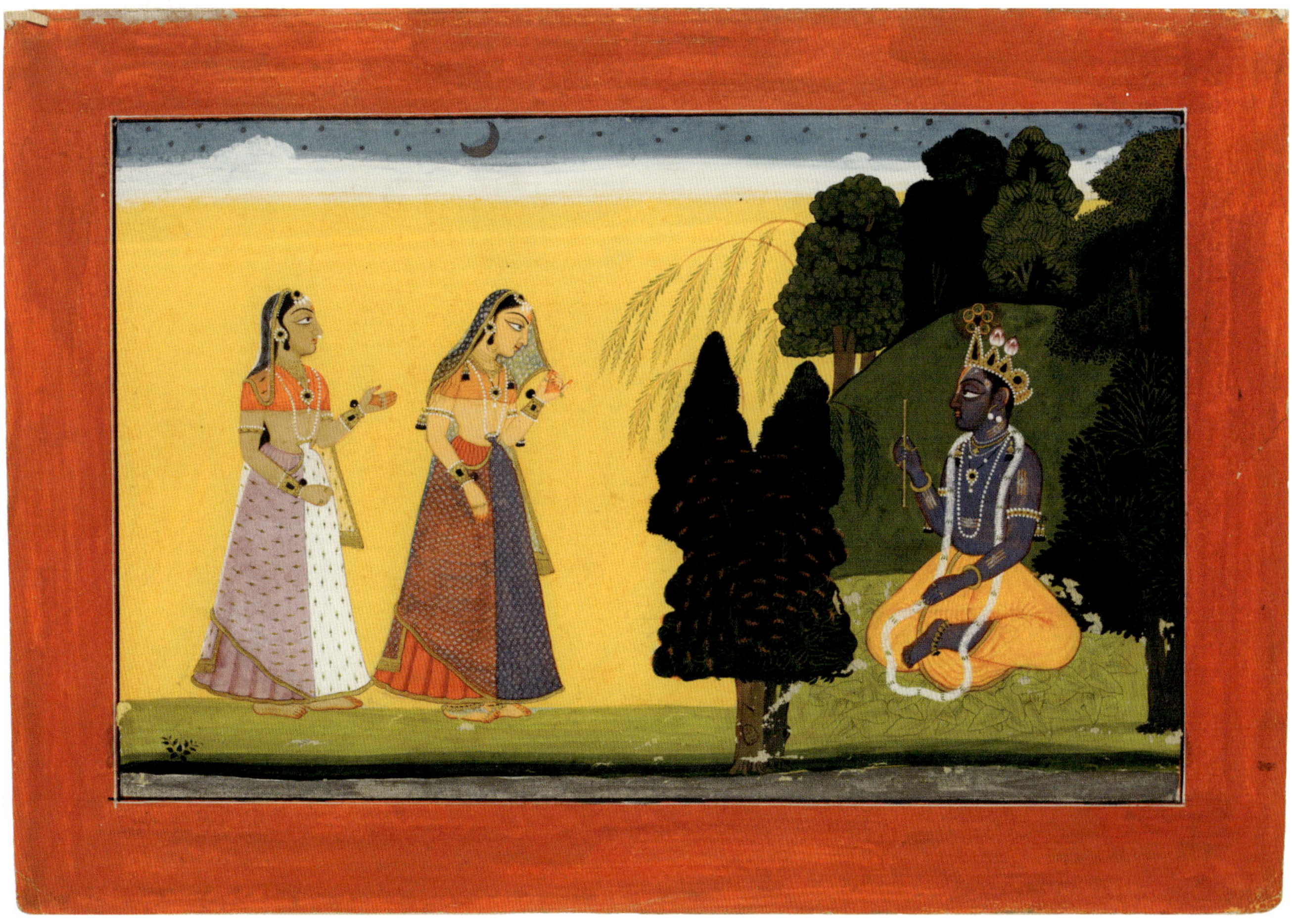

RUKNUDDIN & ASSISTANTS

59 The private pleasure of the son of Raja Bhagwandas

c.1687–98 | watercolour with metallic paints on paper | 19.6 × 13.3 cm | Fitzwilliam Museum

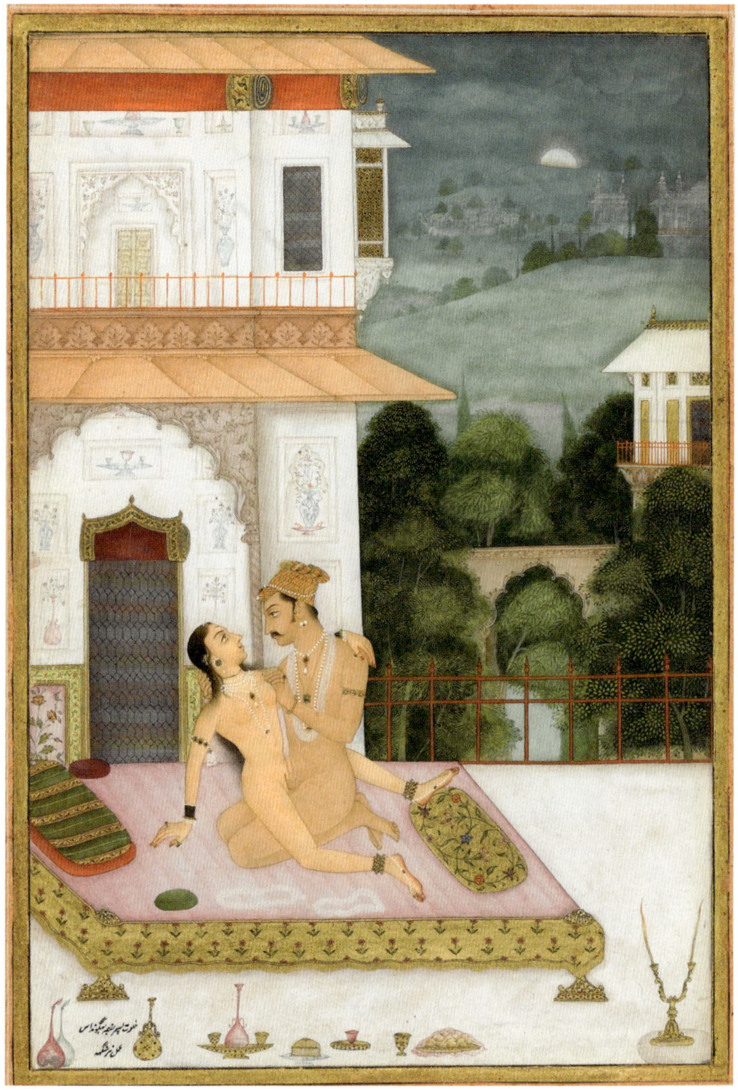

Among the 150 Indian paintings bequeathed to the Fitzwilliam Museum by Percival Chater Manuk and his partner Gertrude Coles (see p. 23) were a set of 40 erotic miniatures. Commissioned by Maharaja Anup Singh of Bikaner (r.1669–98) at the end of the seventeenth century, the series probably remained for most of its history in the royal library at Bikaner until Manuk purchased the set in the 1930s or 1940s.[206]

Emperor Alamgir appointed Anup Singh as a general in his imperial army during the Deccan campaigns and stationed him permanently in Hyderabad from 1681 to 1698. This unusual series was painted for the maharaja in Hyderabad by the group of retained artists he brought with him, led by the Delhi-trained painter Ruknuddin.[207] Inscriptions name each of the 40 male lovers as specific figures from the Mughal court during the sixteenth and seventeenth centuries, from the emperors and princes to minor members of the nobility. But the images are not intended to be satirical, with the patron himself depicted among them. Instead, they depict mastery of erotic pleasure as noble craft that men practise in the pursuit of ultimate self-fulfilment.[208]

The specific imagery of the paintings reflects the teachings of an influential Indian erotic text, the *Ananga Ranga*, similar to the *Kama Sutra*, which stresses the Hindu understanding of *kama* (pleasure) as one of the fundamental goals of human existence, along with *dharma* (duty), *artha* (wealth) and *moksha* (liberation).[209] The author, Kalyana Mala, offers advice on how to optimize *kama* during the sexual encounter: 'both man and woman should contend against any reserve, or false shame, giving themselves in complete nakedness to unrestrained voluptuousness.'[210]

RUKNUDDIN & ASSISTANTS

60 The private pleasure of the Raja Karan

*c.*1687–98 | watercolour with metallic paints on paper | 19.6 × 13.3 cm | Fitzwilliam Museum

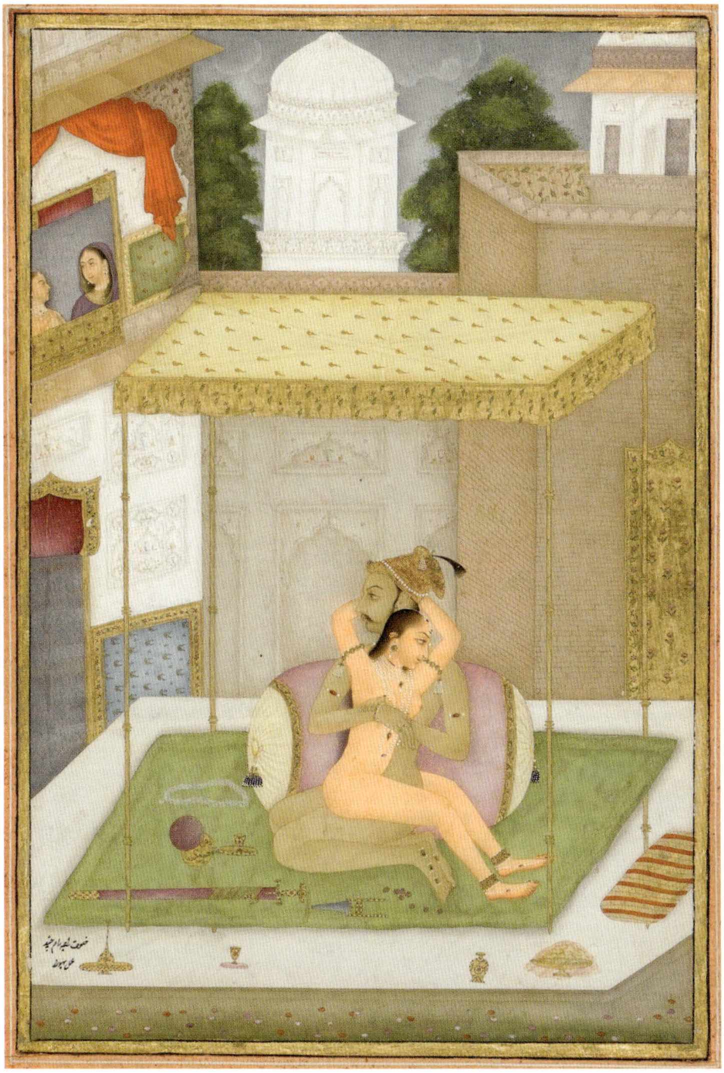

RUKNUDDIN & ASSISTANTS

61 The private pleasure of Raja Bhagwant Singh

*c.*1687–98 | watercolour with metallic paints on paper | 19.6 × 13.3 cm | Fitzwilliam Museum

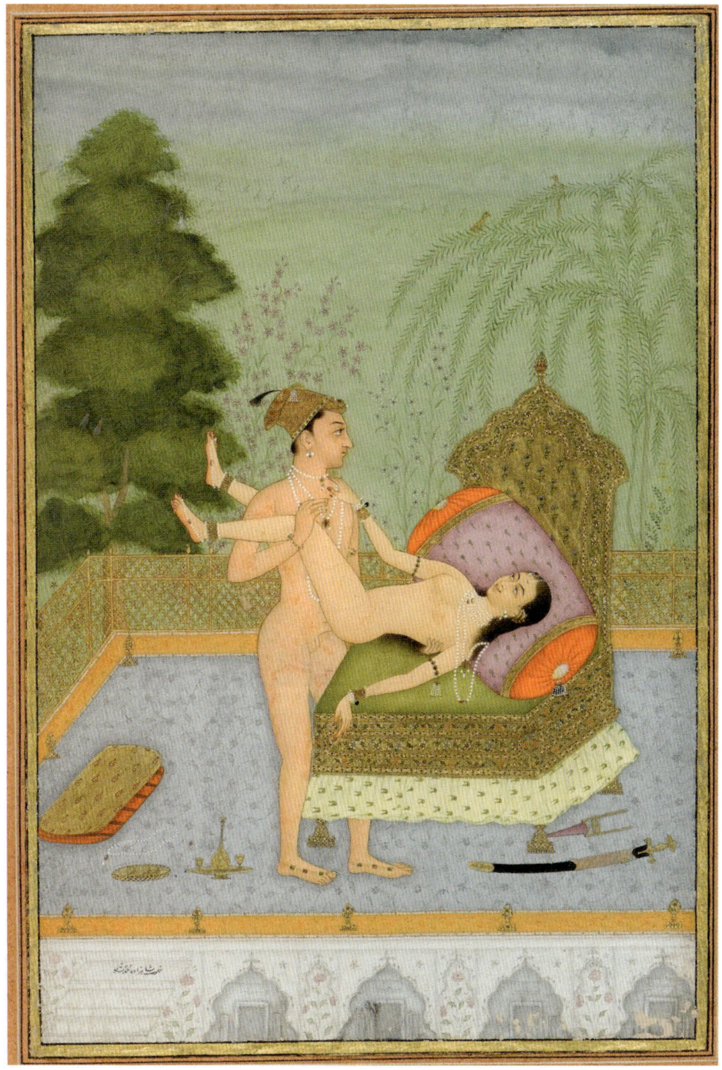

'The setting should be 'furnished [with] many pillows and covered by a rich *chatra* [canopy], the sheets being sprinkled with flowers' and he suggests refreshments, 'cocoa-nut, betel leaf and milk, which is so useful for treating and restoring vigour; bottles of rose water and various essences.'[211]

The series can therefore be understood as depicting erotic pleasure as an art form in itself, something to be learned and mastered. In homage to his forebears and as a play on the depiction of historic figures, Ruknuddin ascribed the paintings not to the artists who painted them, but to sixteenth- and seventeenth-century Mughal masters, including Govardhan and Chitarman.

NANDALAL BOSE

62 Santiniketan

c. 1930s | watercolour on paper | 26.8 × 17.4 cm | private collection, London/Karachi

An early student of Abanindranath Tagore, Nandalal Bose (1882–1966) was a major protagonist in the evolution of the Bengal School of Art. In 1909 Tagore sent him to assist Lady Christina Herringham in her project to copy the frescoes of the Ajanta Caves, sparking a deep and lifelong interest in mural paintings. When he later became a teacher, he emphasized the importance of copying 'ancient Indian masterpieces' and encouraged his students to gain a strong understanding of the sense of rhythm used by ancient and historic Indian painters before embarking on any individual or personal experimentation.[212]

For almost thirty years (from 1922 to 1951), Bose was principal of the *Kala Bhavana*, the school of arts and crafts at Santiniketan in West Bengal, founded by Abanindranath's uncle, Rabindranath Tagore (1861–1941). This miniature painting on handmade paper is a utopian vision of the school and its students, painted in the style of a local Bengali *pata* (painting) and rendered in an earthy colour palette evoking the pastoral atmosphere of Santiniketan.

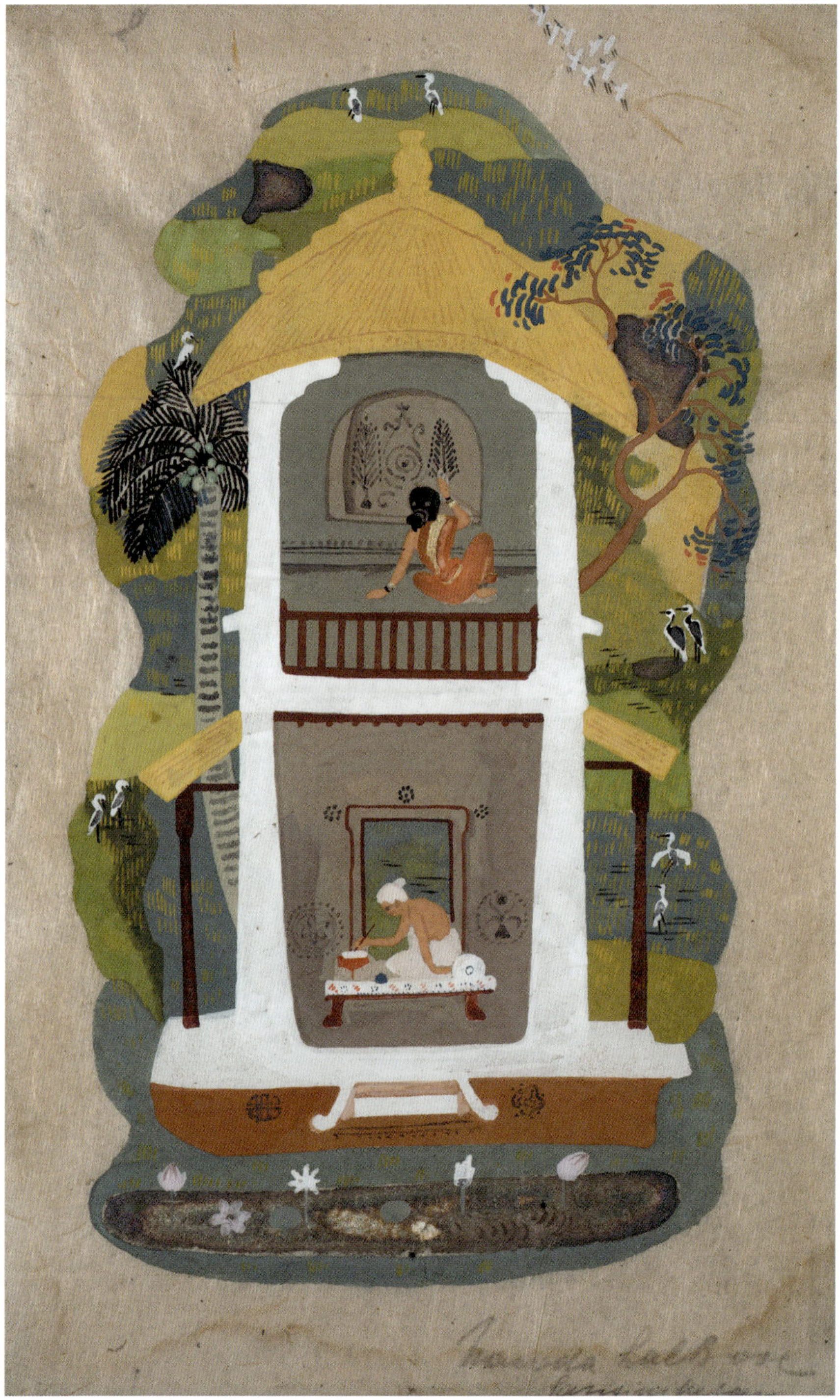

UNKNOWN ARTIST

63 Bhishma sleeping

c. 1800 | watercolour and metallic paints on paper | 36.4 × 51.2 cm | Victoria and Albert Museum

In 1951 the V&A purchased 111 paintings and drawings from Lady Alice Rothenstein from the collection of her late husband, the painter Sir William Rothenstein (see p. 21), with the assistance of the Art Fund. This is one of two consecutive paintings in his collection from a series painted in the Himalayan state of Garhwal depicting the Hindu epic the *Mahabharata*.[213] The warrior king Bhishma sleeps inside the palace with his crown laid beside him. He was renowned for his vow of lifelong celibacy; he and the princes and princesses of the court sleep alone watched by their servants, apart from two women who snuggle together on the far left.[214]

Rothenstein regularly lent his Indian miniatures to exhibitions in Britain in the hope of widening appreciation of the art form, although not all critics were wholly sympathetic to his efforts. One member of the Bengal press who previewed the 1931 *Art of India* exhibition at the Burlington Fine Arts Club remarked that 'Sir William Rothenstein's Moghul paintings, which must now be getting a little shop-soiled, are to be once again paraded before the wondering British public.'[215]

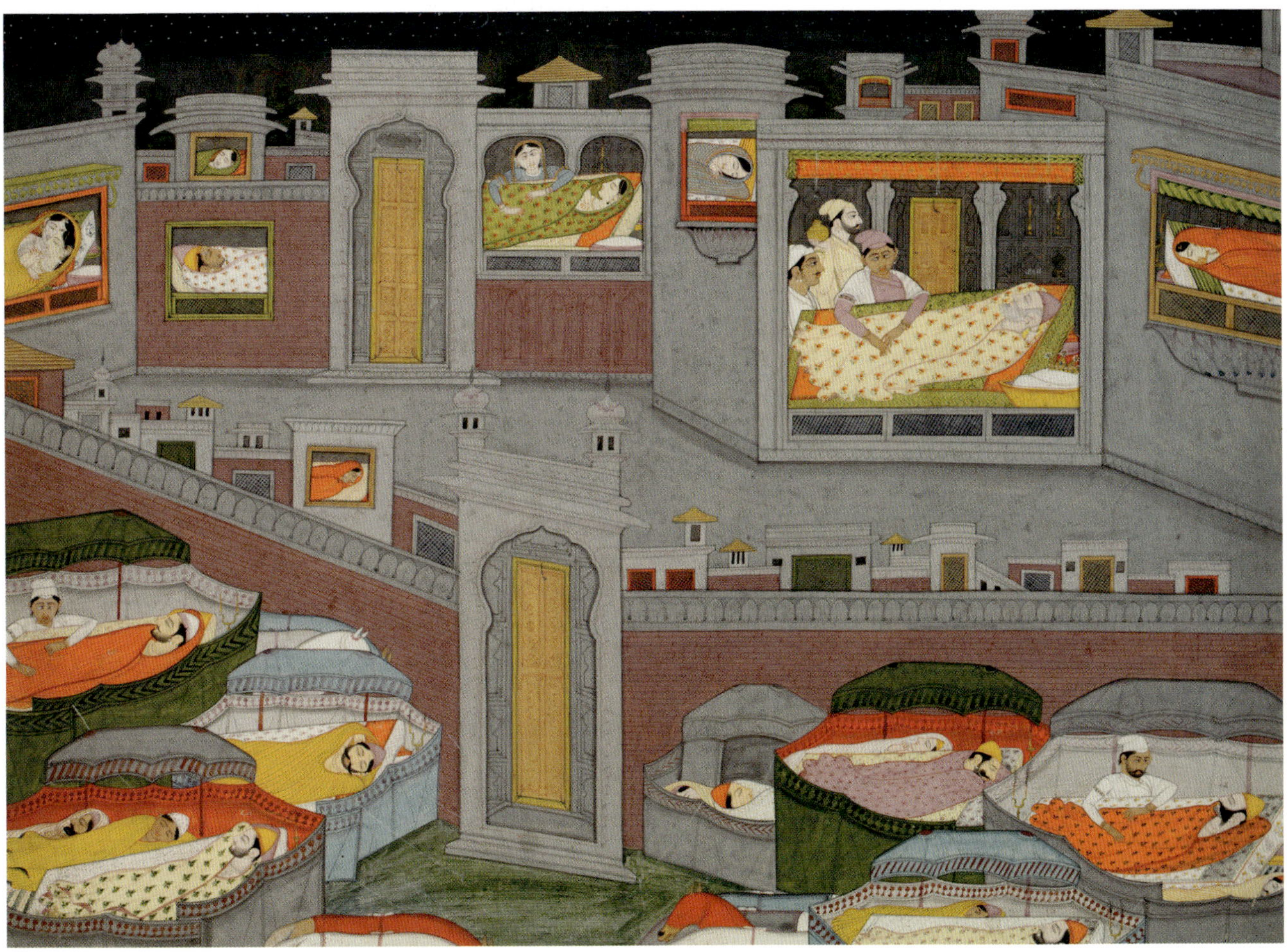

ATTRIBUTED TO PURKHU

64 Radha makes love to Krishna in a grove

c. 1820 | gouache with gold | painting 24.8 × 15.1 cm | British Library

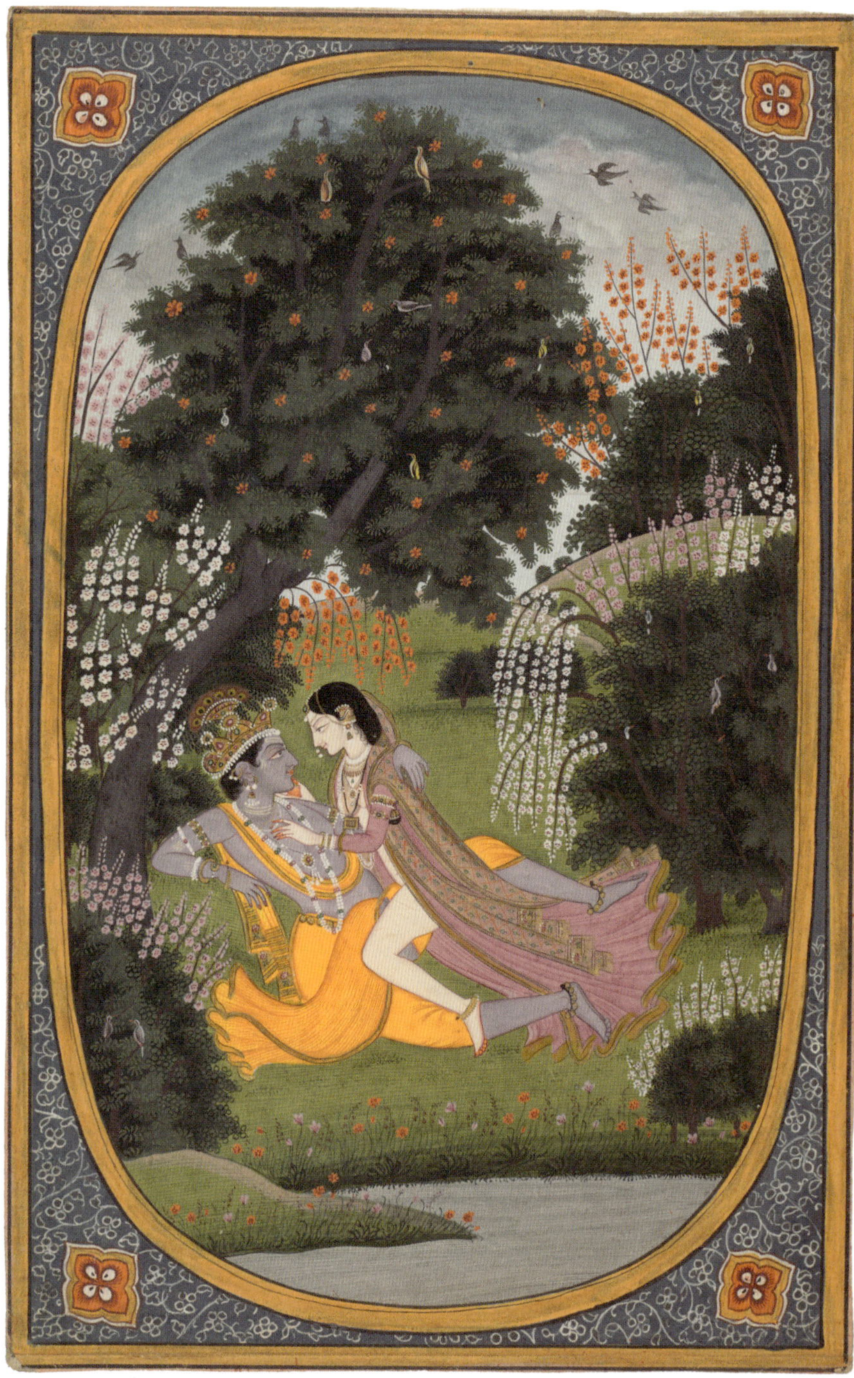

The India Office Library purchased this Pahari painting in 1955 when Mildred Archer was researching its paintings collection. She would have recognized it as a page from a large dispersed series illustrating the sixteenth-century Hindi poem *Rasikapriya* by Keshav Das, other examples of which had been acquired in the previous decades by the V&A and catalogued there by her husband (see p. 23).[216] Inscribed on the reverse of the painting are seven lines describing *prachanna samyoga sringara* (hidden love in union):

> One day Vrishabhanu's daughter [Radha] and Murari [Krishna] decided to hide in the forest and engage in reverse love play.
> Immersed in each other and groaning with pleasure they were fully enjoying each other.
> During the amorous activity, Radha's sapphire-studded pendant – tied around her neck with a black thread – was moving, and it seemed as though Surya [the sun] and Saturn were swinging.[217]

Several of the works in this series are attributed to Purkhu, an artist at the court of Sansar Chand (1765–1823), the Rajput ruler of Kangra in the Punjab Hills. In 1820 William Moorcroft (1767–1825) of the East India Company visited Sansar Chand and viewed his collection of miniatures (or 'drawings' as he calls them):

> He is fond of drawing, [and] keeps several artists who execute the minute parts with great fidelity but are almost wholly ignorant of perspective. His collection of drawings is very great ... some of which for decency's sake might have been spared.[218]

UNKNOWN ARTIST

65 The marriage of a child to a middle-aged man

c. 1765–90 | watercolour on paper | painting 16.3 × 26 cm | Victoria and Albert Museum

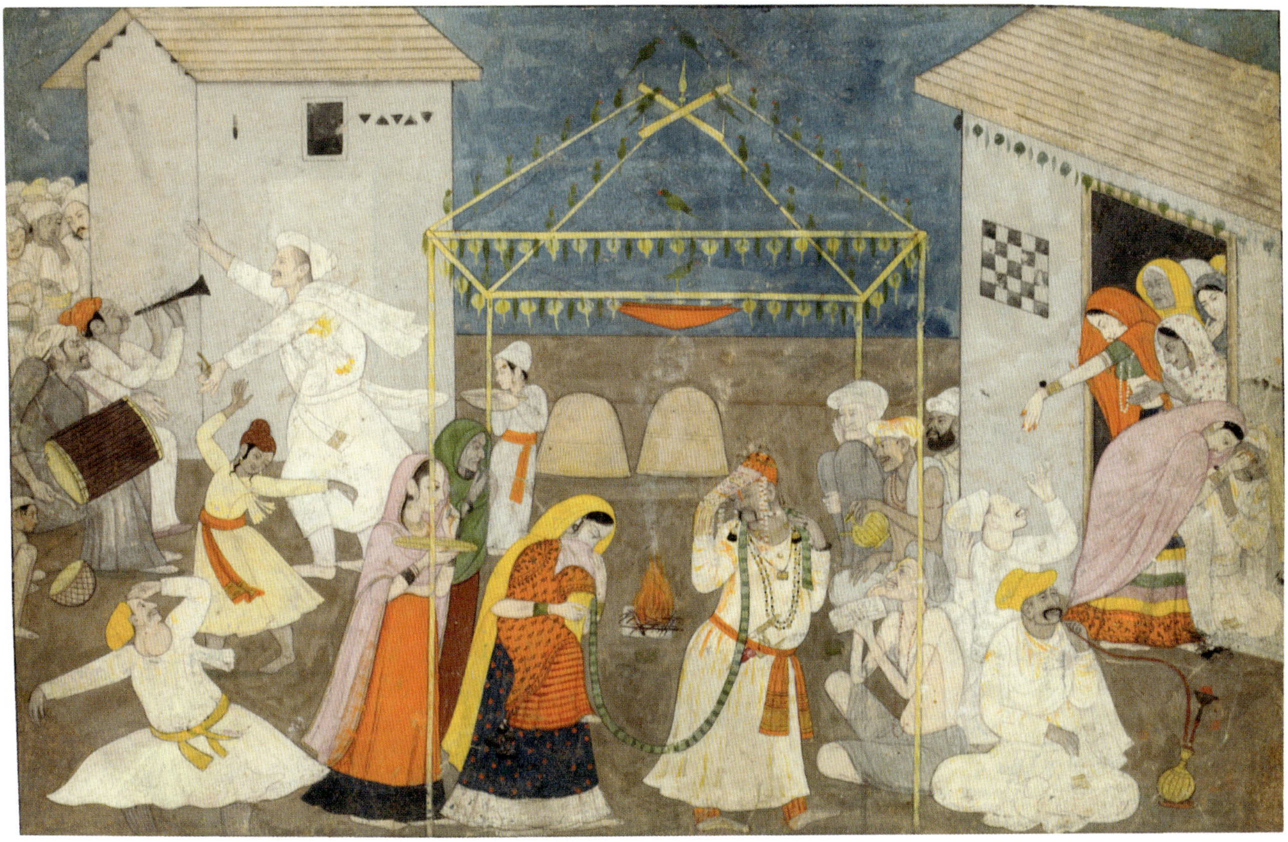

W.G. Archer bought this highly evocative Pahari painting for the V&A in 1956, a time when many Rajput paintings were being sold on the London market.[219] Depicting the plight of a child bride, the haunting scene shows a small, heavily veiled girl being carried by her mother behind a middle-aged man as they circle the sacred marriage fire. He raises his *sihra* (bridegroom's veil) to catch a glimpse of her huddled form. Some of the older women watch the ceremony with palpable unease, sentiments seemingly overlooked by one of the male guests, who encourages the musicians to play louder and faster as the hired dancers twirl and sway.

This is one of the few examples of a Guler artist exploring vivid realism and comes in stark contrast to the romantic and sensual depictions of poetic texts by contemporary Pahari painters. The image is clearly mocking, with elements suggesting the grotesque: the bridegroom's bulging waist and the dancer whose neck is swollen with goitre. A comparable painting in the Lahore Museum depicts the marriage procession of a bridegroom who suffers from goitre, his overweight form riding a half-starved nag, suggesting arranged marriage was indeed a topic of satire.[220]

UNKNOWN ARTIST

66 Maharao Chhatar Sal

c.1870 | watercolour and metallic paints on paper | 44 × 33.6 cm | Victoria and Albert Museum

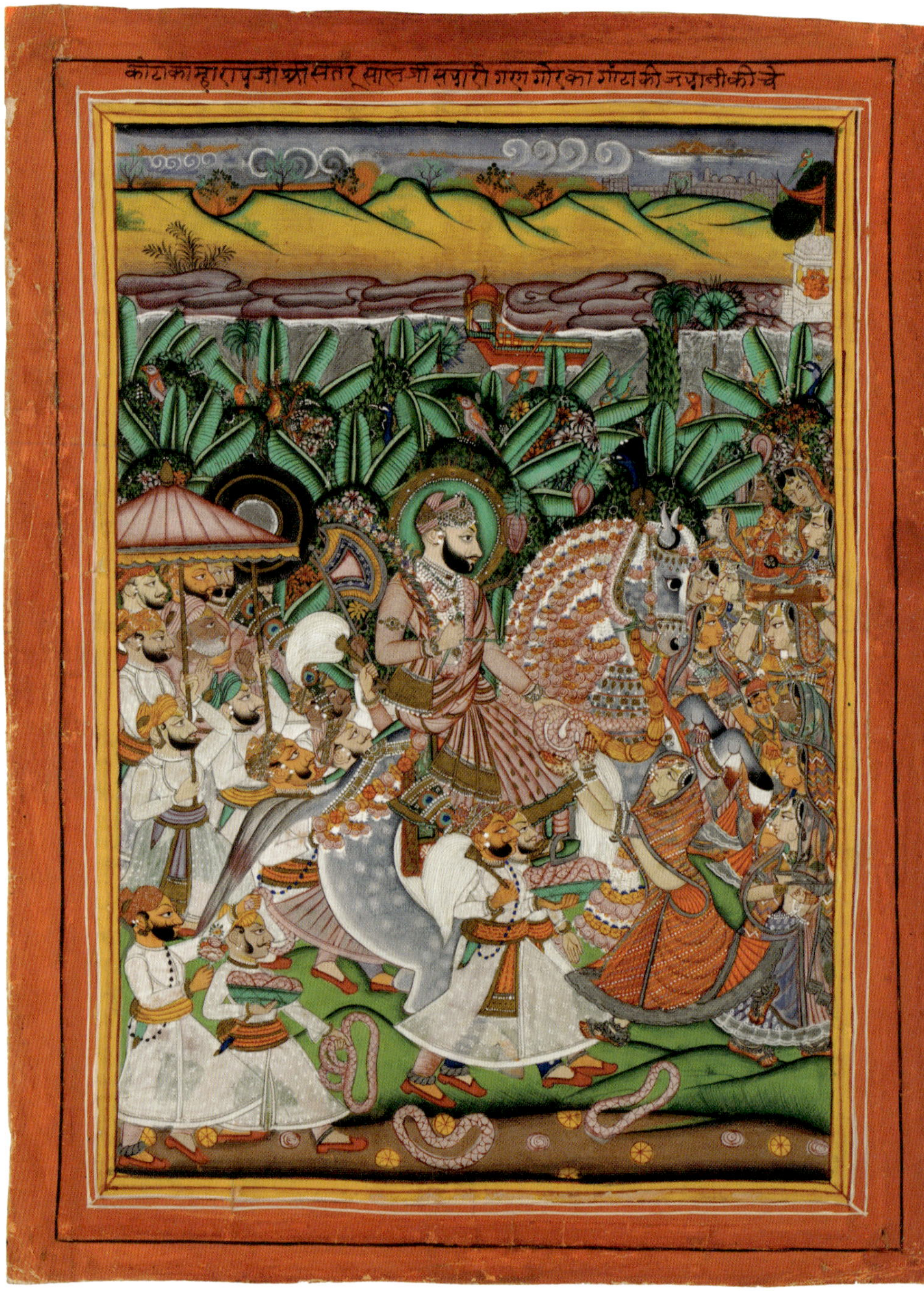

This may be one of the Kota paintings that Robert Skelton showed the artist Gulammohammed Sheikh when he was a student at the Royal College of Art (see p. 106). A late-nineteenth-century work, it shows Maharao Chhatar Sal of Kota (r.1866–1869) riding in a procession during the festival of Gangaur, a holiday celebrated in Rajasthan in honour of the Hindu goddess Gauri (Parvati).

The portrait was one of more than four hundred paintings given to the V&A in 1956 by Colonel T.G. Gayer-Anderson and his twin brother, Major R.G. Gayer-Anderson, both great collectors of South Asian and Middle Eastern art. Colonel Thomas Gayer Anderson had spent the years 1926–30 in Pune at the end of his army career, where he began to collect miniatures, which he continued to acquire in Britain. After his brother died in 1945 the colonel entered into discussions with museum curators to arrange permanent homes for the paintings and objects in their vast collection, and he developed a close relationship with W.G. Archer of the V&A. Archer greatly encouraged Gayer-Anderson's collecting of Indian miniatures, particularly of paintings from Kota, which were up to then largely unknown in Britain.

UNKNOWN ARTIST

67 An elephant in *mast*

c. 1700 | watercolour on paper | 23.8 × 23.9 cm | Ashmolean Museum

This was the last of three Indian paintings that Howard Hodgkin (1932–2017) presented to the Ashmolean Museum in 1995, 2013 and 2016, years when many of his other miniatures were on long-term loan to the Museum.[221] He wrote, 'my favourite and longest lasting enthusiasm has been for Kota painting',[222] and he had a particular fondness for Kota elephants.

A damaged portion of a once larger sketch, this drawing shows a Kota court elephant in its musth season.[223] During this period of peak testosterone levels, bull elephants experience 'intoxicated' surges as the temporal ducts on either side of their heads discharge a thick, foul-tasting secretion and the swollen temporal glands press on their eye sockets causing frantic behaviour. Elephant fighting was a serious combat sport in the courts of Rajasthan, and Kota artists in particular are known for their greatly expressive portraits of champion bulls.

Hodgkin had hoped that after his death the Ashmolean would acquire his entire collection of 122 Indian paintings, but a lack of verifiable provenance information for roughly one-third of them meant the museum was compelled to reject a very generous purchase offer from the artist's estate. Instead, the Metropolitan Museum of Art in New York bought 84 of the paintings, and the 38 without clear ownership histories will be loaned to the Museum but remain owned by the Howard Hodgkin Indian Collection Trust.[224]

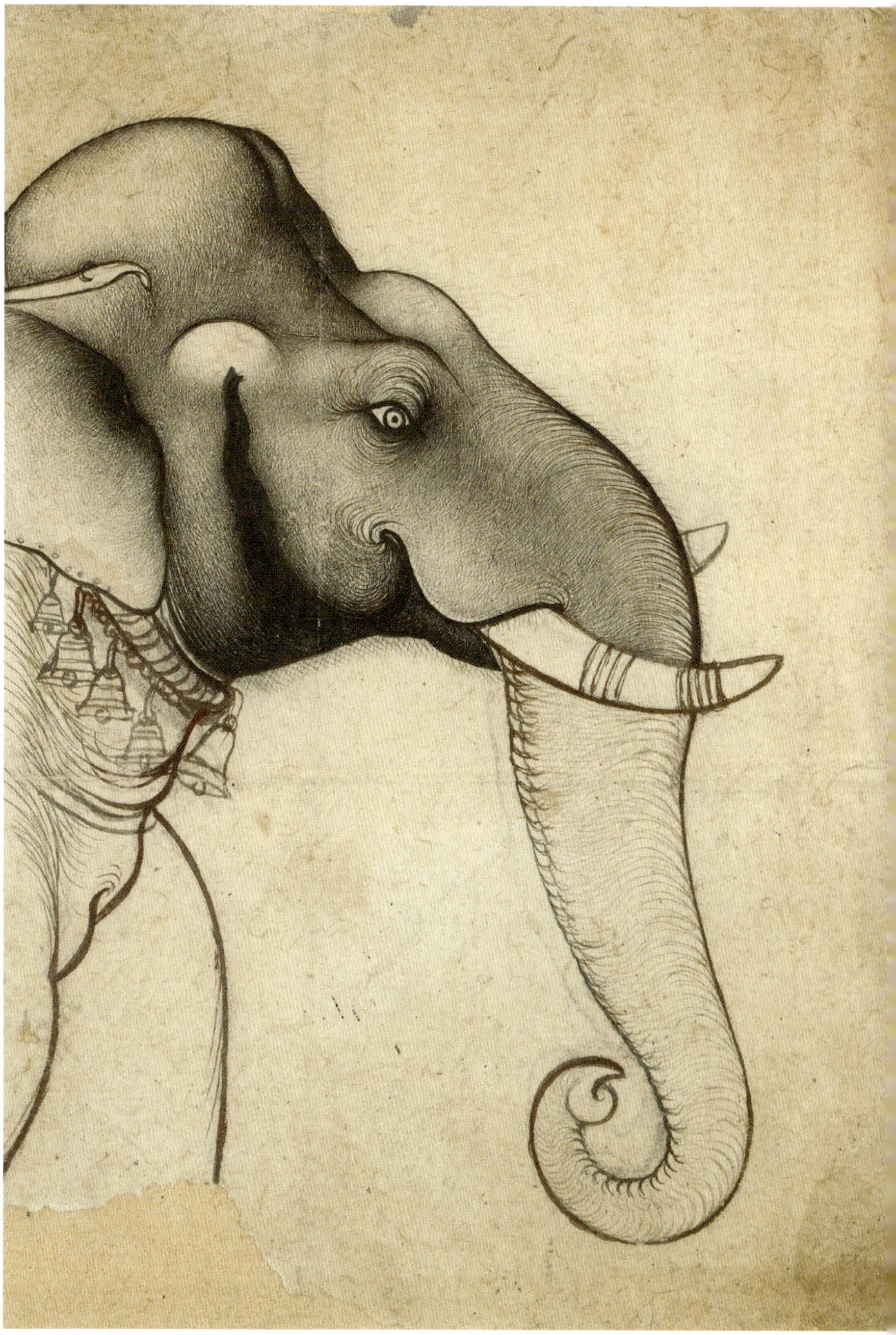

UNKNOWN ARTIST

68 Wild animals are let loose

c.1840 | watercolour on paper | 41 × 29.2 cm | Victoria and Albert Museum

The V&A purchased this *chitrakatha* (picture story) painting in 1991 from Henry Brownrigg (d. 2016), a dealer based in Notting Hill's Portobello Road market.[225] The highly animated picture is the work of a storyteller artist from southern Maharashtra who would have painted a series of narrative images and travelled throughout the local area performing the stories to music. Such paintings were used as visual aids for the audience, propped up alongside the performer. The stories performed were local variations of the Hindu epics. This painting illustrates an episode from the *Mahabharata* after the sage Vishwamitra let wild animals loose in Harishchandra's kingdom: King Harishchandra spent a day hunting and killing the animals, which were already mauling each other and local livestock. The artist dramatically flecked the page with sprays of red paint to imitate the spurts of blood gushing from the animal.

For many years this type of painting was known as a 'Paithan painting' after the father-in-law of collector Dinkar G. Kelkar (1896–1990) received 800 examples as payment from a client in Paithan. Subsequent research has shown that the art form in fact evolved in the early nineteenth century from puppet shows in the small village of Pinguli.[226]

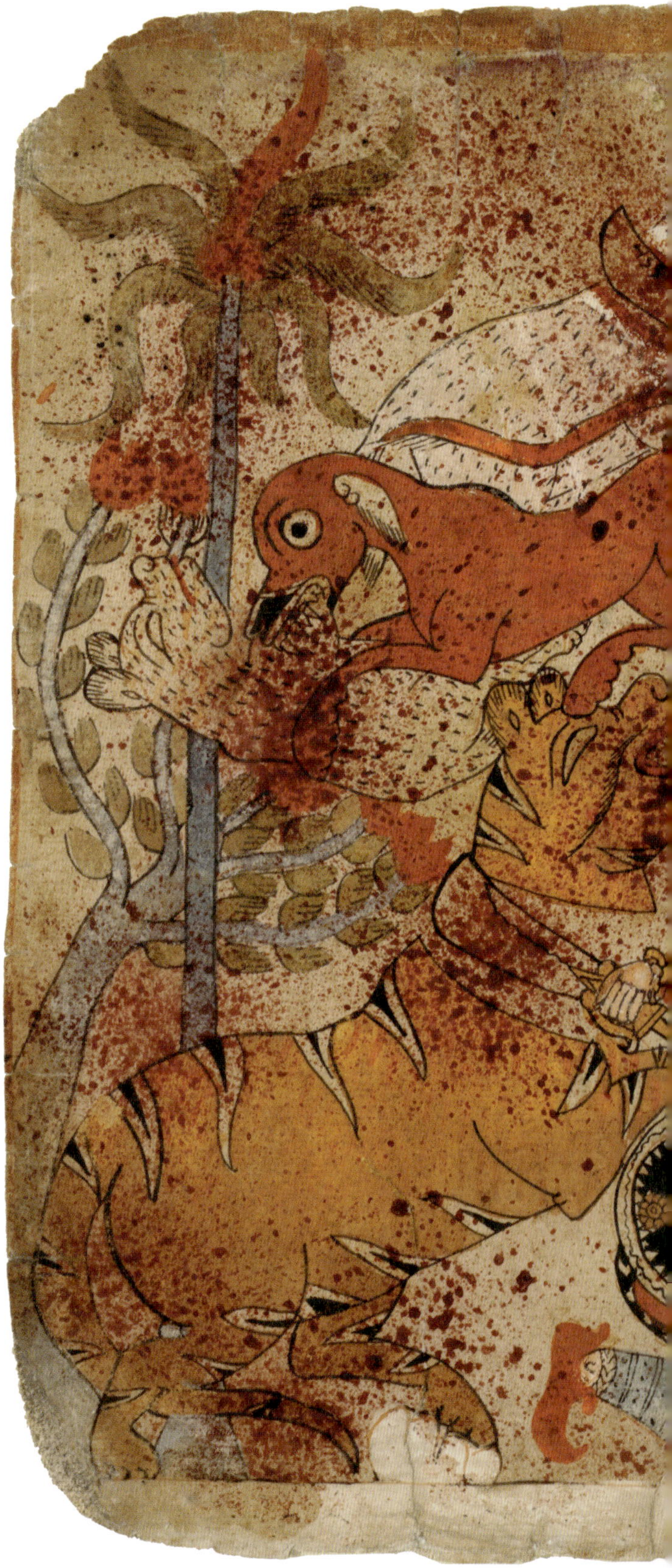

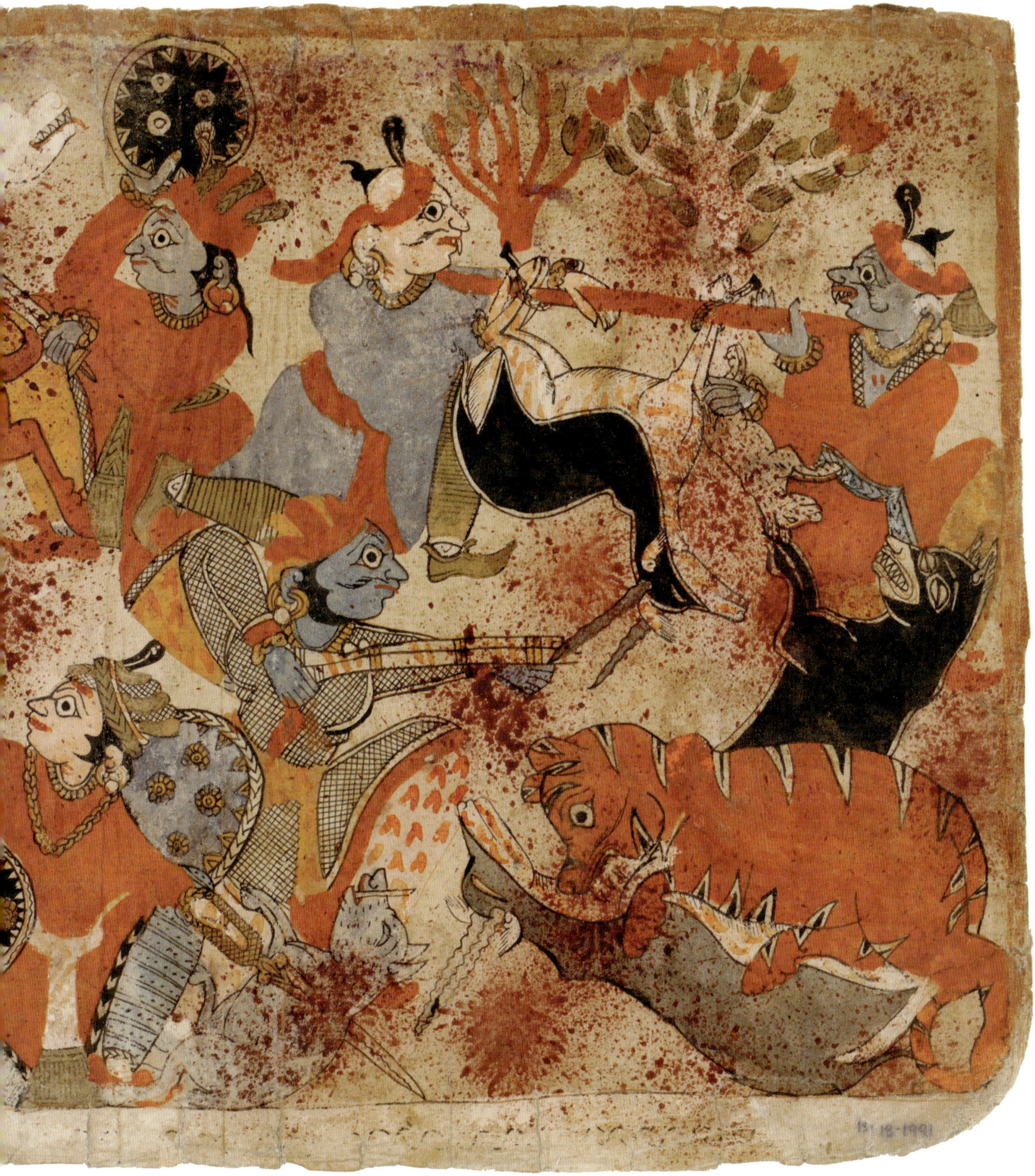

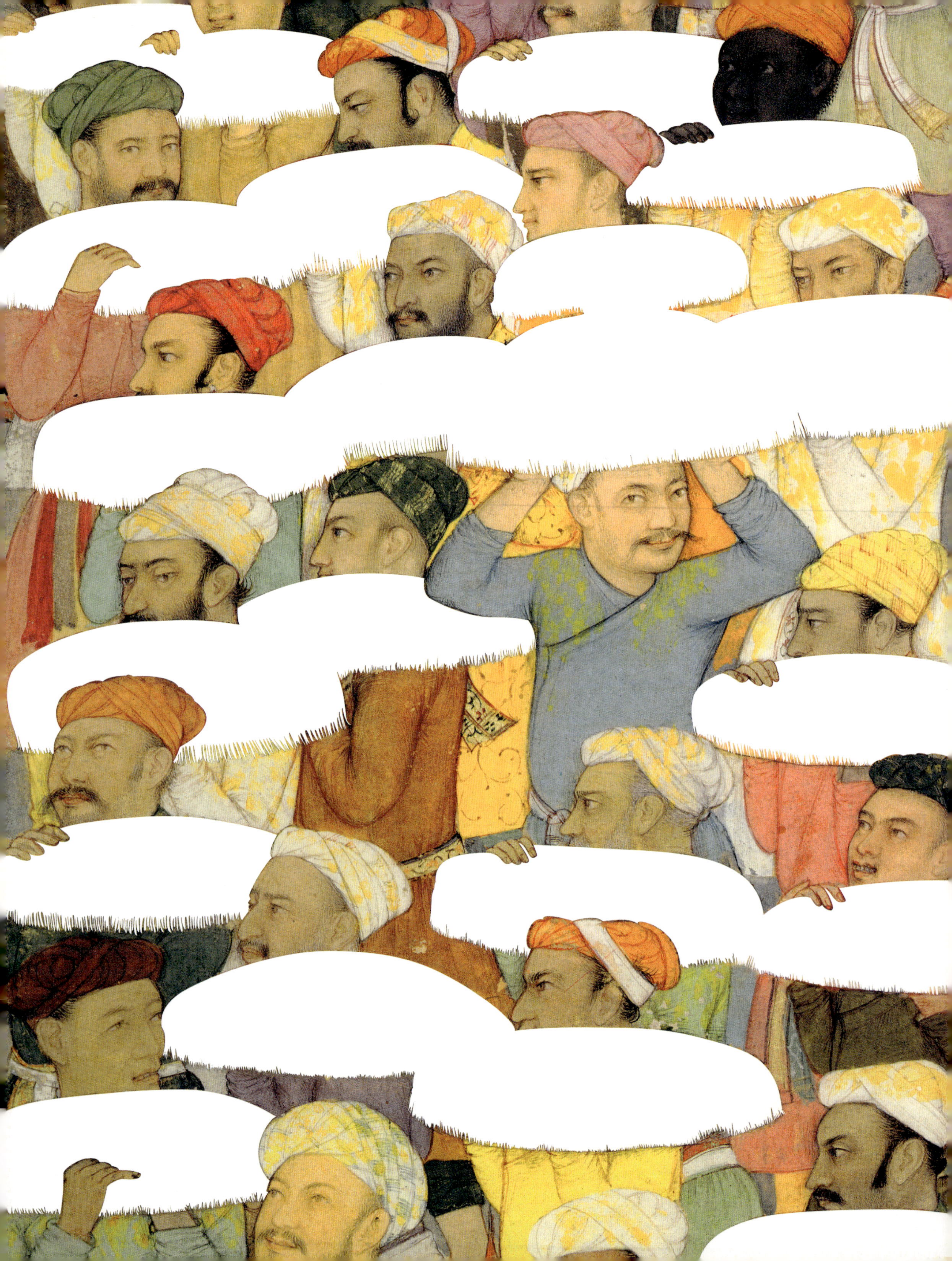

CONTEMPORARY WORKS

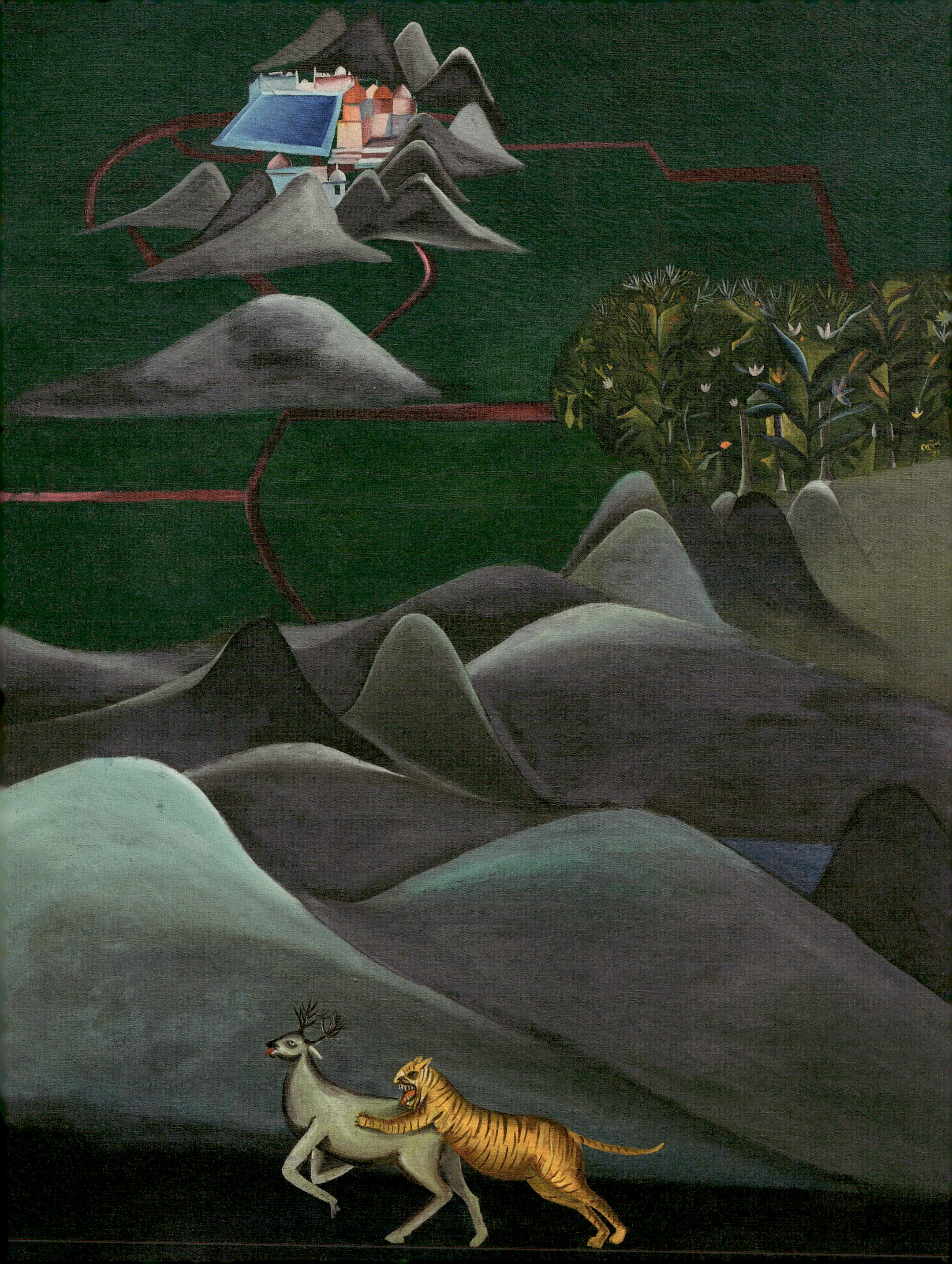

Hammad Nasar

FROM ROOTED MODERNISM TO GLOBAL CONTEMPORARY

Living in India means living simultaneously in several times and cultures.... The past exists as a living entity alongside the present, each illuminating and sustaining the other. As times and cultures converge, the citadels of purism explode. Traditional and modern, private and public, the inside and the outside are being continually splintered and reunited.

Gulammohammed Sheikh[1]

Zahoor played a critical role in a conceptual dialogue with the miniature tradition and my interest grew through watching him do the opposite of what I was pursuing – he was deconstructing miniatures in relation to larger-size painting.

Shahzia Sikander[2]

As artists, teachers, interlocutors and mentors, Zahoor ul Akhlaq (1941–1999) and Gulammohammed Sheikh (b.1937) inspired multiple generations of artists associated with two of South Asia's most significant art schools: the National College of the Arts, Lahore (NCA), and the Faculty of Fine Arts at the Maharaja Sayajirao University (Baroda). Sheikh and Akhlaq were both students at London's Royal College of Art (RCA) in the 1960s: 1963–66 and 1968–69 respectively. During this time, they embarked on independent studies of the neighbouring Victoria and Albert Museum's (V&A) unrivalled collections of Indian 'miniature' paintings, and through a mixture of observation, practice and cogitation fashioned new artistic trajectories for themselves.[3] This text presents an outline of the catalytic impact their personal journeys had on the flourishing of contemporary practice in India and Pakistan that engages with the legacy of miniature painting.

Sheikh's writings and interviews offer a clear window onto his study of the miniature tradition, in particular his close scrutiny of the

V&A's collection.[4] Sheikh had, of course, encountered miniatures before his arrival in London, but, as the art historian John Clark has pointed out, Sheikh's paintings before and during London were in a recognizably international modernist vein: more De Stijl, or the School of London à la R.B. Kitaj and David Hockney, than of the Emperor Akbar's court.[5] As his painting *Returning Home after Long Absence* of 1969–73 (fig. 22) attests, Sheikh's work changed in London. The luxury of distance opened up new windows of engagement with the miniature tradition, as he gave himself permission to tap different histories and practices – for example, the Sienese paintings in London's National Gallery and the *Hamzanama* folios at the V&A – to shape a singular approach to painting that accommodated cultural entanglements and resonances across time and geography.

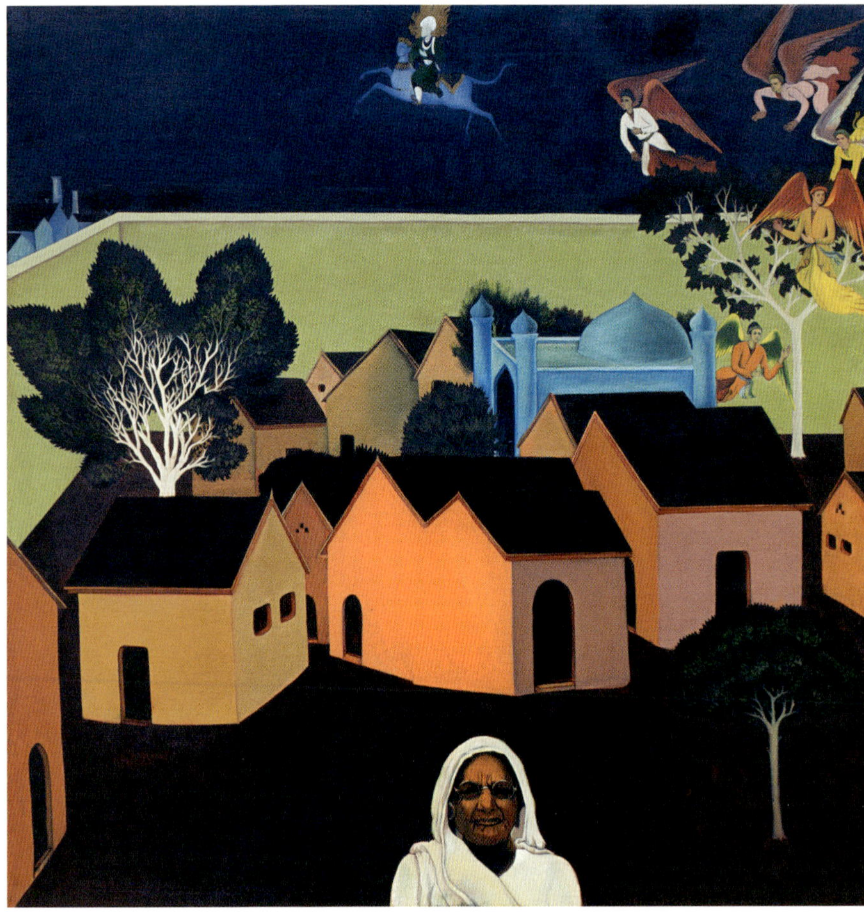

FIG. 22 Gulammohammed Sheikh, *Returning Home after Long Absence* (1969–73).

It was at the V&A where, as Sheikh recounts, his 'interest in Indian painting increased manifold as I continued to discover treasure after treasure' – his dissertation at the RCA was on Kota painting, with the Keeper of Indian Art at the V&A, Robert Skelton (1929–2022), acting as his 'guide'.[6] The capacity of miniature paintings to carry multiple narratives offered Sheikh the ideal vessel for shaping a new mode of practice. In his work different scenes nestle in fragments of the picture plane made possible by what the scholar Anna Sloan has called miniature's 'architectural space'; the unfolding perspective which sits in stark contrast to the European concept of a single-point perspective.[7]

On his return to Baroda, Sheikh initially taught art history, which compelled him to develop an analytic understanding of miniature painting. Sheikh's own investment in writing, as an accomplished poet and writer, and in the form of the book, also provided him with varied trajectories through which to engage the miniature's forms, tropes and formal devices, particularly its capacity to tell multiple stories. In an important text in the *Journal of Arts & Ideas* in 1983, reflecting transhistorically on how we read images, Sheikh writes:

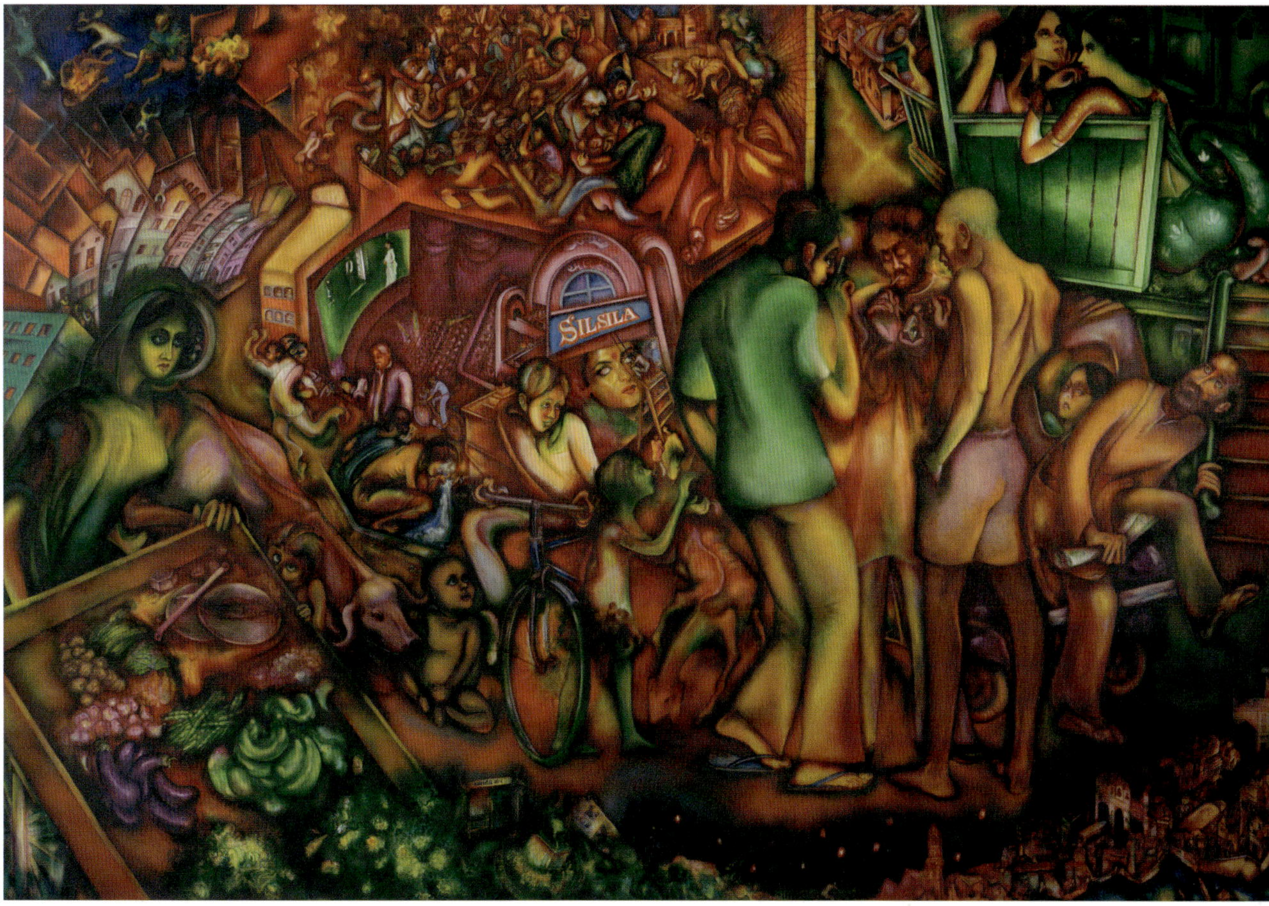

FIG. 23 Gulammohammed Sheikh, *City for Sale* (1981–84).

> The imperatives of the mobility of vision spring from the view of the world in flux rather than in a momentary stasis, in multiple rather than a singular focus. It embraces reality from all possible life perspectives in time rather than printing an optical moment upon a laterally constructed scene. Perception of such art involves greater mobility, hence the process of its viewing necessitates an active participation rather than cool contemplation.[8]

We see Sheikh enacting this thinking in his largest work by that date – the monumental painting *City for Sale* of 1981–84 (fig. 23, cat. 71) – made in response to the relentless communal riots and sectarian violence that Baroda and other places in Gujrat had witnessed; and made at a scale where one has to physically move to see different parts of the painting. The art historian Chaitanya Sambrani offers a polyphonic reading of *City for Sale*.[9] He sees the painting crammed with art-historical quotations: a homage to George Grosz's 1917 *Metropolis* in its colour palette and its 'whirling dynamism'; a reference to Benodebehari Mukherjee's mural *Life of the Medieval Saints* (1946–7) in its combination of large-scale and small figures; and the multi-focal devices used by artists of the *Hamzanama* (cat. 45). But these art-historical filters do not obscure the recognizable phenomenon of a polarized Baroda: in the centre of the painting a cinema is showing a Bollywood film, *Silsila*, set around a love triangle with movie stars playing their real-life roles; just above it we see a communal riot, and a man has been stripped

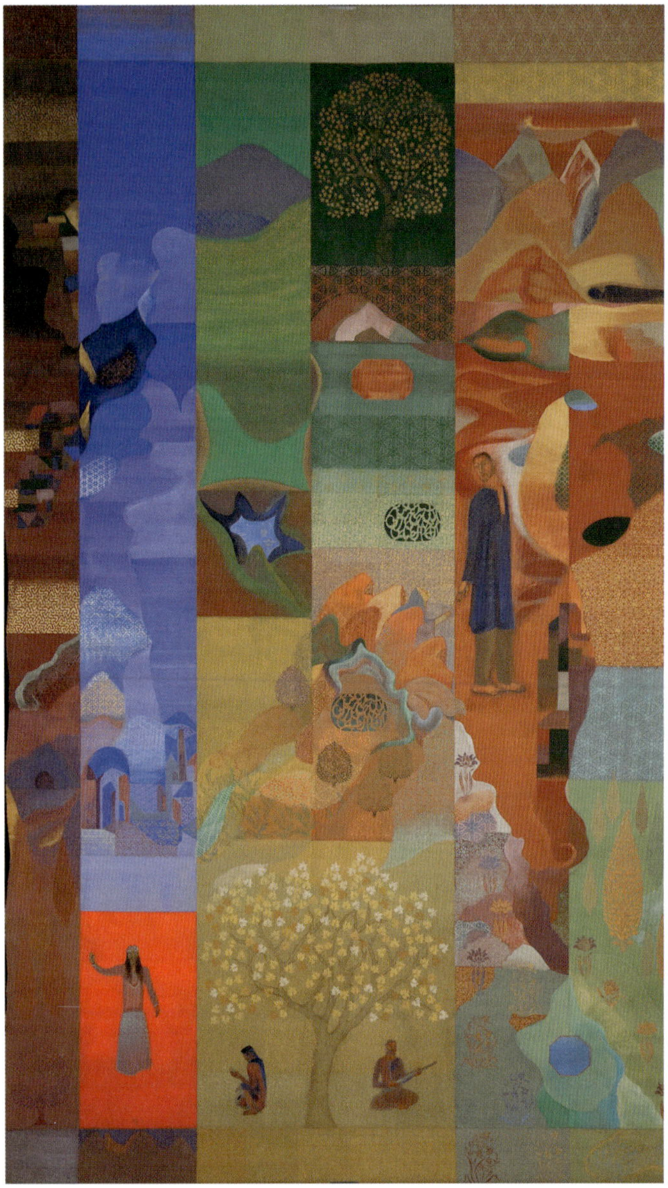

FIG. 24 Nilima Sheikh, *Each Night Put Kashmir in Your Dreams* (2003).

to see if he is circumcised, and hence a Muslim. We are left to imagine what the result of this discovery would be. For a Muslim artist with a commitment to syncretic cultural forms, depicting this unfolding violence in his home city must have been a painful reckoning. It took Sheikh three years to complete the painting, and, as he recalls, he 'developed the superstition that every time I picked up a brush, a riot began to rage'.[10] That the work was acquired for the V&A by Skelton in 1986, two decades after Sheikh first came to London, seems a fitting afterword to Sheikh's relationship with the museum.

Sheikh's multifaceted engagement with the history, form and possibilities of miniature practice also served as a 'catalyst' for his peers and students at Baroda.[11] Foremost among his interlocutors in Baroda was Nilima Sheikh (b.1945), Sheikh's wife, who supplemented her formal academic study at Baroda with learning miniature techniques from painters in the traditional ateliers of Jaipur and Nathadwara, and has remained committed to miniature painting's relationship between text and image, often working in direct inspiration from a wide array of literary traditions, including Indian religious texts, folk tales, song and poetry.[12] The narratives in her paintings are often of resistance from a feminist perspective. In an important early series of paintings, *When Champa Grew Up* (1984) (cat. 90), Nilima Sheikh tells the harrowing tale of the daughter of her housemaid who died mysteriously at the hands of her in-laws and husband; a common enough occurrence to have its own term of reference – a 'dowry death'. Over the last three decades she has engaged with the histories of displacement associated with India's partition and the contested terrain of Kashmir that continue to haunt its present, in works such as the 2003 *Each Night Put Kashmir in Your Dreams* (fig. 24), imbued with a melancholy beauty.

Gulammohammed Sheikh was also a close friend of and mentor to Bhupen Khakhar (1934–2003). When Khakhar moved from Bombay to Baroda to study art criticism, it was Sheikh who introduced him to a lively community of artists, writers, poets and playwrights. They shared a dual interest in literary and visual cultures that included not just miniature and Company School painting, but also that of the Sienese schools. Khakhar, however, was equally drawn to devotional and souvenir paintings found in temples, advertising posters, hoardings and wall calendars, and he has been labelled India's first pop artist.[13] His fascination with capturing everyday scenes imbues his work with an awkward directness that is unburdened by painting conventions or a fetishization of craft skills. Khakhar's work often deploys stylized and fragmentary depictions of space, and readily mixes the flatness of miniature painting with realistically painted elements.

We can see these juxtapositions in the painting *Tiger and Stag* (1970) (cat. 72), a reworking of an image taken from the wrapper of a firecracker, which recalls Henri Rousseau's *The Hungry Lion Throws Itself on the Antelope* (1905), as well as in the foliage and simplified treatment of mountains and buildings from the Pahari school of miniature painting. Khakhar's eccentric use of colour and a flattened bird's-eye view of spatial arrangement is prominent in *Voice of Freedom – Strike* (1972) (cat. 73). The painting is a curiously compelling mixture of scale and visual arrangement. In the bottom right corner of the painting a man looks back at the viewer. His bright white shirt and dark suit jacket suggest he could be part of the aspiring middle classes – perhaps an accountant like Khakhar – equally alienated from the striking workers behind him and the distant suited figures, possibly the owners, on their own inside the factory compound.

N.S. Harsha (b.1969), who studied under Gulammohammed and Nilima Sheikh at Baroda in the 1990s, combines different streams of practice including miniature, temple architecture, murals, popular posters and book illustrations to construct a personal idiom in the spirit of Sheikh's earlier articulation of living in India as 'living simultaneously in several times and cultures'. His interest, as he shares elsewhere in this volume (p. 178), is not in the formal reworking but in 'the way figures were painted and flow of lines'; and in the lack of a central one-point perspective and 'visual flatness', which like Khakhar he sees in both miniature and popular posters and illustration styles. His commitment to the 'flow' of visual storytelling is clearly visible in works like *Women preparing 'hot dye' for shades of blue!* and *Surviving on blueberries from the inverted tree!* (2012) (cat. 130 & 129).

While this deployment of miniatures' spatial and narrative-carrying capacities is much in evidence in the individual practices of artists close to Sheikh, it has not led to the study and practice of miniature painting becoming central to pedagogy in Baroda. In fact, Sheikh's attempts to formally introduce the wider arena of 'Living Traditions' (covering a broad array of craft and artistic traditions including miniature painting) into Baroda's curriculum – for which he submitted a syllabus – failed.[14] In Baroda the storytelling potential of miniature painting was instead absorbed into a wider strand of painting practice centred on the human figure dubbed 'narrative painting' – a term taken from the title of an exhibition organized by British artist Timothy Hyman in 1979, and most cogently articulated by the critic Geeta Kapur in the catalogue for the 1981 exhibition *Place for People*,[15] which travelled beyond Baroda.

The artist Arpita Singh (b. 1937), for instance, did not participate in *Place for People*, but her practice from the 1980s is in dialogue with the ideas and practices it contained. After obtaining

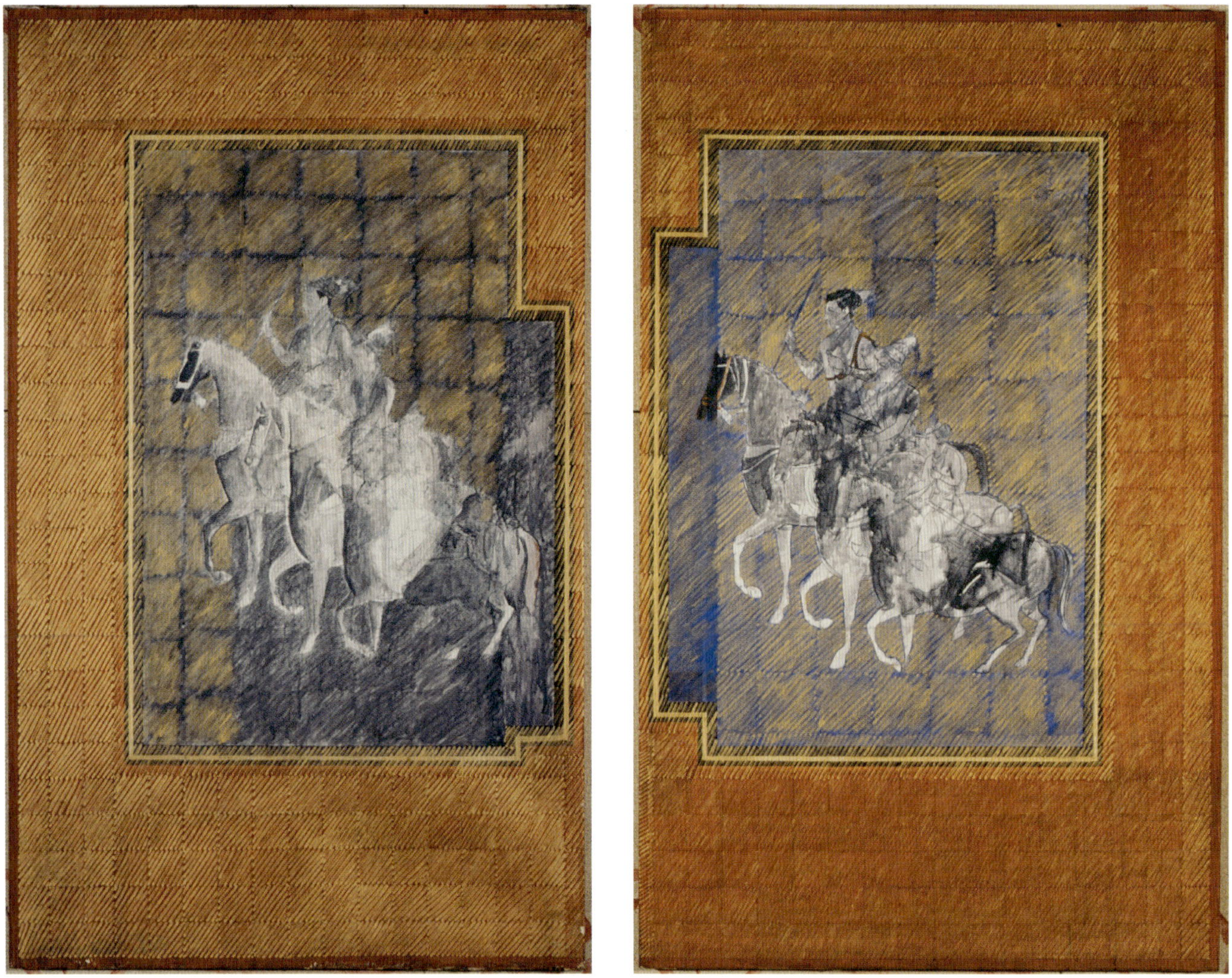

FIG. 25 Zahoor ul Akhlaq, *Untitled* (c.1990).

her Diploma in Fine Art at the Delhi Polytechnic in 1959, she worked initially as a textile designer with the Weavers' Service Centre in New Delhi. And, although Singh was based in New Delhi, her practice developed in complementary ways to artists working in the narrative painting mode from Baroda and elsewhere – for instance she showed with Nalini Malani, Madhvi Parekh and Nilima Sheikh in the influential touring exhibition *Through the Looking Glass* (1987–9). She developed a distinctive style of figurative painting informed by multiple traditional art forms, including textiles, miniature painting and folk art. Her paintings – in watercolour on paper and oil on canvas – are built on a scaffolding of repetitive mark-making that recall weaving, quilting and other forms of textile art. Her works often centre feminist narratives in surreal settings where time, figures and objects seem to be free-floating. Her use of simple floral and vegetal motifs recalls illuminated borders in traditional miniature painting; and in *Noor Jehan* (2001) (cat. 94) we see Singh's subversion of the familiar conceit of a Mughal emperor astride the globe. In Singh's rendering, it is a confident middle-aged woman, unashamed of her naked body, visible through her diaphanous sari, who takes centre stage.

In Lahore, miniature painting's engagement with contemporary practice followed a different trajectory. Zahoor ul Akhlaq, as the art historian Simone Wille argues, was 'a key proponent of artistic modernism in Pakistan', whose artistic legacy has informed trajectories of contemporary practice.[16] Salima Hashmi (b.1942), the artist, educator and close friend of Akhlaq, has traced a genealogy of Akhlaq's practice, highlighting: his childhood training in calligraphy with Yousaf Dehlvi (1907–1991); his interest in the relationship between the etched form and the ground it was embedded in, developed through his studies in England; his investment in the miniature tradition of painting; and his experiments with sculpture and public monuments – in particular an exploration of 'geometric principles which stem from Islamic art of all kinds', including architecture.[17]

While Akhlaq's tragic untimely death (he was brutally murdered in 1999) and fragmentary archive have so far resisted the close textual readings and density of scholarship that Sheikh's works and writings elicited, even a casual perusal of Akhlaq's work reveals his study of the V&A's collection, as well as the nature of his interest in the paintings he was studying. Balchand's *Shah Shuja, Awrangzeb and Murad Bakhash* (*c.*1635), for instance (cat. 53), was a subject of intense fascination for Akhlaq, and he produced two large-scale works, the *Shah Jahan Triptych* (1981) and the diptych *Untitled* (1990) (fig. 25), which removes the three princely riders and their steeds (whose relative size to each other is dependent on their rank in court) from the landscape and deposits them in the middle of a grid. Both works use the grid as a structuring device, but also as a painterly scaffolding to explore the application of paint, the intensity of mark-making, and variations in light and dark created through a limited set of colours.

Akhlaq often used a fine brush to paint in short diagonal strokes, approximating the laborious *pardakht* technique of paint application in historic miniatures. The squares of the grid have been filled with diagonal cross-hatching, recalling, as Virginia Whiles has pointed out, the drawing exercises where miniature students spend hours and days 'drawing parallel lines into square-inch boxes'.[18] The latter diptych takes on the form of an open manuscript across two pages, but, unlike the highly decorated margin of the Balchand painting, Akhlaq leaves his empty – allowing space for the viewer to enter.

> Dialogue is important between the painting and the viewer, and the imagery is only part of that dialogue. The underlying structure is also something that communicates and helps create this dialogue.[19]

For Akhlaq, unlike Sheikh, it was not the possibility to tell or hold multiple stories that attracted him to the miniature, but its formal properties and tropes – its use of borders, margins and framing devices; its application of paint in layers; the looseness or tightness of its brush strokes – that could help him construct conceptual, imaginary worlds for the viewer to enter. Akhlaq's frequent use of rectangular 'windows' serves as a spatial invitation for viewers to enter these dream-like worlds, populated by shapes, figures and motifs that recall the miniature paintings' geometric designs and calligraphy that populate manuscripts, but in a language of his own making – as exemplified by *Untitled (2)* (cat. 78).

This commitment to language and to the art of writing can also be seen in a series of small untitled works (cat. 79–82) that share the format of a *takhti*, a small wooden slate traditionally used in rural schools for children to write on, erase and reuse. In these works Akhlaq uses the window frame to hold abstracted forms, including trees and cactus-like foliage, while experimenting with colour and modes of paint application, including gestural drips.

It was this approach to painterly 'deconstruction' in Akhlaq's painting practice that Shahzia Sikander (b.1969) describes as being important in shaping her own interest in the form. But in parallel to developing his own interests in experimenting with the formal features of miniature painting in his own painting practices, Akhlaq used his position as Head of Fine Arts at the NCA to institute a full-fledged miniature department.[20] He encouraged a young miniature painter, Bashir Ahmed (b.1954) – who had trained with Sheikh Shujaullah, who in turn had trained with Haji Mohammed Sharif, and could trace his lineage of practice back to the ateliers of the Mughal courts – to give the formerly artisanal practice an academic overhaul. Miniature practice was subsequently afforded the same standing as painting, sculpture and printmaking.

In the hands of a generation of artists trained at the NCA since the establishment of this department in the 1980s, miniature painting has moved beyond its tropes, to become an *attitude*.[21] One characterized by a rejection of the tyranny of binary choices to embrace both: the monumental and intimate; exquisite craft skills and expressive gestures; reference and irreverence; history and contemporaneity. There are few artists who better embody this ability to toggle between these seemingly binary states than the New York-based Shahzia Sikander (who graduated from the NCA's miniature department

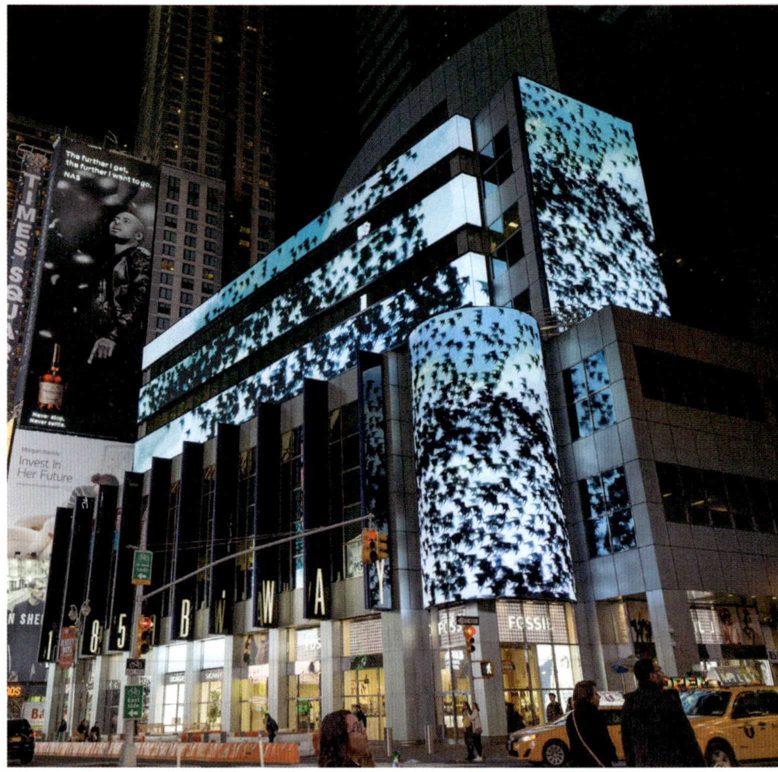

FIG. 26 Shahzia Sikander, *Gopi-Contagion* (2015).

in 1991) and the Lahore-based Imran Qureshi (b.1972; class of 1993), who now heads the miniature department at the NCA.

Sikander's thesis work, *The Scroll* (1991–2) (cat. 96) – a large-scale intricately executed narrative painting depicting daily life through a personal and feminist perspective – managed to be both 'highly traditional' and 'modern' and is considered a breakthrough in the development of contemporary miniature at the NCA.[22] In her early works such as *Riding the Written* (1992–3) (cat. 97) we see Sikander experimenting with the word and the horse, tropes familiar to us from Akhlaq's larger-scale canvases (see cat. 76), and their entangled fragments on the more intimate scale of the handmade wasli paper.

Sikander has moved from personal narratives of domestic space to theatrical installations recalling Mughal gardens. She has explored the postcolonial condition in manuscript-style large-scale paintings such as *The Explosion of the Company Man* (2011) (cat. 99) before transforming the same ideas into ambitious digitally animated meditations. Her animation of hundreds of digital drawings, *Gopi-Contagion* (fig. 26), took over the electronic billboards of New York's Times Square in 2015. And in 2023 she created twin sculptures for a major public commission, *Havah... to breathe, air, life,* in Madison Square Park and the courthouse rooftop on Madison Avenue and 25th Street.

Imran Qureshi's modest-sized painting *Musawwir ka Chota Bhai, The Artist's Younger Brother* (1995) (cat. 100), has been painted on a *takhti*. It captures the artist's relationship – teetering on the edge of deference and contestation – with the tradition of miniature painting. The painting's central figure and the landscape he stands in are both rendered in the manner of a Mughal-era court painting. This seeming conservatism, however, is juxtaposed with the youthful insouciance of his brother's fashionably ragged flared trousers. There is a knowing mischief that shimmers on the painted surface.

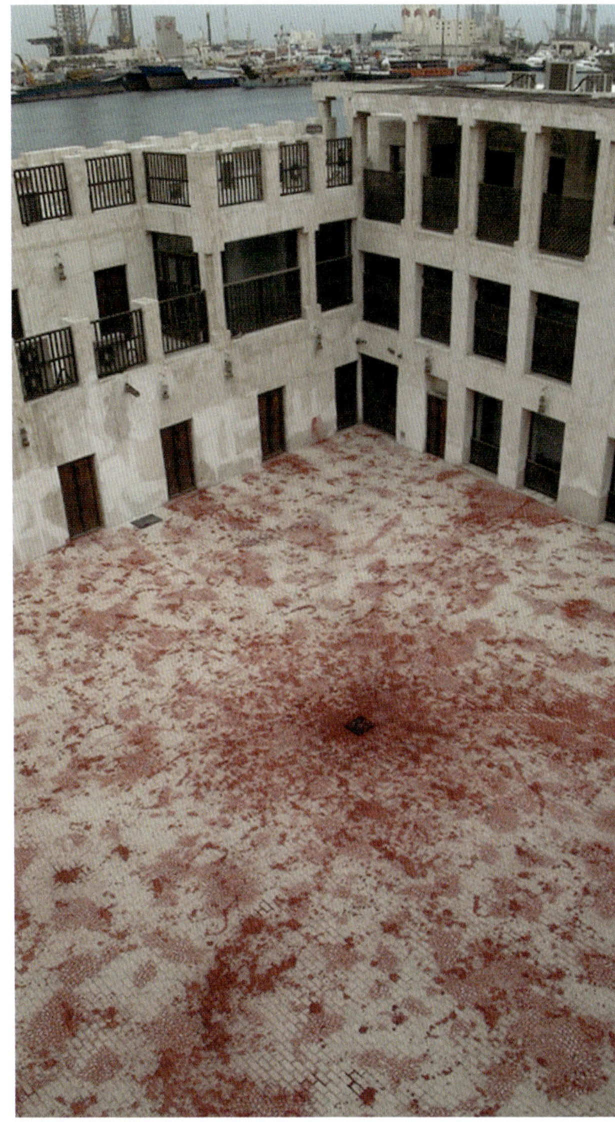

FIG. 27 Imran Qureshi, *Blessings Upon the Land of My Love* (2011).

Qureshi burst into global prominence with *Blessings Upon the Land of My Love* (2011) (fig. 27) at the 11th Sharjah Biennial. His site-responsive treatment of a courtyard floor suggested the bloody remnants of an Arab Spring gun battle, or the aftermath of a bomb attack in his native Lahore. Closer examination revealed morbidly beautiful foliage growing from pools of red pigment – delicate white tendrils that seemed to be plucked straight out of seventeenth-century Basohli miniatures. He has since shown widely across the world, including numerous biennials and the prestigious Roof Garden commission for the Metropolitan Museum of Art in New York in 2013. He even entered the wider public imagination outside the confines of the art world when London Underground used his artwork for the cover of the Tube map in December 2013. In 2019, celebrated fashion designer Christian Louboutin named his flat shoes, inspired by the ubiquitous Peshawari chappal, 'Imran Sandals'. In 2022

Qureshi collaborated with the Pakistan Super League cricket franchise Islamabad United to design the pink and red cricket kits for the men's team – bursting with bright blue floral patterns that seem to have leapt off the painted page of a Mughal painting.

Sikander and Qureshi are perhaps the most highly visible alumni of this specialization at the Fine Arts Department of the NCA. It is beyond the scope of this text to even sketch out the practices of the corona burst of talent – including Nusra Latif Qureshi (b.1973; class of 1995), Aisha Khalid (b.1972; class of 1997), Muhammad Zeeshan (b.1980; class of 2003), Khadim Ali (b. 1978; class of 2003), Noor Ali Chagani (b.1982; class of 2008) and Rehana Mangi (b.1986; class of 2007) – that has followed. And this is before acknowledging the impact that having a miniature department in the NCA has had on the practice of artists who have chosen not to specialize in it, for example Hamra Abbas (b.1976) and Ali Kazim (b.1979), but who engage with its techniques, ideas and visual tropes. To say nothing of artists like Rashid Rana (b.1968), who worked closely with Akhlaq as a student at the NCA, and whose landmark work, *I Love Miniatures* (2002), is a critique of the celebratory impulse of contemporary miniature (cat. 108). In this photomosaic digital print presented in a gilded frame, Rana has marshalled thousands of images of advertising billboards in Lahore to construct a portrait of the Mughal emperor Shah Jahan. Each pixel acts as a single dab of paint, building a picture as per the miniature's *pardakht* technique. The dynamic tension between the macro (the Mughal portrait) and micro (the banal commercial billboards) images is activated by the viewer moving backwards and forwards. In *I Love Miniatures* Rana honours both: his mentor Akhlaq's interest in creating a structural dialogue with the viewer, and Sheikh's ambition to hold multiple realities that 'necessitates' the viewer's 'active participation'.

This density of practice and practitioners, and a growing critical discourse, have played an important role in injecting the miniature-painting department at the NCA with a certain vigour. With the notable exception of Sikander, most of the NCA-trained miniature painters developed their international careers while working and living in Pakistan. To supplement their incomes, many of them taught miniature painting; in the NCA, but also in numerous similar departments established in art schools across the country in the wake of the perceived success of the NCA. This critical mass of practitioners and prospective students, and the resulting teaching and exhibition opportunities, have helped establish a supportive ecosystem in Pakistan.

This group of artists also benefited from a discernible generosity exhibited by senior faculty members at the NCA (Akhlaq and Hashmi) and teachers in the miniature department (Ahmed and Qureshi) playing multiple roles as mentors, cheerleaders, teachers, employers and collaborators. This encouraged an openness to collaboration and horizontality that has infused contemporary miniature. This collaborative impulse is perhaps best exemplified by the *Karkhana* project (cat. 117): conceived by Imran Qureshi and initially realized as an exhibition, *Karkhana: Contemporary Pakistani Miniatures* at the Touchstones Art Gallery in Rochdale, UK (2003–4). It was subsequently developed as a larger exhibition, *Karkhana: A Contemporary Collaboration*, at the Aldrich Contemporary Art Museum in Ridgefield, Connecticut, and the Asian Art Museum, San Francisco (2005–6).[23]

Karkhana is a series of 12 collaborative paintings by six artists who trained in miniature at the NCA – Aisha Khalid, Hasnat Mehmood (b.1978), Imran Qureshi, Nusra Latif Qureshi, Talha Rathore (b.1969) and Saira Wasim (b.1975) – who, at the time, were based in five cities on three continents. The project was inspired by the cooperative nature of miniature painting during the Mughal era (early sixteenth–early eighteenth centuries) in India, and catalysed by a series of correspondences between the artists in Pakistan and those who had moved abroad, discussing the aftermath of the attacks on the World Trade Center on 11 September 2001 – and the invasions of Afghanistan and Iraq that followed. Each artist started work on two new pieces of wasli paper, and then sent the paintings (by courier) in succession to the five other artists in the group, each of whom added a layer of imagery, marks or other processes. Their work was a groundbreaking collaboration, an 'improvisational act involving creative destruction, semiotic play and dynamic adaptation' that garnered considerable critical attention and general interest.[24]

GOING GLOBAL

Karkhana: A Contemporary Collaboration marked a significant node in the international circulation of contemporary miniature. It came on the heels of the exhibition *The American Effect* (2003) at the Whitney Museum of American Art in New York, exploring global perspectives on America through the work of 50 international artists and artist groups. Two of these artists were Qureshi and his erstwhile student Saira Wasim (b.1975; class of 1999). In speaking of this selection – a notable focus on one mode of artistic expression within a global survey – the exhibition curator Lawrence Rinder shared:

> I had put my finger inadvertently on a scene by choosing these two people, two very different manifestations of a tendency of an old tradition ... it suggests to me that this is a very healthy and vibrant part of the culture.[25]

Museums in some parts of the world (Australia, India, Japan and the UK) had already 'put their fingers on this scene', and others (Canada, Germany, Hong Kong, Italy, Singapore and the UAE) began to do so shortly thereafter; with numerous exhibitions devoted to, or prominently featuring, contemporary miniature from Pakistan.[26] In more recent years, with a greater number of artists reaching prominence in the field, the survey exhibition has been replaced with displays focused on individual artists' works; in 2016, public museums in the UK staged six solo exhibitions of Imran Qureshi's work alone.

This pattern of global interest was reflected in the new geographies of contemporary art; for example, Imran Qureshi and Aisha Khalid's presentations at the Sharjah Biennial (2011) had greater art-world visibility than their showing at the Venice Biennale (2009). Contemporary miniature, with its exquisite displays of skill and often politically charged content, was also notably 'other' enough to feed this expanded contemporary art world's insatiable appetite for the new. As contemporary miniaturists started being represented by commercial galleries in Australia, Hong Kong, India, the UK and the USA, their work began to be collected all around the world; not just by contemporary art museums but also by venerable universal museums finding contemporary resonances with historic collections, and by private collectors of all shades, everywhere. Miniature painting's attractions were heterogeneous and multifarious, appealing to: East Asian aesthetics

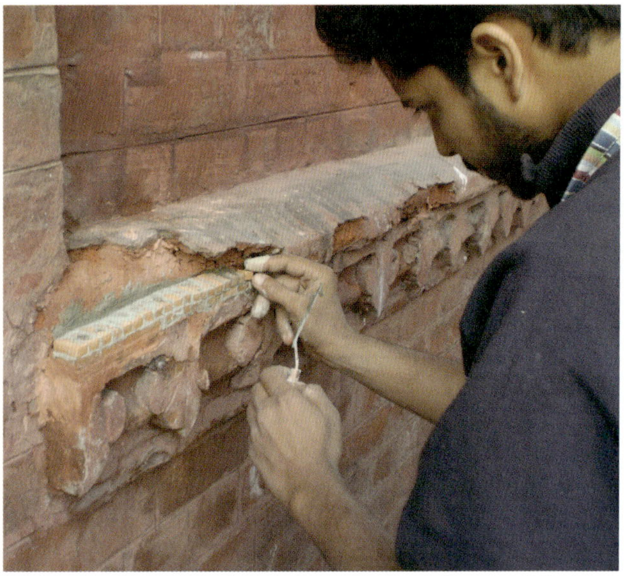
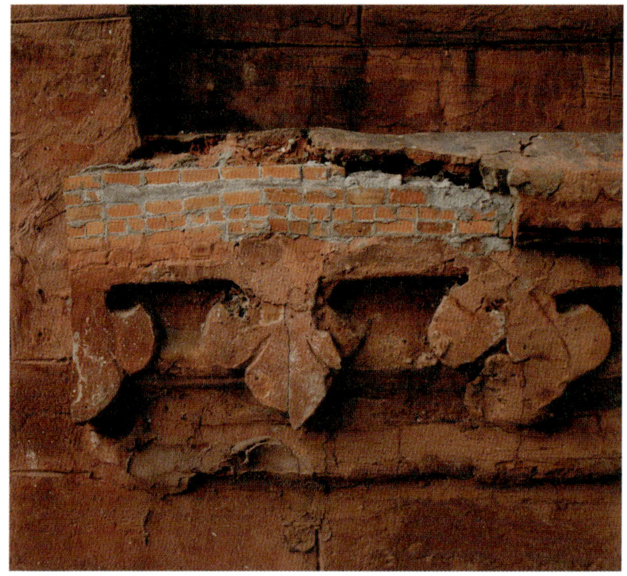
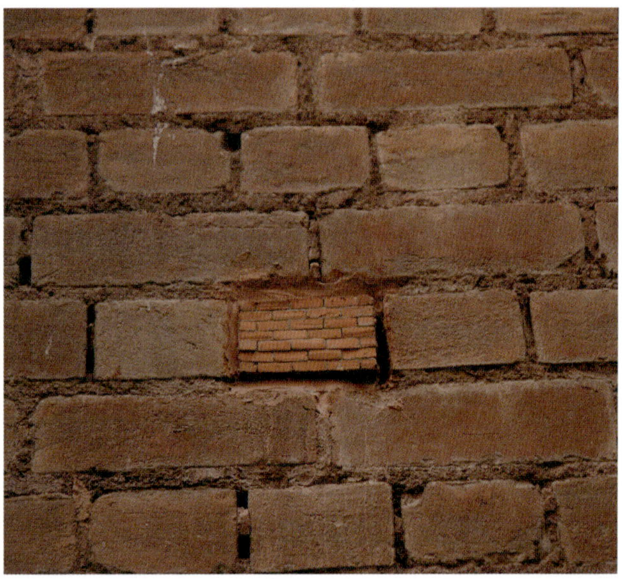
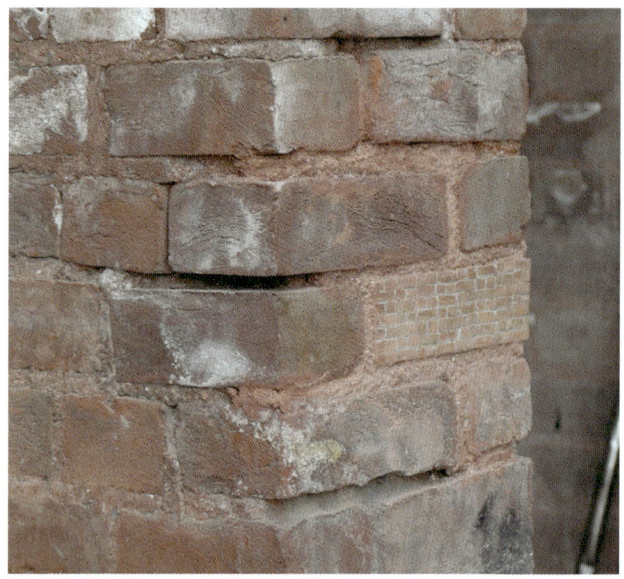
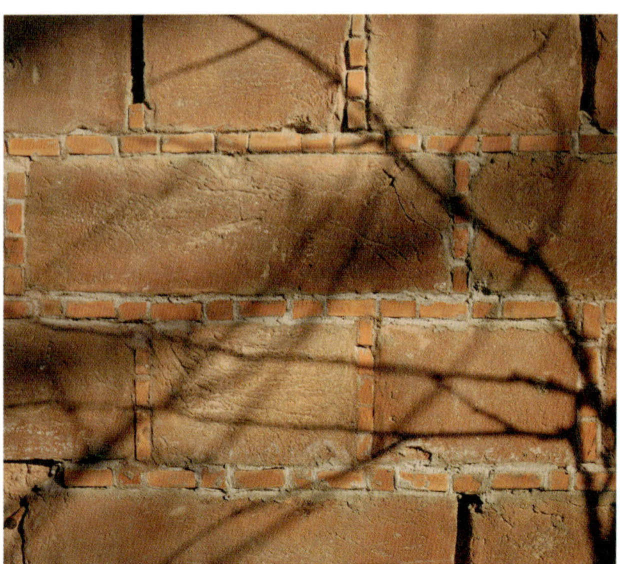
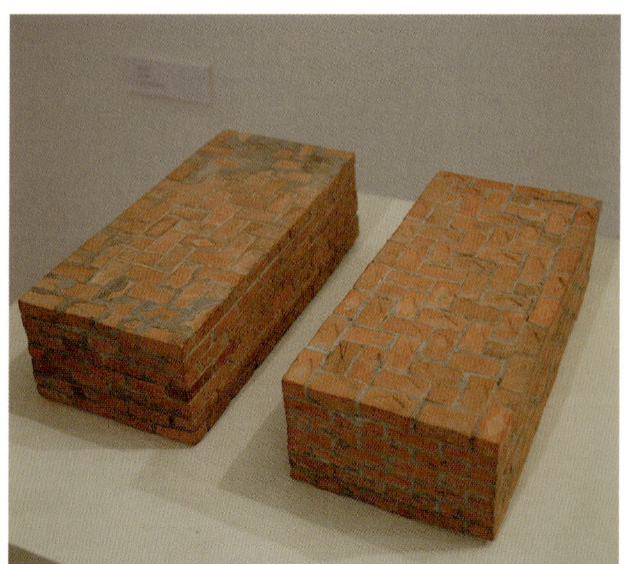

that recognized miniatures' visual rhyme with ink painting; South Asian sensibilities that drew on the long Indo-Persian tradition; aficionados of Arabic calligraphy in West Asia; and fans of gestural painting in the Euro-American canon.

The surge of international interest resulted in the opportunity for artists to show in biennials, take part in residencies and produce site-specific installations that, as Anna Sloan has so insightfully analysed, allowed miniature artists to manipulate 'the architectural structure of the historical miniature' in new ways and build on its status as a hybrid practice (historically as illustrations in a bound book) in innovative new approaches.[27] With dramatic new and multimedia installations alongside exquisitely rendered paintings on an intimate scale, contemporary miniature offered museums and audiences multiple ways of entering this imaginative and innovative world – transporting it beyond the cultural boundaries of the Indo-Persian tradition it came from.

A CONCLUSION, OR NEW BEGINNINGS?

This story started with two artist-teachers (Sheikh and Akhlaq) and the transformative impact on their practices of the study of South Asian miniature paintings in London.

What does it mean for artists from India and Pakistan to engage with artistic 'treasure after treasure' from the subcontinent in London? What would it mean, in a parallel thought experiment, if Turner's best paintings were in Lahore or New Delhi?[28]

While these questions have no easy answers, it seems appropriate to turn to art itself to suggest ways forward. Noor Ali Chagani, while a student of Imran Qureshi's at the NCA, developed a mode of practice that included making sculptural objects and site-aware installations with miniaturized terracotta bricks. Chagani's graduation project, *Be a Part of It* (2008), comprised repairing the walls of the NCA's historic building with his tiny bricks (fig. 28).

The NCA started life as the Mayo School of Art, a colonial-era school established alongside the Lahore Museum in 1875. Its first principal, and the curator of the Lahore Museum, was John Lockwood Kipling, made immortal as the curator figure in his son Rudyard Kipling's classic novel *Kim* (1901). The creation of the Mayo School and the Lahore Museum was as part of the efforts of Britain's Department of Science and Art to 'reinvigorate the existing artisanal groups' of the Punjab and the North-West Frontier Province, and then train them for industrial design.[29] This in turn was part of an overall imperial effort to enhance British design that included the development of institutions we now know as the V&A and the RCA.

Be a Part of It is at once simple and profound. Chagani's touching act of material and cultural repair is also a metaphor for engaging the past in a critical dialogue without being restrained by it.

Contemporary miniature – the product of individual and institutional effort, and nurtured through international interest and collaborative potential – offers the hopeful possibility of expanding our imagination of what the global can be; beyond the aesthetic regimes that presently dominate the contemporary art world.

FIG. 28 Noor Ali Chagani, *Be a Part of It* (2008).

THE CATALOGUE ENTRIES THAT FOLLOW ARE BY
CLEO ROBERTS-KOMIREDDI & ELIZABETH BROWN

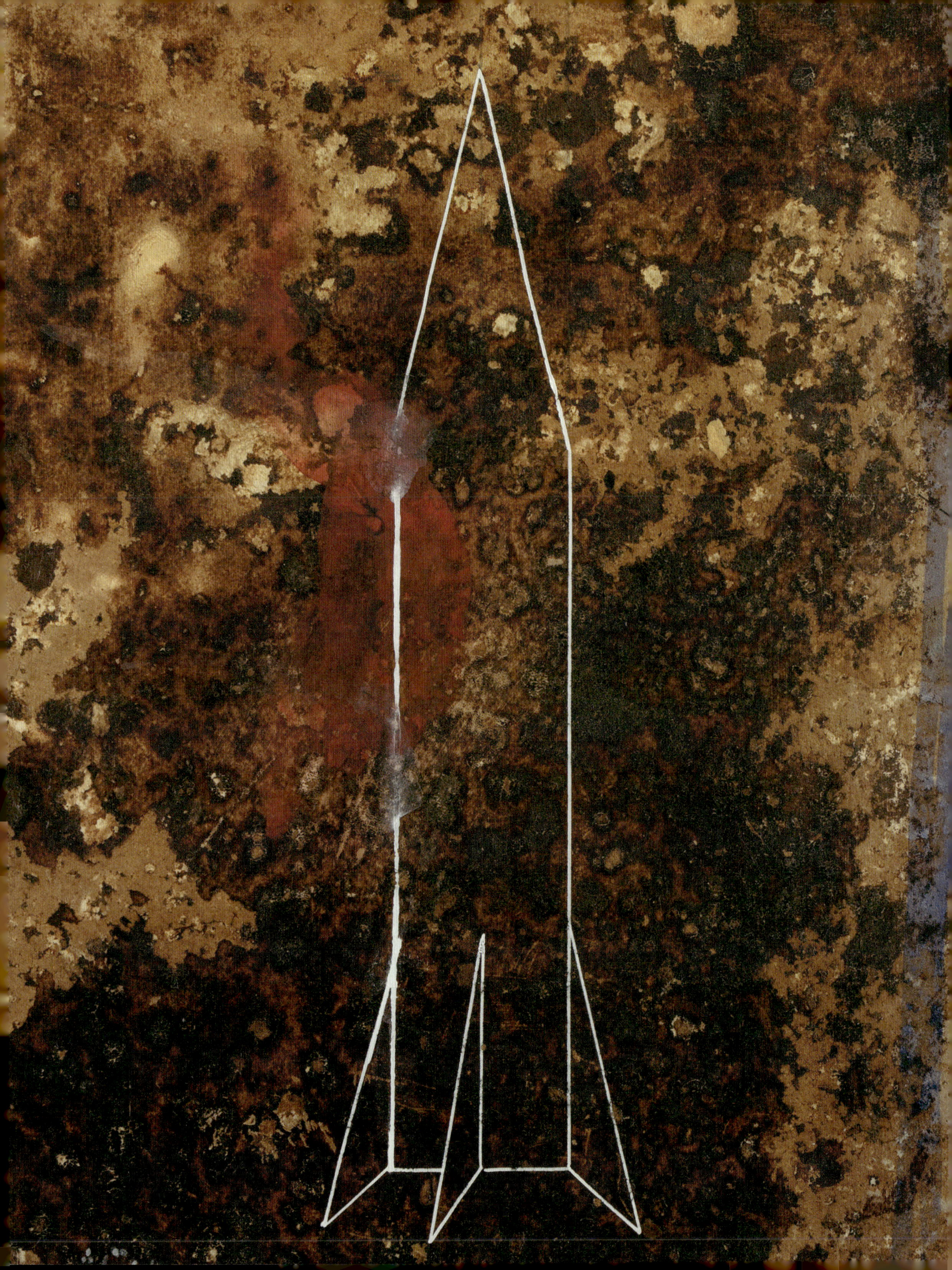

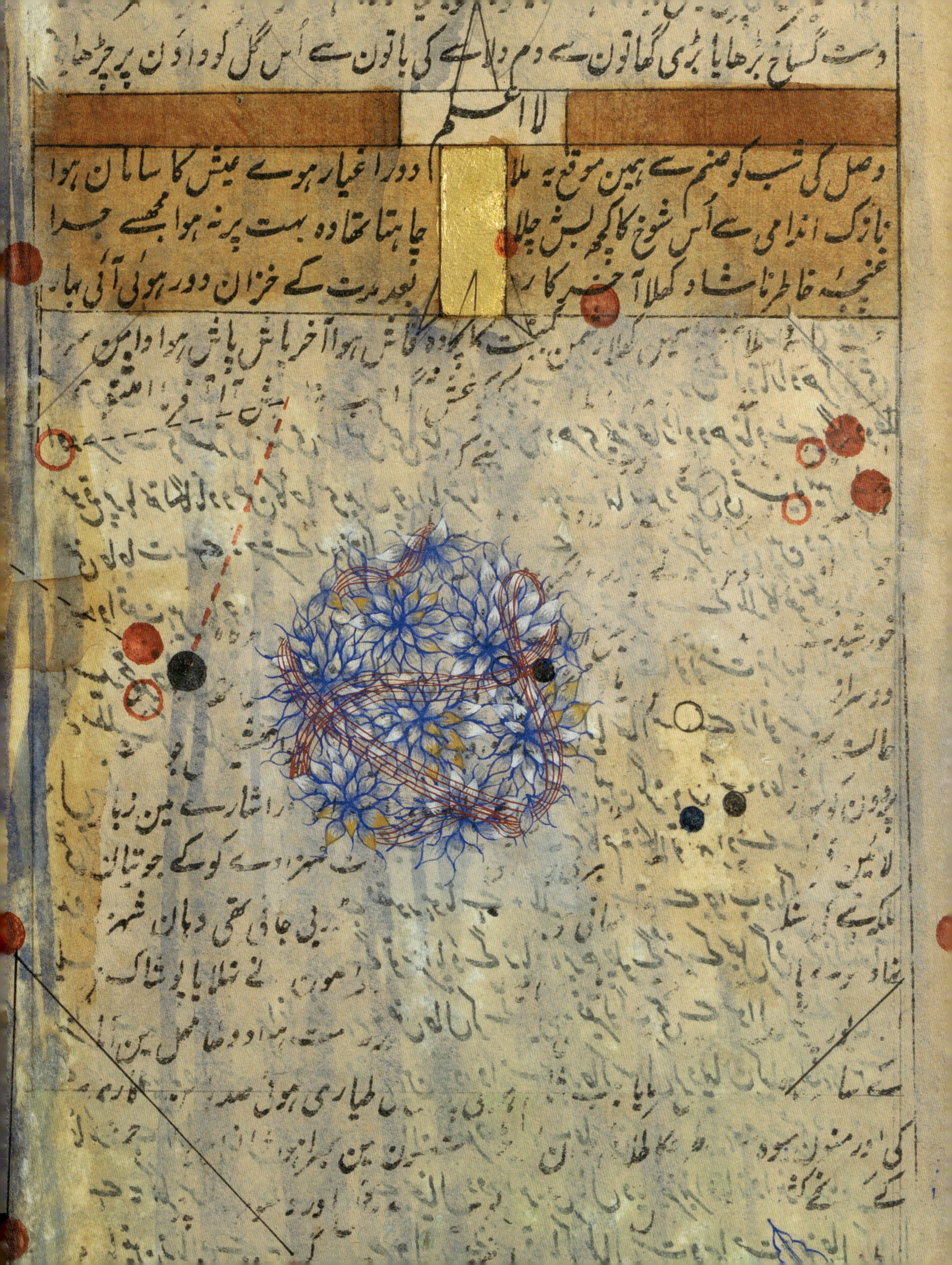
دست گستاخ بڑھایا بڑی گھاتوں سے دم دلاسے کی باتوں سے اس گل کو واؤں پر چڑھایا
وصل کی شب کو صنم سے ہمیں موقع یہ ملا
دور اغیار ہوئے عیش کا سامان ہوا
نازک اندامی سے اس شوخ کا کچھ بس نہ چلا
چاہتا تھا وہ بہت پر نہ ہوا مجھ سے جدا
غنچۂ خاطر ناشاد کھلا آخر کار
بعد مدت کے خزاں دور ہوئی آئی بہار

GULAMMOHAMMED SHEIKH

69 We Two

1970 | oil on canvas | 167.6 × 167.6 cm | courtesy of the artist and Vadehra Art Gallery

The painter, historian, educator and writer Gulammohammed Sheikh (b.1937, Gujarat, India) has been integral to the development of contemporary Indian art. Following his Master's in painting at the Faculty of Fine Arts, Maharaja Sayajirao University of Baroda, Sheikh completed a second Master's at the RCA, London, in 1965, after being awarded the Commonwealth Scholarship. Returning to India, he was a founding member of Group 1890, a collective seeking greater freedom in art. Looking to Persian, Mughal and Pahari miniatures along with Bakhti and Sufi poetry and Renaissance art, Sheikh's work is narrative and multi-perspectival, often combining the fantastical and historical.

We Two (1970), made in the aftermath of Baroda's communal tensions, isolates Sheikh and his wife, the artist Nilima Sheikh. Shown stranded and confined in a disproportional white room, suggestive of a courtyard, the work expresses the couple's vulnerability. The artist borrows from a range of miniature traditions, for example the 'colour field' of Rajput and Pahari paintings (see cat. 58). Delicate trees are dotted across the background and a faint mythical animal leaps through the sky – the *buraq*, ridden by the Prophet Muhammad on his night journey from Mecca to Jerusalem, as depicted in Mughal and Deccani miniatures (see fig. 22).

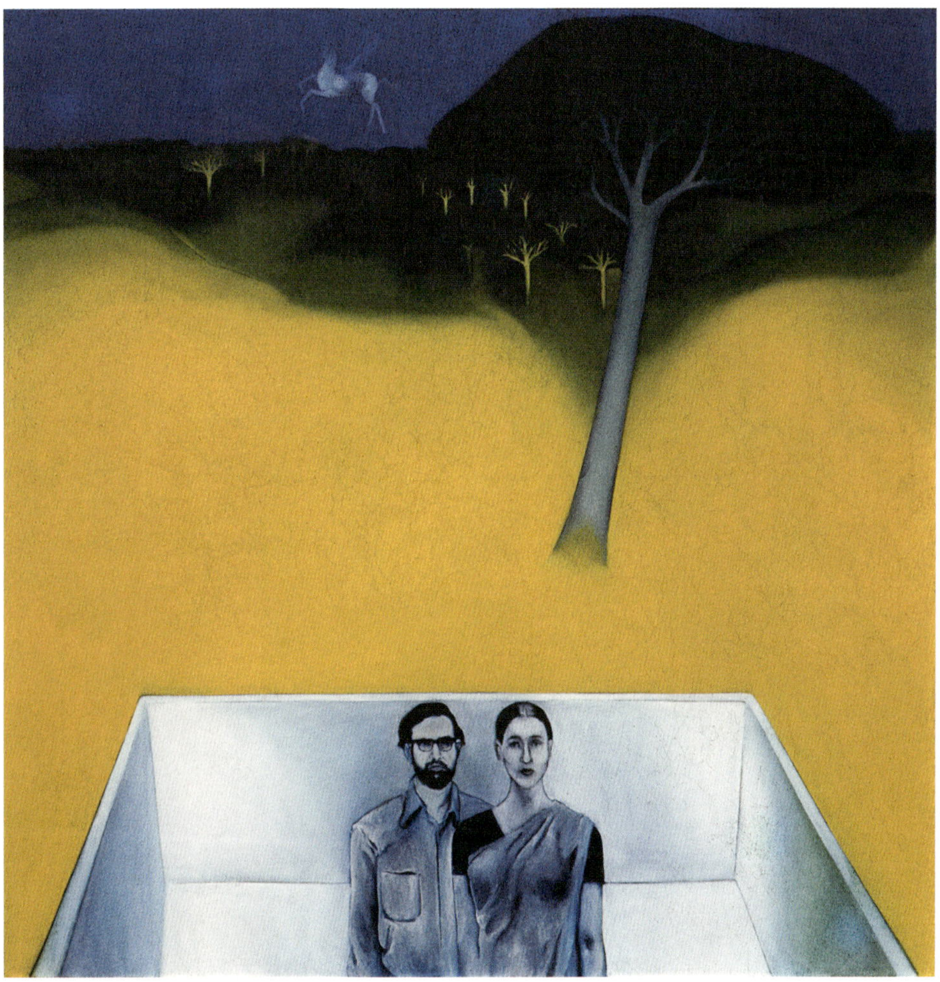

GULAMMOHAMMED SHEIKH

70 Beyond the Ridge

1976 | oil on canvas | 137.8 × 121.9 cm | Collection Kiran Nadar Museum of Art, New Delhi

In *Beyond the Ridge* (1976) Sheikh paints a richly coloured landscape that could be as much imaginary as based on reality. Running through a valley are stylized trees and shrubbery, inconceivably manicured in a way that notes Mughal miniature conventions.

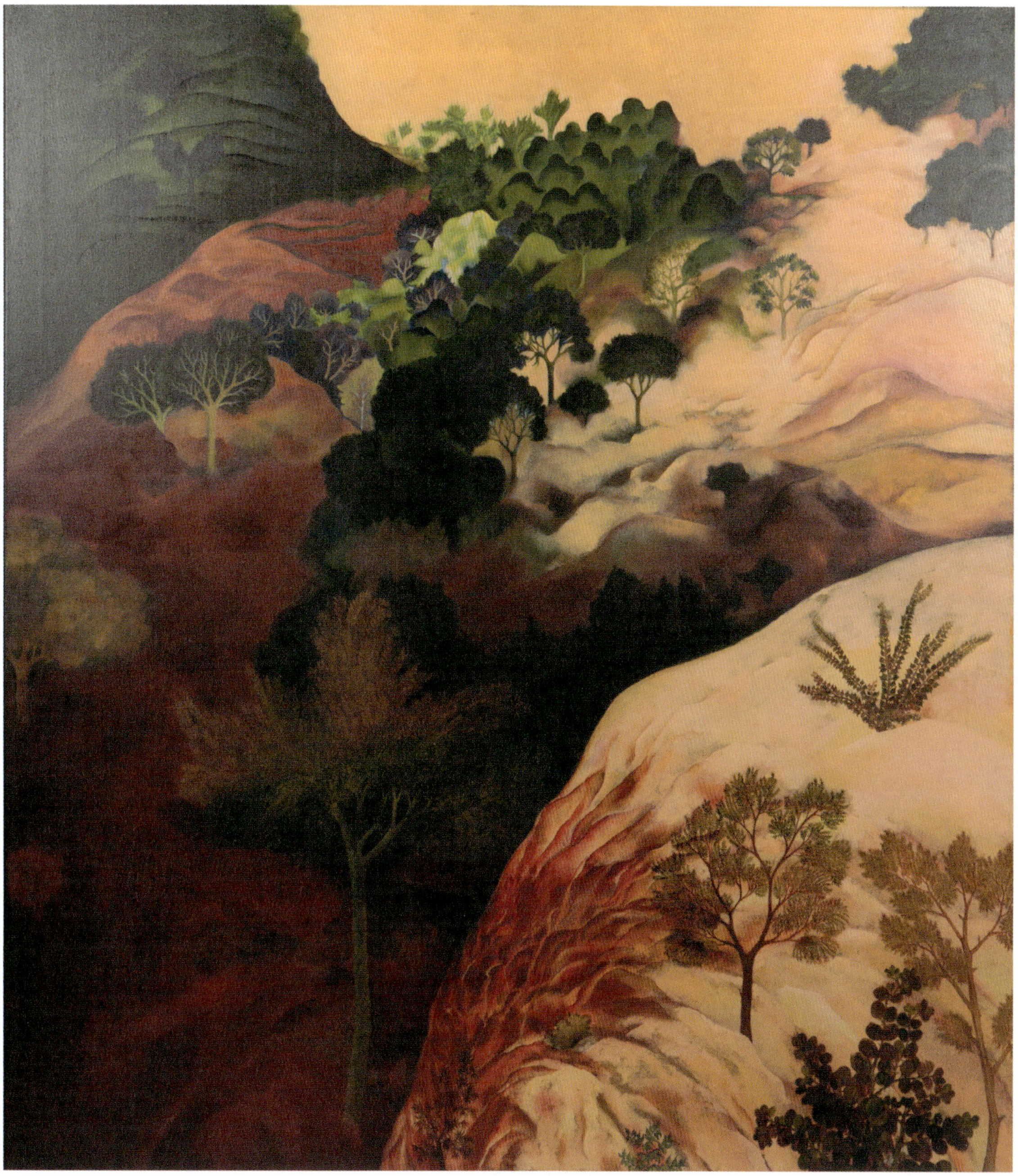

GULAMMOHAMMED SHEIKH

71 City for Sale

1981–84 | oil on canvas | 204.5 × 306 cm | Victoria and Albert Museum

City for Sale (1981–84), one of Sheikh's particularly ambitious works, depicts the city of Baroda rocked by communal riots between Hindu and Muslim communities. As the artist wrote, '*City for Sale* lasted nearly 3 years – the largest painting I have done. It began around the time violent communal riots broke out in Baroda, hence it deals with urban brutalization, its agonies and anguish.' In this dense image, the city is compressed and collapses in on itself around a cinema screening the film *Silsila*. At the time, the film became notorious due to an alleged affair between the two leading actors. Critical of the importance placed on this speculation, Sheikh contrasts the building with the degenerating city; bodies tangle together, vegetables tumble in the foreground, transport is stuck. Heightened by the fiery colour palette, the piece channels feelings of anxiety and fear that Sheikh might have experienced at this time. As he said of the violent clashes, 'For the first time, my identity was questioned. It made me aware of the politics that we had brushed aside until then.'[30]

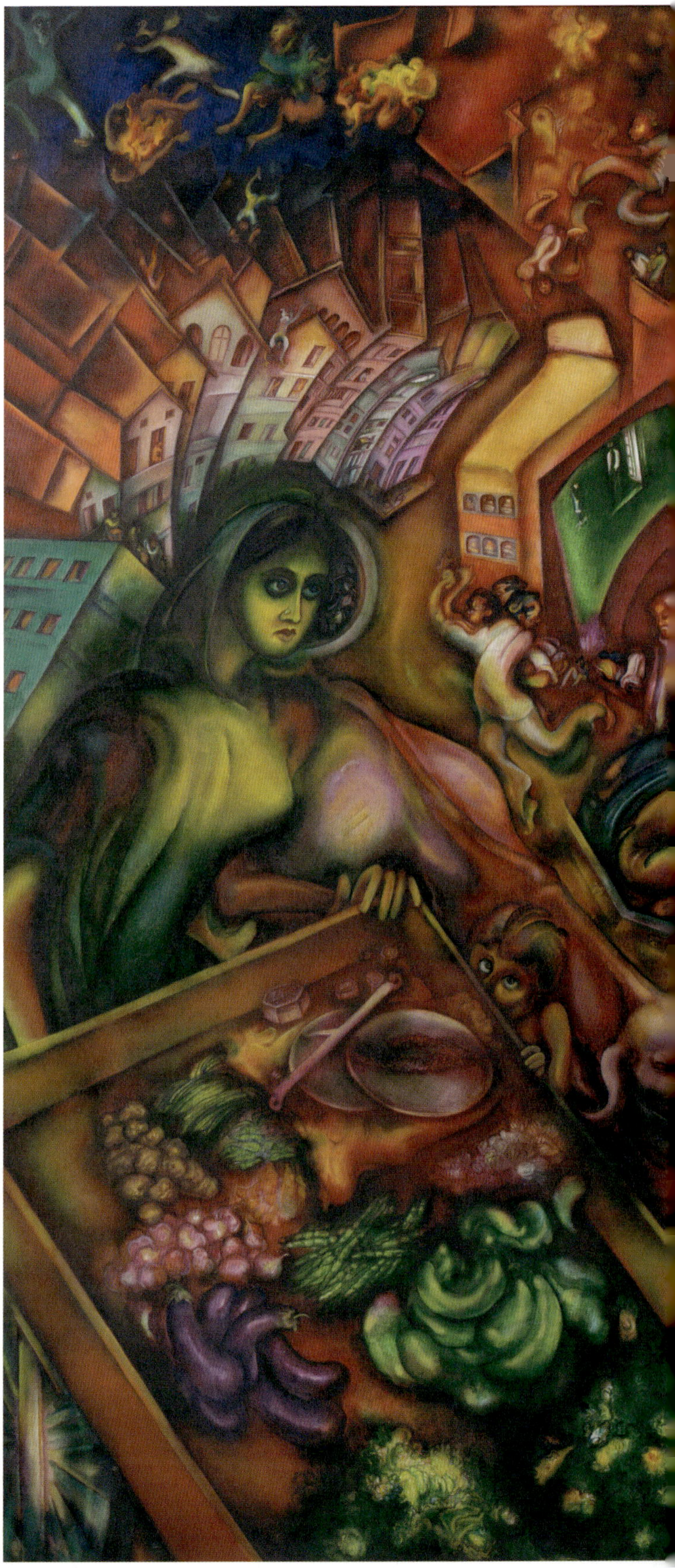

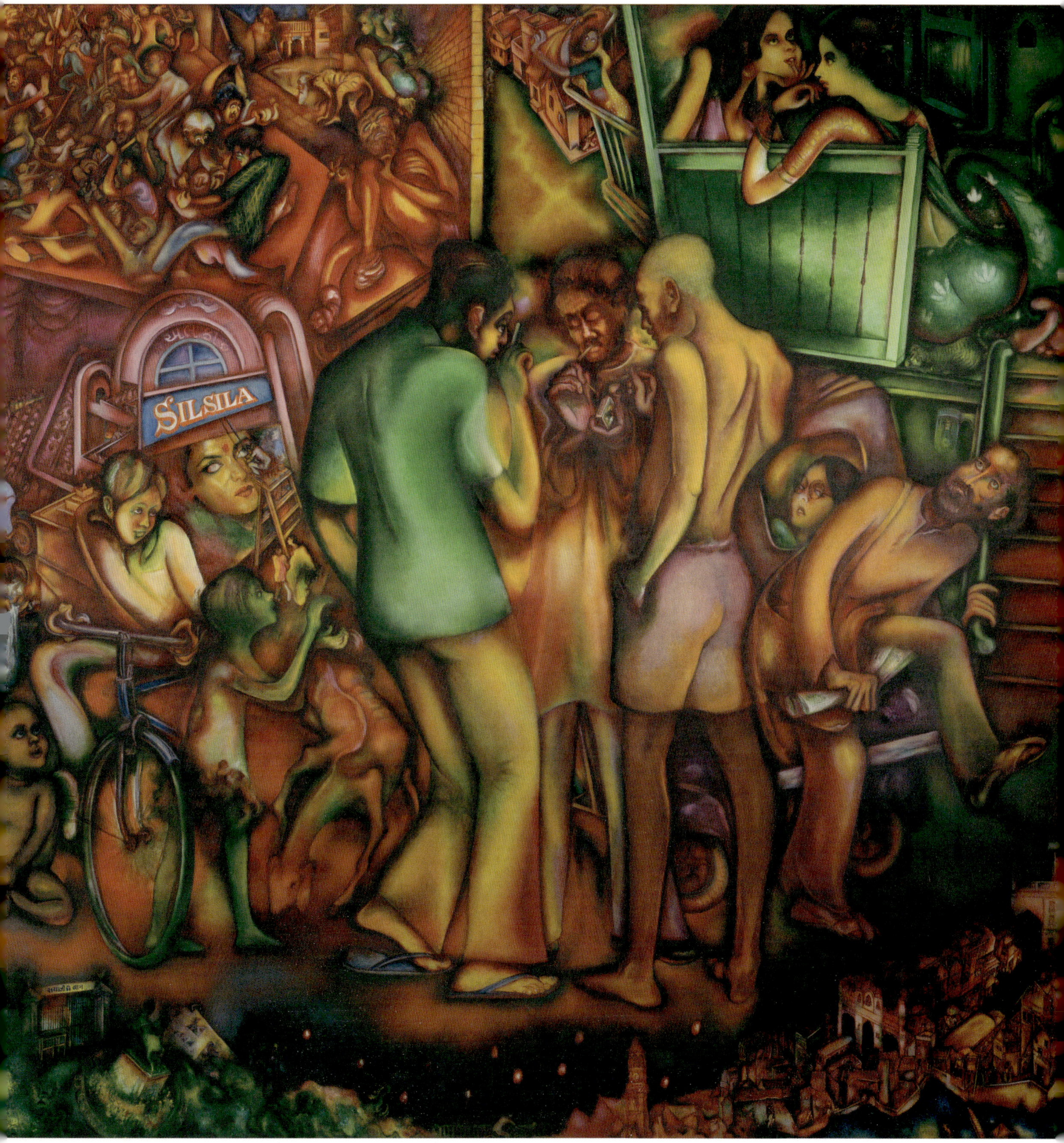
SILSILA

GULAMMOHAMMED SHEIKH

I grew up in a lower-middle-class Muslim family where it was not customary to think of painting as a profession. Baroda, which I joined in 1955, opened up new awareness of the arts of the world: traditional, contemporary, Eastern and Western. And then, the very large presences of my teachers, whose shadows one could not escape. I looked out, and saw other 'heroes' outside, in Delhi or Bombay. So I went knocking at the doors of Tyeb, Hussain and others. After many encounters, when I started painting, I tried to get rid of as many shadows as possible. So I painted as it were in a flush of frenzy; in an expressionist sort of way, thick with impasto. This was a release, but there was still a restlessness. We knew of the great artists of the past, but one would not go back to them. The slogan of the day was to be here in the great moment of modern art, and so, starry-eyed I too plunged into it. It was at this time that I got a scholarship to go abroad to London, at the Royal College of Art. There I saw around me Abstract, Minimal and Pop, and I was in a dilemma as to which world I belonged in.

During that time I used to visit the Victoria and Albert Museum, in fact almost daily; I used to go through the direct passage from the Royal College through its many galleries to the cafeteria. It was not that I had not seen Indian miniature painting before, but I began to spend longer now with increasing absorption. Questions stirred within me. How did this kind of painting come about? Does it have relevance in our times? I began to see more and more *original* paintings, not reproductions that I had been educated on. Ideas about Tachism, and those of easel painting given to us – of the assertion of paint in thick impastos and of a frame in which a painting worked as though the world was set into rectangles – gave way in front of miniatures with incredible dimensions produced through 'flat' expanses of paint and with figures jumping in and out of frames or images spilling out of boundaries, dissolving them in the process. I also learnt that an exclusive image of Indian art created of its spirituality and of the metaphysical nature of its image deciphered only through a code of symbols was not entirely true. I saw that many paintings dealt with the physical world; some even portraying stark, physical violence. Looking at these paintings filled me up with a number of ideas and experience; some I was able to articulate, others remained latent, half-formulated.

So when I came home the reality confronting me overpowered me. That I had seen India through paintings, that some of it in some way was still alive and full of vitality. This I began to probe through painting and writing. Returning to my provincial home town, I found the layers of time past I had seen in painting still present in one or other form; images which were beautiful, serene and deeply moving, images which were disturbing. I began to weave these into my work. There were still many ghost-shadows of my school and college days sitting on my shoulder, expecting me to remain within the confines I was trying to get out of. I wondered how to devise an image which was not academic, or was there only an 'expressionist' alternative? During that period I also travelled a great deal and it was in the landscape I invested my new-found understanding and excitement, sensation and experiences.

During the journeys I realized that the horizon gave way as lands that seemed beyond it emerged in succession, strangely reminiscent of the landscape in Mughal painting which visualized experience of traversing land and not from standing and watching from a given point. This made the academic notion of a vanishing point slightly redundant as it kept on shifting, changing.

At that stage, I dwelt upon colour: yellow attracted me. I felt it had something to do with temperature, perhaps with body temperature (and not with empirical notions of spectrum) that again I had gathered from looking at paintings. And then the question was – what images shall I paint? I liked painting people but the people I liked were people I knew: my family and friends. Should one paint one's family or friends? ... Subsequently there have been images of trees, one such painted leaf by leaf on an eight-foot-long canvas. And then a series of paintings of walls. These have served as a leitmotif in the confrontation between the two worlds. The world I live in now or the world where I grew up. There is always a plural, always a something other which is constantly present. The East and the West, the past and the present. This engagement preoccupies me.[31]

BHUPEN KHAKHAR

72 Tiger and Stag

1970 | oil on canvas | 105.4 × 85.1 cm | private collection, London/Karachi

Acclaimed painter Bhupen Khakhar (1934–2003, Mumbai, India) began his practice in Baroda in west India, after moving there in 1962 to pursue a Master's in art criticism at the Faculty of Fine Arts, Maharaja Sayajirao University of Baroda. Practising as an accountant part-time and otherwise painting, with artist contemporaries including Gulammohammed Sheikh, he associated with the Baroda Group, who focused on developing a narrative figurative style. Khakhar, unencumbered by formal art training, fused the flattened pictorial plane associated with miniature painting and Renaissance illusionism in a style that has often been referred to as 'Indian Pop'. With a characteristically bright palette, Khakhar's work captures the intricacies of habitual Indian life and its myriad communities, and in later years became a way of expressing his homosexuality.

Tiger and Stag (1970) exemplifies Khakhar's ability to combine multiple perspectives in one work akin to many miniature traditions. In this flattened perspective, the two animals tussle in a verdant landscape that extends and surrounds a cityscape. The crude rendering of tiger and stag along with the rendering of the foliage are reminiscent of French painter Henri Rousseau, whom Khakhar cited as an influence. Khakhar gave clues to the meaning of this imagery, writing in an exhibition catalogue from his 1972 show *Truth is Beauty and Beauty is God* at Mumbai's Gallery Chemould that it could be interpreted as 'A rich man attacking a poor man', 'India, an undeveloped country, threatened by a developed country', 'the slightest unawareness leads to death', 'might is stronger than right'.[32]

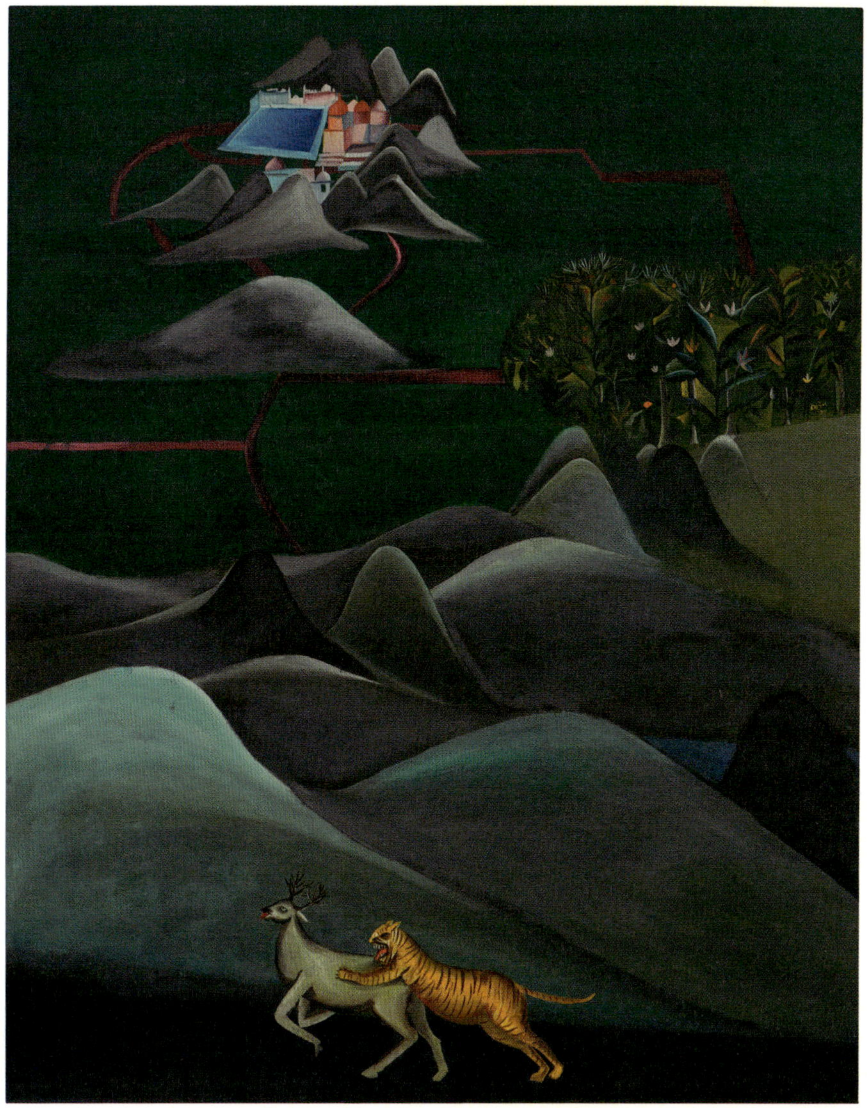

BHUPEN KHAKHAR

73 Voice of Freedom – Strike

1972 | oil on canvas | 91.5 × 91.5 cm | private collection

Voice of Freedom – Strike (1972) is part of Khakhar's notable *Trade* series that depicted everyday professional men in India. Drawing on conventions of nineteenth-century Company paintings, which recorded India's people and customs for a European market (see cat. 37–38), the series includes images of tailors and barbers – those often not depicted in art. It was in the year this piece was painted that Khakhar's style distinguished itself, synthesizing a variety of visual sources and developing its documentary aspect. In this work, a group of striking workers cluster by a factory waving flags while two suited men stand beyond the factory's locked gate. Khakhar's engagement with social issues and labour conditions is not entirely clear, for, as he said himself, 'I am at a loss to know exactly what my feelings are towards these people. At one time I feel fully sympathetic towards these people; but at other times I also feel against their hypocrisy.'[33]

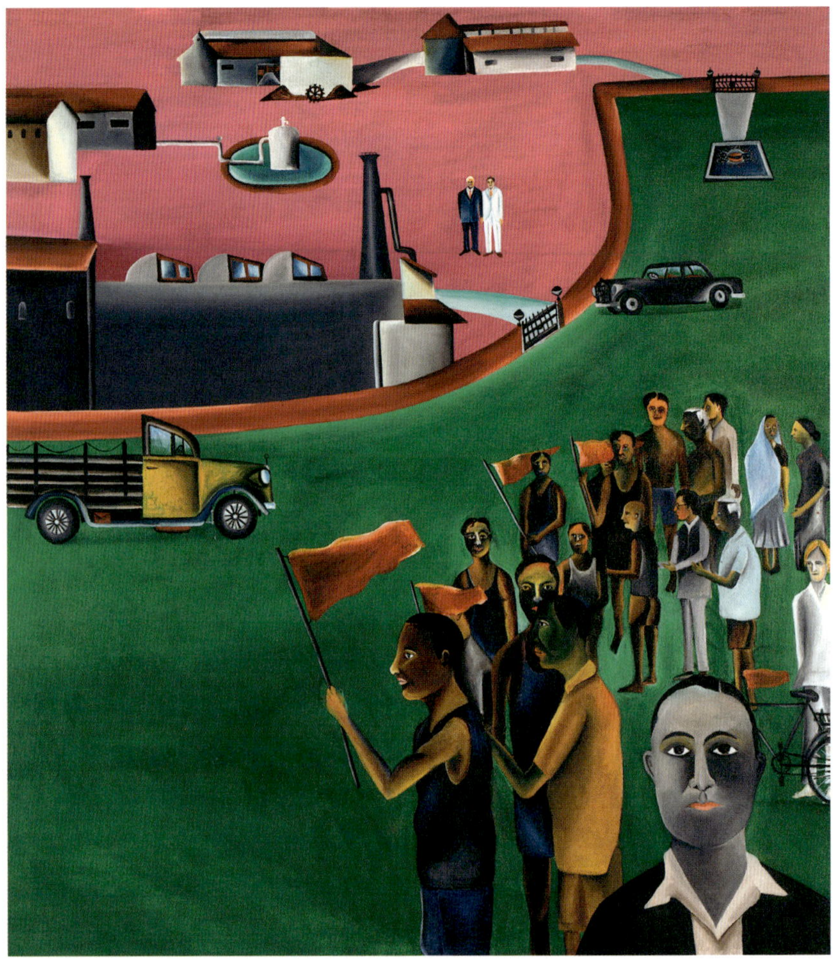

Untitled (1975), a delicate watercolour, was owned originally by Khakhar's close friend and peer, artist Howard Hodgkin, and is inscribed on the reverse 'To / Howard / With love / Bhupen.' The pair first met in New Delhi in 1968 at the First Triennale-India and struck up an enduring friendship. The work depicts a canopied daybed in a sprawling garden, recalling romantic Mughal and Rajput scenes (see cat. 22 & 60). Khakhar would later stay with Hodgkin at his Wiltshire home during a residency in 1979. This was a formative time in his personal life, after which he openly referred to his homosexuality.

BHUPEN KHAKHAR

74 Untitled

1975 | watercolour on paper | 25 × 35.2 cm | private collection, London/Karachi

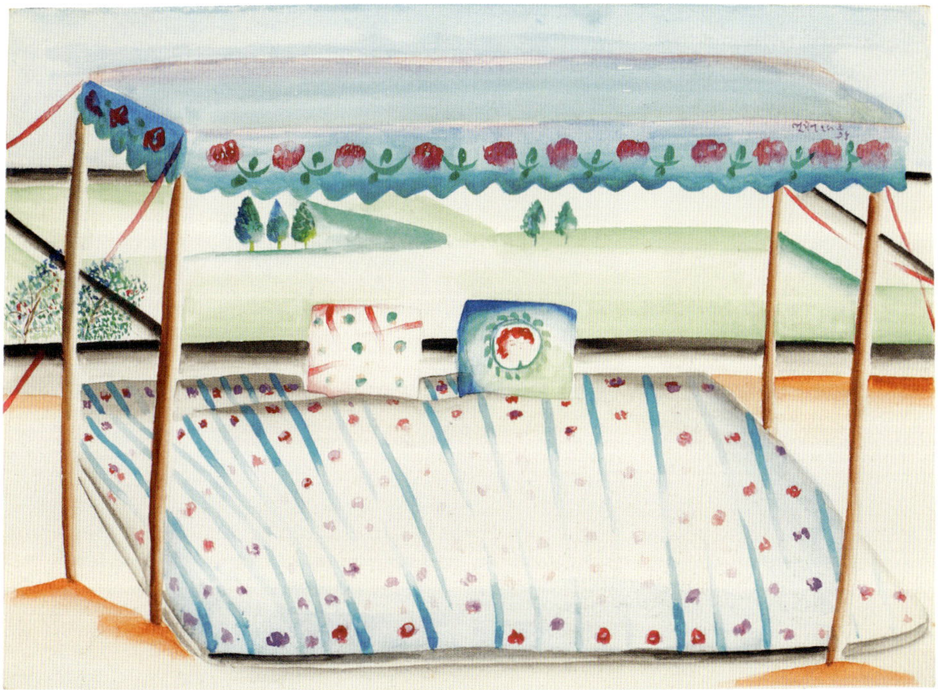

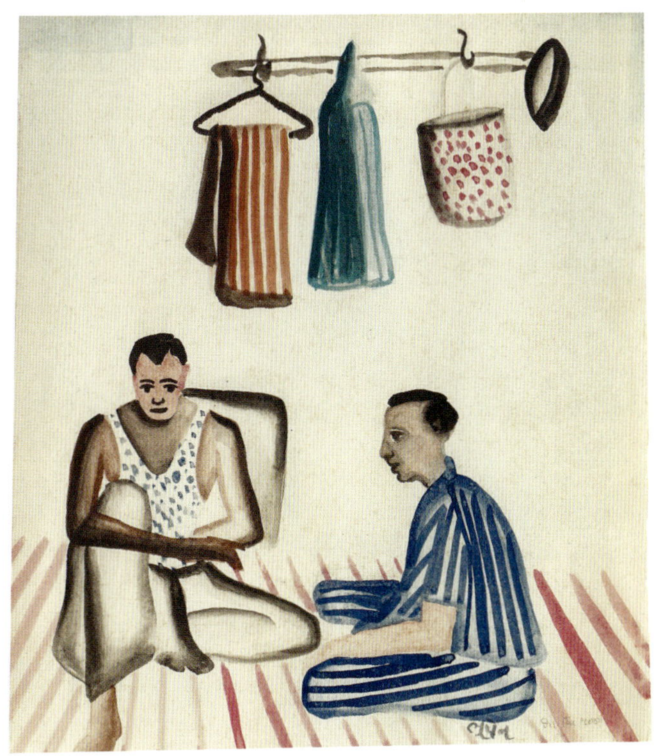

BHUPEN KHAKHAR

75 In the Room

1979 | watercolour on paper | 30.5 × 26.9 cm | private collection, London/Karachi

In the Room (1979), featuring two men sitting together in a domestic setting, is an example of Khakhar's confident use of watercolour. The medium lent Khakhar a painterly speed unachievable with oil and was used by the artist for more spontaneous recordings of his surroundings. Khakhar's watercolours are numerous and, often small scale, can be considered diaristic in their nature.

ZAHOOR UL AKHLAQ

76 Untitled

1974 | acrylic on canvas | 144.75 × 101.6 cm | private collection, London/Karachi

ZAHOOR UL AKHLAQ

77 Untitled

c.1975 | acrylic on canvas | 152.5 × 105 cm | private collection

ZAHOOR UL AKHLAQ

78 # Untitled (2)

1990 | acrylic on canvas | 137 × 91.5 cm | private collection, London/Karachi

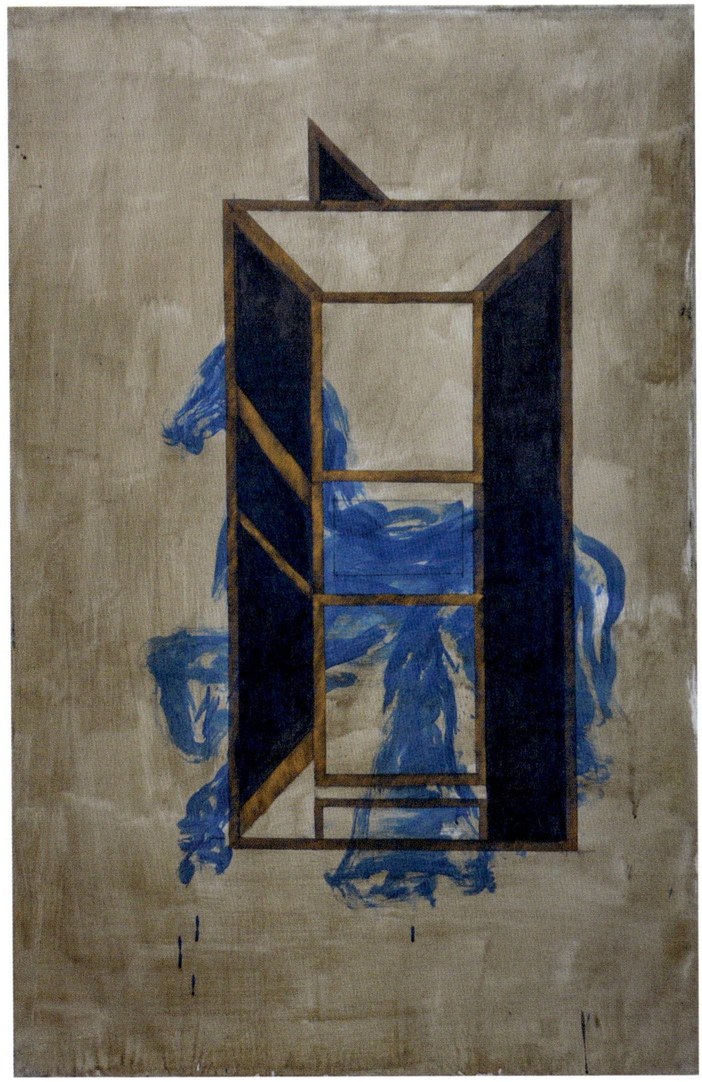

Zahoor ul Akhlaq (1941–1999, b. Delhi, India; d. Lahore, Pakistan) is credited with being a defining force in the contemporary engagement with South Asian miniature painting. Departing from his studies at the NCA, Lahore, and studying at the Hornsey College of Art, the RCA in London, and Yale University, New Haven, Akhlaq challenged prevailing hierarchies concerning the treatment of traditional art forms and looked to colour field painting to innovate historic techniques. Akhlaq experimented with sculpture, architecture and Islamic geometry, setting a precedent for subsequent generations of artists, many of whom he taught at NCA.

Untitled (1974) and *Untitled* (*c.*1975) are enigmatic early works. The artist customarily avoided defining himself and it is possible that this work was, as suggested by Iftikhar Dadi, a means of negotiating pressing social and moral issues at a time when public debate was curtailed.[34] In *Untitled* (1974) the calligraphic marks suggest sword-like forms; there is also an interplay between riding and writing (see cat. 97). The artist often worked in monochrome and used black-and-white photocopies to develop his paintings as a way of disrupting the value in traditional miniature training placed on artists creating true and accurate copies.

Untitled (2) (1990) is a quintessential visual play created by Akhlaq through the use of a window frame. Informed by the layout of Mughal album pages (see cat. 5, 15, 53) and suffused with the language of abstraction, the painting shows how Akhlaq's experimentation echoes with younger generations of artists.

ZAHOOR UL AKHLAQ

79 Untitled

1992–93 | acrylic on wood | 31.8 × 22.3 cm | Tate

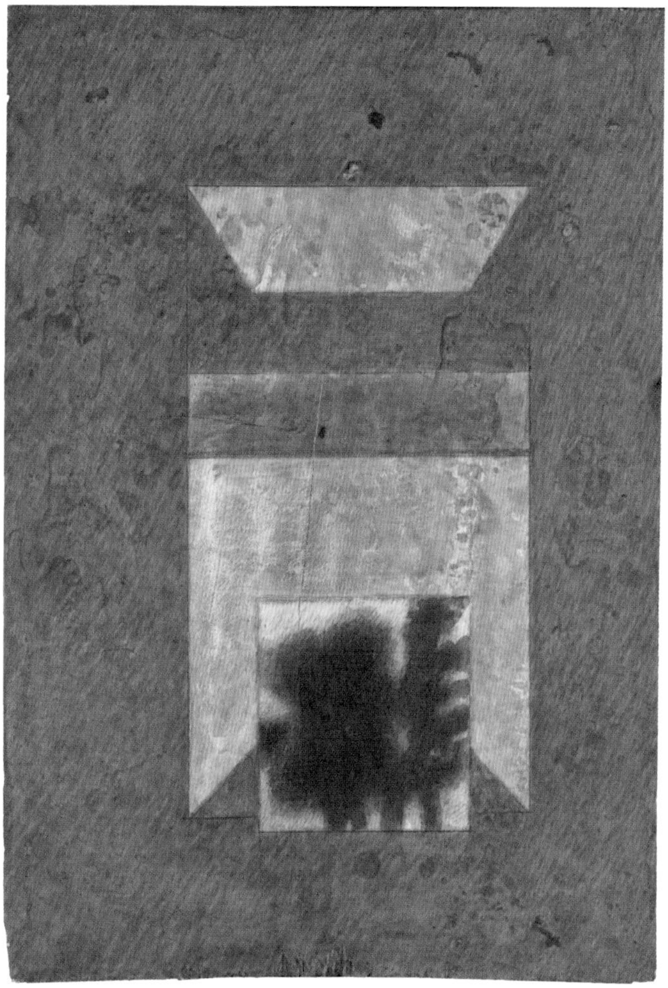

The collection of works *Untitled*, *Untitled* and *Untitled* (all 1992–93) and *Untitled (From the Takhti series)* (1994) are drawn from Akhlaq's *Takhti* series. Each small painting, made during a period of intense travelling, is painted on board in a format derived from the *takhti*, a wooden, wipeable slate still used in some schools for writing. Akhlaq uses multiple layers of quick-drying acrylic to form images that look like educational tools and with thick borders confuse the painting's beginning and end. Discussing his minimal palette, the artist said: 'because black is the beginning – it becomes a challenge. I try not to make it easy for myself. And I become very intensely involved in the structure.'[35]

ZAHOOR UL AKHLAQ

80 Untitled

1992–93 | acrylic on wood | 31.9 × 22.7 cm | Tate

ZAHOOR UL AKHLAQ

81 Untitled

1992–93 | acrylic on wood | 31.8 × 22.6 cm | Tate

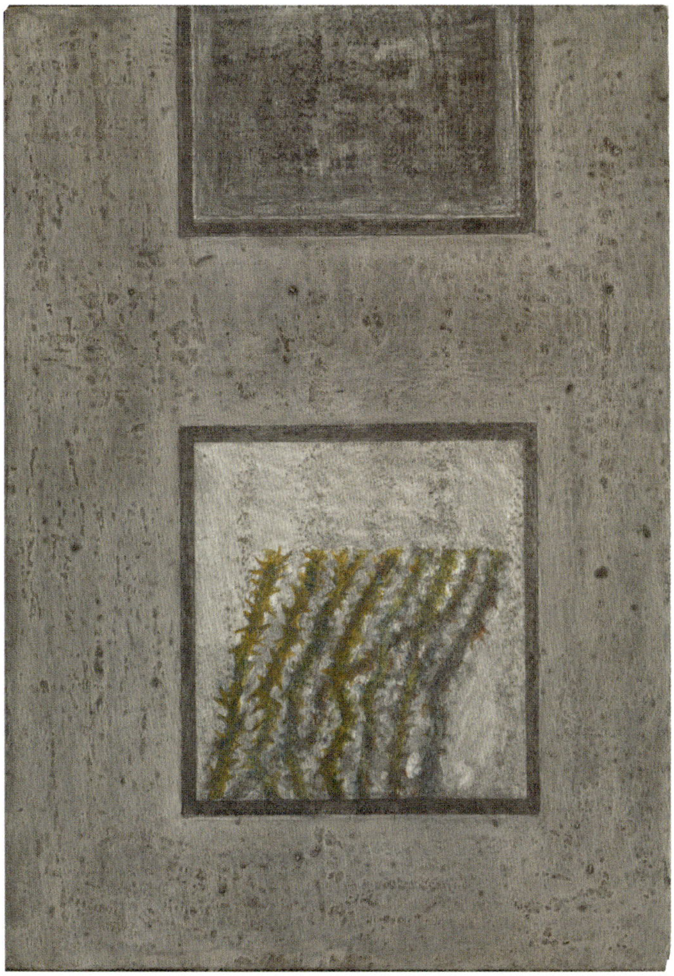

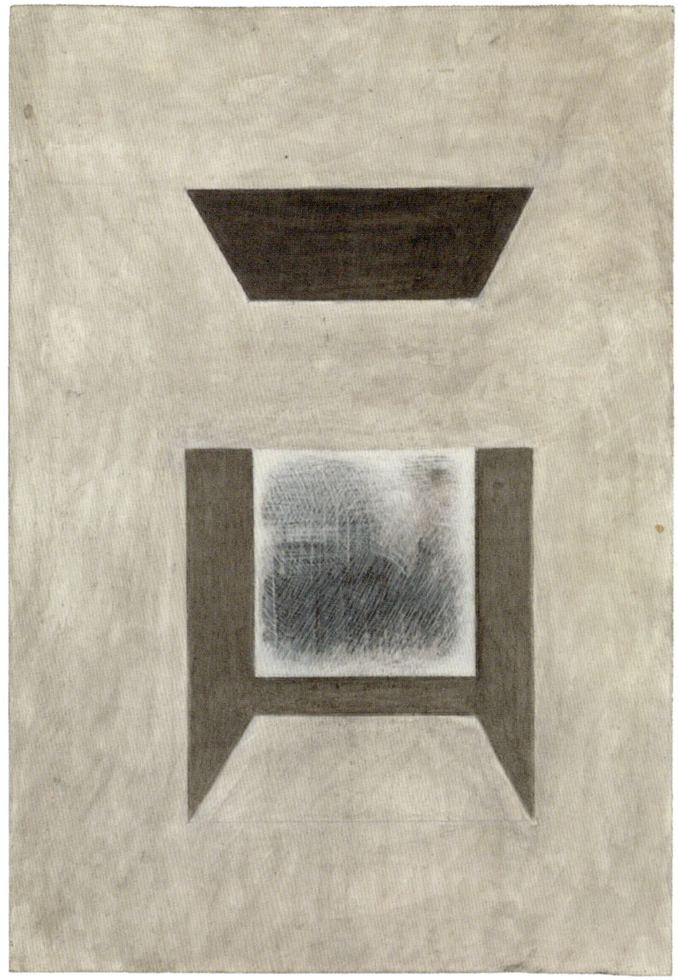

ZAHOOR UL AKHLAQ

82 Untitled (from the Takhti series)

1994 | mixed media on board | 22.3 × 40.6 cm | private collection, London/Karachi

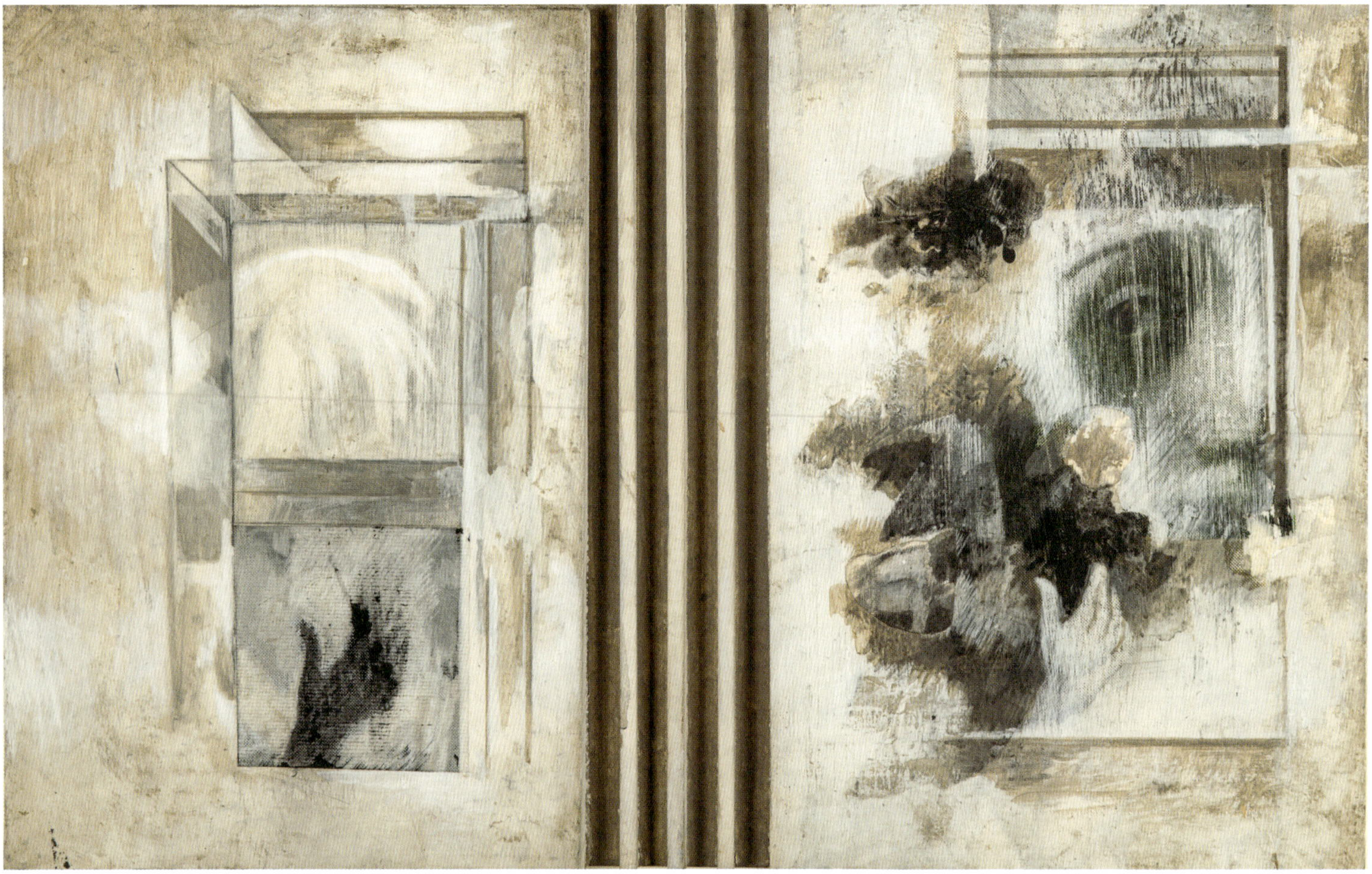

HOWARD HODGKIN

83 Tea with Mrs Parikh (second version)

1974–77 | oil on wood | 46.5 × 51.7 cm | private collection, London/Karachi

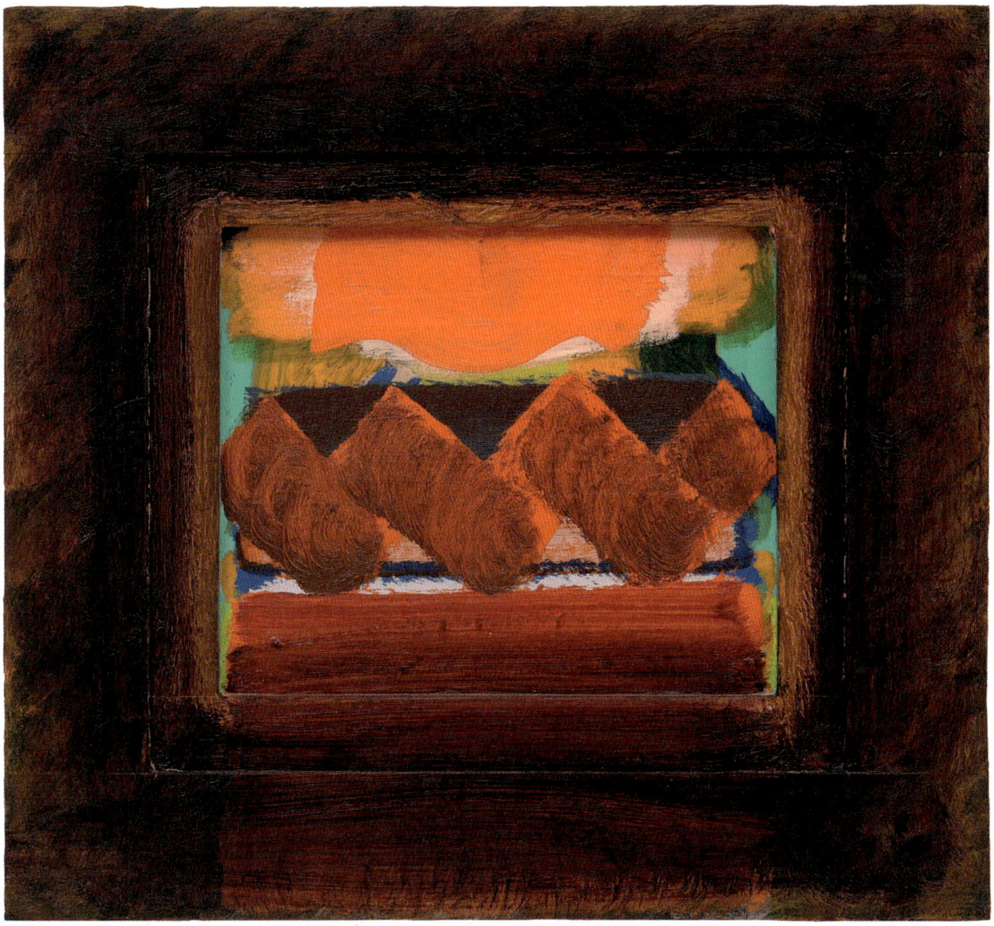

British painter Howard Hodgkin (1932–2017, London, UK) was a devoted collector of Indian miniatures (see cat. 67) and made countless trips to India for more than 50 years. Although an ostensibly abstract work, *Tea with Mrs Parikh* (1974–77) captures the artist's sensory impression of a moment in India: the gaps between the brushstrokes little breaths of natural light permeating an interior space. It was in India that Hodgkin first began painting on wood. The slippery and less absorbent nature of the medium, compared to the grainy weave of a canvas, meant that he could come back to these works over a number of years.

Although the thick red border and hot colours of this reworked panel appear to recall Rajput painting (see cat. 21 & 58), the artist was reluctant to make connections between his famous collection of Indian miniatures and his own artistic practice:

> I use strong colours in my own paintings so people often imagine that Indian painting had a great influence on my work. There are one or two pictures in my collection which have very strong colour which could remotely relate to my own work; but I dislike the comparison because it is made so glibly. Indian paintings are small and painted with gouache or opaque watercolour on paper. My pictures are painted with thick oil paint on wood in bright colours. Many of the Indian pictures in my collection are not in fact very coloured. Their predominant shade is one of those beautiful beige colours, the tinted cream of Indian hand-made paper.[36]

HOWARD HODGKIN

84 Kerala

1992 | oil on wood | 23.5 × 35.6 cm |
private collection, London/Karachi

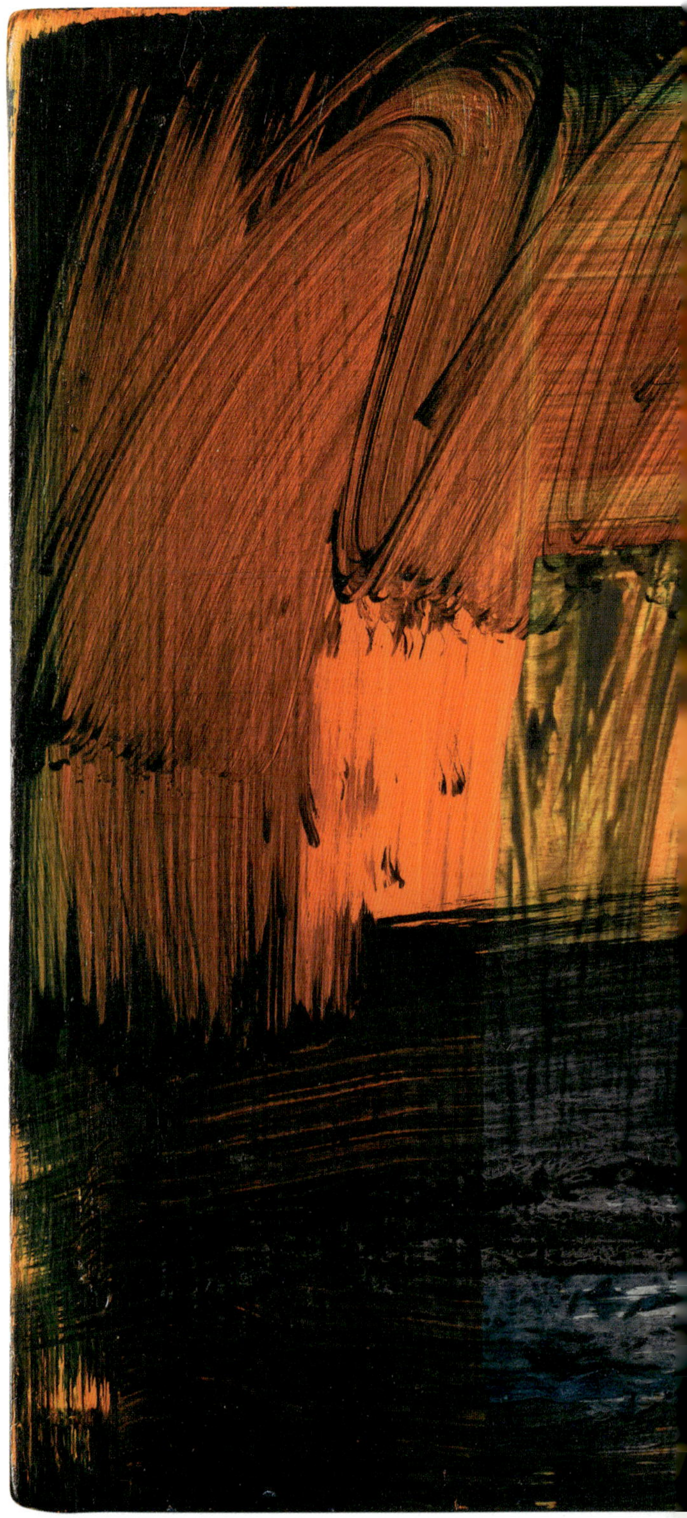

The title of *Kerala* (1992) specifically grounds this painting to Hodgkin's travel in this region and the multisensory experiences of his time there. Andrew Graham Dixon connected this tension between pictorial form and felt reality in Hodgkin's works with the same sensation in a *Ragamala* painting in his collection:

> To see the two lovers who gaze so intensely at each other, rapt in a field of high artifice, ... is perhaps to sense the deeper, unpredictable affinity between the art of the collector and the art he collects. When Hodgkin succeeds, in his own painting, he engineers a tension between the conventions of pictorial form and the pressures of the lived, felt reality which is precisely analogous to the effect of this sixteenth-century picture.[37]

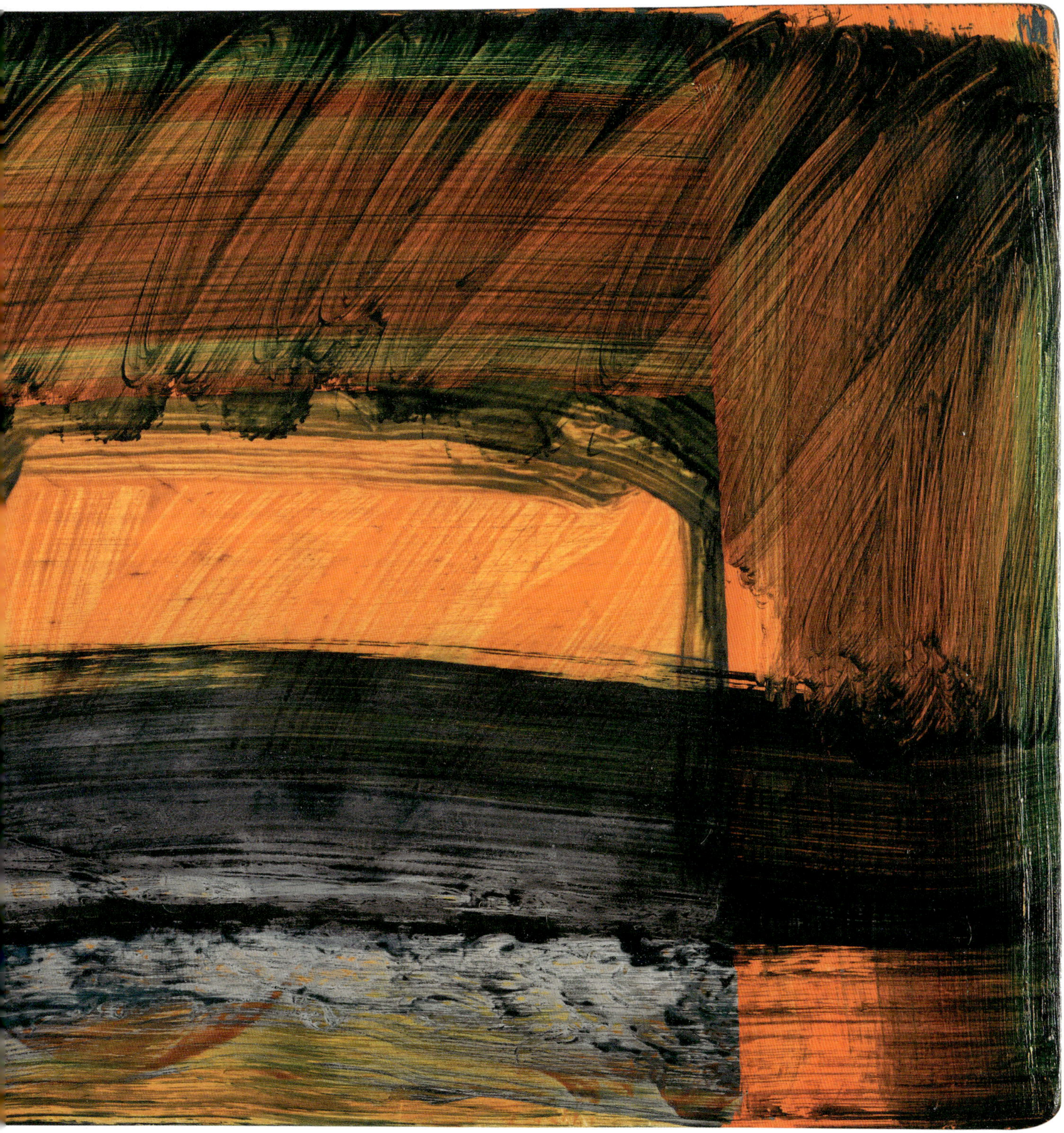

MOHAN SAMANT

85 In the Beginning there was a Man, a Woman, and a Benevolent Ghost

1980 | graphite, watercolour, ink and oil paint on paper on canvas, and paint and sand on canvas | 133.5 × 133 cm | presented by Jillian Samant (Tate Americas Foundation 2020)

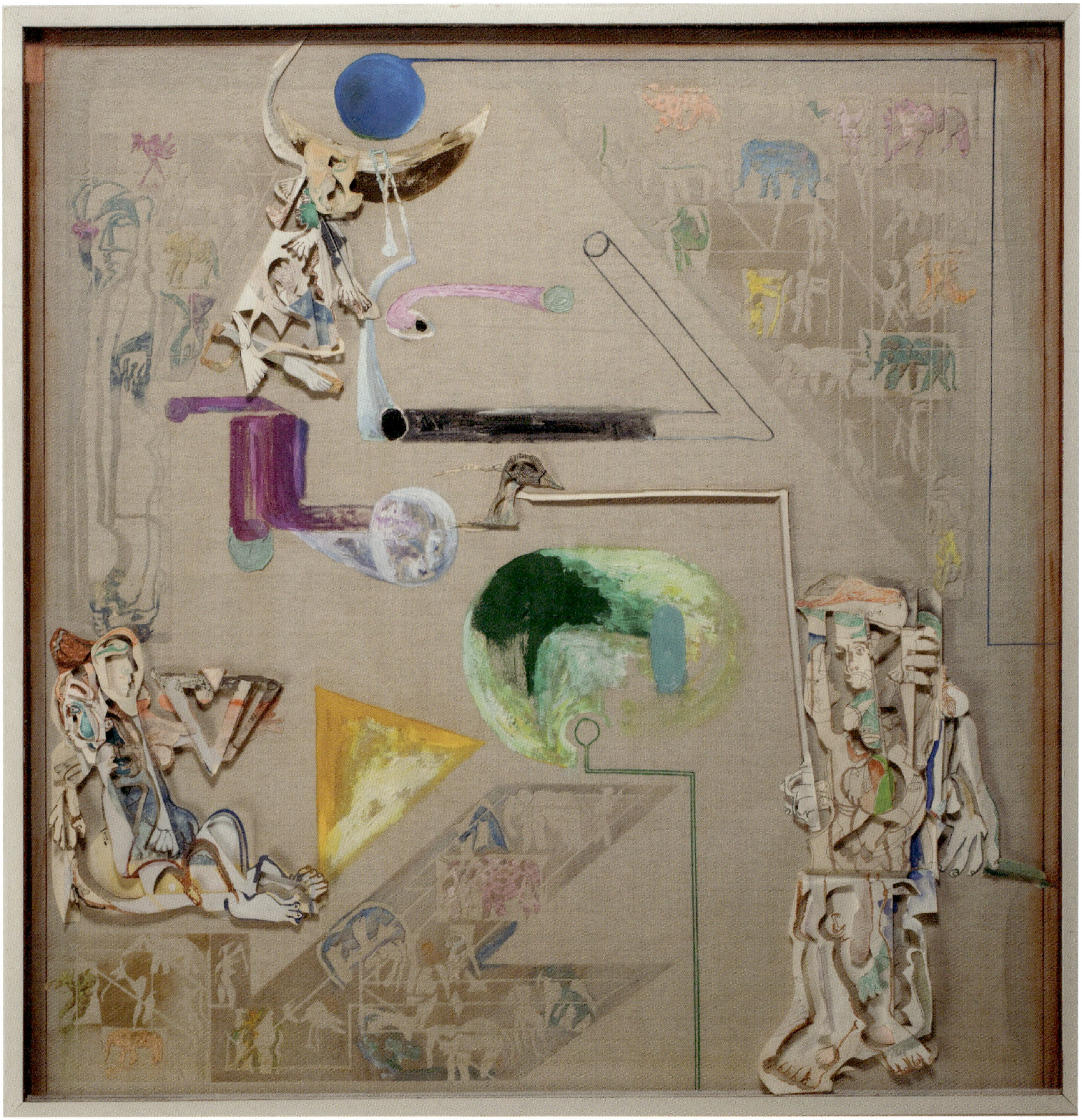

MOHAN SAMANT

86 Untitled

1980–90 | mixed media on paper | 56.5 × 77.5 cm | courtesy estate of Mohan Samant

Mohan Samant (1924–2004, b. Mumbai, India; d. New York, USA), is considered a pioneer of Indian modernism, associated with the Progressive Artists' Group following his diploma from the Sir J.J. School of Art, Mumbai in 1952. With an experimental practice, his style changed throughout his career and drew on diverse visual sources marrying miniature painting with Pre-Columbian sculpture and Egyptian hieroglyphs, among other traditions. Continually shifting processes and approaching each medium with confidence, his paintings became progressively more sculptural with complex wire constructions built into their surfaces, and introducing frieze-like elements of depth with paper and metal. In addition to being an artist, Samant played the *sarangi*, an Indian stringed instrument.

In the Beginning there was a Man, a Woman, and a Benevolent Ghost (1980) demonstrates Samant's singular style born of experimentation with paper relief and wire throughout the 1970s. Unorthodox in approach, this painting is made on unprimed canvas and incorporates oil, watercolour, ink, graphite and sand. As in miniatures, Samant combines several perspectives in his image of man, woman and ghost, and adds sections detailed with animals reminiscent of the lavish ornamentation contained in the borders of miniatures.

Untitled (1980–90) features a man and a small bird, crudely depicted in a manner reminiscent of Picasso. Samant drew on myriad creative sources and painted impulsively, finding pure pleasure in the unplanned act. He explained,

> In my painting, I have swallowed the entire history of thousands of years and synchronised it into a modern idiom. Nobody can tell me I am a copyist because I am just as modern as anyone else except that my influences do not come from the contemporary art world; they come from the entire panorama of art history.

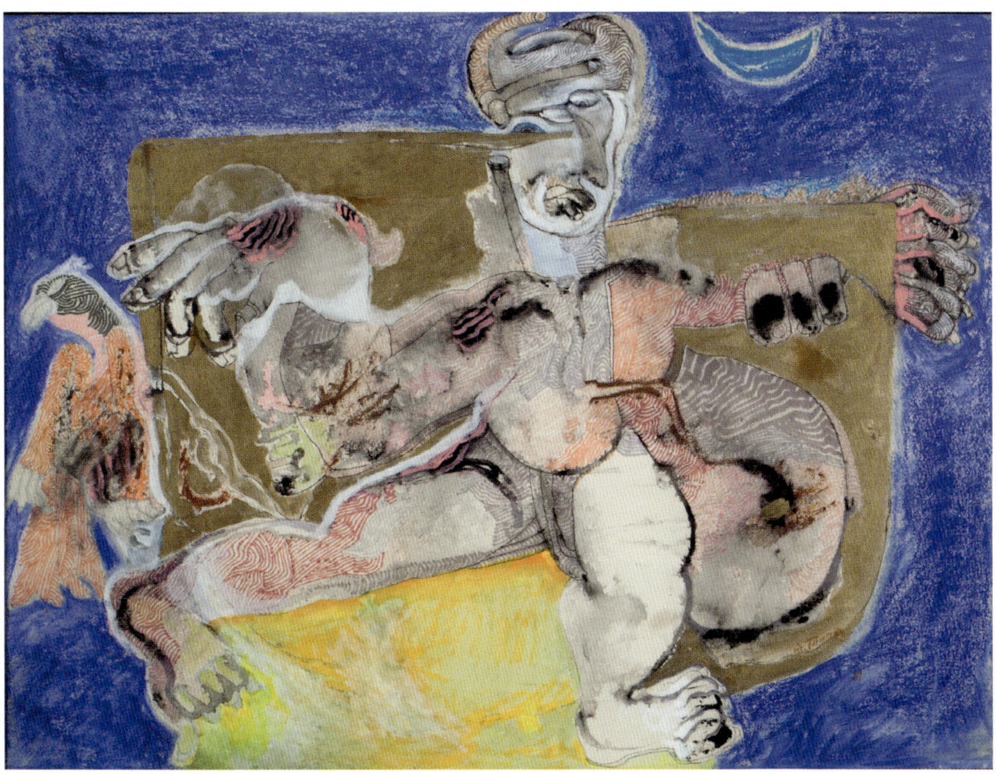

MOHAN SAMANT

87 Untitled

c.1985 | graphite, watercolour, ink and oil paint on paper on canvas, and paint and sand on canvas | 77.2 × 62 cm | presented by Jillian Samant (Tate Americas Foundation 2020)

Untitled (*c.*1985) is a painting that incorporates paper cut-outs and sand among its mixed media. The work's eroticized imagery shows couples engaged in sexual intercourse, echoing erotic works of Pahari painting (see cat. 64). The undulating surface, both carved into and raised, along with the contrast between paper folds against clumps of paint, energizes the work and contributes to its dynamism.

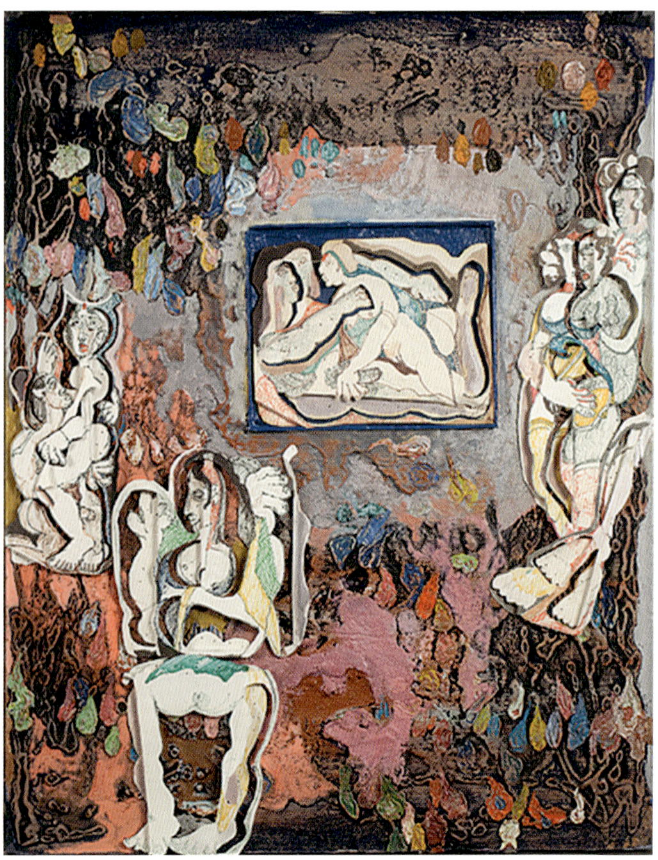

MOHAN SAMANT

88 An Angel and a Firefly

2002 | watercolour on paper | 61 × 45.7 cm | courtesy of the estate of Mohan Samant

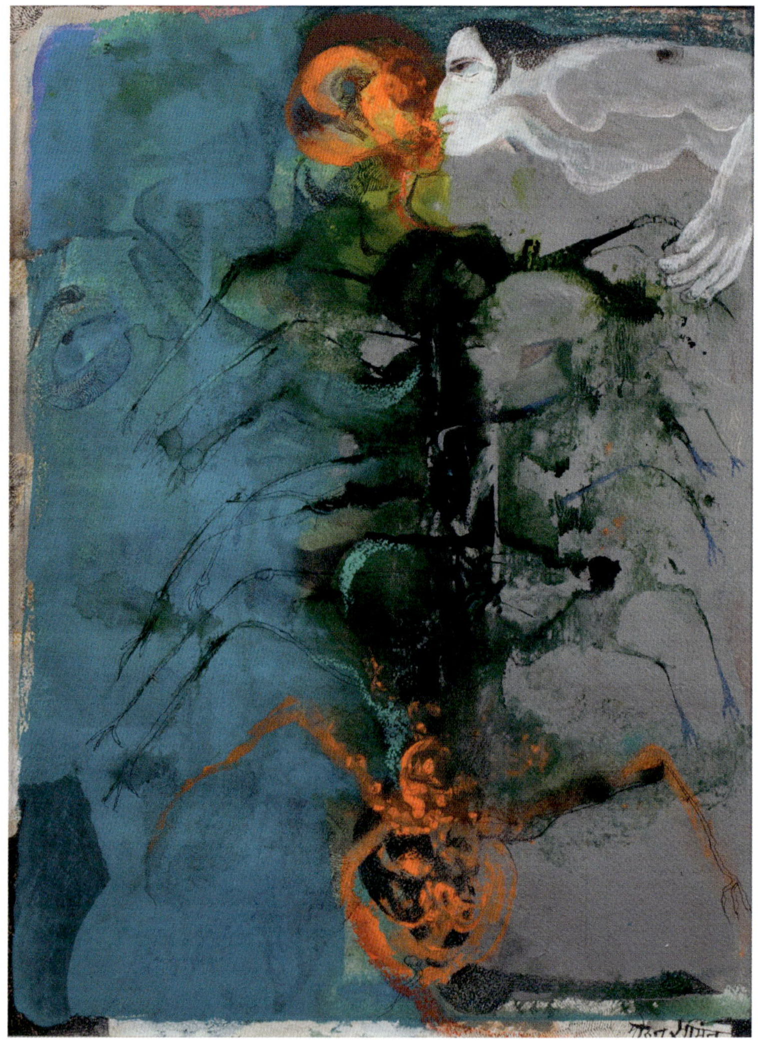

An Angel and a Firefly (2002) is characteristic of Samant's inventive visual language in which he usese watercolour to create a viscous and textured image. Samant brought together diverse references combining the spiritual with the everyday in imagined scenes, as he does in this piece, where an angel hovers and seems to embrace a cluster of elaborate fireflies.

ALAN DAVIE

89 Meditations on Jain Cosmology No. 4 (with Dog and Fox)

1984 | oil on canvas | 174.7 × 215.9 cm | National Galleries of Scotland

The art of the Scottish painter and musician Alan Davie (1920–2014, b. Grangemouth; d. Hertfordshire, UK) famously referenced religious and mystical iconography from a range of world cultures: Navajo Indian, Aboriginal Australian, Coptic, Inuit, Carib, Jain and more. Inspired by Carl Jung's theories of symbolism and the collective unconscious, his paintings are an 'evocation of the inexpressible'.[38] 'What I am doing is fundamentally the same as artists of remote times', he wrote. 'Engaged in a shamanistic conjuring up of visions which will link us metaphorically with mysterious and spiritual forces normally beyond our comprehension.'[39]

Davie first stumbled across Jain painting (see cat. 57) in the window display of a New York gallery in 1984, having never seen such imagery before in Britain. He bought a book on Jain cosmology and in the autumn of that year created a body of work (including five paintings of the *Mediations on Jain Cosmology* series) that incorporated Jain imagery.

In 1993, British artist Ian McKeever wrote of Alan Davie:

> Being a painter in Britain is a strange business. The English don't quite know what to think, or do about painting ... they like it clear cut, either figurative or abstract, a story or a formal problem. Beyond that they get stuck and as the going gets rougher they give up, get lazy ... So when a painter like Alan Davie comes along, who sits full square in the rough ground ... he is seen as an oddball, not quite fitting in or playing the game.[40]

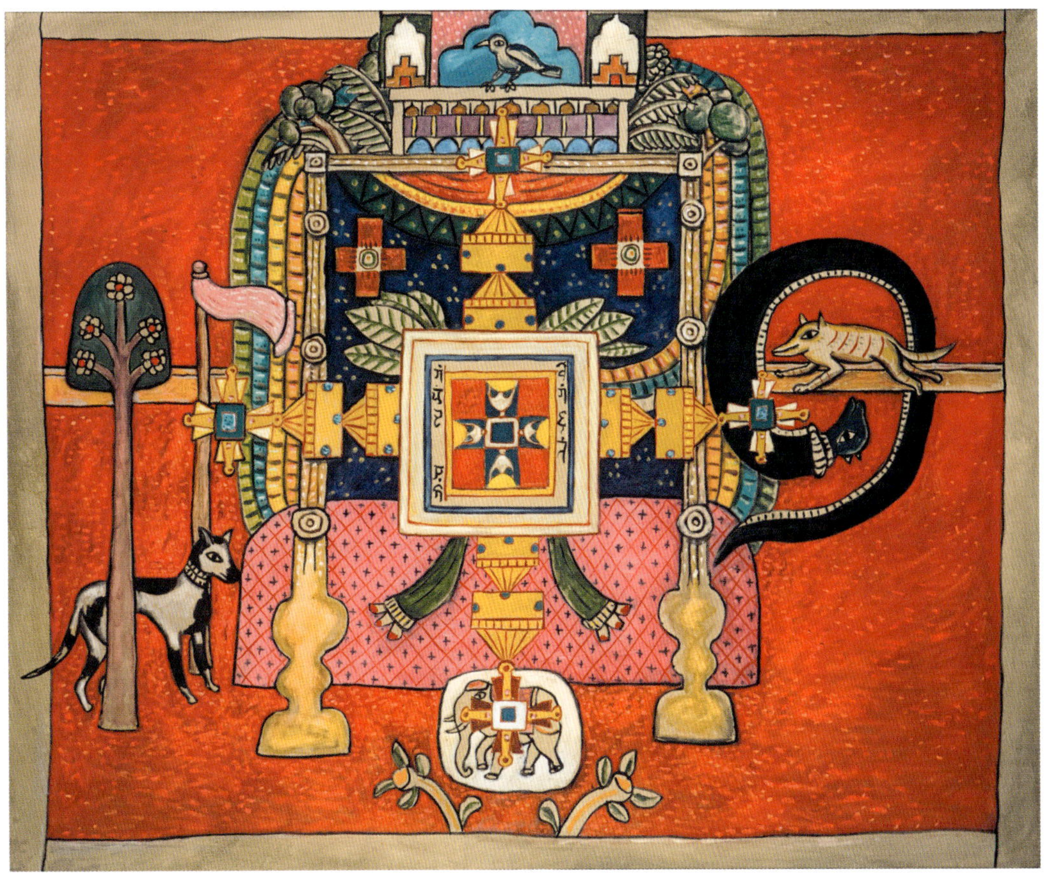

NILIMA SHEIKH

90 When Champa Grows Up

1984–85 | tempera on sanghaneri paper | 12 paintings, each 22 × 35 cm | Leicester Museums and Galleries

Nilima Sheikh (b. 1945, New Delhi, India) studied history at Delhi University before her Master's in painting at the Faculty of Fine Arts, Maharaja Sayajirao University of Baroda in 1971. Sheikh roots her work in South Asian painting traditions, including miniatures and scroll painting. Using tempera, Sheikh translates these painting conventions into narrative works, often including text from folk songs, concerned with feminine experiences in the context of India's customs and politics.

When Champa Grows Up (1984–85), Sheikh's landmark 12-piece work, details the story of a woman, Champa, murdered for her dowry by her parents-in-law after an arranged marriage. Sheikh personally knew the woman and chose a miniature format based on Pattachitra (scroll painting, traditionally done on cloth) to narrate Champa's story, including scenes witnessed by Sheikh. Woven into the delicate paintings is text from Gujarati poems to emphasize the anguish and despair. The work recalls the vivid realism of some Guler painters of the late eighteenth century (such as cat. 65).

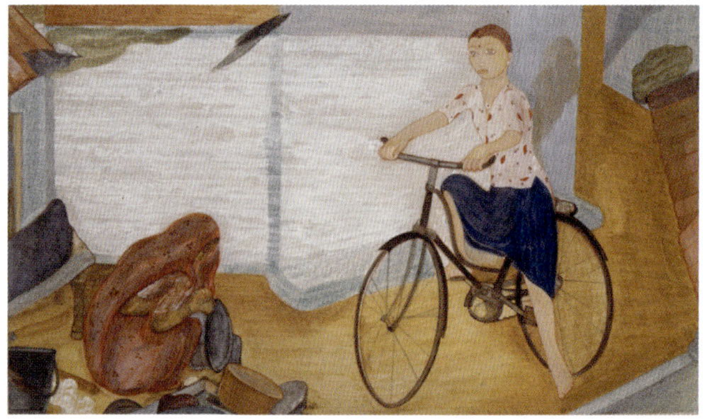

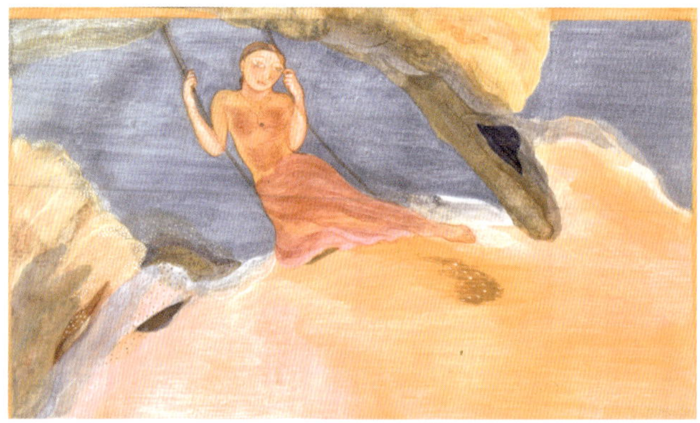

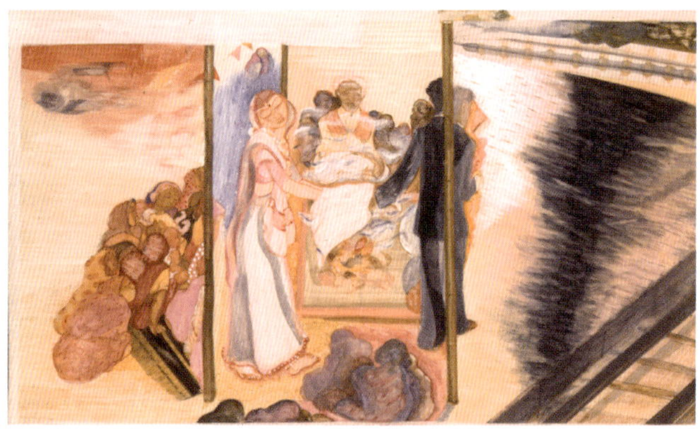

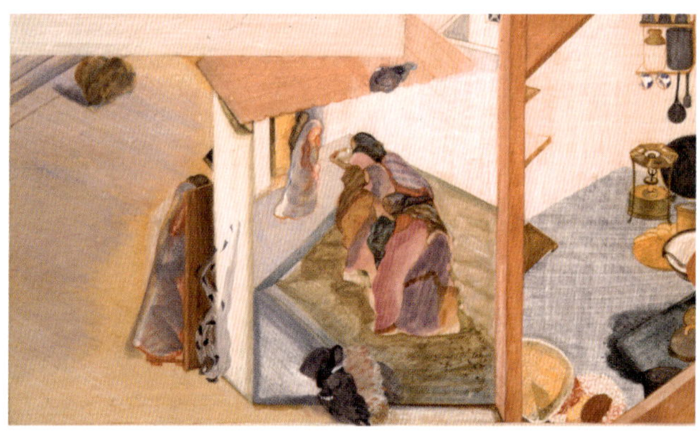

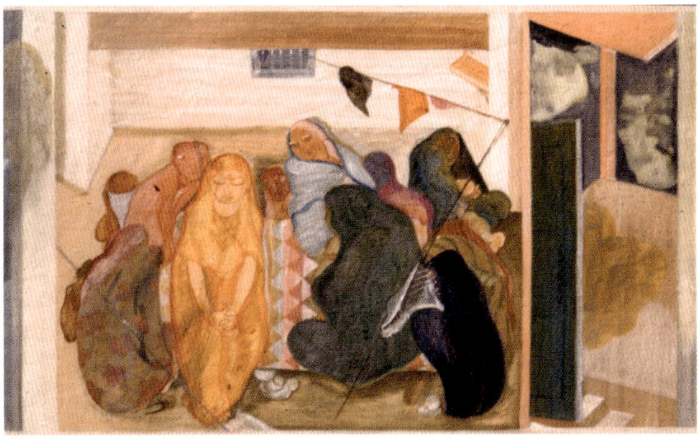

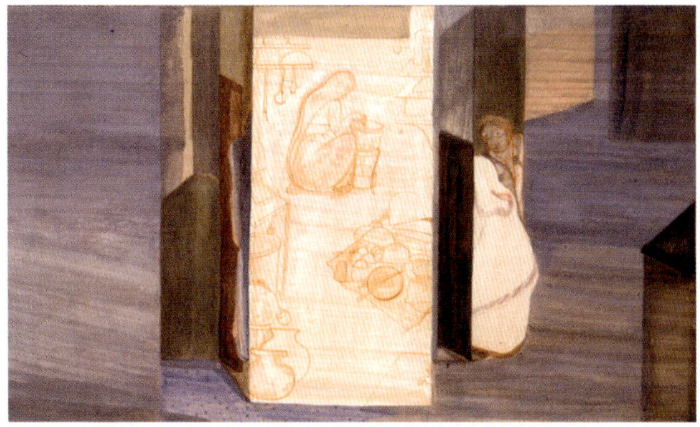

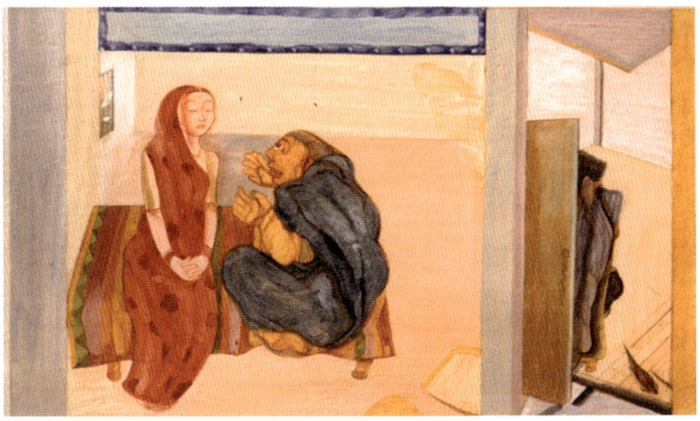

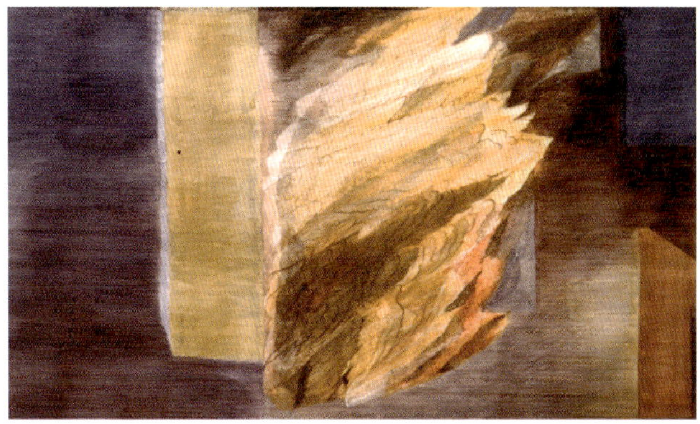

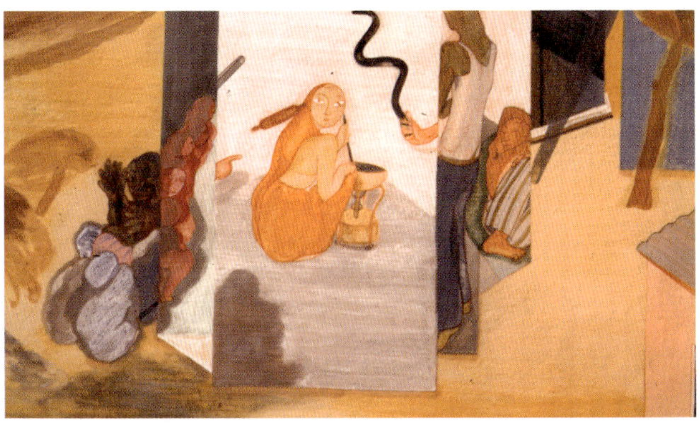

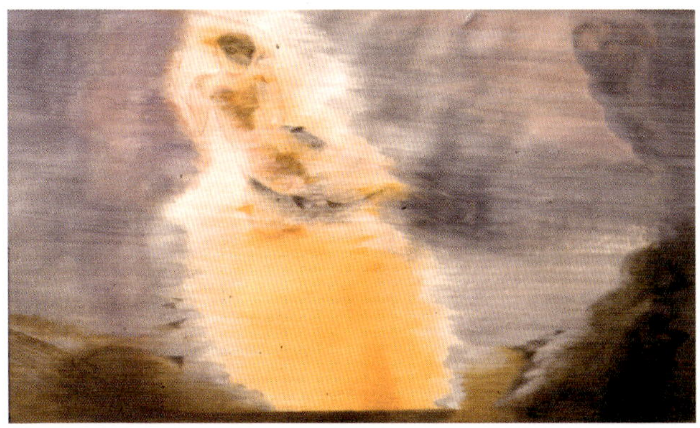

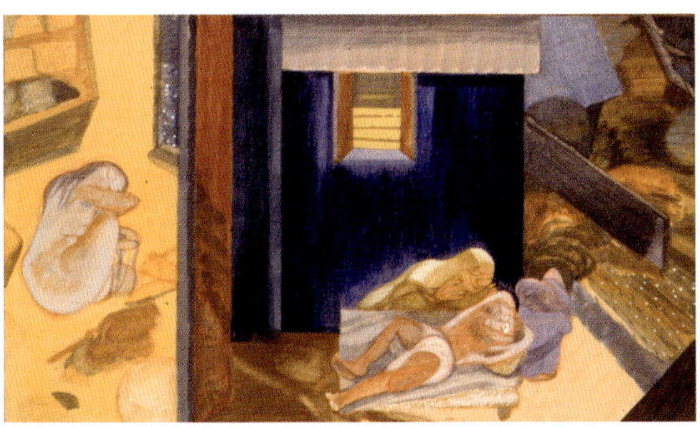

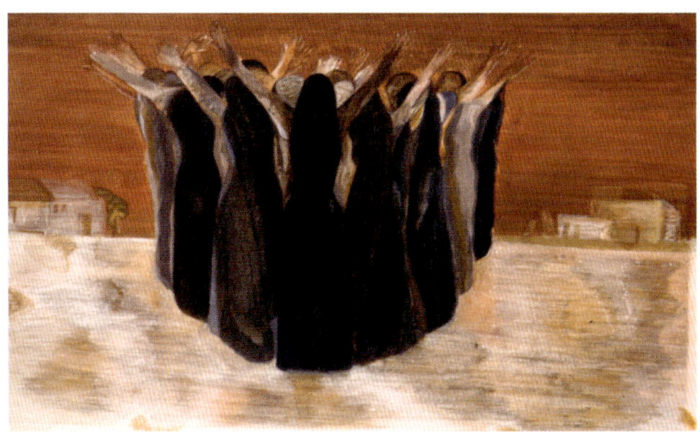

ARPITA SINGH

91 Emergency

1990 | watercolour on paper | 45.7 × 59.7 cm | private collection

In her dense figurative paintings, Arpita Singh (b.1937, Baranagar, India) draws on traditional Indian art forms such as miniature painting and folk art. Her paintings often represent her own complex emotions and childhood memories, as well as a fascination with maps and films. She is also among an important group of women artists who emerged on the artistic scene in 1970s' India, combining personal experiences with feminist and political concerns in their work. She repeatedly includes a range of personal symbols in her paintings, such as cars, planes and watches, which speak of travel and the passing of time; and fruit, flowers and henna, referring to fertility, rituals and cycles of life.

Emergency (1990) presents a complex series of narratives, through multiple, distorted perspectives, related to 'The Emergency', one of the most controversial periods of Indian history. Between 1975 and 1977 Prime Minister Indira Ghandi declared a state of emergency, which provided her with the power to suspend civil liberties, imprison political opponents and censor the media.

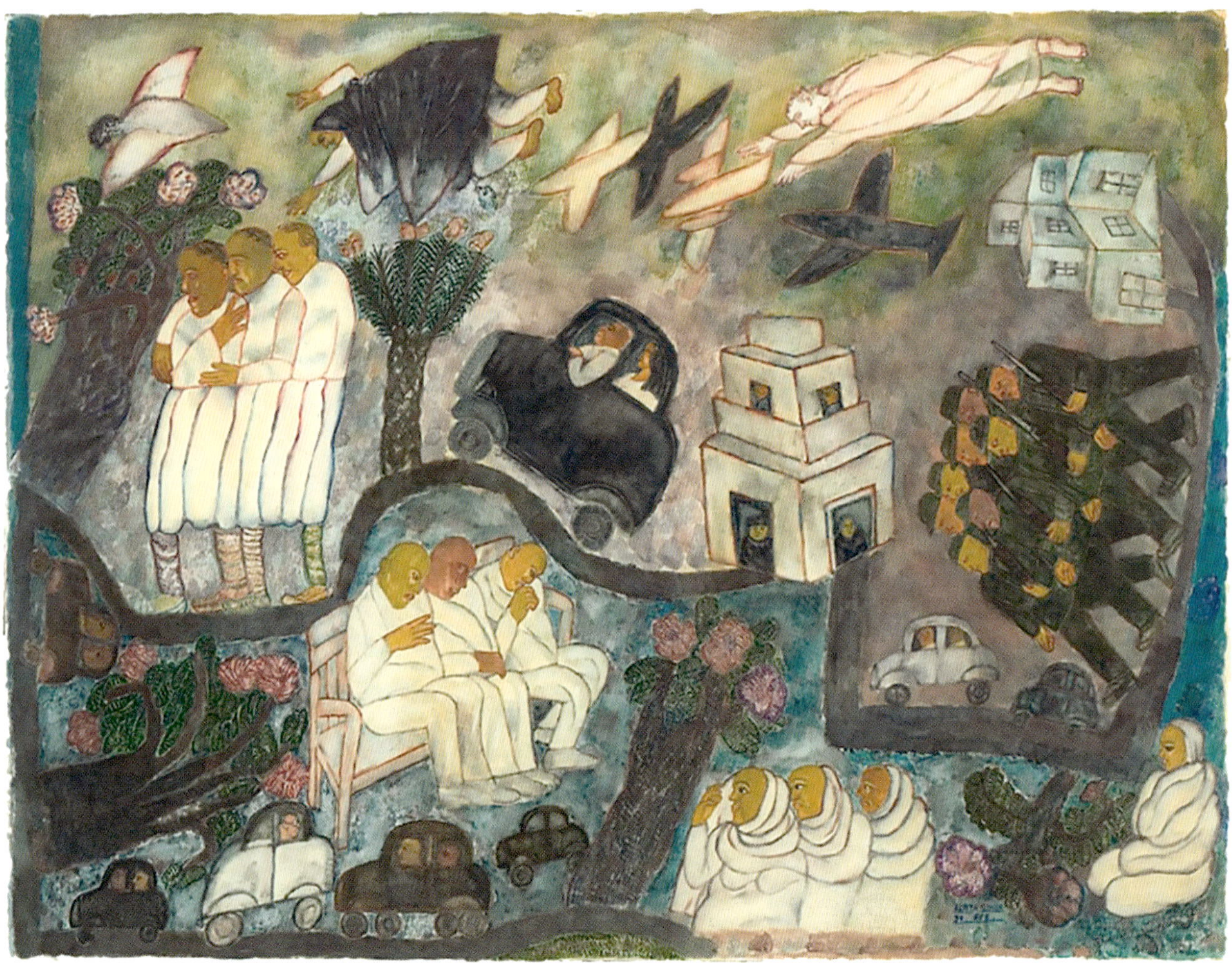

ARPITA SINGH

92 A Feminine Tale

1995 | reverse glass painting | 40.6 × 22.3 cm | private collection, London/Karachi

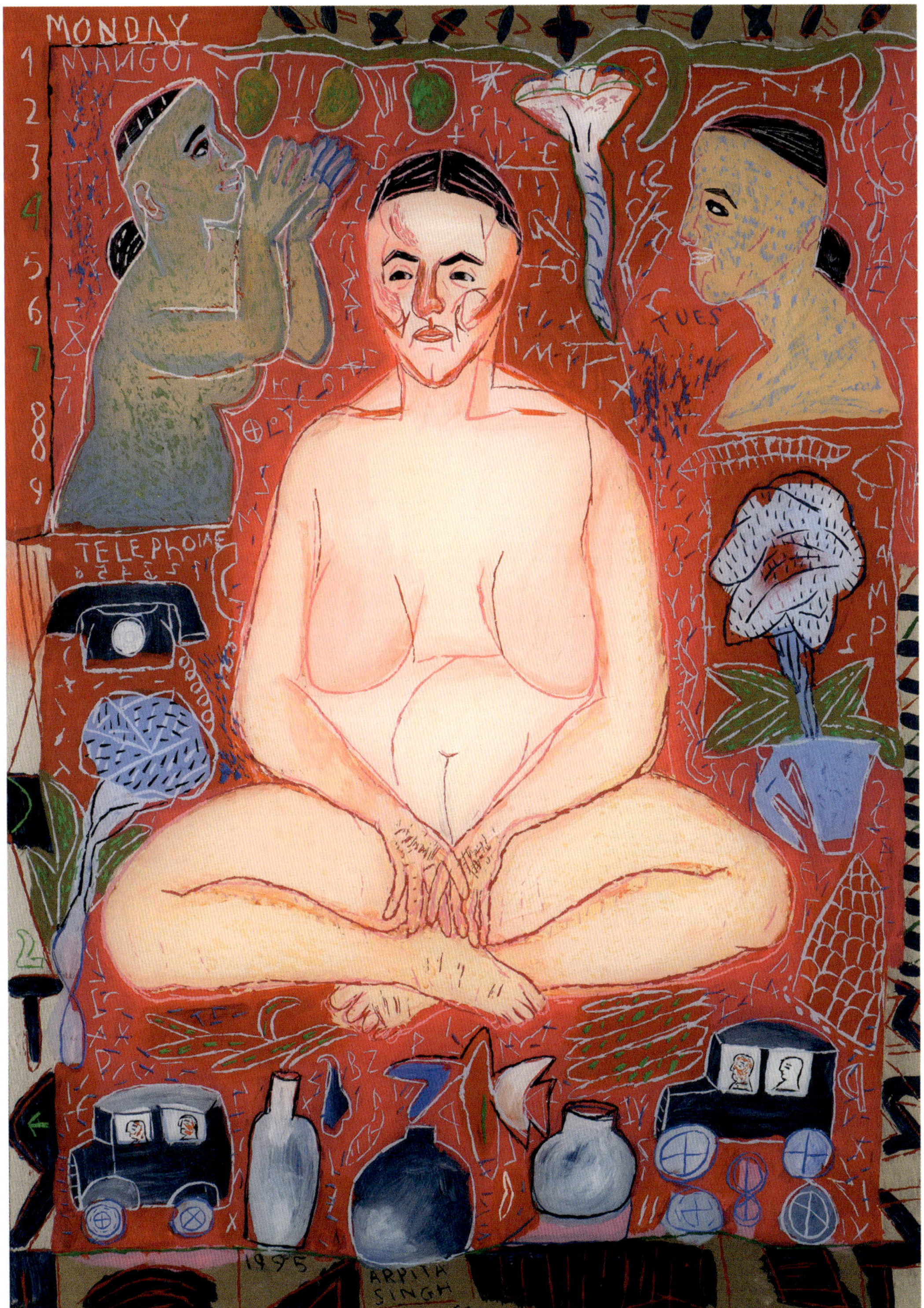

ARPITA SINGH

93 Untitled

1999 | oil on canvas | 130.2 × 121.9 cm | private collection

Singh often presents women in moments of duress and has spoken of depicting 'the secret world of women with their rites and activities'.[41] Critic Gayatri Sinha has written,

> Arpita Singh has pushed the visual lexicon of the middle-aged woman further than almost any other woman artist. The anomaly between the aging body and the residue of desire, between the ordinary and the divine and the threat of the violent fluxes of the impinging external world gives her work its piquancy and edge.[42]

Many of Singh's paintings include ornamental edges that recall both the richly illustrated borders of traditional miniatures and stylistic devices from traditional kantha embroidery.

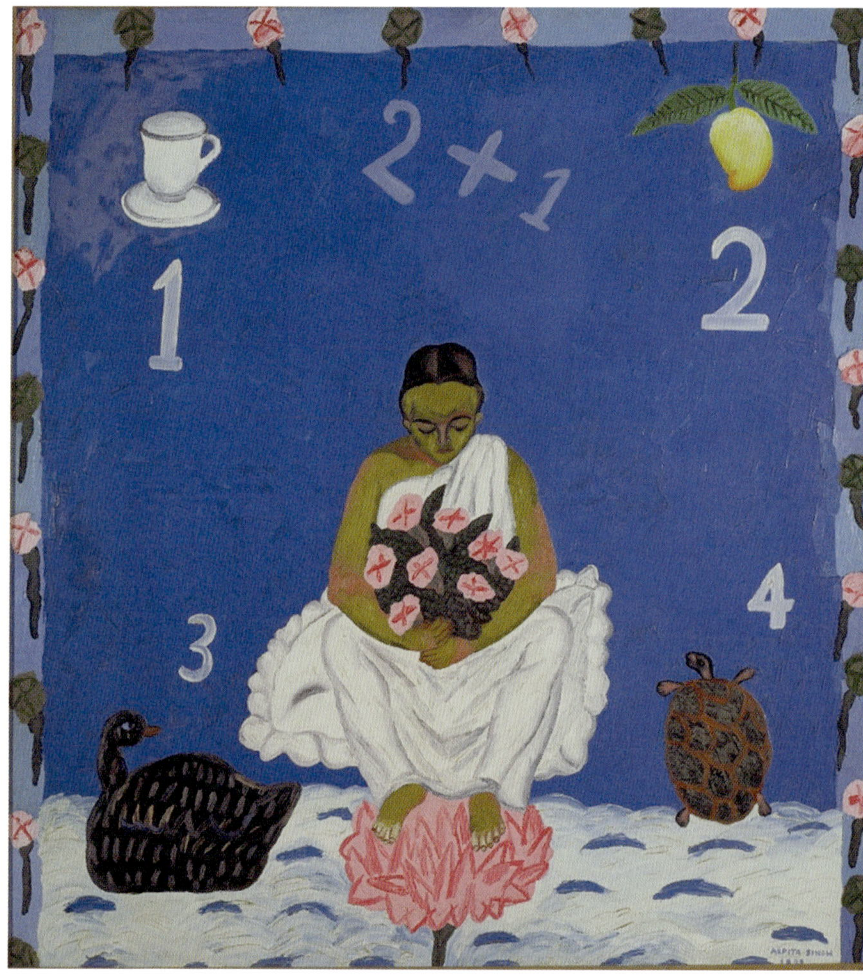

ARPITA SINGH

94 Noor Jehan

2001 | watercolour on mount board | 61 × 40.6 cm | private collection

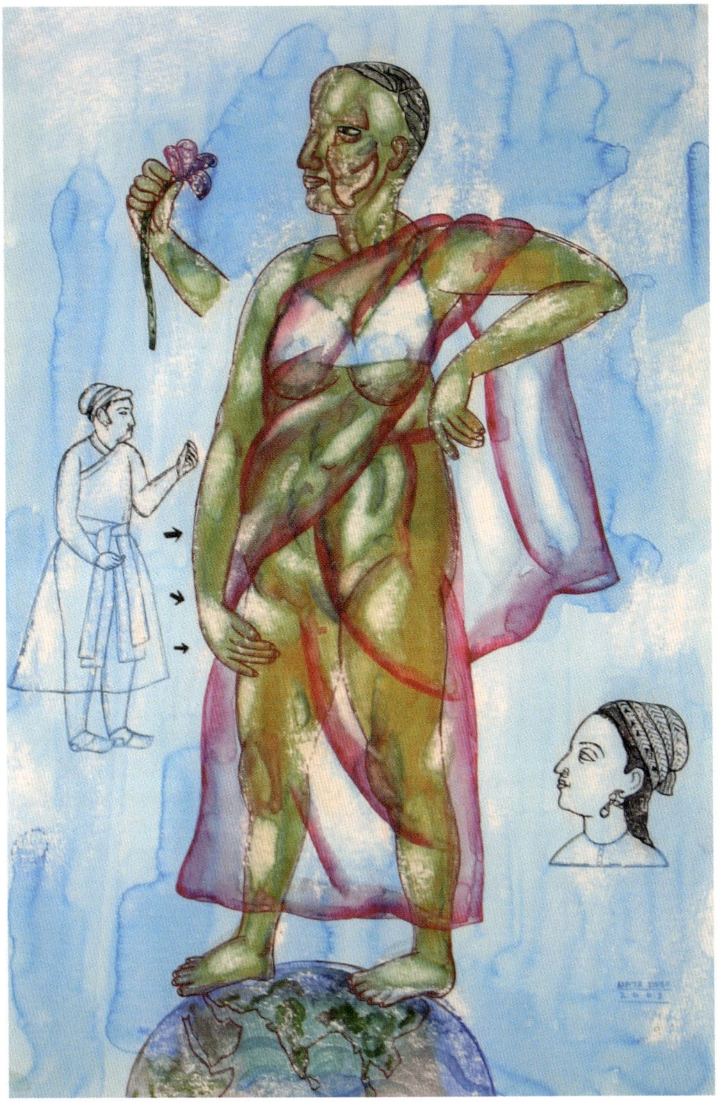

ARPITA SINGH

95 Untitled

2001 | watercolour on mount board | 61 × 40.6 cm | private collection

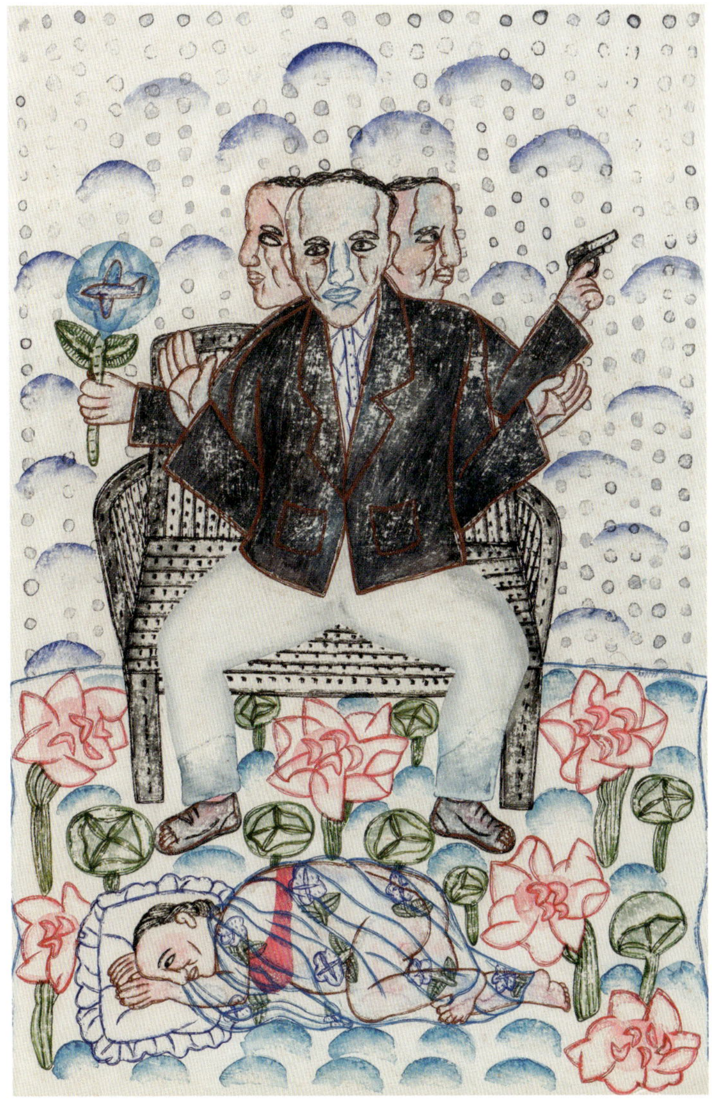

SHAHZIA SIKANDER

96 The Scroll

1989–90 | vegetable colour, dry pigment, watercolour and tea on wasli paper | 34.3 × 162.2 cm | courtesy of the artist

Shahzia Sikander (b.1969, Lahore, Pakistan) was taught at the NCA in Lahore by the miniaturist Bashir Ahmad and became a pioneer in contemporary engagement with the miniature tradition. Reinterpreting the painterly style, Sikander creates animations, sculptures, mosaics, photographs and installations that address a range of themes, including how entrenched orientalist perspectives are replicated and reinforced during world events. In deploying historic techniques to question contemporary debates, her work proposes new associations grounded in feminist and postcolonial thought.

The Scroll (1989–90), a painting that comprised Sikander's undergraduate thesis, draws on early Mughal painting conventions (see cat. 8 & 10) to depict herself moving through a house recalling the place she lived in as a teenager. Painting herself in white akin to a ghostly apparition and never revealing her face, Sikander explains, was 'a statement on the restlessness of youth and the quest for identity. The claiming of the freedom for the female body in the domestic setting.'[43]

In *Riding the Written* (1992–93) groups of horses are pictured in motion as if cantering across a marbled page. The shapes of the animals recount the flourishes of Arabic calligraphy and form an unconventional script recounting Sikander's experiences of memorizing the Quran in Arabic visually and by sound before she could read it in Urdu and English. Sikander says 'It resulted in this amazing visual memory where the beauty of the Arabic script superseded everything else.'[44]

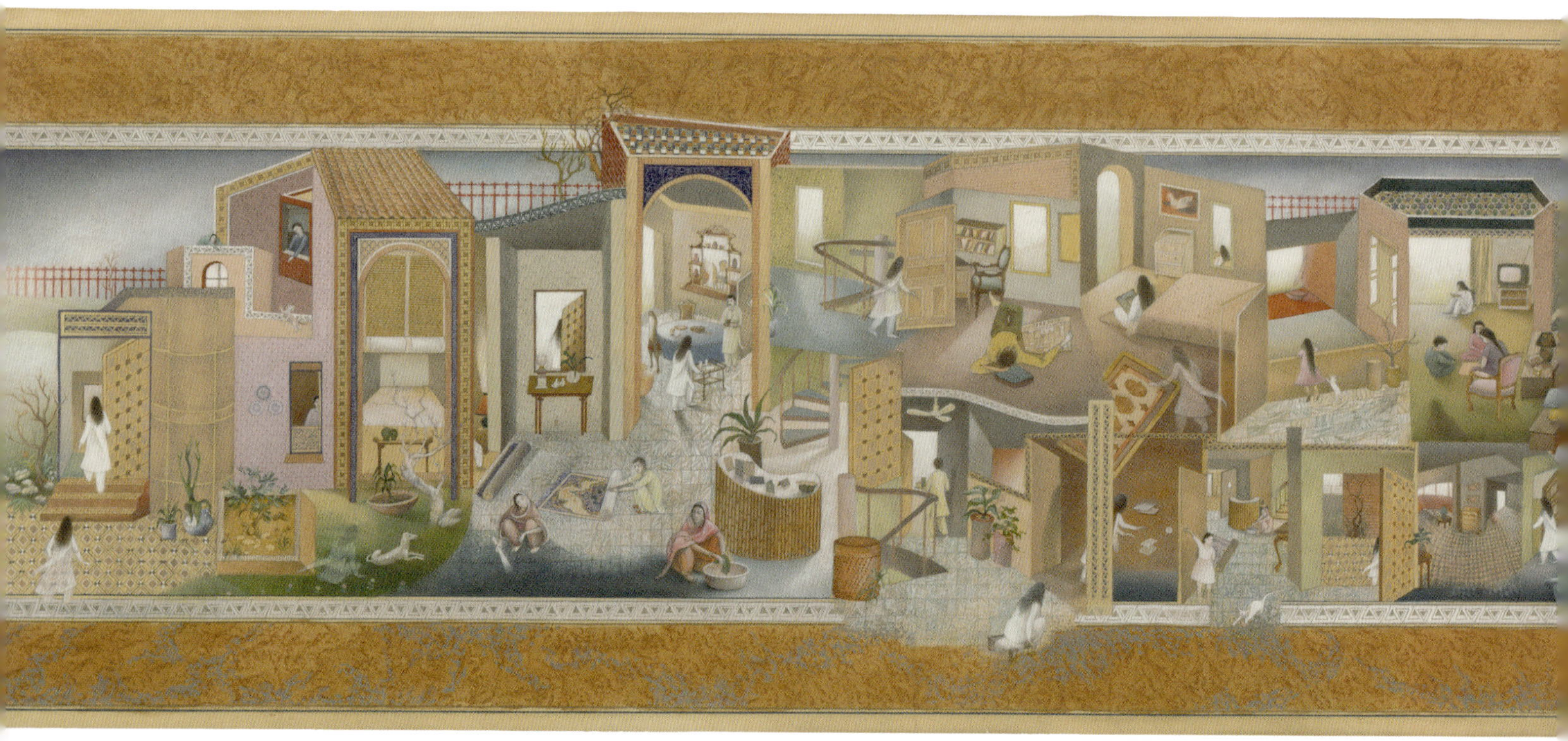

SHAHZIA SIKANDER

97 Riding the Written

1992–93 | gouache with screen printing on marbled paper | 30.4 × 19.3 cm | private collection, London/Karachi

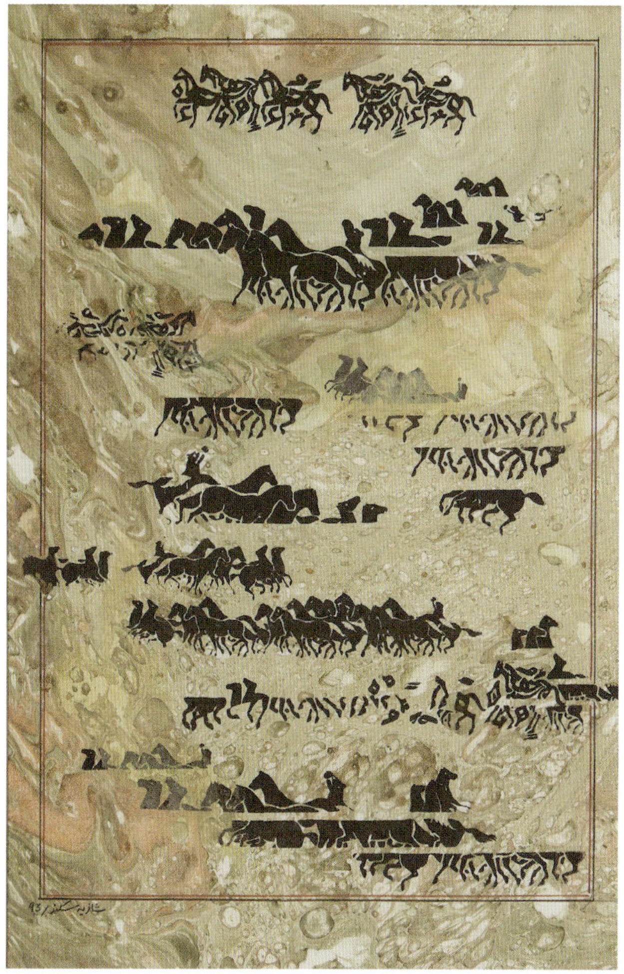

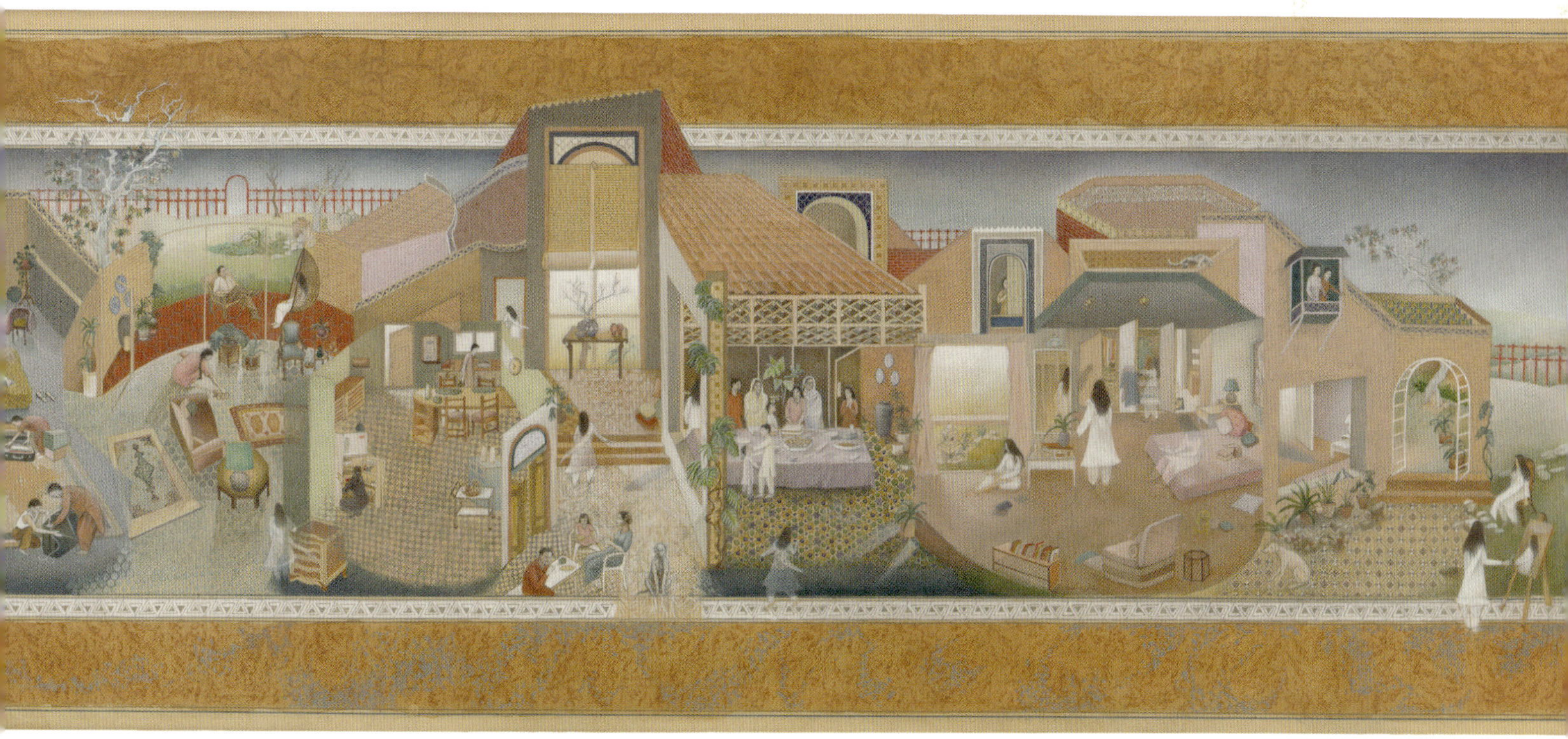

SHAHZIA SIKANDER

Negotiating and understanding the complex inheritance from Pakistan's deep colonial and missionary history drew me to engage with the 'miniature' tradition. My interest in miniature painting began with my own lack of knowledge about the tradition and the dismissive attitude towards non-Western art forms in 1980s' Pakistan. At the NCA in Lahore, traditional miniature painting was stigmatized as kitsch and derivative, but it was clear that the 'tradition' was truncated. 'Miniature' – a colonial term – encompassed pre-modern Central and South Asian manuscript painting and was linked to the English revival of Indian crafts. This deep stigma and unsettled national residue, however, encapsulated the paradox that subsisted along Pakistan's geopolitical landscape. In 1987 no one was elaborating on the merit of pursuing such a tired craft, and the division of who and what could be the 'modernist miniaturist' was highly circumscribed.

Identifying, dismantling and transforming nineteenth- and twentieth-century scholarship around tradition, orientalism and nostalgia towards the miniature, through a feminist lens, fired my imagination. I was also responding to the difficulty of finding female representations of brown South Asians in contemporary culture. This burden was what I carried to the United States in the early 1990s. Historical Indo-Persian paintings existed mostly in institutional storage in the West, interpreted through polarizing Eurocentric East–West, Islamic–Western or Asian–White binaries – deeply exclusionary constructions that propagate the oppressive dynamics of the past.

The female protagonists in my work resist simplistic categorization, deconstructing racial representation and stereotyping, and refuting the colonial and male gaze. There is an attention to the gendered body: androgynous, confident and playful women flourish in the virtuosic manuscript traditions of Central, South and East Asian contemporary culture. Erotics and the landscape, practices of concealment, staging, erasure and ornamentation in the miniature painting, provide ways to resignify 'woman'. Connected to the past, and layered with heterogeneous multi-faith visual histories, the figures veer from a heteronormative origin or parochial representations of nation and diaspora and reimagine archetypal characters in prolific stories. Miniature has emerged for me as an anti-monument in which I reference the past without glorifying history. Space, velocity, magnitude, direction become active in different ways through installation and public space.

My commitment to the pre-modern manuscript tradition has confronted its material history, infrastructural contexts of training and pragmatic apprenticeship through which South Asian art and aesthetics have classically pursued the study of miniature versus the pedagogy of the art school. I have also looked at art making as embodied labour, examined the relationship between decolonial art practice and the archive, the archive and its porousness for creative repurposing, and the interrelation of the miniature, its provenance and the museum. My practice through the broader manuscript tradition casts intersections of poetry, dialogues of how to view the miniature, calligraphy in relation to the philosophy of line, expansions in media to animation, music and sculpture, and speaks also to the loss of access to South Asian art collections in the global South.[45]

SHAHZIA SIKANDER

98 The Many Faces of Islam

1999 | gouache, vegetable colour, watercolour, gold leaf, graphite and tea on wasli paper | 30.5 × 43.2 cm | courtesy of the artist

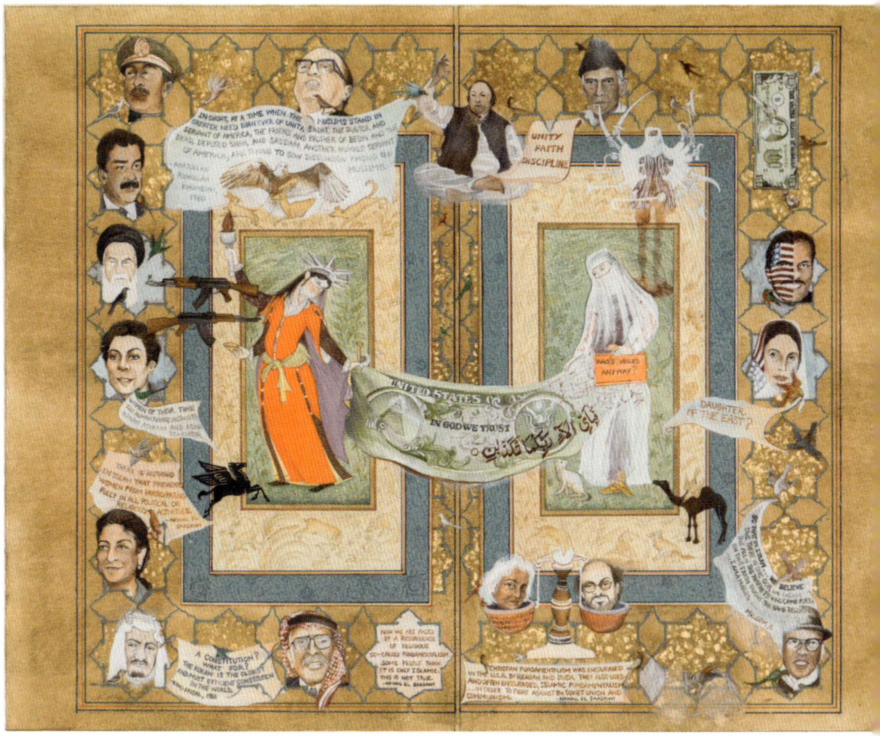

The Many Faces of Islam (1999) reimagines an opening of a Mughal album to examine the geopolitical relationship between America and the Islamic world. Originally published in the *New York Times Magazine*, the work shows a hybrid Statue of Liberty figure and a veiled Muslim woman holding an American banknote embellished with a quotation from the Quran: 'Which, then, of your Lord's blessing do you both deny?' Portraits of notable figures from Muslim cultures or heritage, including Nusrat Fateh Ali Khan, Malcolm X, Salman Rushdie and Benazir Bhutto, fill the borders. Sikander explains,

> The 1990s was about war, coalitions, alternating friends and foes, imposed sanctions, debts forgiven, and human rights brushed under the carpet as America flexed its military muscle around the world. This work took this history into account, and I proposed that American policy in Islamic countries would become a defining issue in the new millennium.[46]

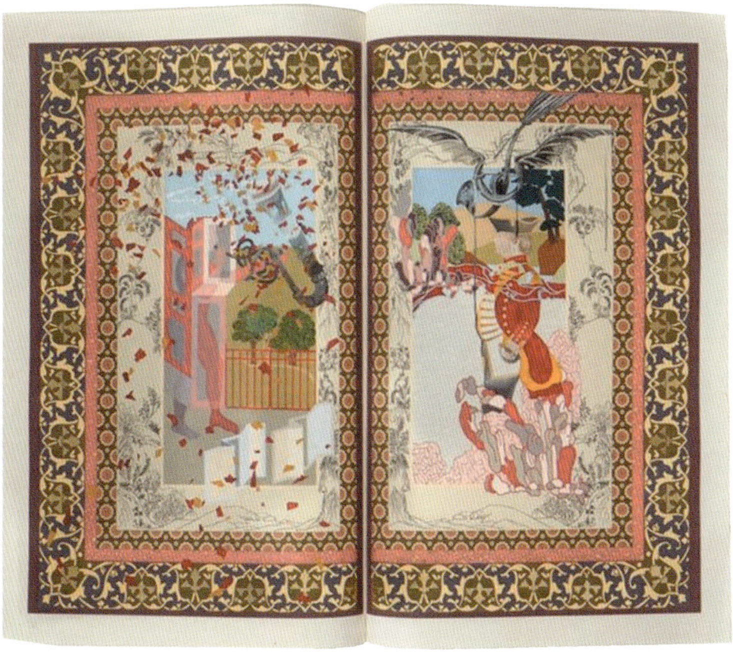

SHAHZIA SIKANDER

99 The Explosion of the Company Man

2006 | gouache, hand painting, gold leaf and silk-screened pigment on paper | 159.4 × 190.5 cm | private collection, London/Karachi

The Explosion of the Company Man (2006) is presented like an open Mughal album with two pages visible. The focal point is an image of a British colonial official from the East India Company encroached by graphic patterns and painted as if fading away. Sikander's act of visual defacement can be considered a form of rebalancing and metaphorical retribution for the extractive and aggressive policies pursued by such actors across South Asia.

IMRAN QURESHI

100 The Artist's Younger Brother

1995 | gouache on paper | 18.5 × 11.5 cm | private collection

Imran Qureshi (b.1972, Hyderabad, Pakistan) trained in miniature painting at the NCA, Lahore, under Bashir Ahmad. Qureshi has forged a style that abstracts miniature motifs and loads them with conceptual ideas. Embracing a range of mediums, including installation, painting and drawing, Qureshi characteristically makes use of red pigment and gold leaf, in part symbolic of the relationship between the mortal (lifeblood) and immortal (celestial plane).

The Artist's Younger Brother (1995) captures Qureshi's sibling in profile against a verdant outdoor setting. Made on wasli paper with the image contained in thick, decorative borders, the work directly references seventeenth-century Mughal portraits (see cat. 1). As Qureshi recalls, 'While rehearsing a performance from the 1970s, I saw my younger brother standing at the back of the stage waiting for his turn. He looked so cute in a 1970s' outfit that I thought why not replace the traditional kings and queens in miniature painting with common figures from our daily life.'

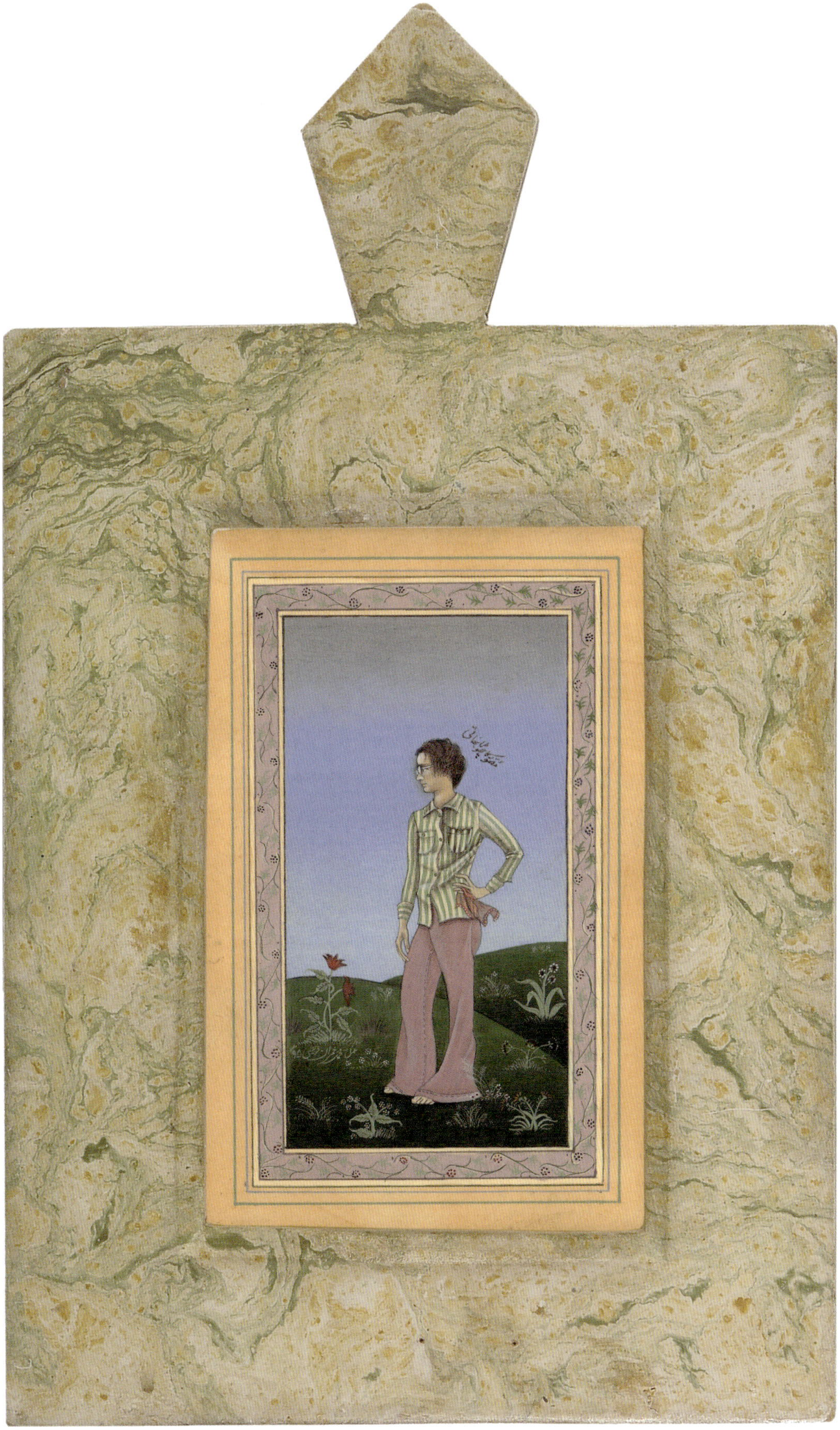

IMRAN QURESHI

101 A Lover Waiting for His Beloved

1999 | gouache on wasli paper | 25.4 × 19.1 cm | private collection, London/Karachi

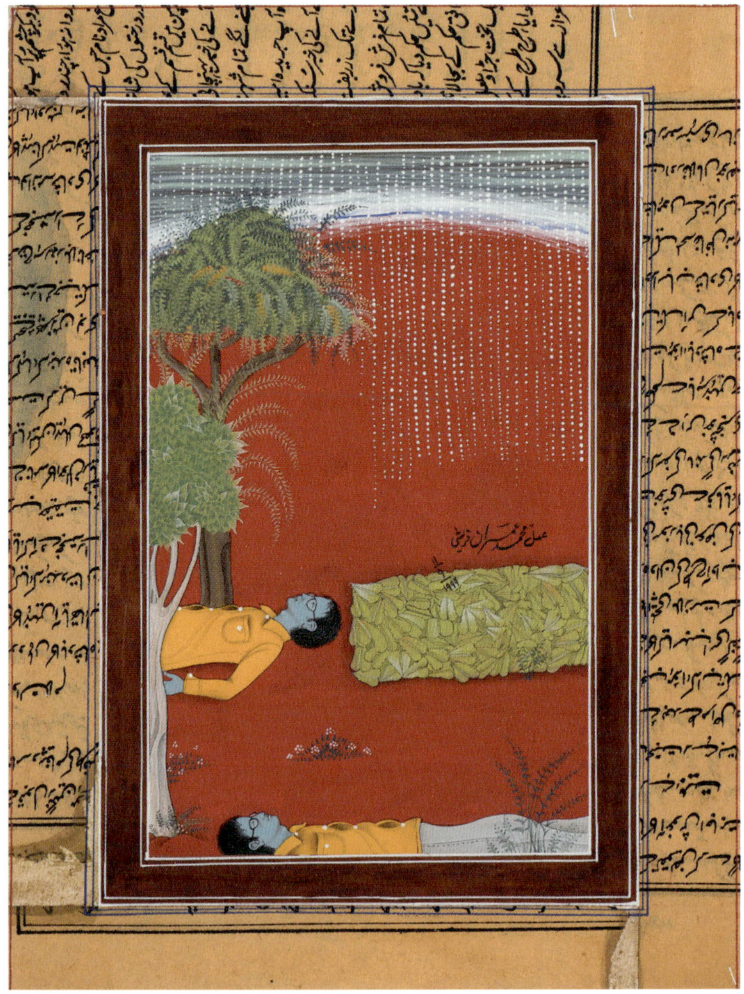

A Lover Waiting for His Beloved (1999) appears as if taken out of a Rajput miniature painting. Around the central image are sections of Urdu script, possibly taken from second-hand books. Qureshi deploys miniature conventions to conjure a surreal romantic reverie featuring a young man with blue skin, perhaps a reference to the Hindu god Rama or Krishna (see cat. 21, 58, 64).

IMRAN QURESHI

102 Blessings Upon the Land of My Love

2011 | gold leaf and gouache on wasli paper | two paintings, each 39.5 × 32.5 cm | Deutsche Bank Collection

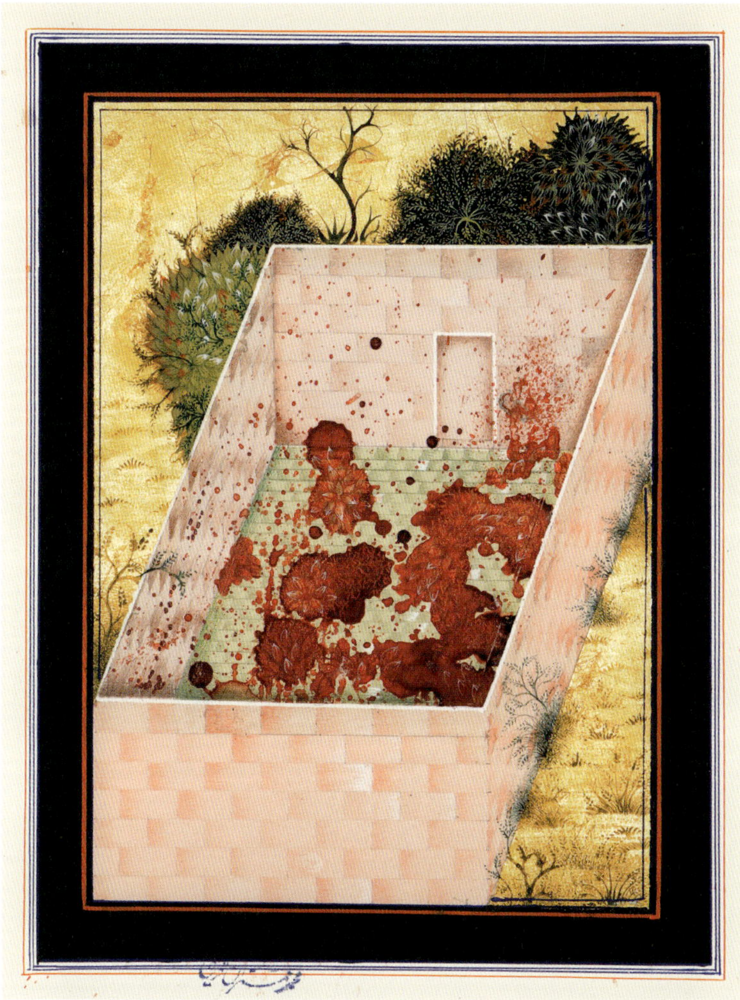

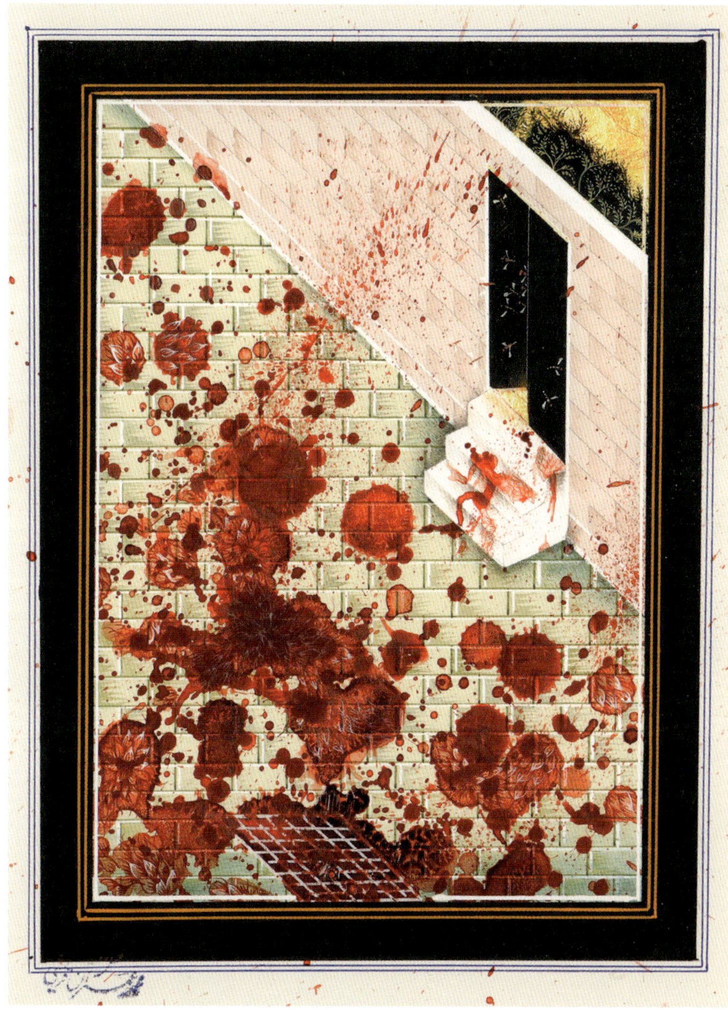

Blessings Upon the Land of My Love (2011), two small paintings on wasli paper featuring a courtyard splashed with red pigment, are indicative of Qureshi's experimentation with scale and reference a site-specific installation commissioned by the Sharjah Foundation, Sharjah. Made in response to a courtyard, it is a form of action painting, in which Qureshi gesturally applied red paint across the architecture. Floral visions emerge from the spatters of blood-red that soak the courtyard's walls and brick pavement. The work's various forms have a haunting effect; blood spots quicken before your eyes whether on paving stones or paper.

IMRAN QURESHI

103 Spots

2000 | gouache on wasli paper | 24 × 30 cm | private collection

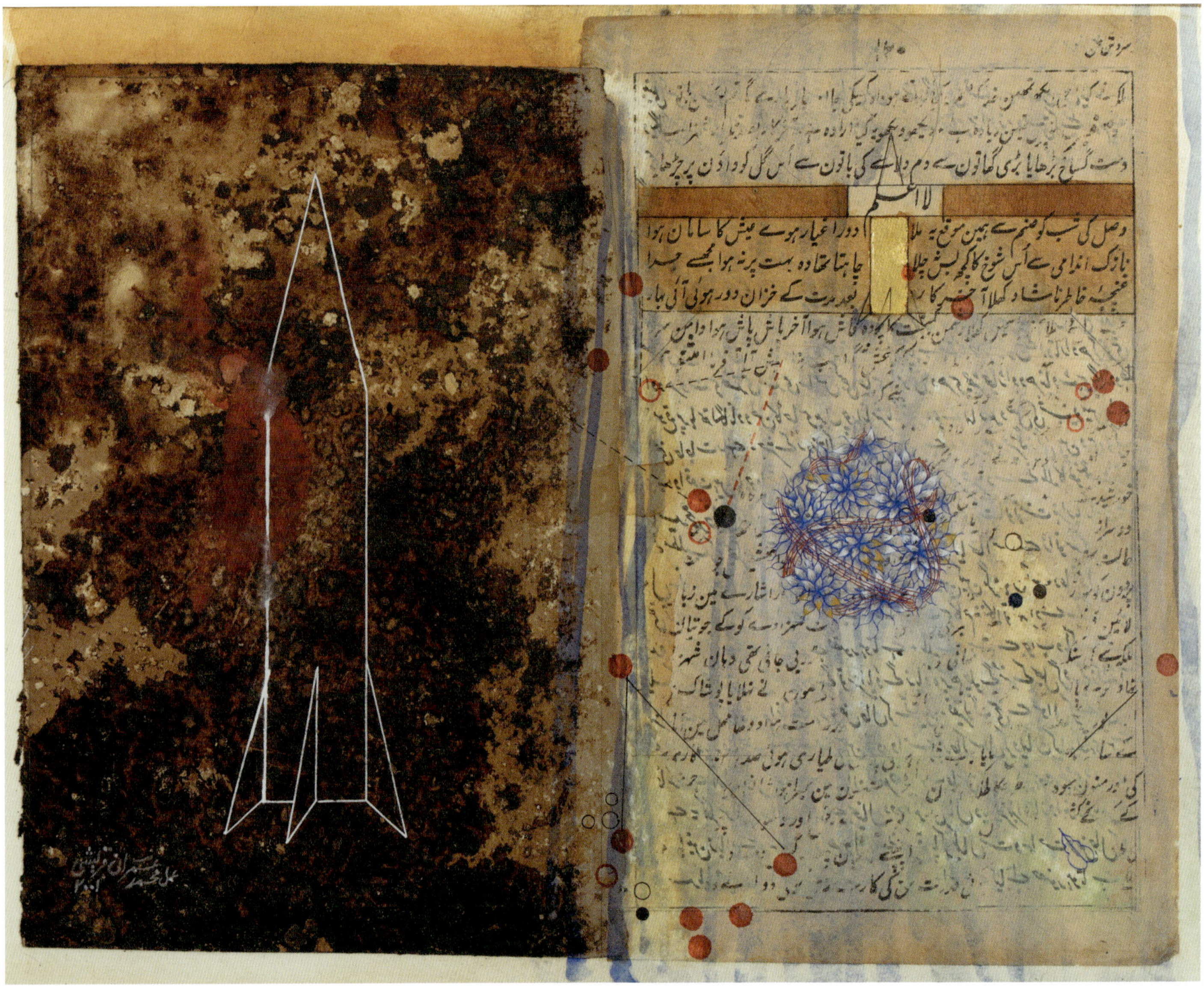

IMRAN QURESHI

104 Kagaz ke Sanam

2000 | gouache on wasli paper | 24 × 14.1 cm | private collection

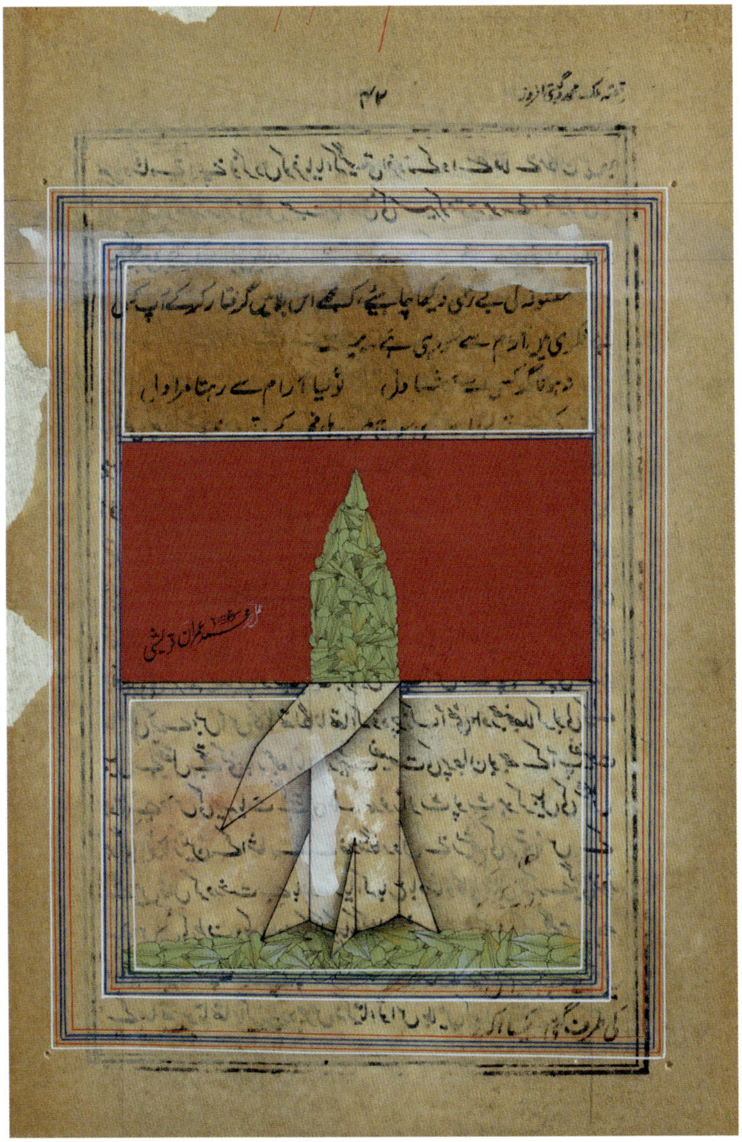

IMRAN QURESHI

105 Missile in Series

2000 | gouache on wasli paper | 25 × 16.5 cm | private collection

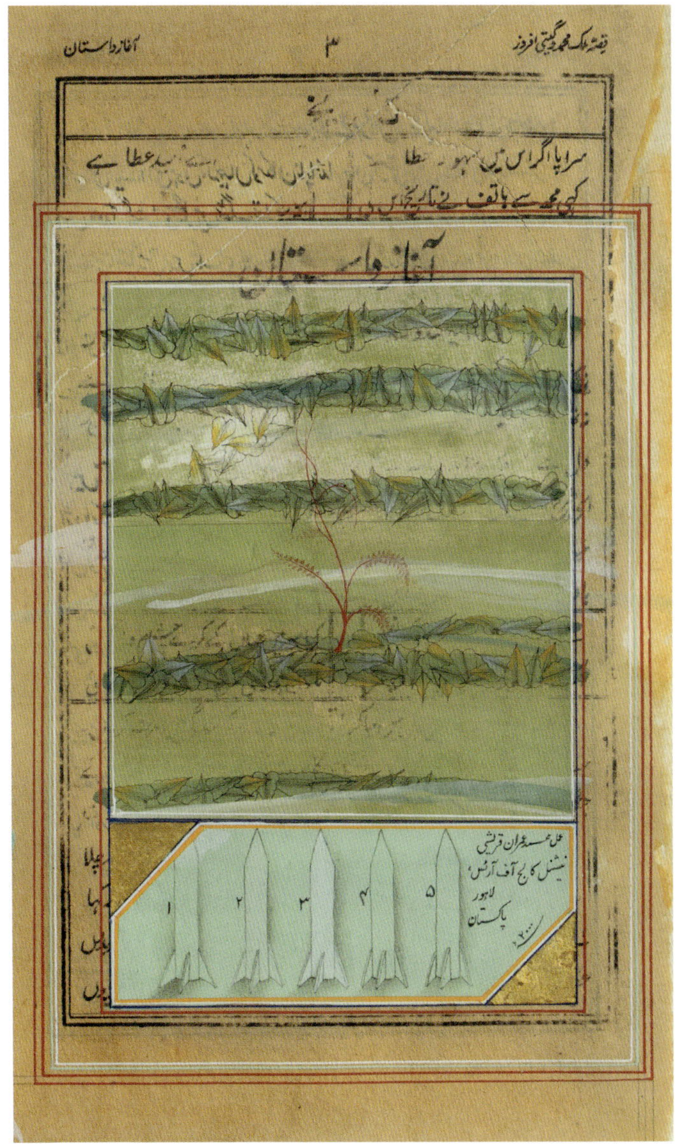

Both Pakistan and India possess nuclear weapons and obsolete or replica rockets are found as statues decorating the public realm in Lahore. In this series of paintings Qureshi mixes imagery of missiles with landscaped gardens, placing the missile in the prominent role previously occupied by Mughal emperors.

OLIVIA FRASER

106 The Street

2001 | watercolour on paper | 20 × 29 cm | private collection

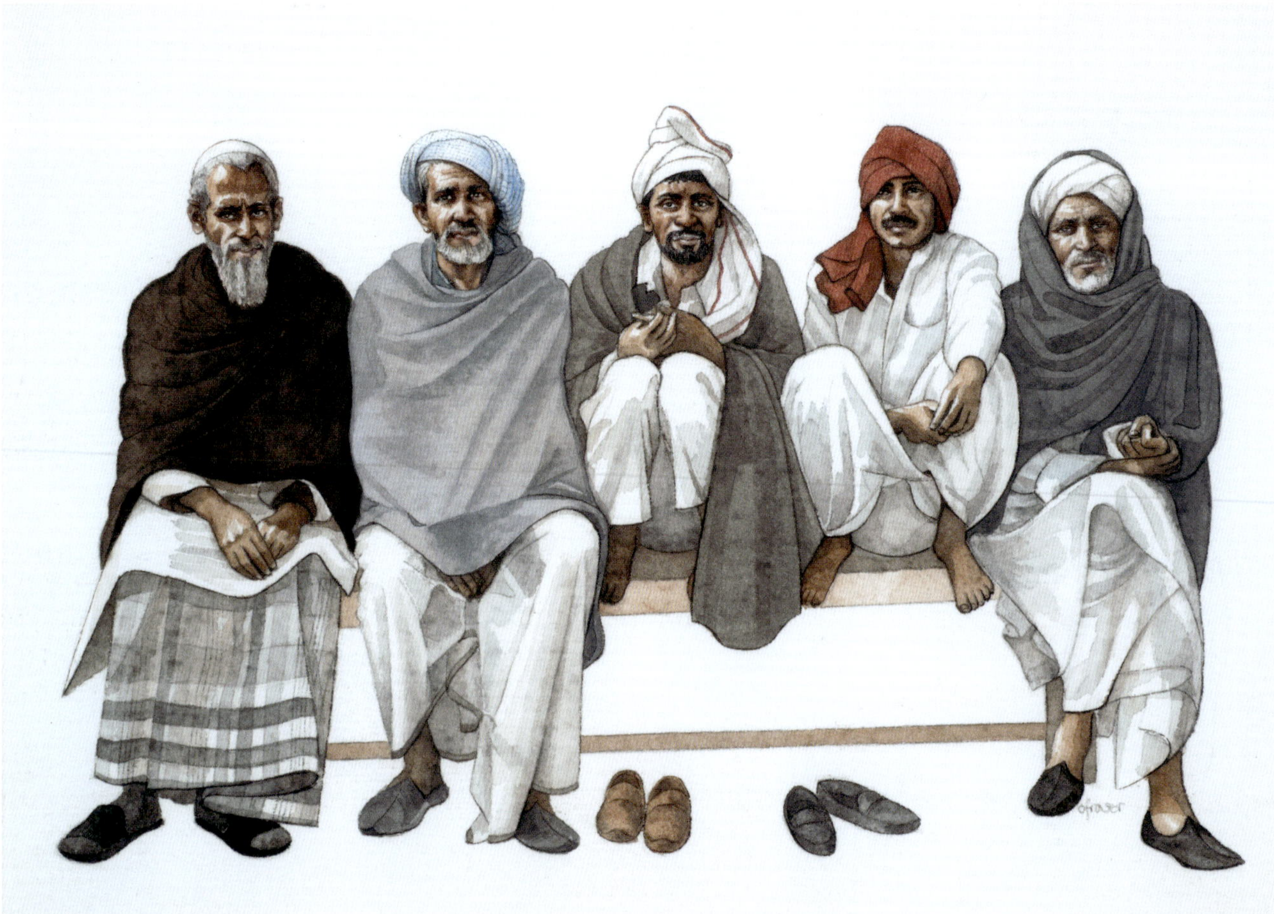

Olivia Fraser (b.1965, London) is a Scottish artist based in New Delhi. Her watercolour portraits of people and places in India painted in the 1990s and early 2000s recall the series of paintings commissioned in the early nineteenth century by her famous kinsmen, the Fraser brothers (see p. 15). The artist wrote:

> I first travelled to India in 1989 clutching a book about my kinsman James Baillie Fraser, a 19th-century landscape painter who painted the Himalayas and cityscapes of Calcutta and who commissioned one of the greatest collections of Company School paintings known as the *Fraser Album*. This hybrid form of painting, where Indian artists created something that mixed techniques and ideas from the East and the West, taking great trouble with the portraiture of ordinary folk excluded from the courtly miniatures of the past, greatly influenced my early work.[47]

Like many of the Fraser brothers' artists, Olivia Fraser places her subjects against a plain white ground, focusing on their physical features and clothes. *The Street* (2001) depicts five men whom the artist met in Haryana, near the former country retreat of the Fraser brothers' friend Colonel James Skinner (see p. 16).

OLIVIA FRASER

107 Singing the Phad

2001 | watercolour on paper | 19 × 42.4 cm | private collection

Fraser began her study of Rajasthani painting in the early 2000s, including the folk traditions of *phad* painters. *Phad* paintings on cloth usually depict local gods or folk heroes and form the backdrop for village entertainments. On *Singing the Phad*, the artist informs us:

> I'm reflecting on past miniature paintings which depict musicians performing for emperors or maharajas. But here ... I'm depicting a rural devotional performance where the musicians are singing the story of the local desert deity in front of local dignitaries.[48]

The *phad* depicted in the scene is by renowned painter Sri Lal Joshi, whom Fraser depicts in the bottom left corner, where Mughal artists sometimes placed self-portraits in their own paintings.

The highly saturated colours recall the burnished stone pigments used by Mughal and Rajput painters. Fraser later gained an intimate working knowledge of miniature painting during her apprenticeship with the master artist Ajay Sharma in Jaipur and a Delhi-based studio painting *pichwais* (temple backdrops), and has since applied her technical miniature skills to the 'esoteric world of Tantric Art'.[49] Similar to Alan Davie's exploration of Jain iconography (see cat. 89), Fraser's interest in Tantra was based in metaphysical curiosity:

> In my search to really understand the roots of this world, it seemed to me that they were built on a very strong, rigorous backbone of arcane knowledge and that Tantric art could contain answers to my questions.[50]

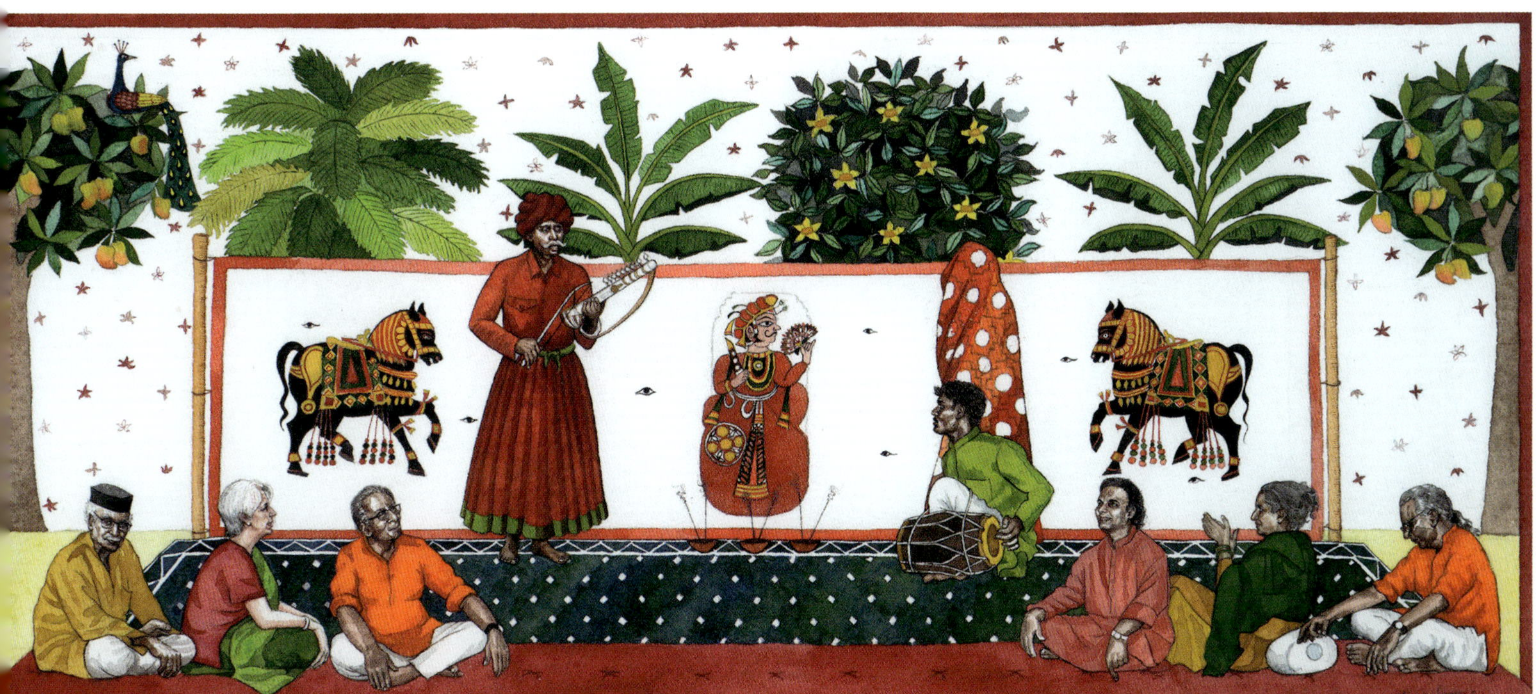

RASHID RANA

108 I Love Miniatures

2002 | digital print | 34.5 × 25.3 cm | private collection

Rashid Rana (b.1968, Lahore, Pakistan) examines the social stereotypes and cultural paradoxes operating in a globalized world. Taught by Zahoor ul Akhlaq at NCA, Lahore, before receiving a MFA from Massachusetts College of Arts, Boston, Rana highlights the politics of representation and demands placed on non-Western artists to respond to their heritage. Spanning many mediums, including sculpture, installation and photography, Rana's practice challenges, confronts and ridicules these expectations.

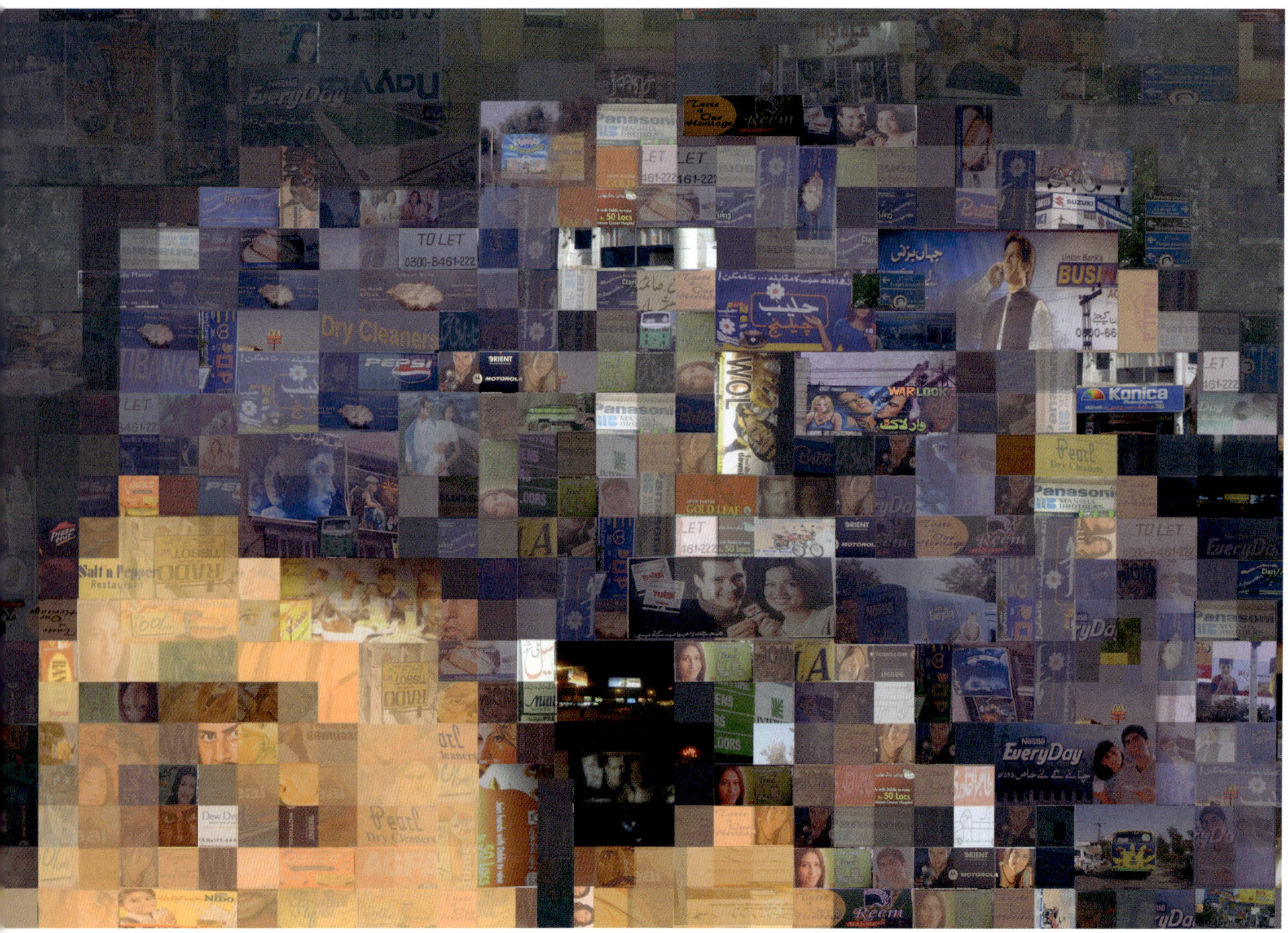

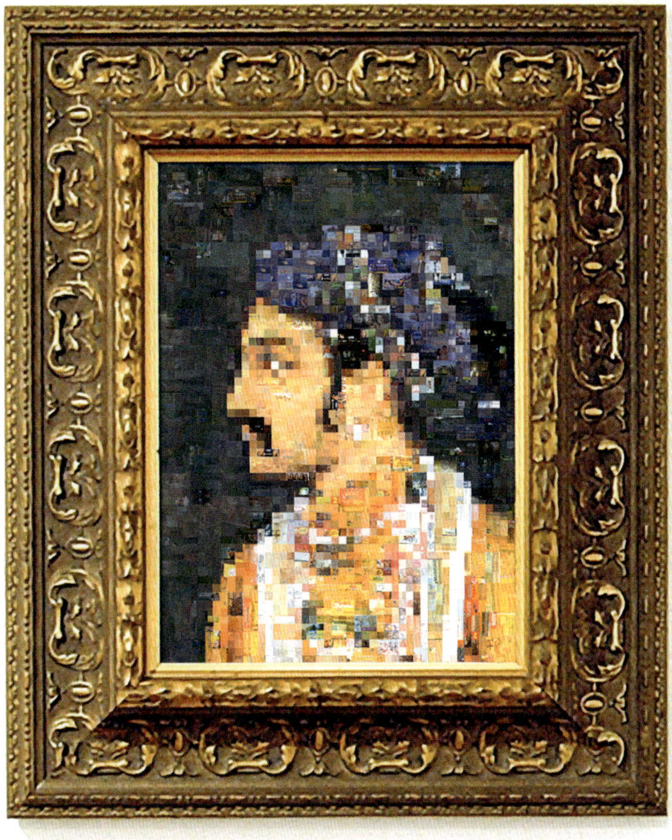

In *I Love Miniatures* (2002) Rana uses a panoply of everyday images to construct an image that from afar looks like a portrait of the Mughal emperor Shah Jahan (see cat. 61). Confusing the relationship between part and whole, appearance and reality, Rana puts pressure on the authenticity of miniature painting and challenges assumptions made about the contemporary imagination and relevance of the past and tradition.

Rana explains,

> A European artist born and raised in Amsterdam is not expected to produce works that visually resemble those of Rembrandt or Van Gogh but the same expectation of subscription to tradition is present for an artist from Pakistan or other regions that were colonized in the past. *I Love Miniatures* is a critique of this burden.[51]

NICOLA DURVASULA

109 Agarbatti

2002 | watercolour on paper | 35.5 × 51 cm | courtesy of the artist and Joost van den Bergh, London

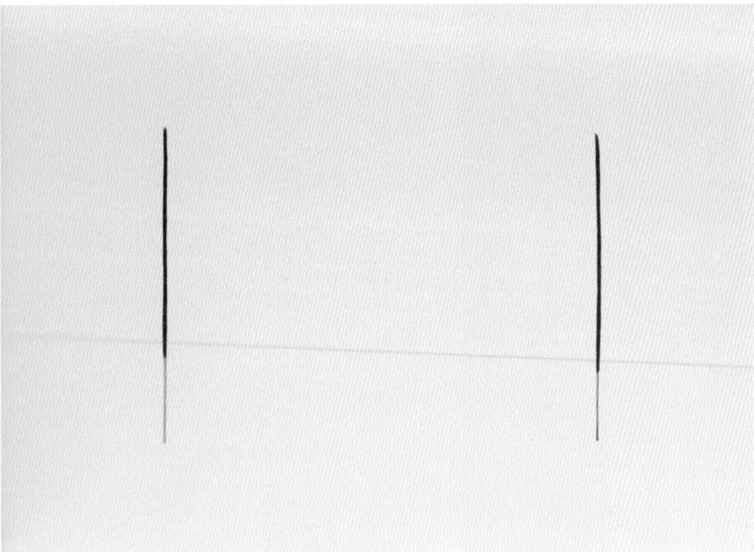

NICOLA DURVASULA

110 'No Search' study for black glass

2011 | inks, graphite on paper | 38 × 51 cm | Payal and Anurag Khanna collection, India, courtesy Joost van den Bergh, London

British artist Nicola Durvasula (b.1960, Jersey, British Isles) moved to India in 1992 and lived there for ten years teaching fine arts at the University of Hyderabad. While there she was struck by artist Laxma Goud's ability 'to capture energy and sensuality following the Indian tradition of a sensual response to surface, one that is implied and symbolic rather than analysed'. Her own artistic practice ranges across drawing, sculpture, ceramics, film and painting, often making reference to aspects of South Asian culture, from *agarbatti* (incense sticks) to Mughal miniatures.

Durvasula's work shifts from the mundane to the profound and across high and low art forms, often with a humour that brings both lightness and depth. Inspired by ubiquitous Indian objects such as the mosquito coil and incense sticks, Durvasula has, since the mid-1990s, made drawings of *agarbatti*, explaining that 'The precision of the lines and the deep layers of colours produce a meditative effect.'

NICOLA DURVASULA

111 Portrait of C.K. Rajan

1999 | watercolour on paper | 27.5 × 27.5 cm | private collection

Durvasula describes *Portrait of C.K. Rajan* as

> A tongue in cheek deconstruction of traditional miniature portraiture: Holding a freshly plucked Champa flower from the garden, Rajan, a member of Kerala Radical Group of the 1980s, known for his edgy political collages, sat/posed in the studio one afternoon. His profile was drawn/painted from this one sitting and photos were taken as reference used for completing of work. I'm deeply interested in the quality of fine line used in preparatory drawings for miniature painting, and without training/instruction in miniature painting, this is one of the early brush drawings made using an extremely fine brush (da vinci 10/0) and watercolour on ordinary paper.[52]

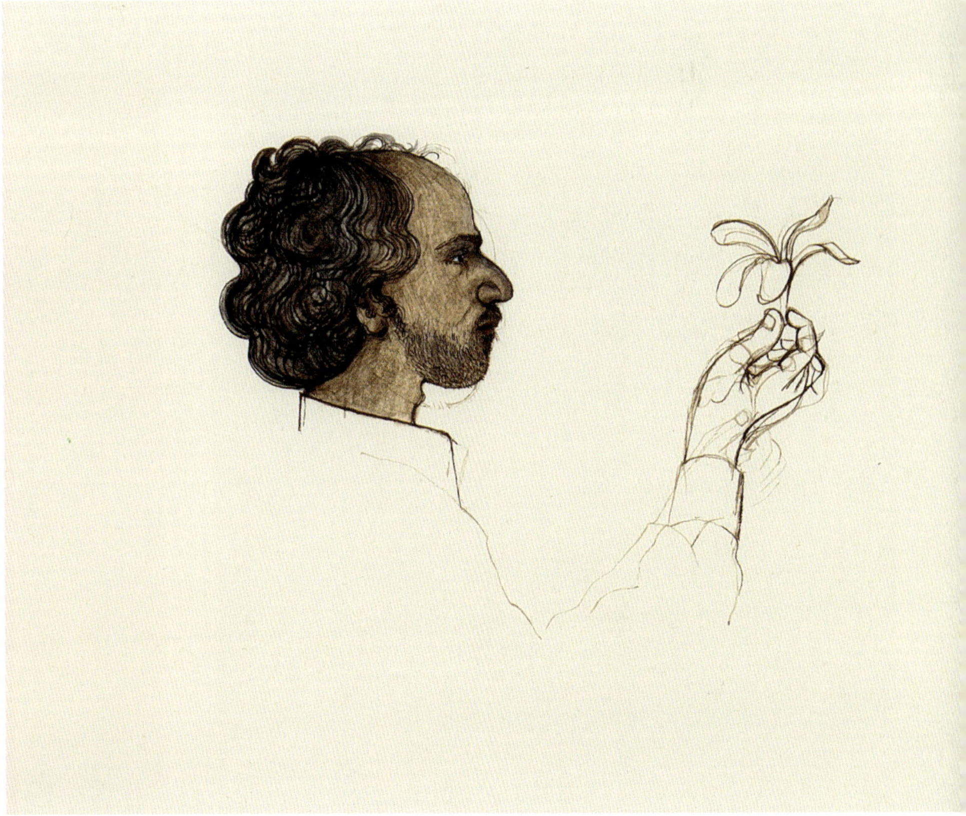

NICOLA DURVASULA

112 Untitled (red 1)

2018 | watercolour, gouache, Gangajal (Ganga water) on toned paper | 33 × 24 cm | Payal and Anurag Khanna collection, India, courtesy Joost van den Bergh, London

113 Untitled (burnt orange)

2018 | watercolour, gouache, Gangajal (Ganga water) on toned paper | 28.5 × 25.5 cm | Payal and Anurag Khanna collection, India, courtesy Joost van den Bergh, London

114 Untitled (green 3)

2018 | watercolour, gouache, Gangajal (Ganga water) on toned paper | 29 × 30.5 cm | Payal and Anurag Khanna collection, India, courtesy Joost van den Bergh, London

NICOLA DURVASULA

115 लाल लीला Lāl Līla (melody VII)

2020 | watercolour pencil on paper | 17 × 23 cm | private collection UK, courtesy Joost van den Bergh, London

116 Untitled (zip red)

2022 | pencil on toned paper | 33 × 45 cm | Payal and Anurag Khanna collection, India, courtesy Joost van den Bergh, London

Durvasula's work often lies somewhere between materiality and abstraction, an inner life and the external world. This group of monochromes was produced during a Shelagh Cluett Residency at the Alice Boner Institute, Varanasi, in 2018.

> Every morning I would leave the house around 5.20 a.m. and head straight to the ghats to attend the morning Aarti followed by Morning Ragas and Yoga. Aarti is said to have descended from the Vedic concept of fire rituals and young pandits wearing saffron robes conduct this early morning ritual in front of the Ganges. Conch shells are blown, then in succession, multi-tiered oil lamps, snake hood lamps, peacock feathers and Yak Tail fans are circulated in slow, synchronised motion, accompanied by the repetitive sound of a gong, bells and Vedic chanting by girls instead of young boys (breaking hundreds of years of tradition). ... I found it mesmerising to watch, absorbing through sight, sound and smell this most ancient of ceremonies set against the backdrop of the Ganges with twilight gradually merging into daylight.
>
> ... At Varanasi it is said that the Ganges flows backwards, from south to north, towards its source of origin in the Himalayas, a phenomenon considered to be very auspicious by the Hindus. Filling a large plastic container (sold specifically for this purpose) with Ganges water I began a series of drawings and paintings combining this sacred water with water-colour. Using a single colour, I soaked Indian handmade paper a number of times, watching the chemistry of inactive pigment come to life in the water, colour gradually increasing in density. Some of these paintings have been/will be used as a background for fine line drawings and the others remain as themselves: 'Monochromes'. Having straddled Abstract, Figurative and Conceptual art for the past 30 years, this is the first time I explored total abstraction; reducing the painting to its purest physical elements; colour, form, texture and the conceptual manner in which it was made.

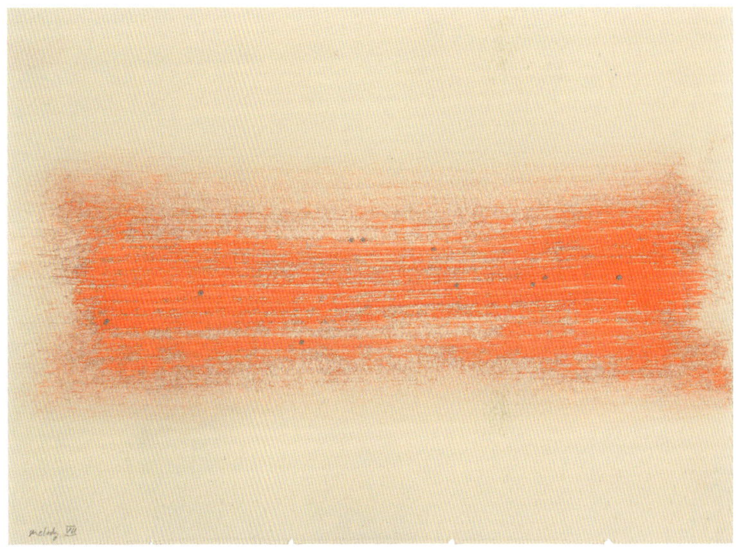

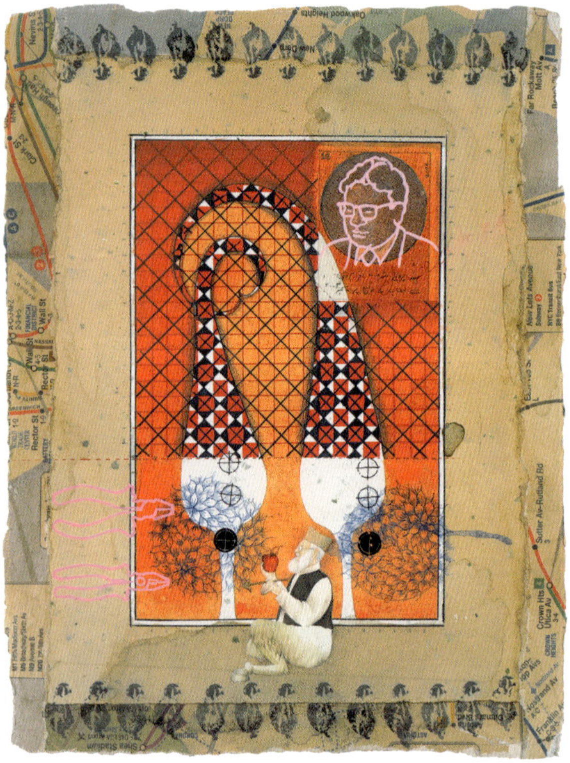
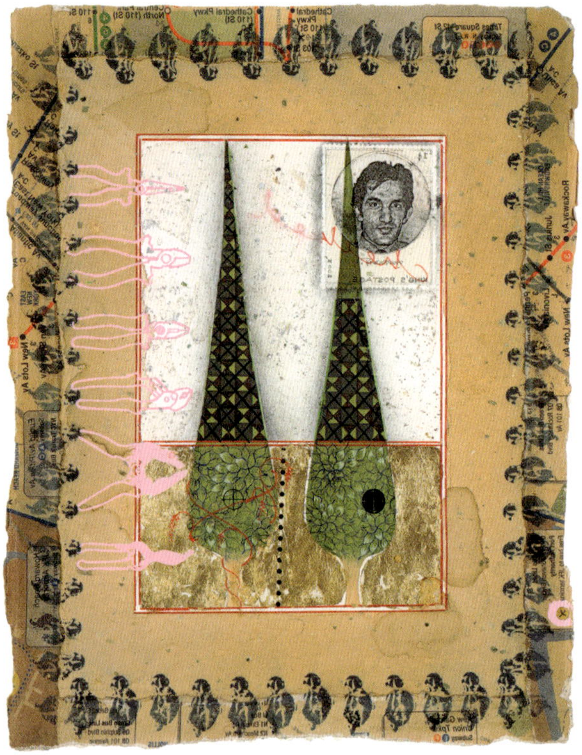
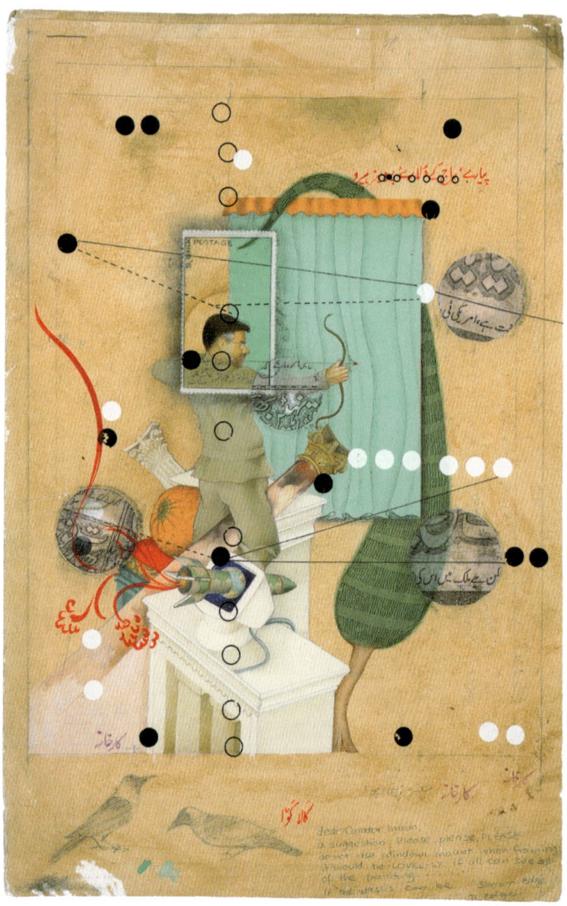
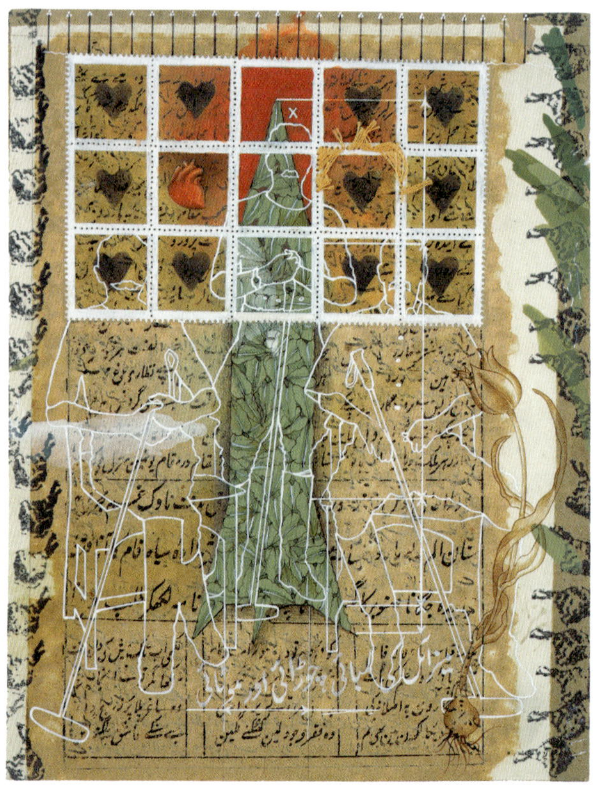

MUHAMMAD IMRAN QURESHI, AISHA KHALID, HASNAT MAHMOOD, NUSRA LATIF QURESHI, TALHA RATHORE & SAIRA WASIM

117 Karkhana

2003 | mixed media on wasli paper | 12 sheets, each 28 × 20 cm | Guggenheim Abu Dhabi

Karkhana (2003) is a collaboration between six artists, all alumni of NCA, Lahore, a school renowned for teaching miniature painting techniques. The project was initiated by Imran Qureshi, inspired by historic miniature painting workshops called *karkhanas* that brought together groups of painters who worked together under the supervision of an *ustad* (master).

Imran Qureshi invited each artist to begin two paintings on handmade wasli paper before sending them on to the next artist to continue adding, subtracting and adapting layers and imagery. With each artist based in a different location across the world, this global circulation resulted in 12 collaboratively made miniatures. As curator Hammad Nasar noted, 'The nature of the *Karkhana* project is vast and multi-faceted. It explores the possibilities of collaborative practice and political resistance, the reinvention of a "tradition", and the expression of diasporic identity.'[53]

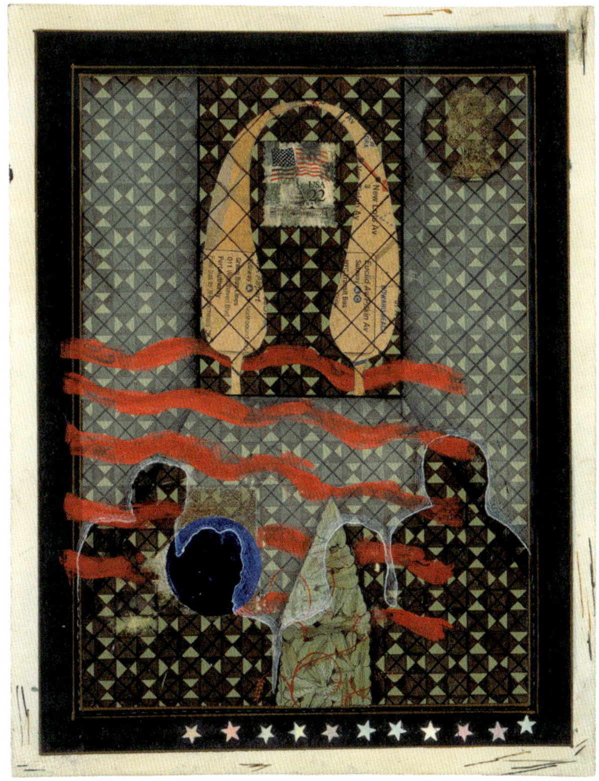

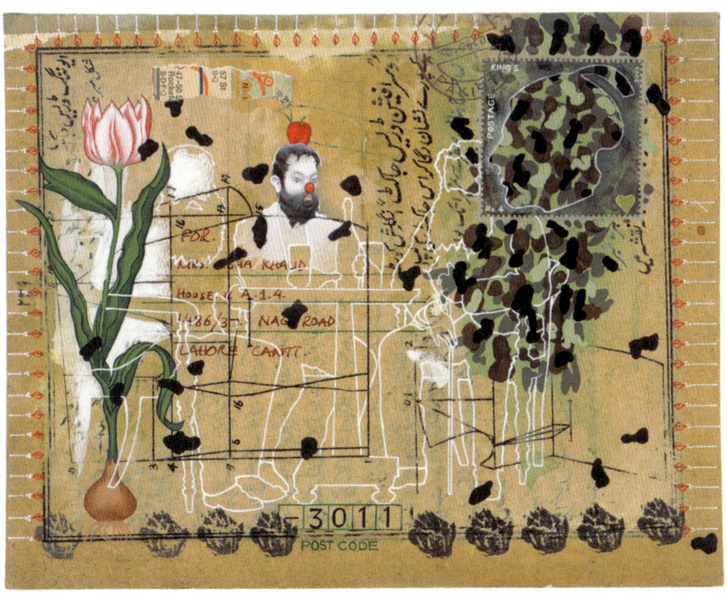

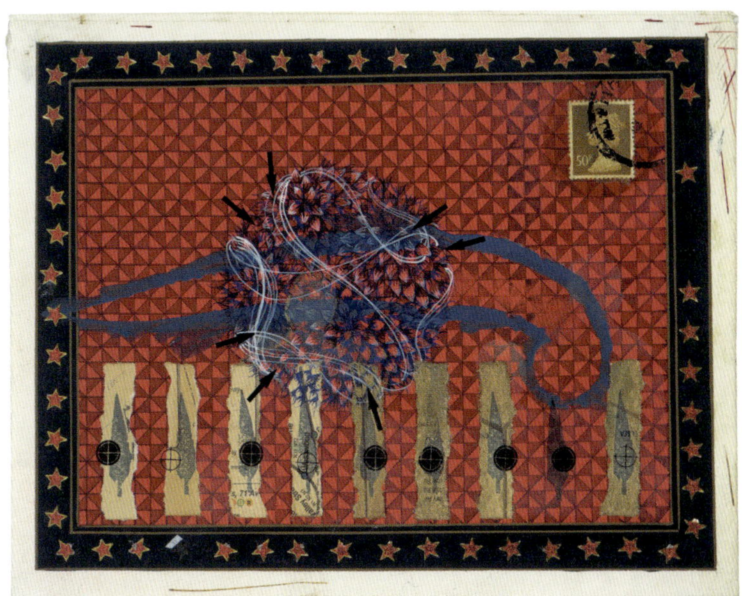

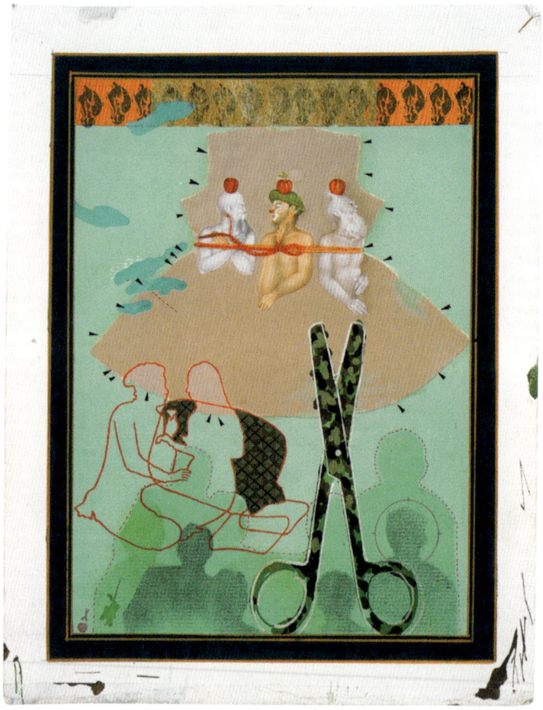

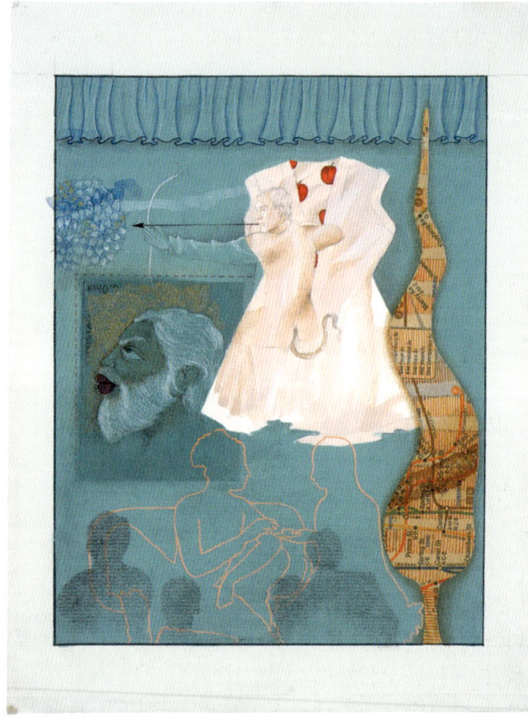

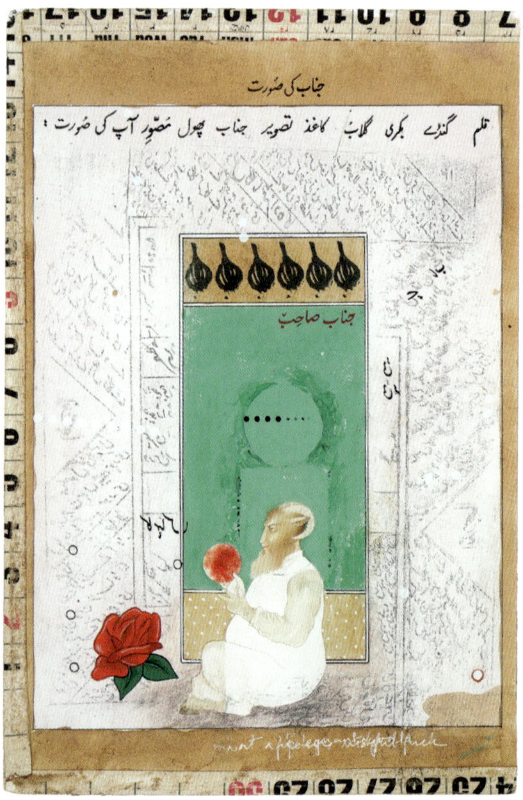

جناب کی صورت
قلم گنڈیرے بکری گلاب کاغذ تصویر جناب پھول مصوّر آپ کی صورت :
جناب صاحب

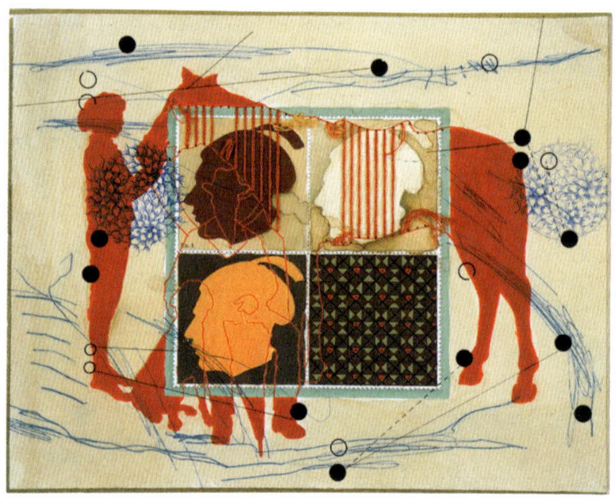

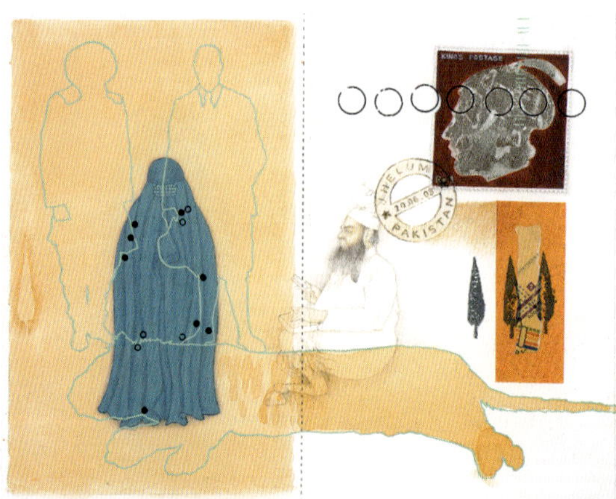

PAKISTAN

AHSAN JAMAL

118 Beards

2003 | gouache on wasli paper | 5 works, 7×5 cm each | private collection

Ahsan Jamal (b. 1975, Jhang, Pakistan) received a BFA in Miniature Painting from the NCA, Lahore, in 2003. Jamal's contemplative studio practice examines the genre of portrait painting under the discipline of Indo-Persian miniature painting. Jamal is known for his portrait paintings. He creates portraits that are moved by his interest in socioreligious ideologies and class dynamics of Pakistani society. Often working in series, Jamal sometimes thoughtfully picks up characters from his surroundings to develop his themes, so that a found photo of a person becomes a meaningful insertion in his series to grow a satiric socio-political commentary with religious undertones.

Beards (2004) is a group of five cameo portraits featuring men with facial hair. Each figure sports a different style intricately painted by Jamal. In focusing on this aspect of the male appearance, Jamal brings together a diverse group of men; for some, the beard is associated with religious beliefs, for others it is an aesthetic choice. This cross-section speaks to self-construction as much as it does requirements of faith.

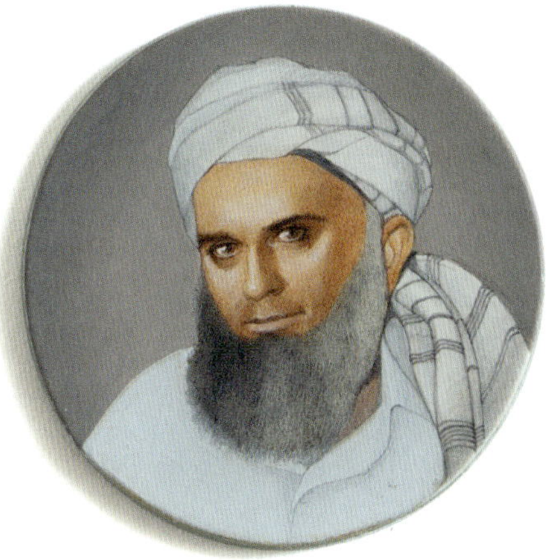

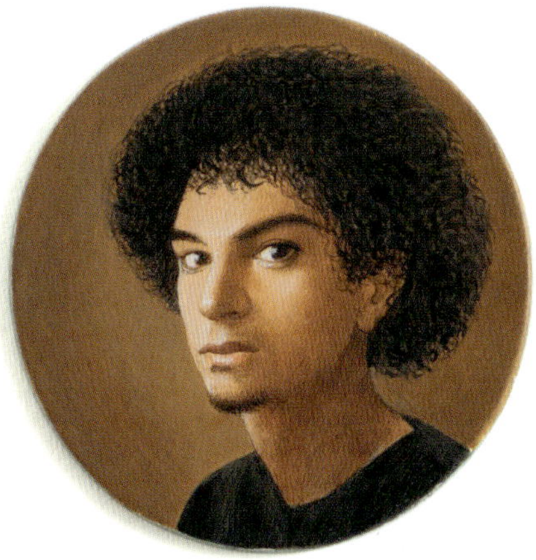

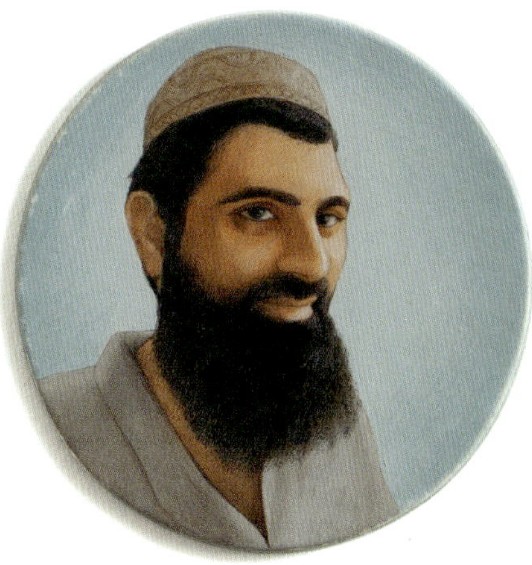

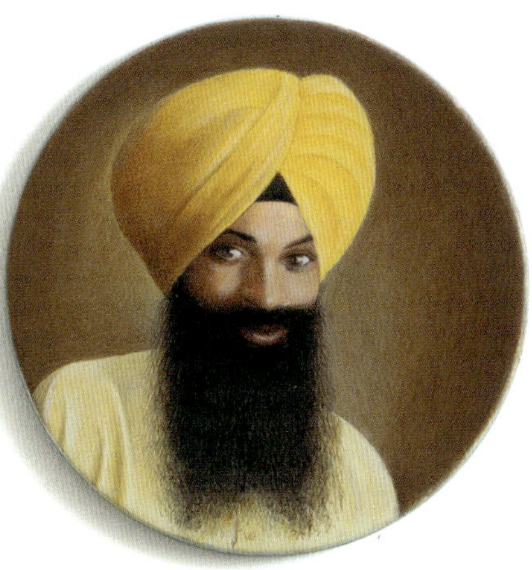

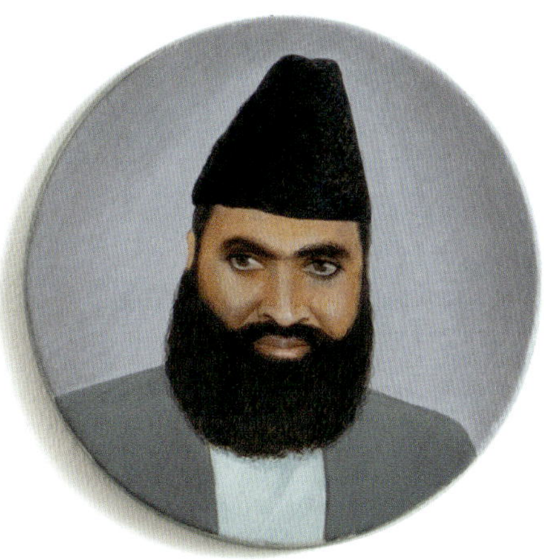

HAMRA ABBAS

119 All Rights Reserved

2004 | 4 × digital prints | each 81.7 × 57.4 cm | collection of Kamran M. Anwar

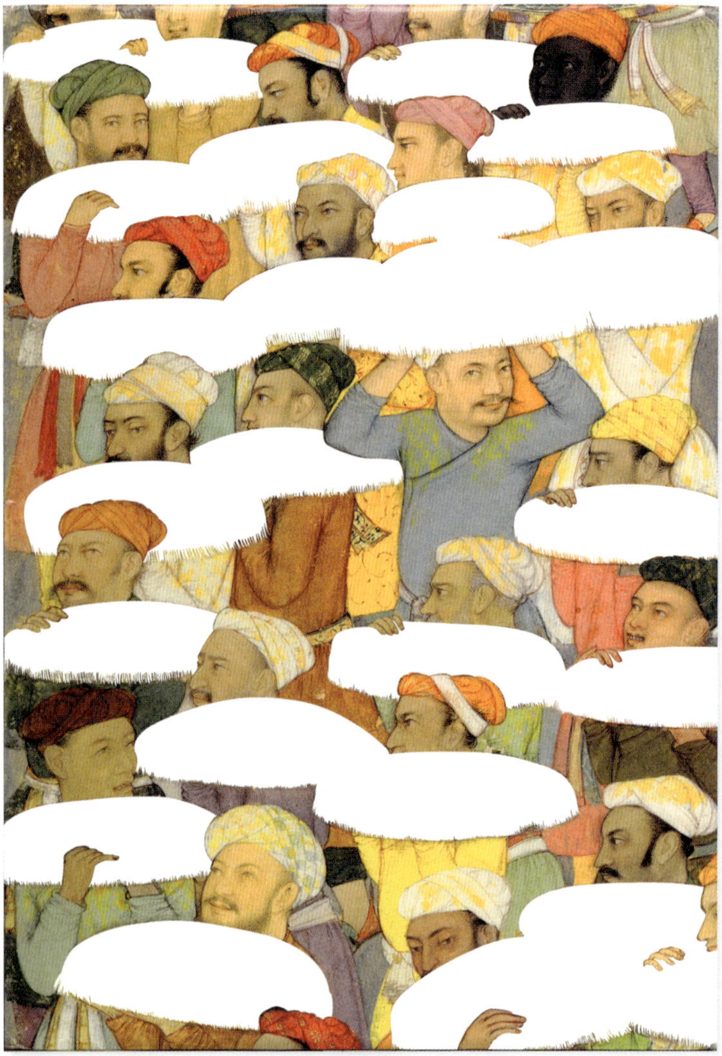

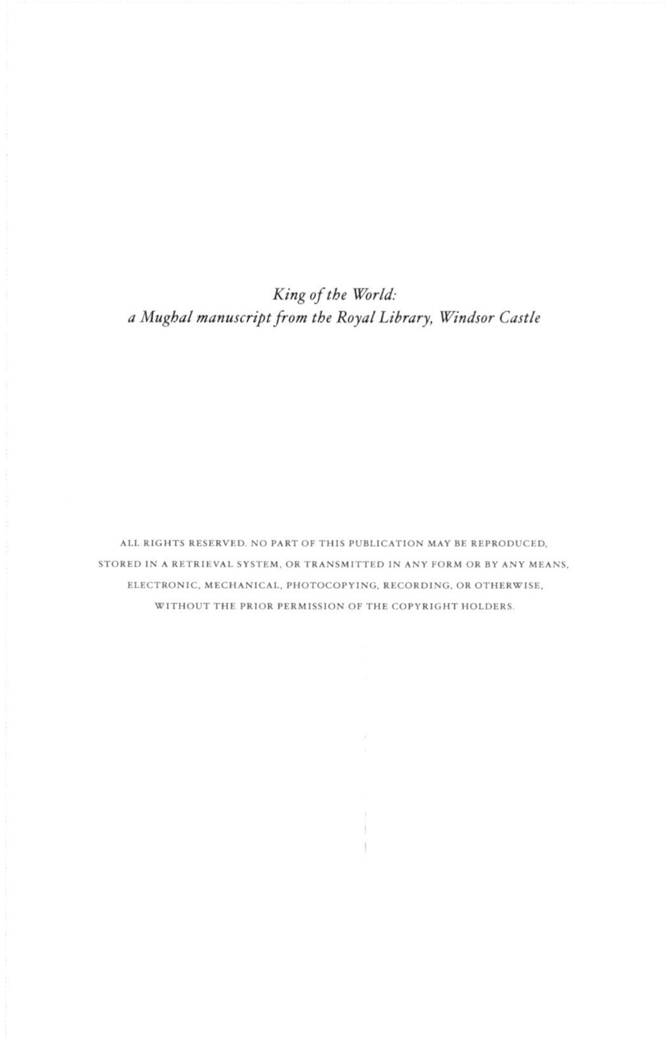

Hamra Abbas (b.1976, Kuwait) completed her BFA studies in sculpture and MA in visual arts at NCA, Lahore, between 1999 and 2002, before studying at the Universität der Künste Berlin (2002–04). With a playful approach, Abbas explores how Islamic and Western cultures adapt to globalization, adopting a range of mediums, including painting, sculpture and printing and deploying different modes of making including industrial technology as well as craft techniques to tease out the complexities of a changing world. With a rigorous approach to her enquiries, Abbas often produces series that exhaust a single subject, like her immersive installation *Garden* (2021) that reconstructed utopian garden images found in Mughal miniatures.

All Rights Reserved (2004), a four-panel installation, considers the commodification of South Asian art through the famous Mughal manuscript,

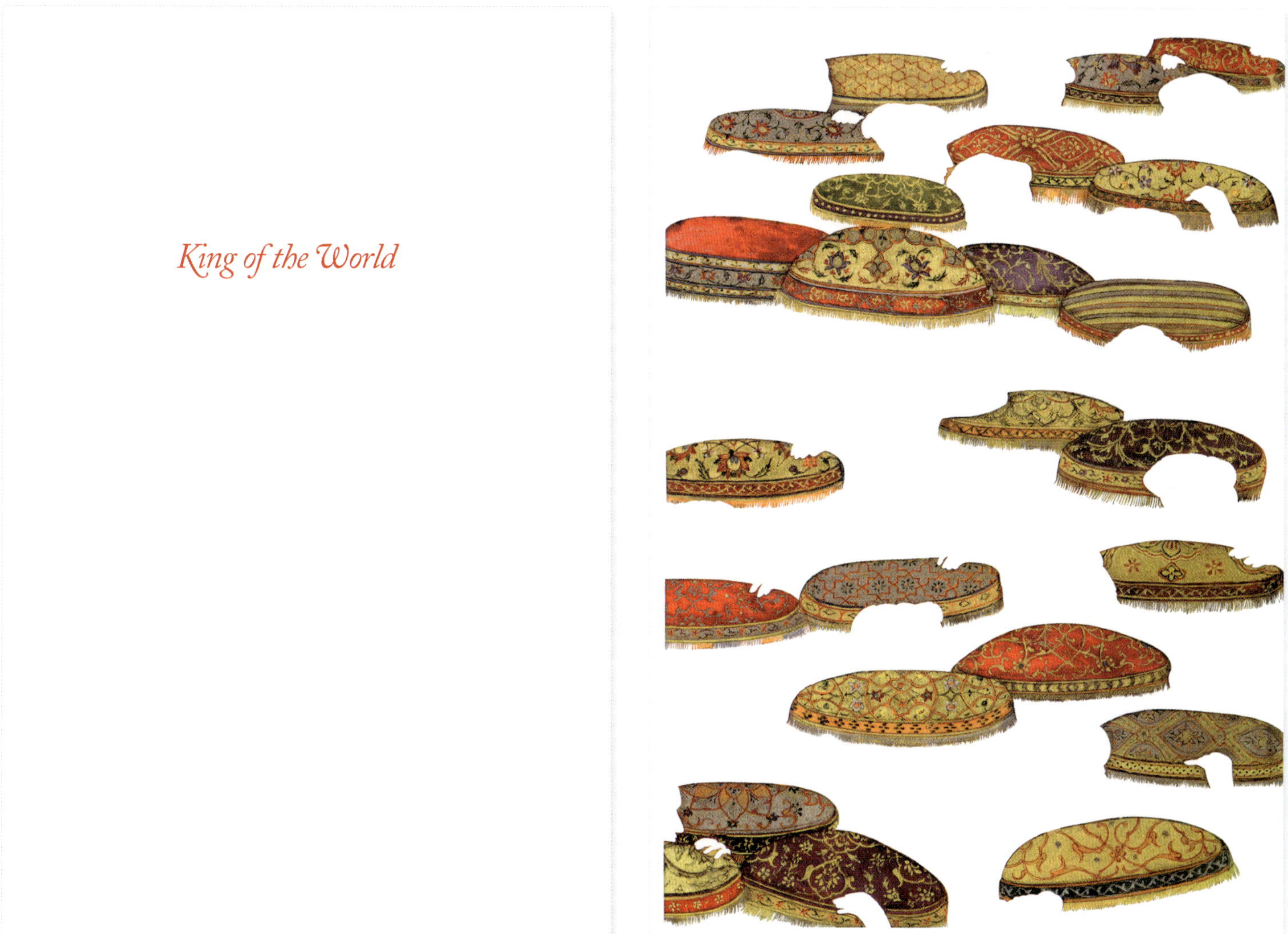

the *Padshahnama* (see cat. 15). The lavish work celebrates the life and achievements of emperor Shah Jahan and was presented as a diplomatic gift to King George III after the death of the Nawab of Awadh. Abbas homes in on and reconfigures a page depicting men carrying presents for the wedding of Prince Dara Shikoh, Shah Jahan's son.

In an echo of the removal of the manuscript from India, in one panel Abbas erases the presents from each guest, transferring them separately onto another panel, suspended in mid-air. Accompanying the images are pages from an exhibition catalogue stating the book's copyright terms prohibiting reproduction, which Abbas clearly ignores.

HAMRA ABBAS

120 Battle Scenes

2006 | digital animation | private collection

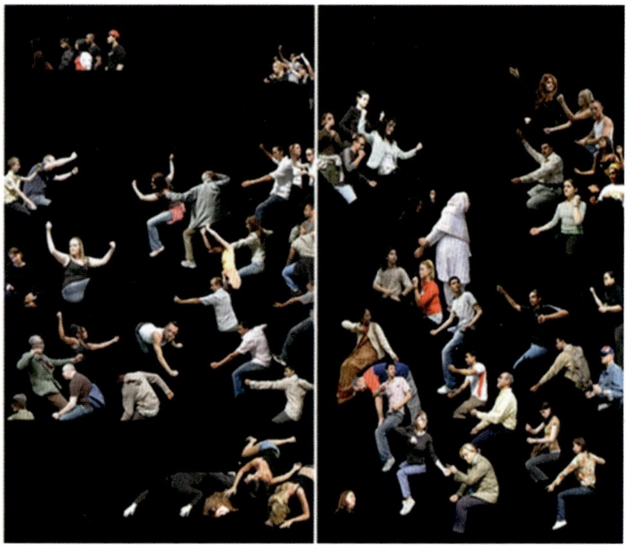

The digital animation *Battle Scenes* (2006) references two miniatures from an illustrated *Akbarnama* manuscript (see cat. 44), that narrates the story of Akbar, the third Mughal emperor. Abbas reimagines a battle scene between Akbar and his enemies, staged using visitors to London parks whom Abbas approached to pose. Drawing on the warrior silhouettes of the *Akbarnama*, Abbas challenges the climate in which she worked in the years immediately following 9/11, critiquing the neo-imperial rhetoric and inaccurate reporting that were rife.

HAMRA ABBAS

121 Lessons on Love

2007–08 | acrylic on high-density resin and wood | 166.5 × 213 × 122.5 cm | Vanhaerents Art Collection, Brussels

In *Lessons on Love* (2007–8) (a rough translation of *Kama Sutra*) Abbas extracts figures from miniature paintings, casting them as three-dimensional sculptures, originally made in coloured plasticine. In isolating the characters from their wider context, Abbas highlights the absurdity of their stance, being in a combined act of amorous embrace whilst hunting. The work simultaneously ridicules contemporary censorship laws by drawing attention to histories of sexually explicit imagery (see cat. 59–61).

Every Colour (2022) is a series of portraits made over the last five years that captures members of Lahore's transgender community during their daily street performances. The luminous miniatures were painted on silk using a courtly Chinese Gongbi technique. On the series, Abbas has explained: 'I want the viewers to experience [the portraits] with a certain level of intimacy and walk away feeling the full extent of the performative engagement I could experience during my interaction with the transgender community in Lahore.'[54]

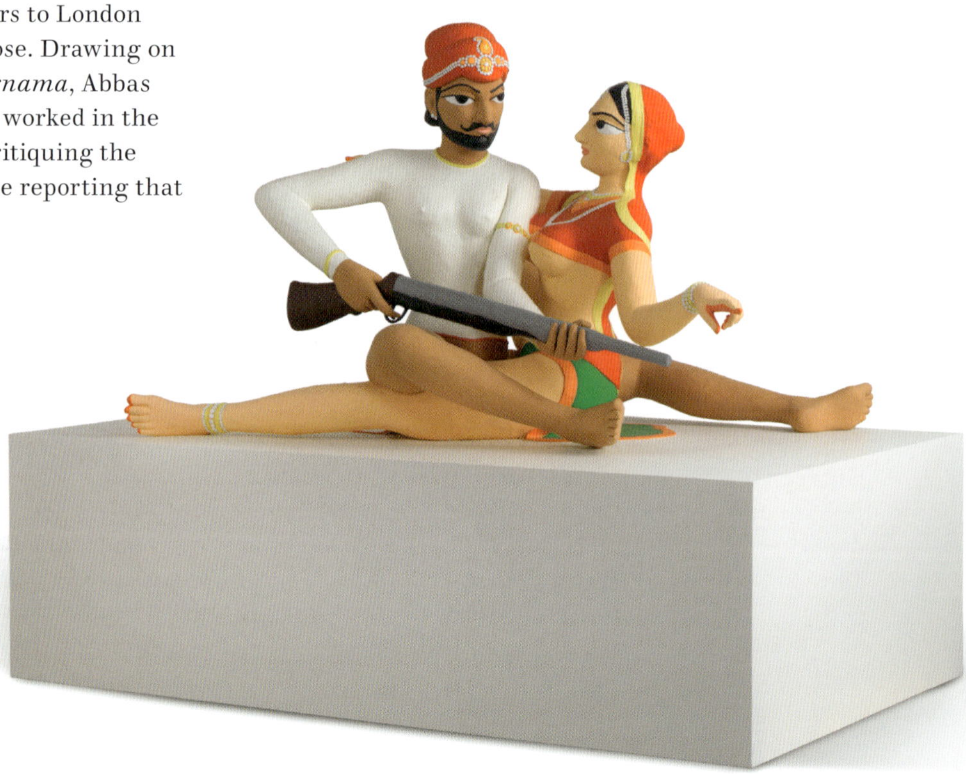

HAMRA ABBAS

122 Every Colour

2022 | gouache on silk | 5 works, each 38 × 34 cm | courtesy the artist and Lawrie Shabibi

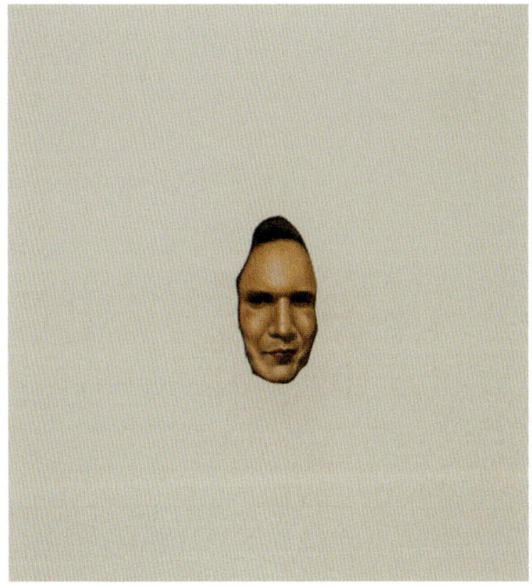

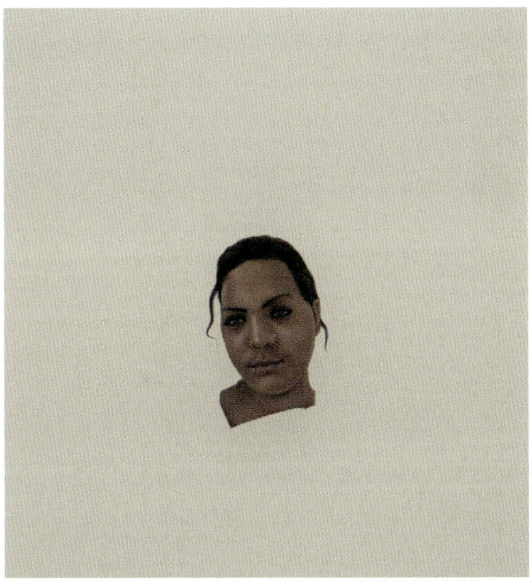

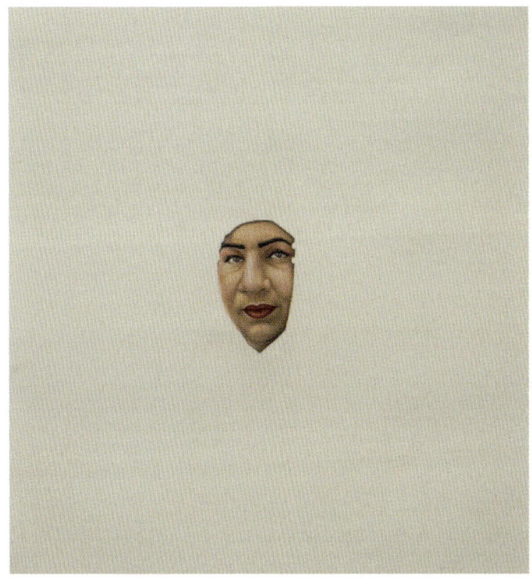

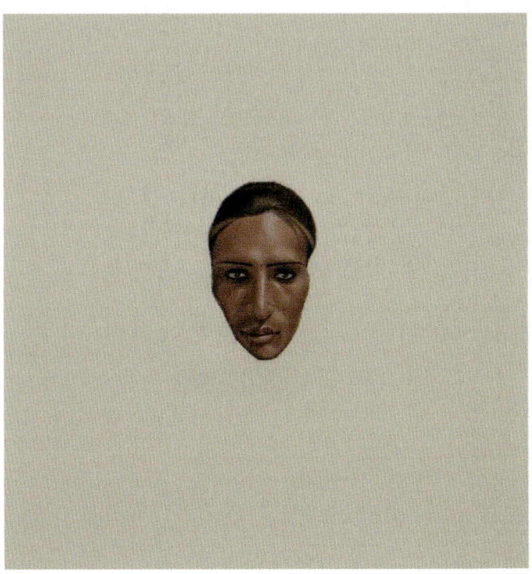

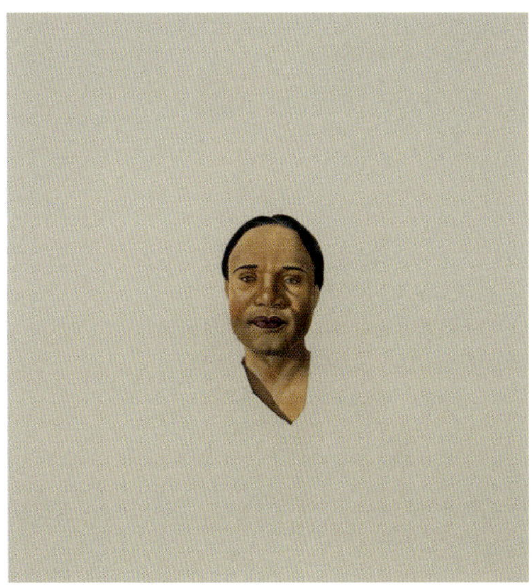

MUHAMMAD ZEESHAN

123 Dying Miniature

2008 | graphite on sandpaper | 132 × 205 cm | private collection, UK

Muhammad Zeeshan (b.1980, Mirpurkhas, Pakistan) explores global socio-politics, examining the exploitation of difference. Zeeshan trained in miniature painting at the NCA, Lahore, with Bashir Ahmed and Imran Qureshi. Working across mediums, Zeeshan experiments with detailed marks, including using a laser to score wasli paper. Concerned with the intensification of social polarity and division, Zeeshan's work highlights cultural similarities and human connection across the ages.

The *Dying Miniature* series (2008–09) is a satirical response to an art-world debate in Pakistan concerning the 'death of the miniature' and directly quotes famous Mughal paintings, including those from the *Padshahnama* (see cat. 11).

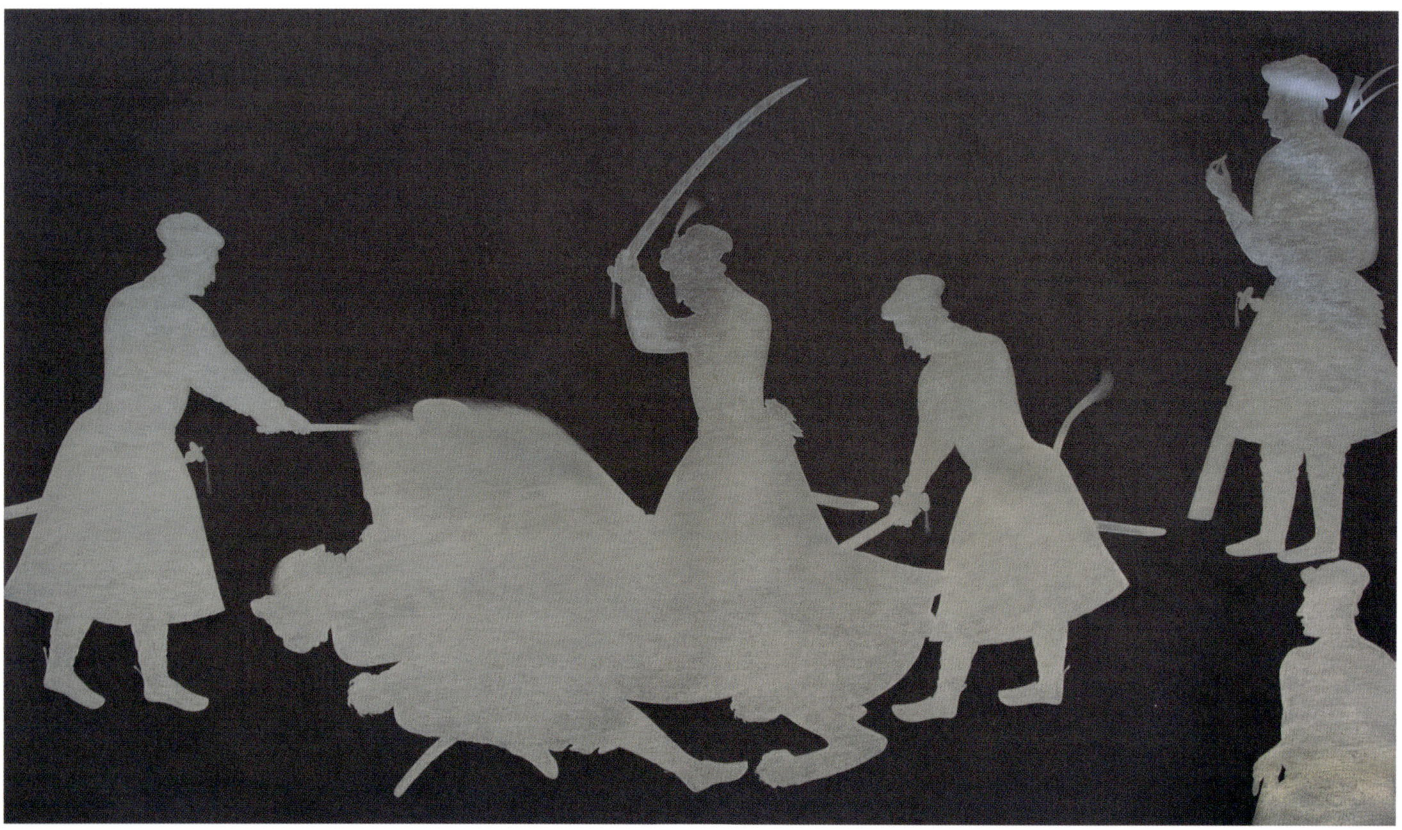

MUHAMMAD ZEESHAN

124 Dying Miniature

2009 | graphite on sandpaper | 101.6 × 167.6 cm | courtesy of the artist/Kirstin Hjellegjerde Gallery

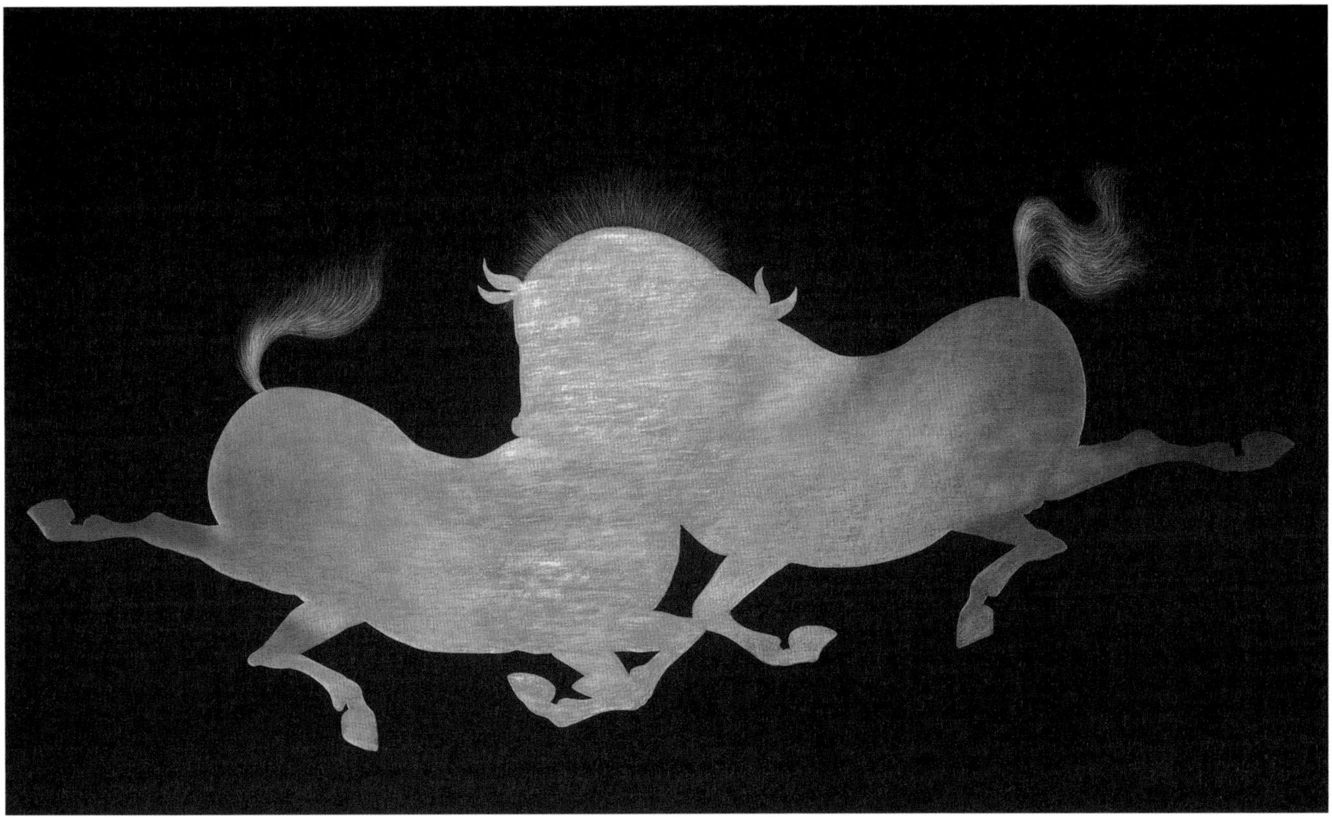

On a base of sandpaper, rather than wasli, Zeeshan applies graphite, silver leaf and copper. The base paper is particularly pertinent, as Virginia Whiles comments:

> Forgoing the smooth surface of the polished wasli ... for the roughness of a paper used usually to strip painted surfaces is an ironic gesture in its reversal of the actual material process. Zeeshan's use of such unlikely material is deliberately set up as a challenge to the mythical aura created around miniature practice today.[55]

JESS MACNEIL

125 The Shape of Between

2006 | digital video with sound, 12 minutes 57 seconds on an infinite loop | courtesy the artist

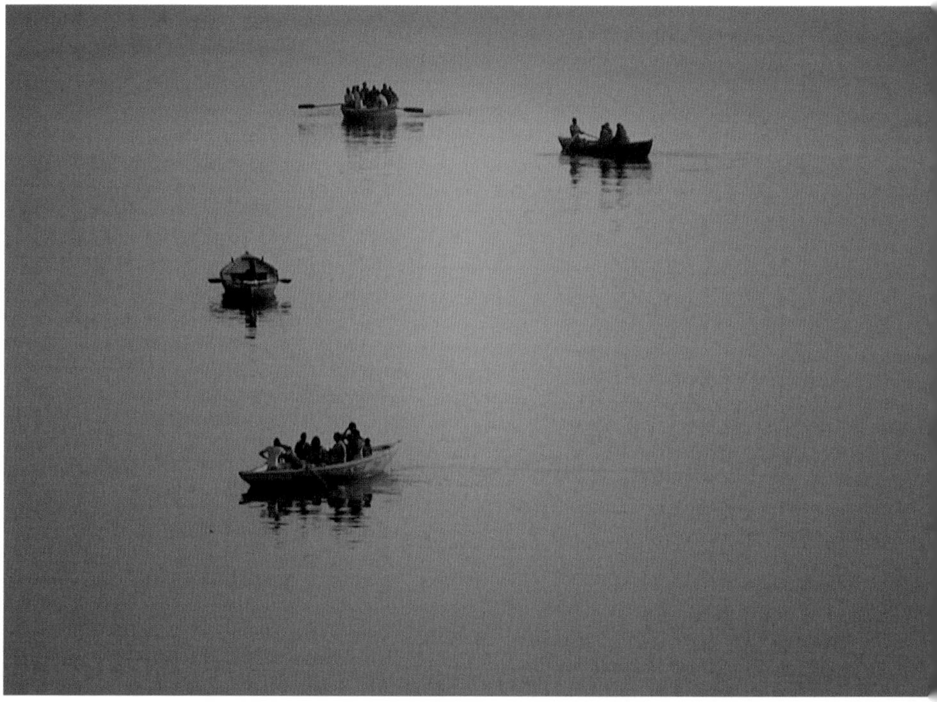

Jess MacNeil (b.1977, Inverness, Nova Scotia, Canada) currently lives and works between London and Sydney, Australia. Her interest in recording human traces in the environment is manifested in painting, installation, video and photography.

In the film *The Shape of Between* (2006), four rowing boats drift ambiguously across water. Shot from a single vantage point, on the sacred waters of the Ganges river, the film plays with our perceptions as 100 seconds of footage is digitally altered and stretched to 13 minutes. Each boat pulls in and out of focus, disrupting our sense of distance and time in a way that evokes the multiple perspectives often found in miniature painting. The work was filmed in India, which holds personal significance for the artist, mixing emotion and mythology with occasional glimpses of reality.

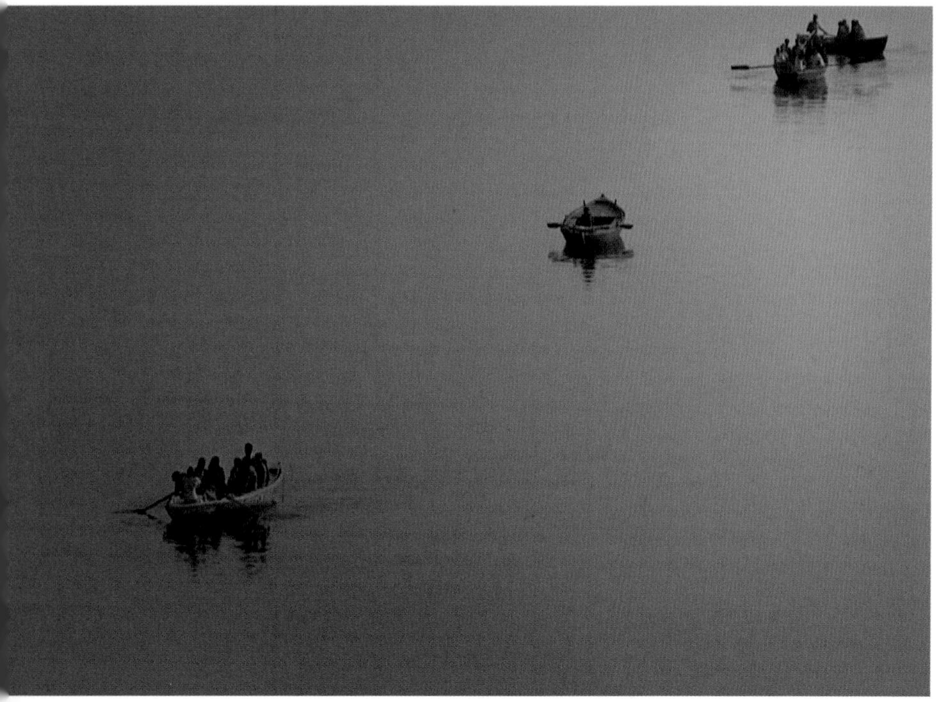

NUSRA LATIF QURESHI

126 Did You Come Here to Find History?

2009 | digital print on transparent film in the form of a scroll | 65 × 870 cm | courtesy of the artist

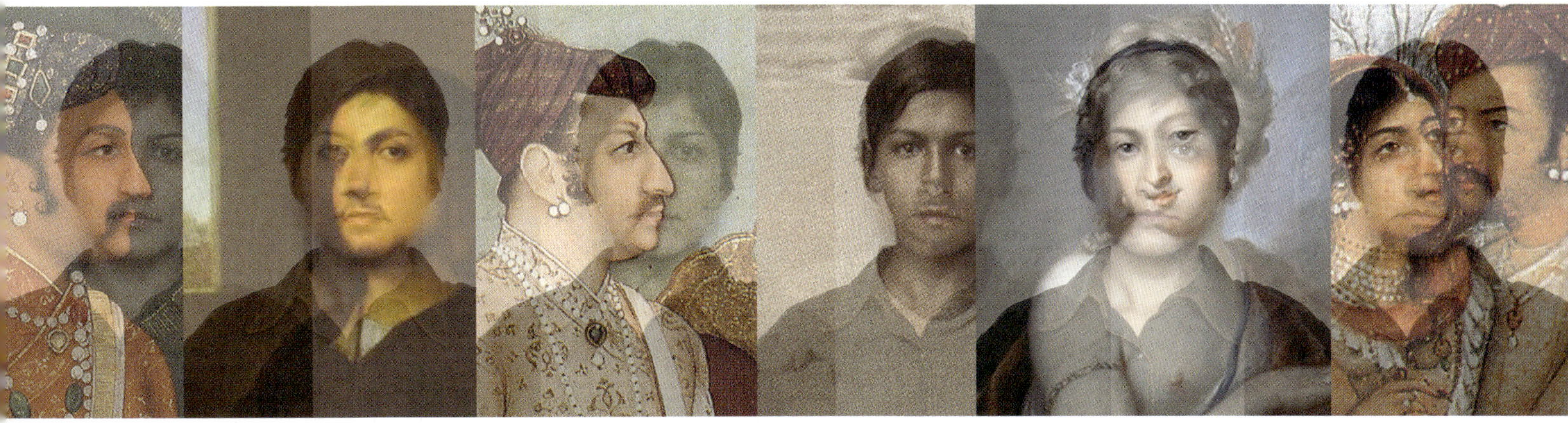

Nusra Latif Qureshi (b.1973, Lahore, Pakistan) critically engages with art history using miniature techniques to question cultural assumptions and invert the conventions of the genre. Trained at the NCA, Lahore, and the University of Melbourne's Victoria College of Art, Australia, Qureshi culls figures, patterns and objects from disparate sources including textiles, miniature paintings and colonial photographs to create fanciful juxtapositions; often inserting female figures into historical contexts. In presenting visual complexity, Qureshi explores the way narratives can be disrupted and reconstructed.

Did You Come Here to Find History? (2009) is a digital print on film in scroll form, stretching to almost 9 metres in total length. Transposed onto the film are the artist's passport photographs, the image of a nineteenth-century acrobat, and fifteenth- to seventeenth-century Venetian and Mughal portraits. In creating shifting, composite portraits, the artist denies any linear mapping of time and instead folds the images into a more layered temporality that incorporates those typically erased from historical narratives.

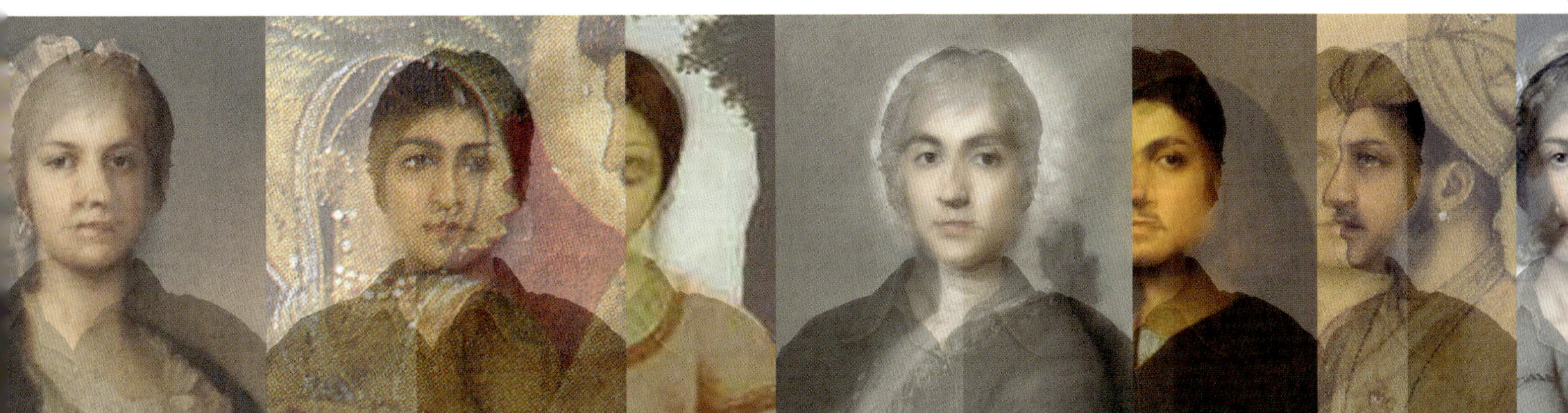

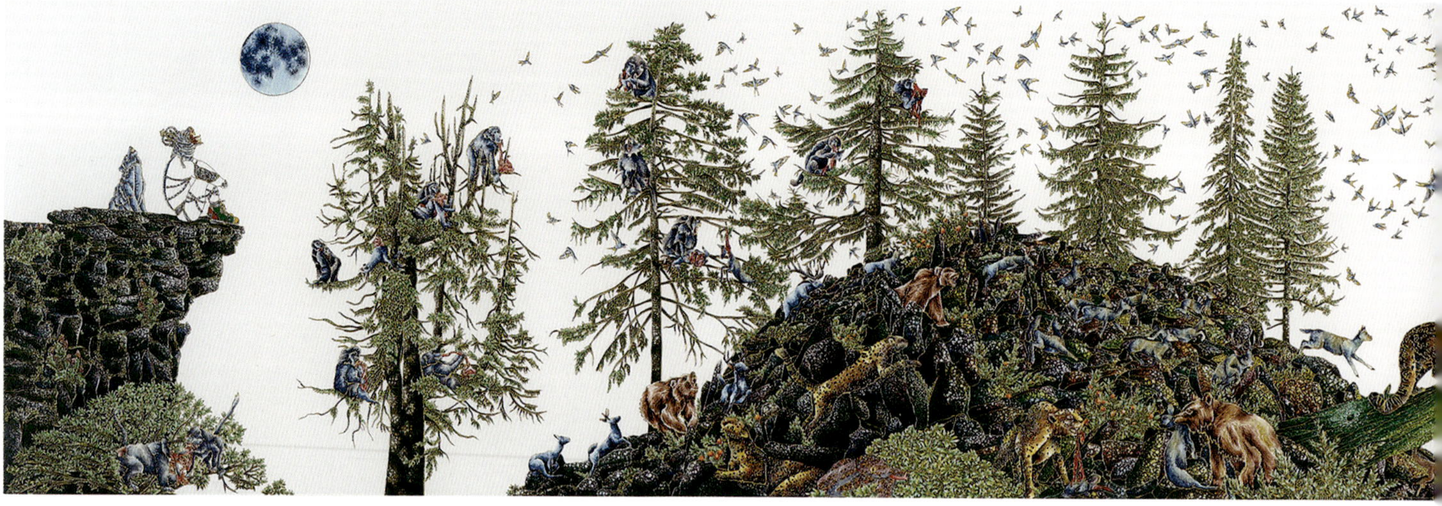

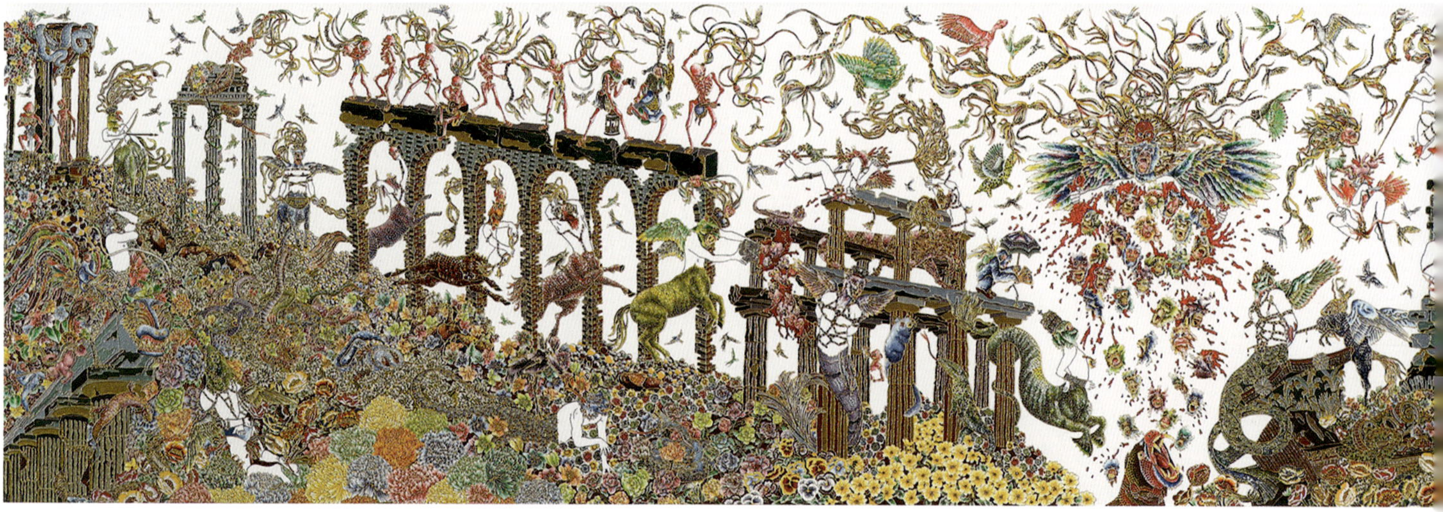

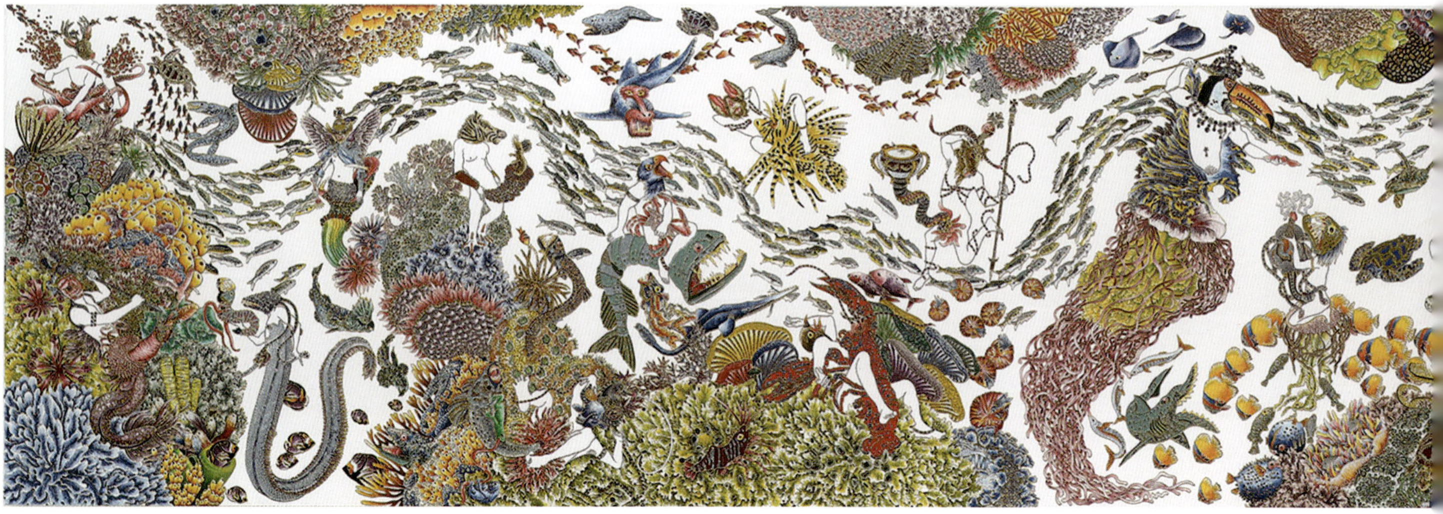

RAQIB SHAW

127 Synopsis Triptych

2010–12 | acrylic, glitter, enamel and rhinestones on paper | 3 parts, each 65×255cm framed | courtesy of the artist and White Cube

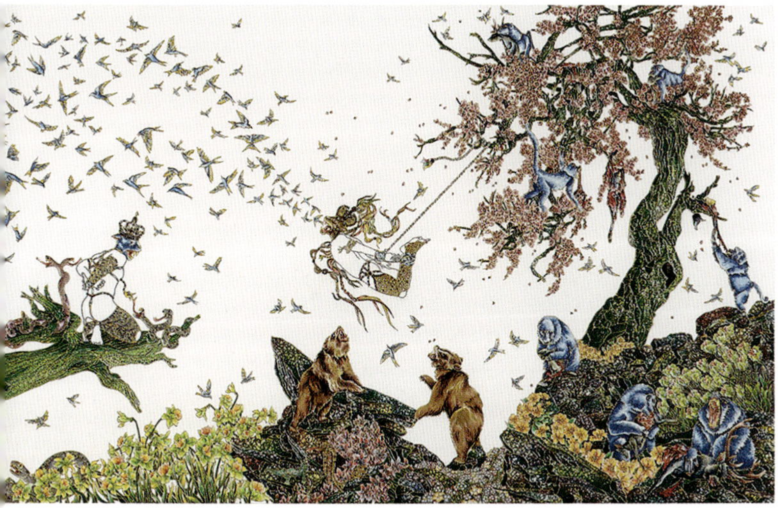

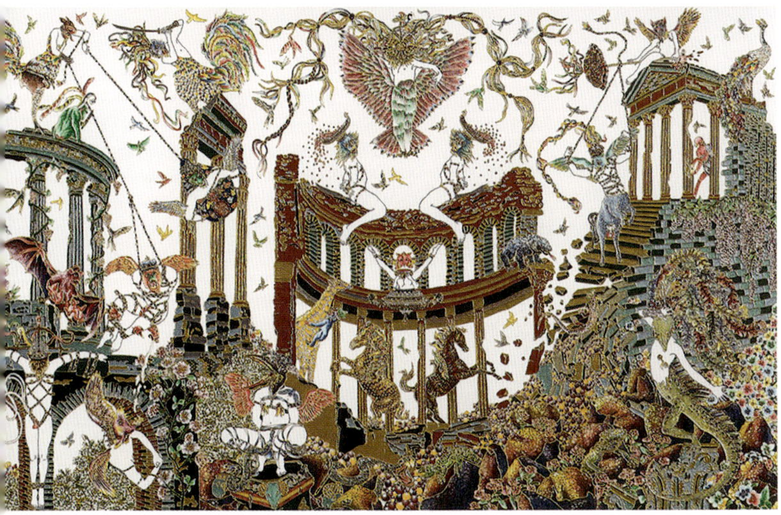

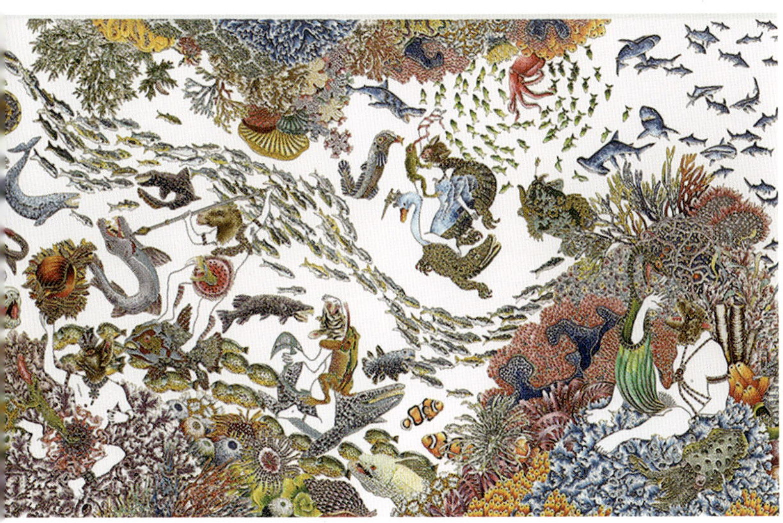

Raqib Shaw (b.1974, Kolkata, India) is a London-based artist of Kashmiri decent. From afar, his otherworldly paintings have the appearance of large Indian miniatures: their richly coloured detail, flatness of form and uncanny hybrid creatures recall Mughal and Deccani traditions (see cat. 19–20). The glitter, rhinestones and enamel paint (which the artist manipulates with a porcupine quill) evoke the decorated and iridescent surfaces of Basohli paintings (see cat. 58). Yet, on close inspection, the fantastical worlds recall the hellish visions of Hieronymus Bosch and archaeological ruins of ancient Greece and Rome. As Shaw describes it, the paintings are 'a commentary on my own experience of living in this society and of being alive'; his characters finding themselves either in a 'ballad of pleasure and pain' or in a 'dance of beauty and violence'.[56]

Shaw studied at Central Saint Martins School of Art and Design in London. As Dr Petr Nedoma writes, he

> stands astride his own Indian past and his deep knowledge of European culture, knowledge that far exceeds the norm among educated Europeans.... Two worlds which, in a British setting, seem quite logically linked, but never entirely interconnected.... With his deep knowledge of two worlds of such different cultures, [Shaw] poses pressing questions about possibilities in the way art is interpreted.[57]

N.S. HARSHA

My formal exposure to miniature painting was during my MFA in Baroda (1992–95). It was more of an academic interest than an actual painting interest during that time. Only after returning to Mysore in 1995 did I experiment with a certain painterly language inspired by temple architectural forms, popular posters, textbook illustrations and murals, which eventually resulted in repetition of forms as a painterly device. During my Master's in Baroda I was working under the influence of Transavanguard painters. After returning to Mysore there was a sense of vacuum in my language so I started revisiting the above-mentioned areas of interest.

My teachers, like Gulam and Nilima Sheikh, were revisiting miniature paintings as a primary painterly interest. I was not that interested in reworking the formal elements of miniature paintings, but more so in the way figures were painted and the flow of lines in these paintings. Lack of central 'perspective' and visual 'flatness' is a visual device I still use now. But these elements could also be observed in popular posters and illustrations.

Sometimes I wonder about the terminology of 'miniature'. How did this term get fixed to this kind of painting? What is the 'normal size' of painting then? If so, are Renaissance paintings 'Western extra-large paintings'? Then I remind myself that these terminologies are more of a communicative device rather than their actual state of being.

I'm not sure if 'Time' can overrule painterly qualities of a painting or painted surfaces. So, there is always a spark of inspiration in all kinds of paintings. We have seen artists getting inspired by historical paintings, pure flat distemper wall painting, worn-out painted surfaces or a glittering glamorous car paint. All painted surfaces offer equal opportunities for an artistic gaze.

N.S. HARSHA

128 Distress Call from Jupiter's Neighborhood

2011 | acrylic on canvas and gold foil on processed leather, wood (musical instrument) | 290 × 168 cm | courtesy the artist and Victoria Miro

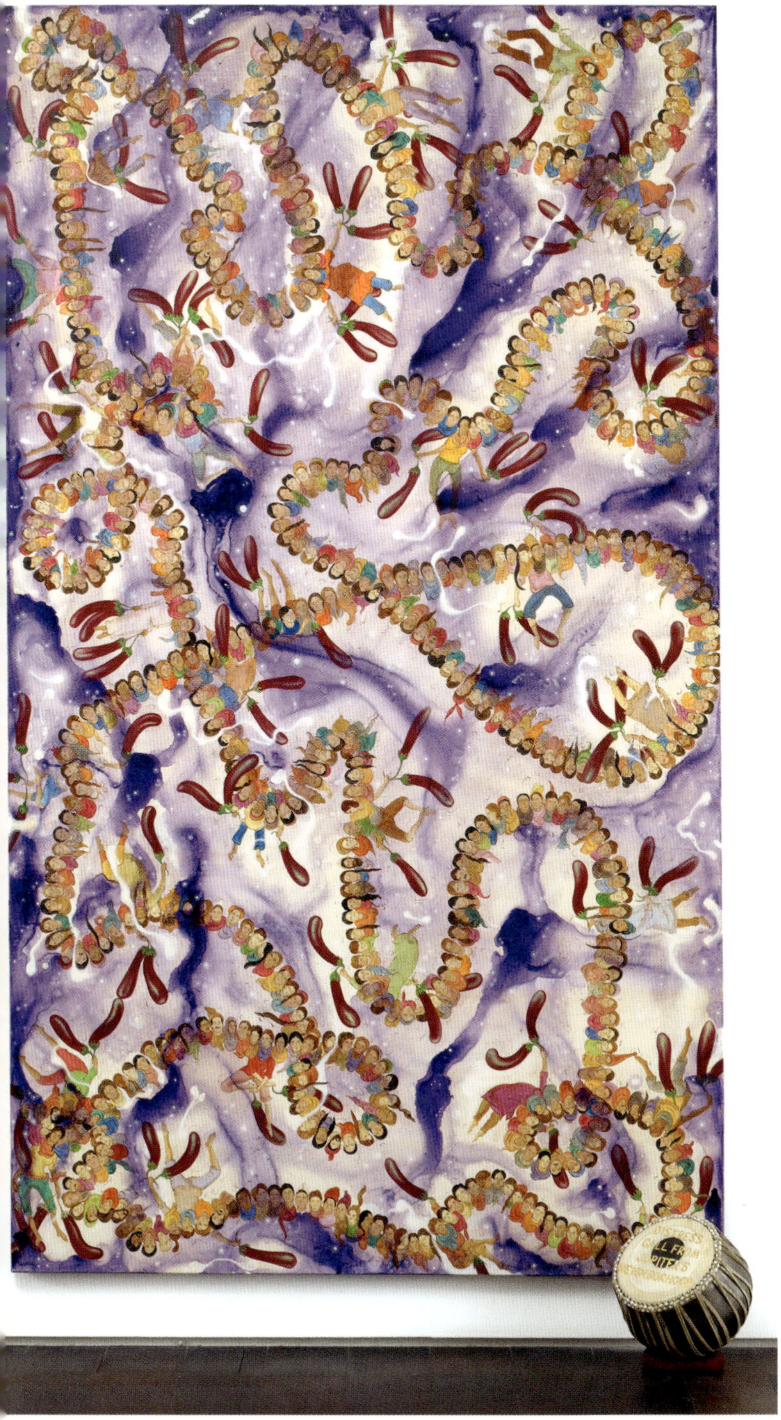

N.S. Harsha (b.1969, Mysore, India) looks to India's spectrum of painting traditions, incorporating pop references as well as courtly styles alongside the Western art canon in works that examine the tensions running through human experience in the context of global modernization. Taught by Gulammohammed and Nilima Sheikh during his studies at the Faculty of Fine Arts, Baroda, Harsha produces detailed paintings, sculptures and site-specific installations that question the binaries that define the contemporary condition: local and global, traditional and contemporary, and the individual and the collective.

Distress Call from Jupiter's Neighborhood (2011) is based on a popular Hindu image, Vishvaroopa, which visualizes the universe as a body with multiple heads. In Harsha's interpretation continuous chains of miniature heads and bodies float rhythmically against a cosmic purple background, some of the figures holding seemingly weightless bunches of aubergines. Harsha embraces the absurd and uses the vegetable icon as a purely aesthetic, almost abstract motif, specifically chosen for its lack of symbolic association. Devoid of religious or political significance, the object serves an aesthetic function and gives a festive tone to the work. Harsha tethers the painting with a *dhol*, a drum specifically used in Indian rituals and celebrations, installed beside the work.

N.S. HARSHA

129 Surviving on blueberries from the inverted tree!

2012 | watercolour and pencil on paper | 29.7 × 21 cm | courtesy the artist and Victoria Miro

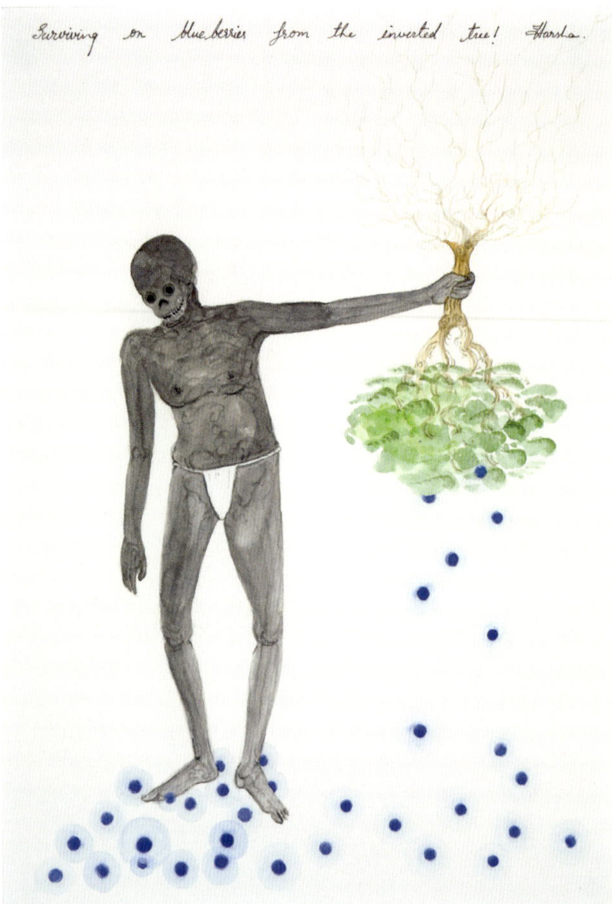

N.S. HARSHA

130 Women preparing 'hot dye' for shades of blue!

2012 | watercolour and pencil on paper | 29.7 × 21 cm | courtesy the artist and Victoria Miro

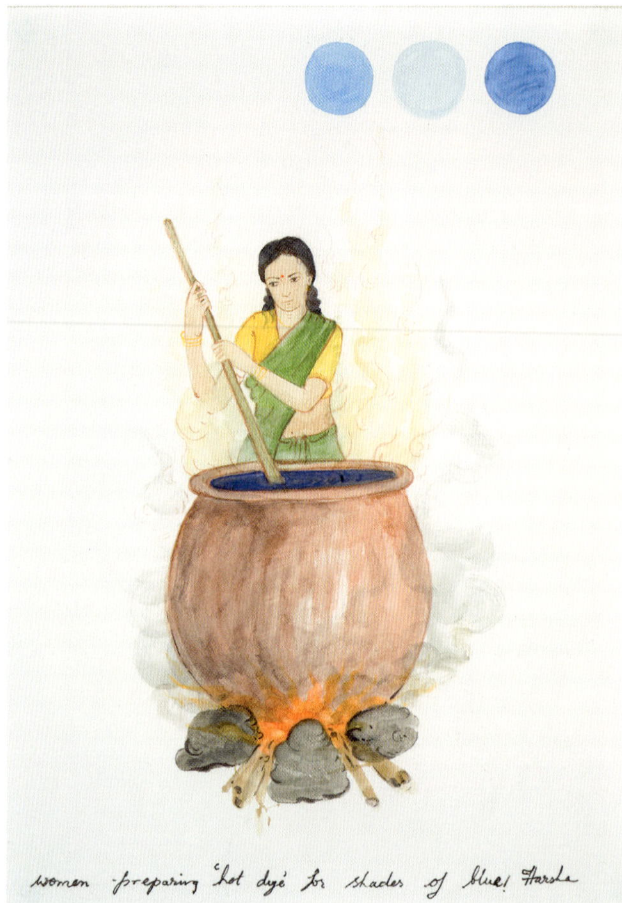

Surviving on blueberries from the inverted tree!, *Women preparing 'hot dye' for shades of blue!*, *She sold her cow and started squeezing magenta into her farm!* and *Coming out of the forest, laying arms down for dignity and honour!* (all 2012) are a suite of surreal miniature drawings rendered in watercolour. The narrative titles, handwritten alongside each image, suggest that these vignettes could be pulled from a storybook or folkloric tale. Harsha uses this visual trope to communicate socio-political issues faced by India's tribal and agrarian communities. *She sold her cow and started squeezing magenta into her farm!*, for example, notes the changes in work as new markets for milk produced on an industrial scale have pushed women into chemical dye processing.

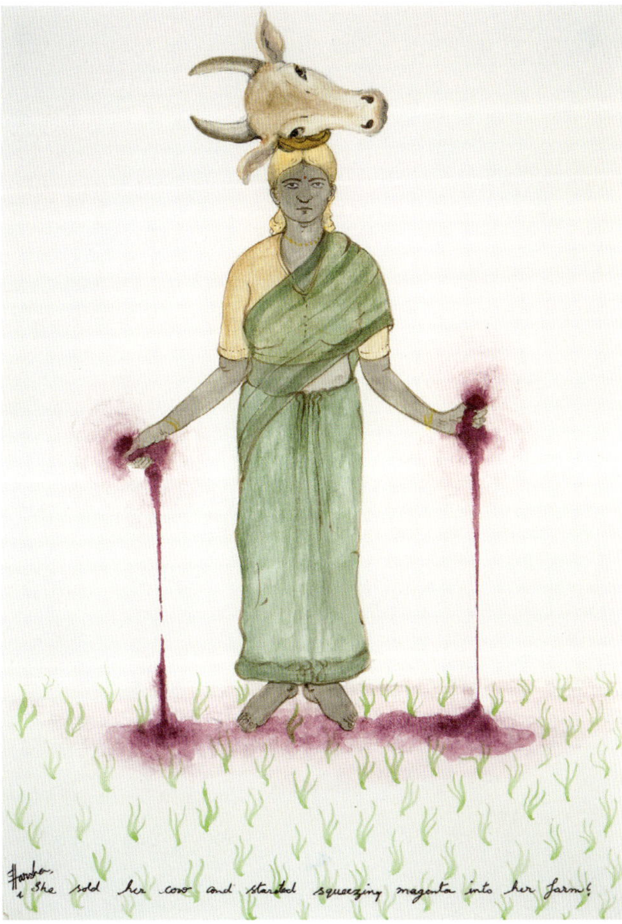

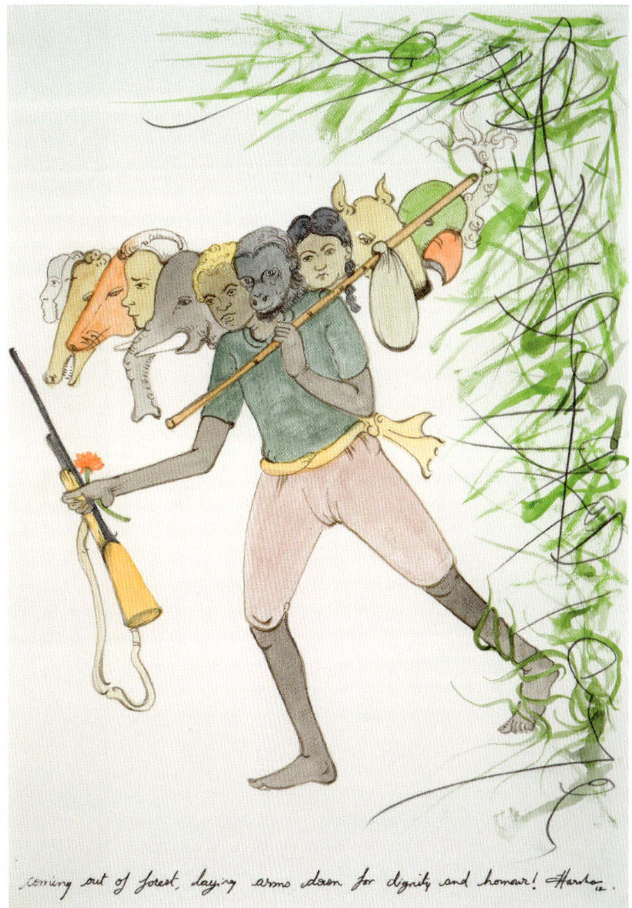

N.S. HARSHA

131 She sold her cow and started squeezing magenta into her farm!

2012 | watercolour and pencil on paper | 29.7 × 21 cm | courtesy the artist and Victoria Miro

N.S. HARSHA

132 Coming out of the forest, laying arms down for dignity and honour!

2012 | watercolour and pencil on paper | 29.7 × 21 cm | courtesy the artist and Victoria Miro

NOOR ALI CHAGANI

133 Lifeline

2011 | handmade miniature kiln bricks and nylon strings | 220 × 97 x 40 cm | Joost van den Bergh, London

Noor Ali Chagani (b.1982, Karachi, Pakistan) sculpturally reinterprets miniature painting, a form he trained in at the NCA, Lahore. Using handmade miniature terracotta bricks he deems 'transforming units', Chagani translates his ideas for paintings into sculptural forms of connected bricks that reflect on the necessity of shelter and the symbolism of walls. At times he applies delicate brush strokes to the surface to record the streets of his home town and practises a form of weaving with the terracotta blocks.

Chagani describes *Lifeline* (2011) as a 'turning point in my practice'.[58] Made from tiny bricks, the work resembles a shrugged-off blanket, or a rug roughly kicked aside. Chagani hand-makes the bricks from red clay and embosses them with his own initials and those of his wife before firing them in the kiln. The bricks are then woven together with wires, allowing them to roll and undulate as a fabric and suggest its stiffness. The 'lifeline' may provide protection, akin to the walls and roof of a house, whilst also noting the absence of universal shelter and the daily human struggles for survival.

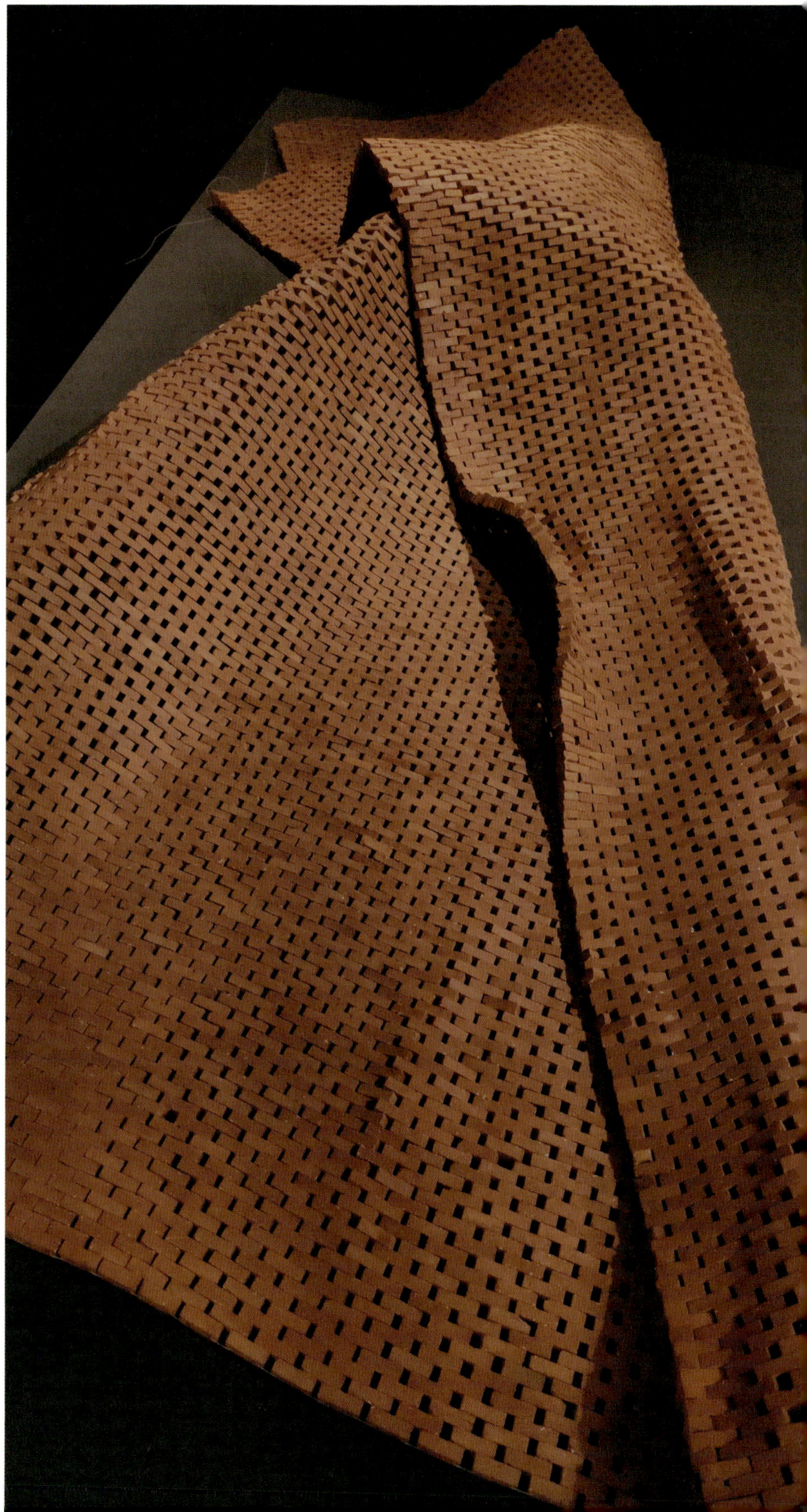

BHARTI LALWANI

134 Bagh-e-Hind

2018 | collaborative curatorial project | courtesy of the artist

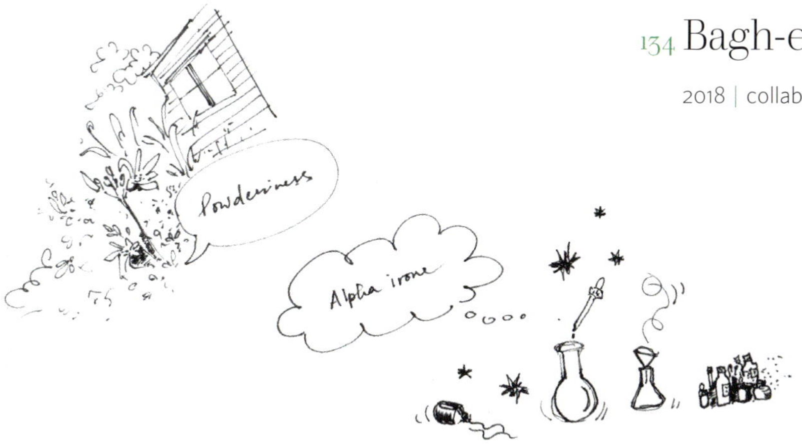

Bharti Lalwani (b. Lagos, Nigeria) is an art critic and perfumer who first trained as an artist at Central Saint Martins School of Art, London, before studying at Sotheby's Institute of Art, Singapore. Her writing focuses on South East Asian contemporary art and in 2018 she established Litrahb Perfumery to explore new languages of fragrance. She combines her interests in art and olfaction in the research initiative *Bagh-e Hind: Scent Translations of Mughal and Rajput Garden Paintings*, launched in collaboration with Dr Nicolas Roth, historian and gardener, in 2021.

The project reinterprets and contextualizes miniature painting through smell, sound and taste. This sketch, part of Lalwani and Roth's curatorial planning of an online exhibition, shows how a selection of historical Mughal and Rajput artworks were translated into their sensual character. As Lalwani says, 'such paintings are abundant with olfactive cues that signal a world of sensorial pleasure'.[59] In the drawing a group of flowers is annotated with the word 'powderiness', a reference to their smell. Beneath, a cluster of bottles and implements indicates a perfume recipe that will use the chemical 'alpha irone'. For the exhibition, five scents – roses, narcissus, iris, kewra, smoke – were isolated and made the basis of a series of 'synesthesia boxes' containing fragrances, food, music and objects. The recreation of the sensorial richness of the periods offers a comprehensive experience of art and history that enriches perceptions of this time.

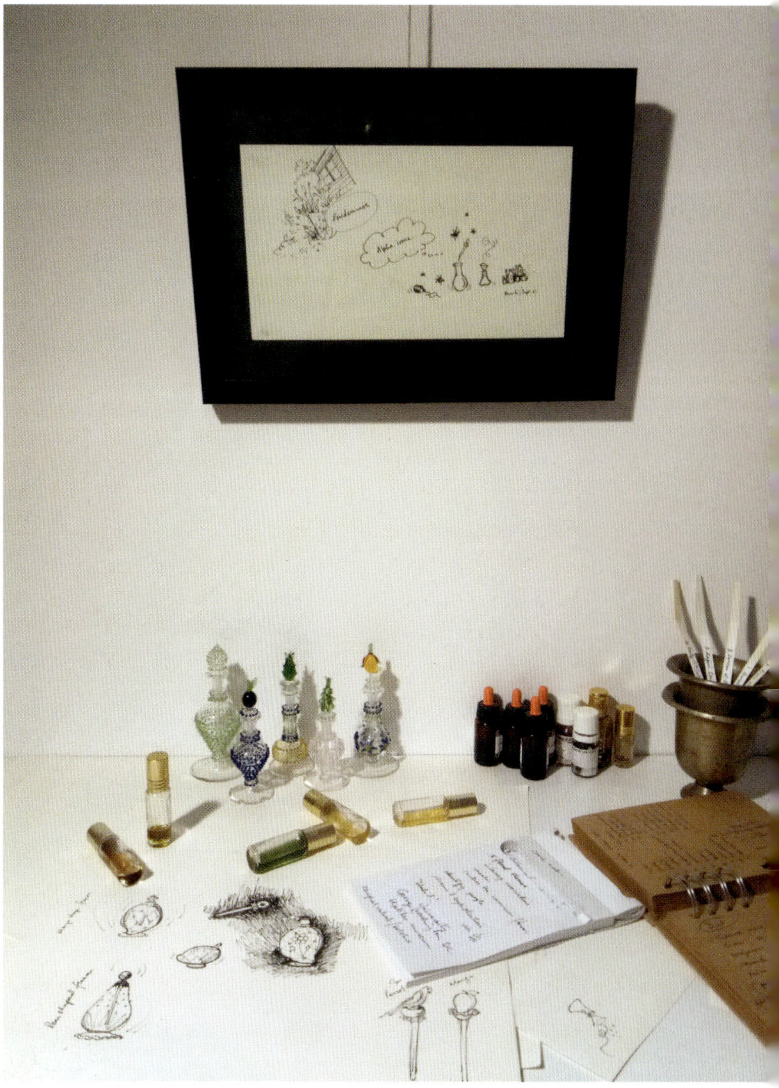

THE SINGH TWINS

135 Because You're Worth It? II

2022 | digital dyed fabric lightbox | 180 × 180 cm |
The Singh Twins - Amrit and Rabindra Singh, MBE, DFA, LittD, D.Arts

The Singh Twins (b.1966, London, UK) first encountered miniature painting at the National Museum in New Delhi during a family holiday in 1980. They describe their style as Past Modern (as opposed to Post-Modern), drawing on traditional Indian and European art forms while engaging with contemporary critical debates. They recall:

> when the time came to develop our own style during our university days, we immediately wanted to go back to that miniature tradition so we referenced some more historical examples to teach ourselves the technique, resulting in our own interpretation of the miniature style. We had our own hurdles pursuing the miniature style as it was considered 'old, backward and outdated' by our tutors who dismissed the tradition as having 'no place in contemporary art' and pressured us to follow Western role models in art history. It's not been easy to gain acceptance for our style of art within a contemporary art world dominated by a Eurocentric outlook.[60]

Because You're Worth It? II uses the well-known marketing slogan to condemn global consumerism and its impact on the environmental crisis. It employs the Indian convention of composite animals (see cat. 19) to sharpen the irony: death rides an elephant made of brand logos and household products while firing a crossbow at a desperate family of orangutans.

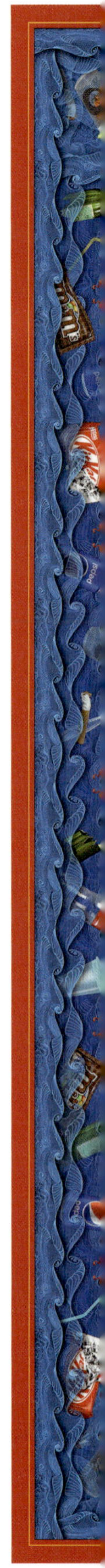

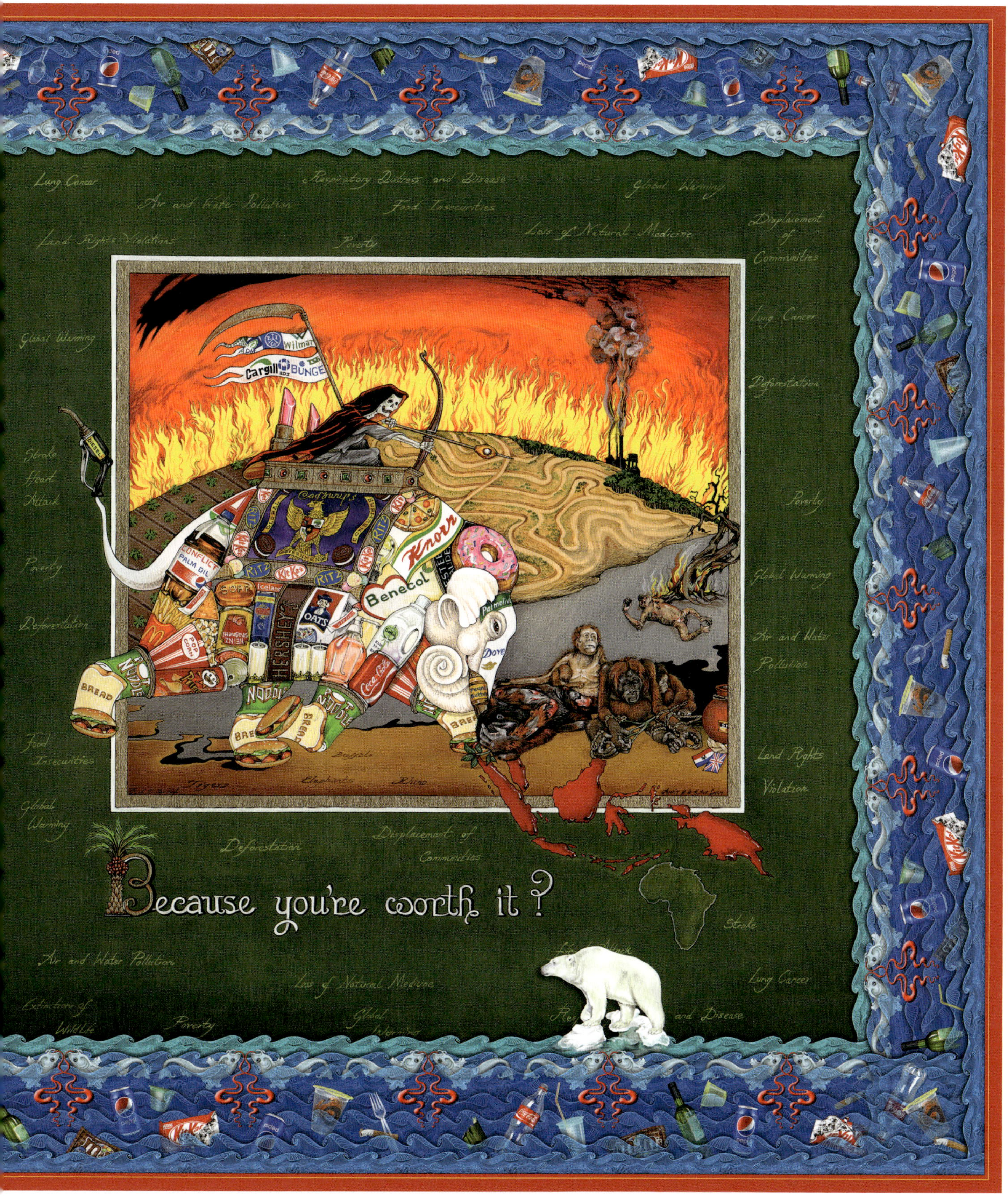
Lung Cancer
Air and Water Pollution
Respiratory Distress and Disease
Food Insecurities
Global Warming
Land Rights Violations
Poverty
Loss of Natural Medicine
Displacement of Communities
Global Warming
Lung Cancer
Deforestation
Stroke
Heart Attack
Poverty
Poverty
Global Warming
Deforestation
Air and Water Pollution
Food Insecurities
Land Rights Violation
Global Warming
Deforestation
Displacement of Communities
Because you're worth it?
Stroke
Air and Water Pollution
Loss of Natural Medicine
Lung Cancer
Extinction of Wildlife
Poverty
and Disease
Wilmar
Cargill
BUNGE
CONFLICT PALM OIL
Knorr
Benecol
HERSHEY'S
OATS
Coca-Cola
Dove
Palmolive
KitKat
RITZ
NOODLE
BREAD
Tigers
Elephants
Rhino
Buffalo

ALEXANDER GORLIZKI

136 A Medieval Paradox

2018 | gouache on paper | 41×31.5 cm | courtesy of the artist and Joost van den Bergh, London

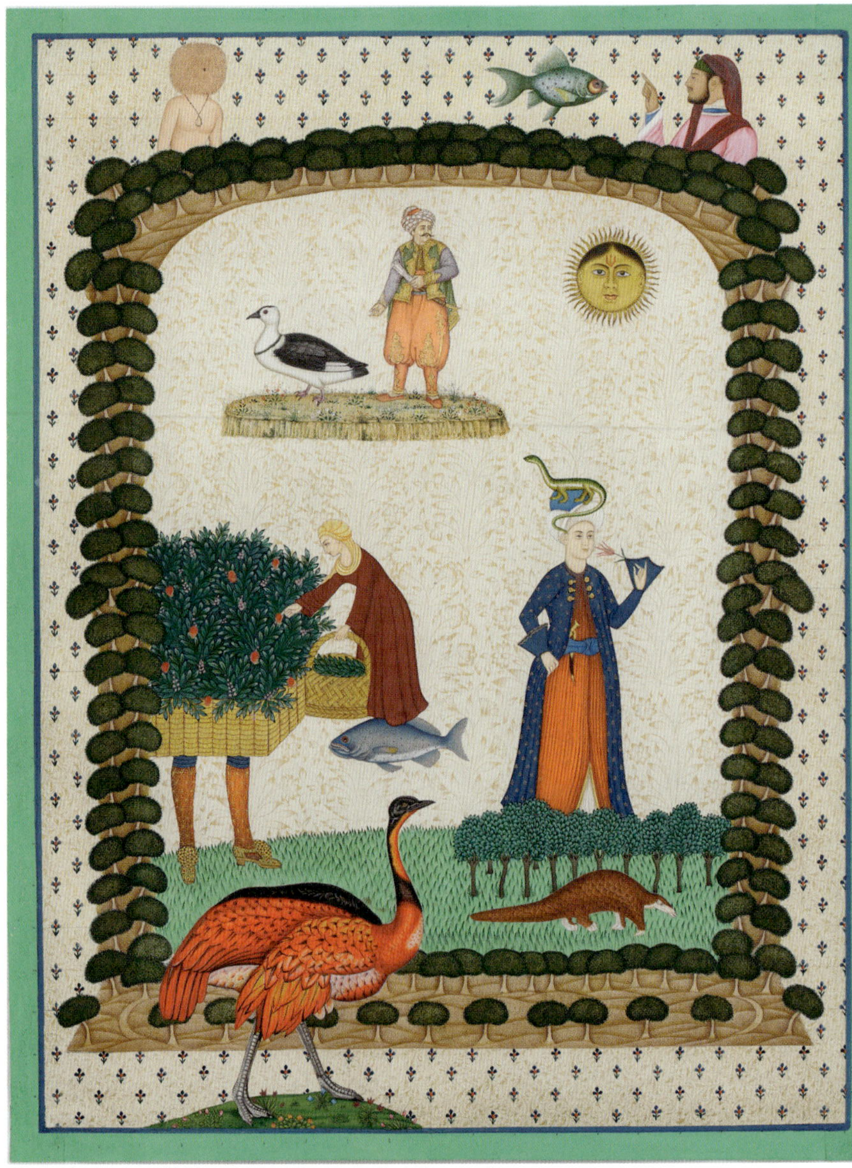

Alexander Gorlizki (b.1967, London, UK) currently lives in New York, working in collaboration with miniature painter Riyaz Uddin (b.1972, Jaipur, India), with whom he established a studio in Jaipur in 1996. Gorlizki became interested in miniature painting as a teenager through his mother's friend Francesca Galloway, a dealer specializing in Indian art:

> I don't specifically remember my earliest encounter with Indian Miniatures – and I'm sure it was in reproductions – but I can imagine how, as a child, the depiction of these fantastic, idiosyncratic worlds were absolutely captivating and rather magical.

His collaboration with Riyaz Uddin began in the mid-1990s after he became interested in artisanal skills and traditions during his visits to Asia:

> After working with a number of artisans from various traditions in Pakistan and Northern India, I was interested in finding a skilled miniature painter to 'translate' some drawings I had and was introduced to Riyaz in Jaipur. He was an extraordinarily gifted miniature painter and at the time was exclusively making copies of copies of classical paintings for the tourist market. As talented as he was he was very much beholden to the dealers in the City Palace so our meeting presented itself as a new opportunity for him too.... We work together in Jaipur some of the time and at others drawings are sent back and forth, sometimes over a period of years. As the project has evolved, so has the studio which functions like a traditional atelier with a number of other artists, men and women, Hindus and Muslims. There's now a social dynamic to the studio, which has also become very important to me.[61]

ALEXANDER GORLIZKI

137 This Much I Know

2020 | gouache on paper | 30×35.5 cm | courtesy of the artist and Joost van den Bergh, London

ALEXANDER GORLIZKI

138 Just Dropping By

2021 | gouache on paper | 39.5×30 cm | courtesy of the artist and Joost van den Bergh, London

Gorlizki first draws his witty and surreal figures onto photographs, found paper, or pages from books. His imagery draws heavily on Indian miniatures:

> I spend a lot of time looking at historical Indian miniature paintings. For all the different styles, subjects and themes within the tradition, they do have certain features in common, quite apart from the exquisite intricacy of the brushwork. I'm struck by the sense of intimacy, and quiet – even in the most brutal war scenes or mythological paintings. This is partly to do with the way the figures are staged in relation to one another (and very often in profile) and also the use of borders, windows and arches that create an impression of entering into another world, as if through a portal.[62]

Uddin and his team paint over the compositions and patterns with colour pigments and gold leaf, using the traditional slow and meticulous methods that have been practised for centuries.

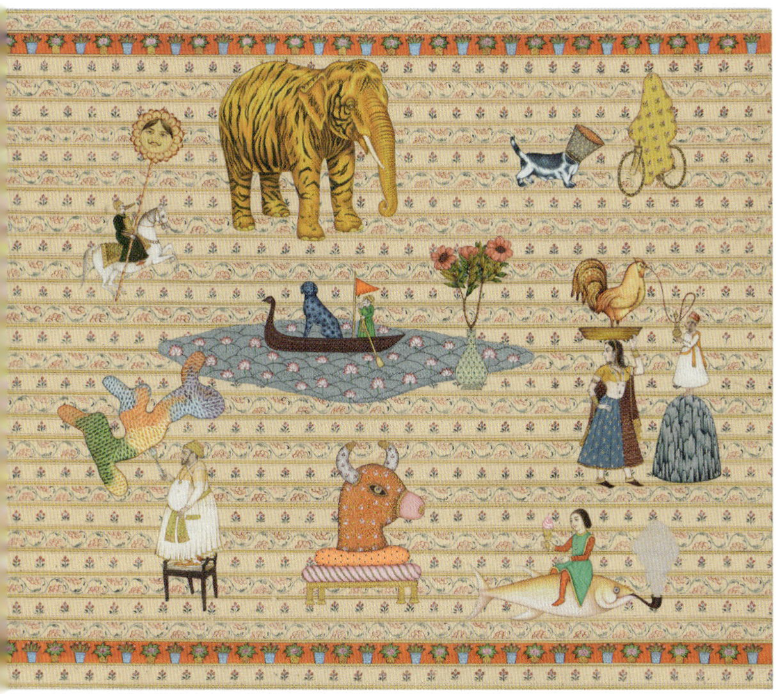

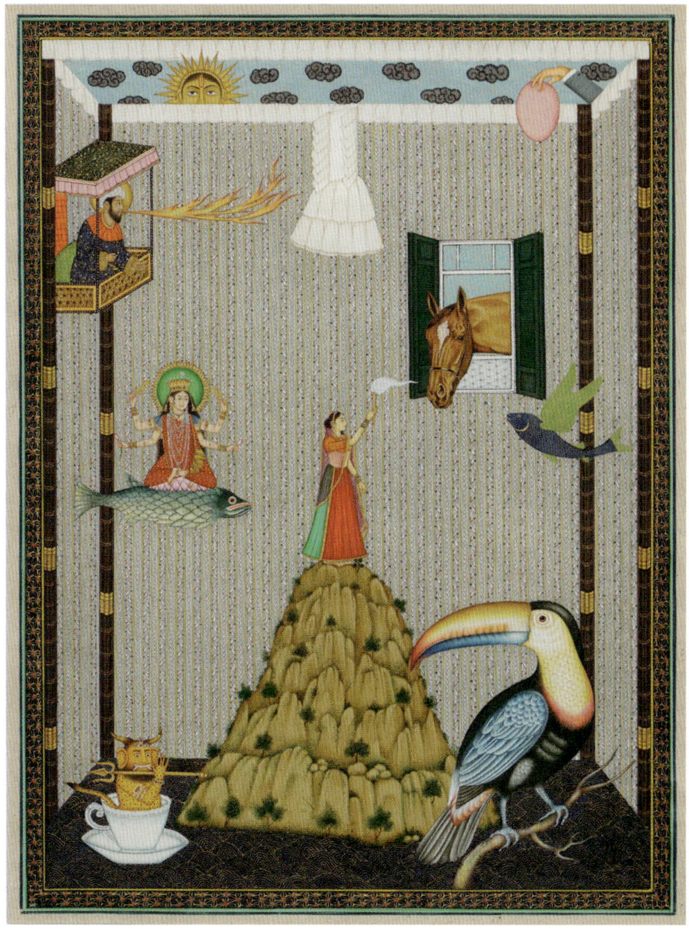

MATTHEW KRISHANU

139 Church Tower and Field

2019 | oil on board | 40 × 30 cm | private collection, Kent

MATTHEW KRISHANU

140 Church and Palm Tree

2020 | oil on board | 40 × 30 cm | private collection

Matthew Krishanu (b.1980, Bradford, UK) is a London-based painter whose work explores themes of childhood memory and the history of empire. The paintings of his *House of God* series recall the landscapes of Bangladesh, where he spent his early childhood in the 1980s with his father (an English priest) and mother (a Bengali Indian theologian), then employed by the Church of Bangladesh.

The artist lists among his artistic influences South Asian miniatures and Indian painters who have drawn directly on Indian miniatures, like Bhupen Khakhar and Lalu Prasad Shaw:

South Asian miniatures give me licence to experiment formally in my paintings with colour, representational styles and the picture plane.

My parents had framed prints of Indian miniatures on the wall when I was a child, growing up in Dhaka, Bangladesh. I have continued to look at miniatures throughout my life. I am particularly interested in the way both the Muslim and the Hindu traditions of miniature painting have included depictions of Christian subjects, which relate somewhat to my *Mission* and *House of God* series, which

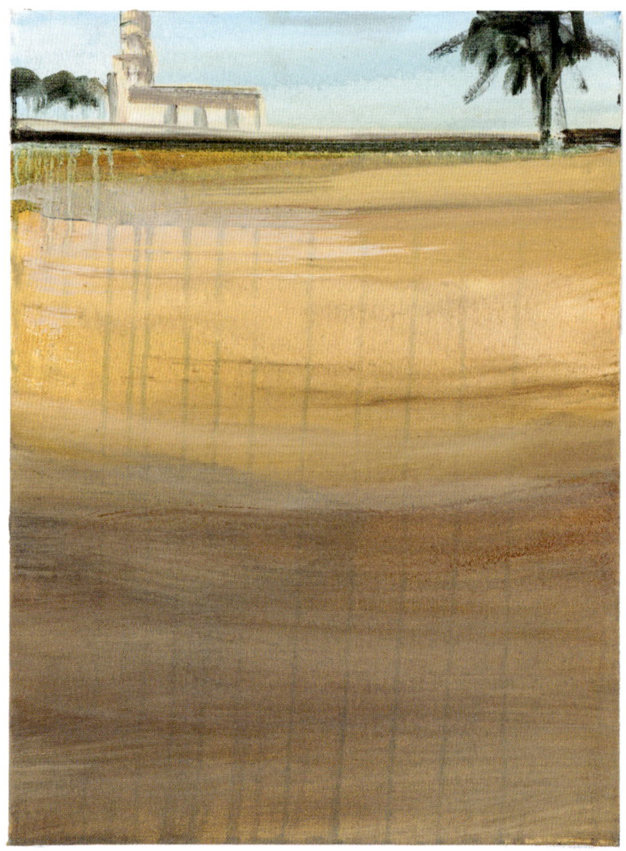

MATTHEW KRISHANU

141 Church and Lake

2020 | oil on board | 40 × 30 cm | private collection

MATTHEW KRISHANU

142 Church, Tree and Field

2020 | oil on board | 40 × 30 cm | Gordon Watson Ltd

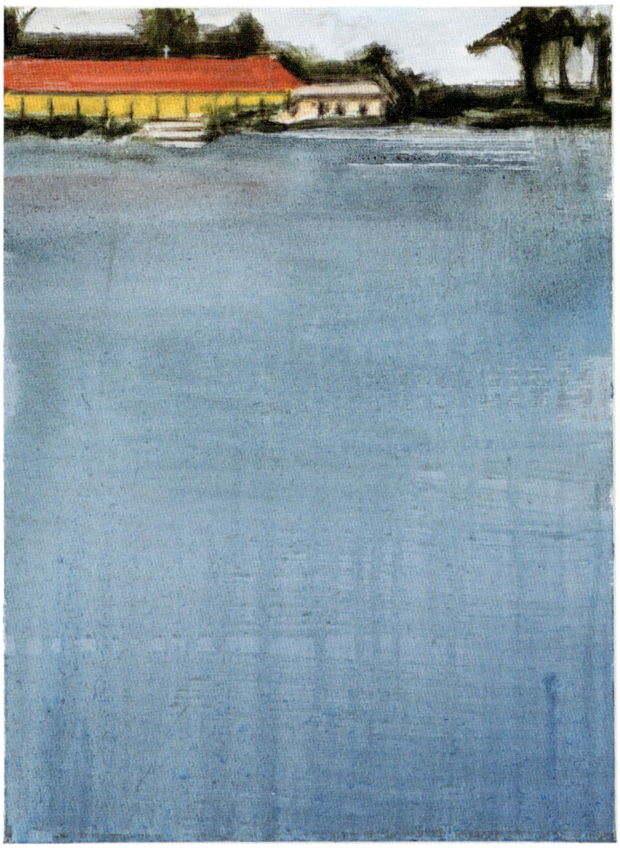

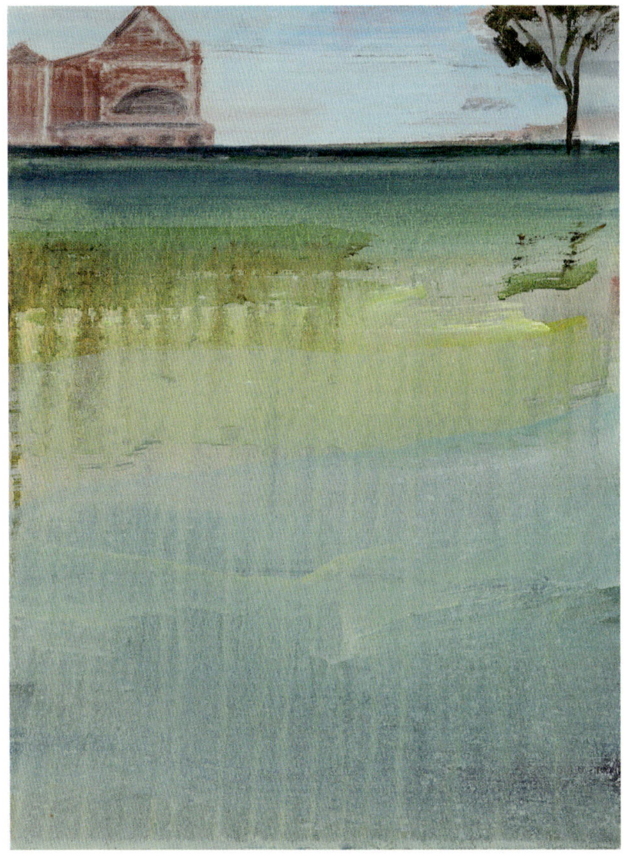

are about painting Christian religious subjects within Indian settings – alluding to histories of colonialism and Christian Mission in India and Bangladesh.

I am drawn to the simplification of forms in depictions of people in Indian miniatures. I like to keep the 'drawn' elements of my figures pared down and essentialized, while also containing a mood or emotion. In my *House of God* paintings I flatten the picture plane in the landscape, drawing on the flatness I find in miniature landscapes. I abbreviate the buildings, often high up in the picture plane, to suggest their distance. I use colour 'fields' that reference both American and European colour-field painting and the thinned washes of paint in miniature landscapes. Like miniatures, I like to apply my paint relatively thinly, but with high areas of contrast, brightly coloured accents in often muted grounds, and with areas of empty space to create atmosphere and tone.

MUHANNED CADER

143 The Lesser Adjutant Stork

2020–21 | charcoal on paper | 50 × 50 cm | courtesy the artist and Jhaveri Contemporary

144 The Common Coucal

2020–21 | charcoal on paper | 50 × 50 cm | courtesy the artist and Jhaveri Contemporary

145 The Forest Eagle Owl

2020–21 | charcoal on paper | 50 × 50 cm | courtesy the artist and Jhaveri Contemporary

146 The Ceylon Frogmouth

2020–21 | charcoal on paper | 50 × 50 cm | courtesy the artist and Jhaveri Contemporary

Muhanned Cader (b.1966, Colombo, Sri Lanka) experiments with scale and detail, reducing and abstracting aspects of his physical surroundings into painted, drawn and collaged fragments. Cader received his BFA from the School of the Art Institute of Chicago. Through his practice he subtly critiques the impact of neocolonial policies on the Sri Lankan natural environment.

The Lesser Adjutant Stork, *The Common Coucal*, *The Forest Eagle Owl* and *The Ceylon Frogmouth* (all 2020–21) record a range of Sri Lankan birds taken from *A Guide to the Birds of Ceylon* by G.M. Henry (1971). Using charcoal and a cameo format, an approximation of the particular bird's egg, the images are humanizing. As if sitting for Cader, the birds' depictions invest the animals with personality (see also cat. 28).

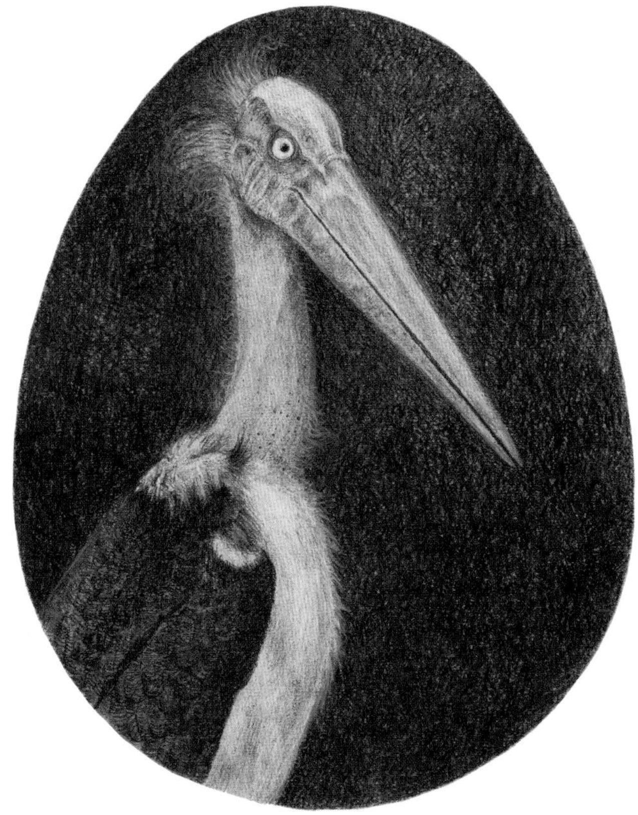
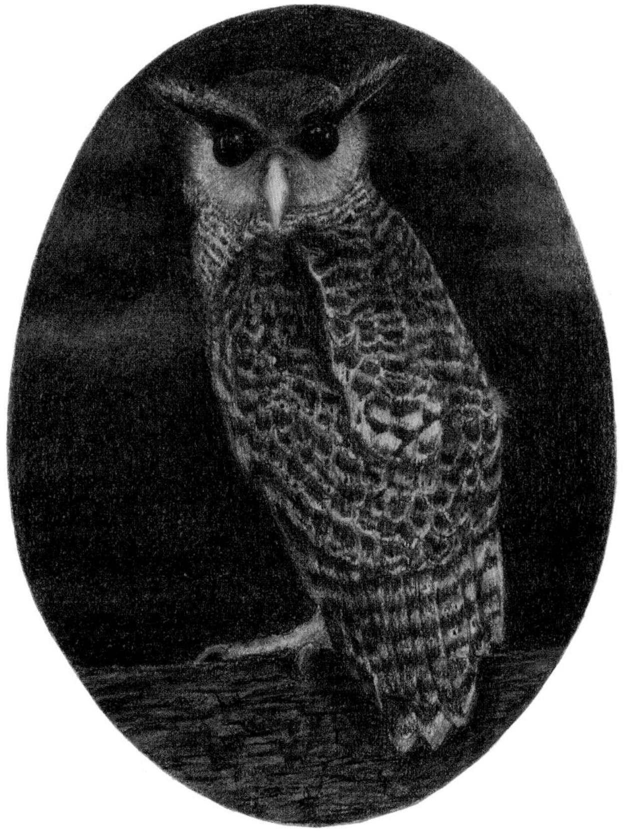
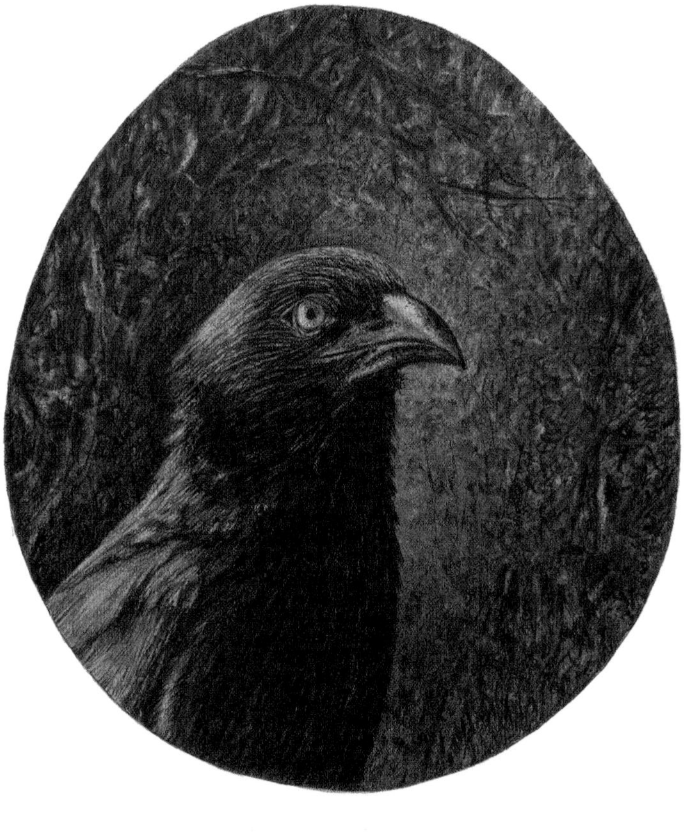
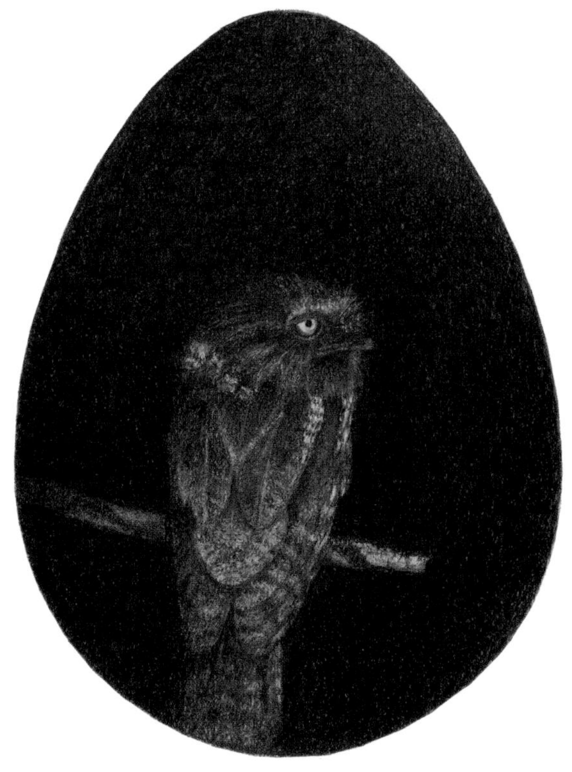

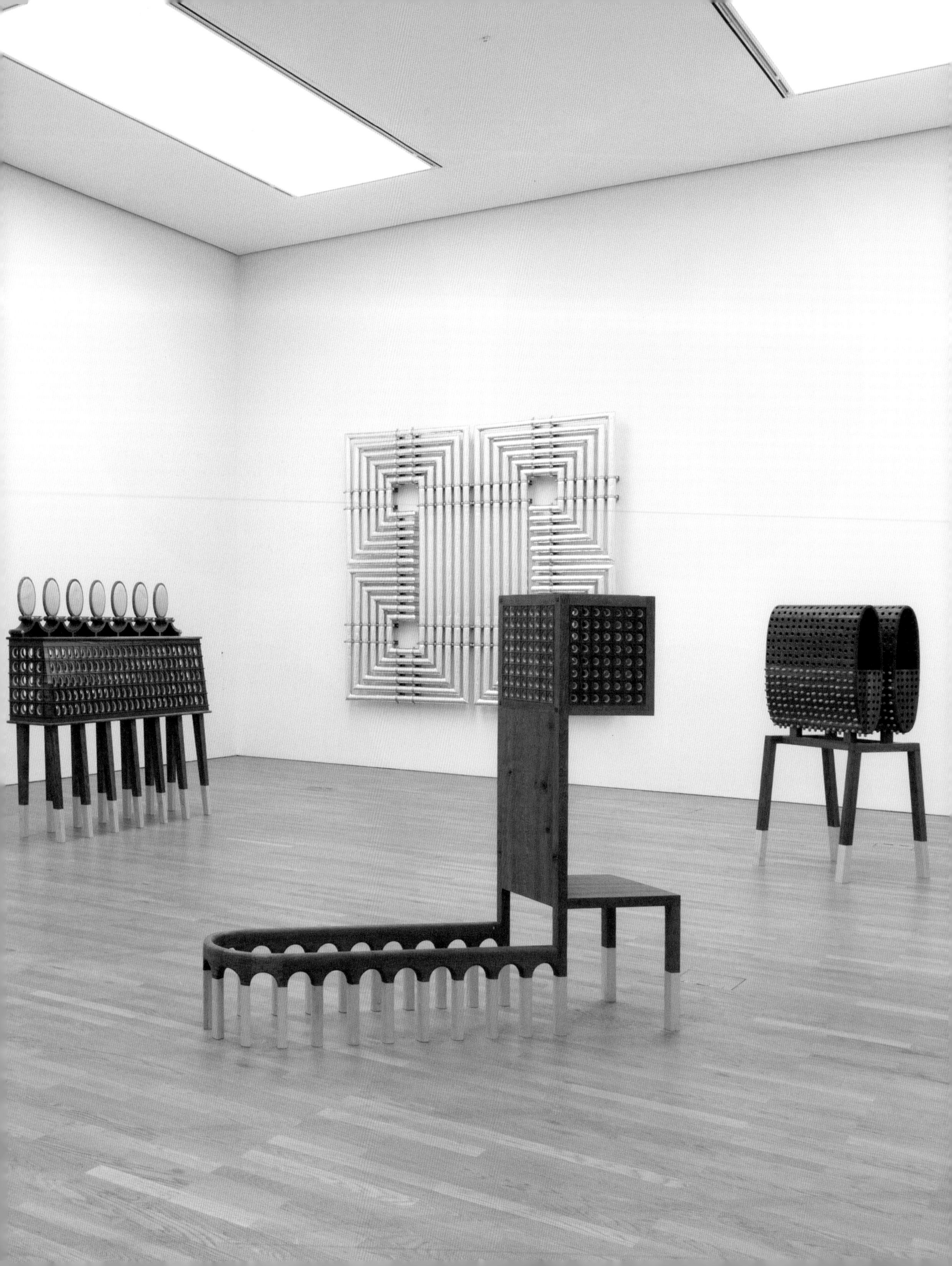

LUBNA CHOWDHARY

147 # Erratic III

2021 | wood | 149 × 66 × 60 cm | courtesy the artist and Jhaveri Contemporary

Lubna Chowdhary (b.1964, Tanzania) has a Masters degree from the Royal College of Art, London. Chowdhary became fascinated by colonial Anglo-Indian furniture during a ceramics residency at the V&A in 2017. The hybrid references of the Indian furniture-makers resonated with her own cultural experience as an Asian Muslim who moved to Rochdale from Tanzania as a child:

> When Europeans arrived [in India], they came with their own culture of furniture and a new set of ergonomics that were unfamiliar to the Indian craftsmen they commissioned. Within the objects, there is a complete merging of aesthetic and cultural understanding, or lack of understanding. When I first saw these hybrid objects I recognised my own botched together aesthetic and formal language in them.[63]

Her series of wooden sculptures *Erratics I, II & III* reimagines the Indian craftsmen's interpretation of British designs as if pushed beyond the limits of practicality. Chowdhary uses the geological term 'erratic' (meaning a rock that has been transported by ice from one place to another), for both its sense of dislocation and of blending. 'It is', she says, 'a useful analogy for a diaspora artist.'[64] The sculptures were initially intended as a collaboration with Indian designers, but due to Covid restrictions the artist created them with a team in the UK.[65]

ALI KAZIM

148 Hudhud

2023 | watercolour pigments on paper | 198 × 110 cm | courtesy of the artist and Jhaveri Contemporary

Ali Kazim (b. 1979, Pattoki, Pakistan) practises a distinctive painting technique, combining miniature practices with watercolour washes to create images of lone figures and desolate landscapes inspired by Pakistan's ancient civilizations. The process, originating from his studies at the NCA, Lahore, and Slade School of Fine Art, London, begins with a pencil outline made on paper overlaid with black pigment applied with a fine brush. After adding watercolour pigments in a granulated form, the whole work is bathed in shallow water. Kazim continues these washes, which changes the colour intensity leaving layers of textural hues that Kazim paints over with small dots using a technique called *paradakht*.

In *Hudhud* (2023), Kazim presents a dazzling array of birds in flight, inspired by the twelfth-century Persian poem *Conference of the Birds* (1177) written by Sufi poet Farid uddin Attar. The hudhud is referred to in the Quran as a messenger between the prophet Sulayman (Solomon) and the Queen of Sheba. The dense flock references the subject of natural-history paintings made for the East India Company during the eighteenth and nineteenth centuries. In these Company paintings, animals were customarily shown in isolation, annotated with their species name. Kazim's piece is less taxonomical; although bleached of colour and muted, it emphasizes the magnitude of the collective.

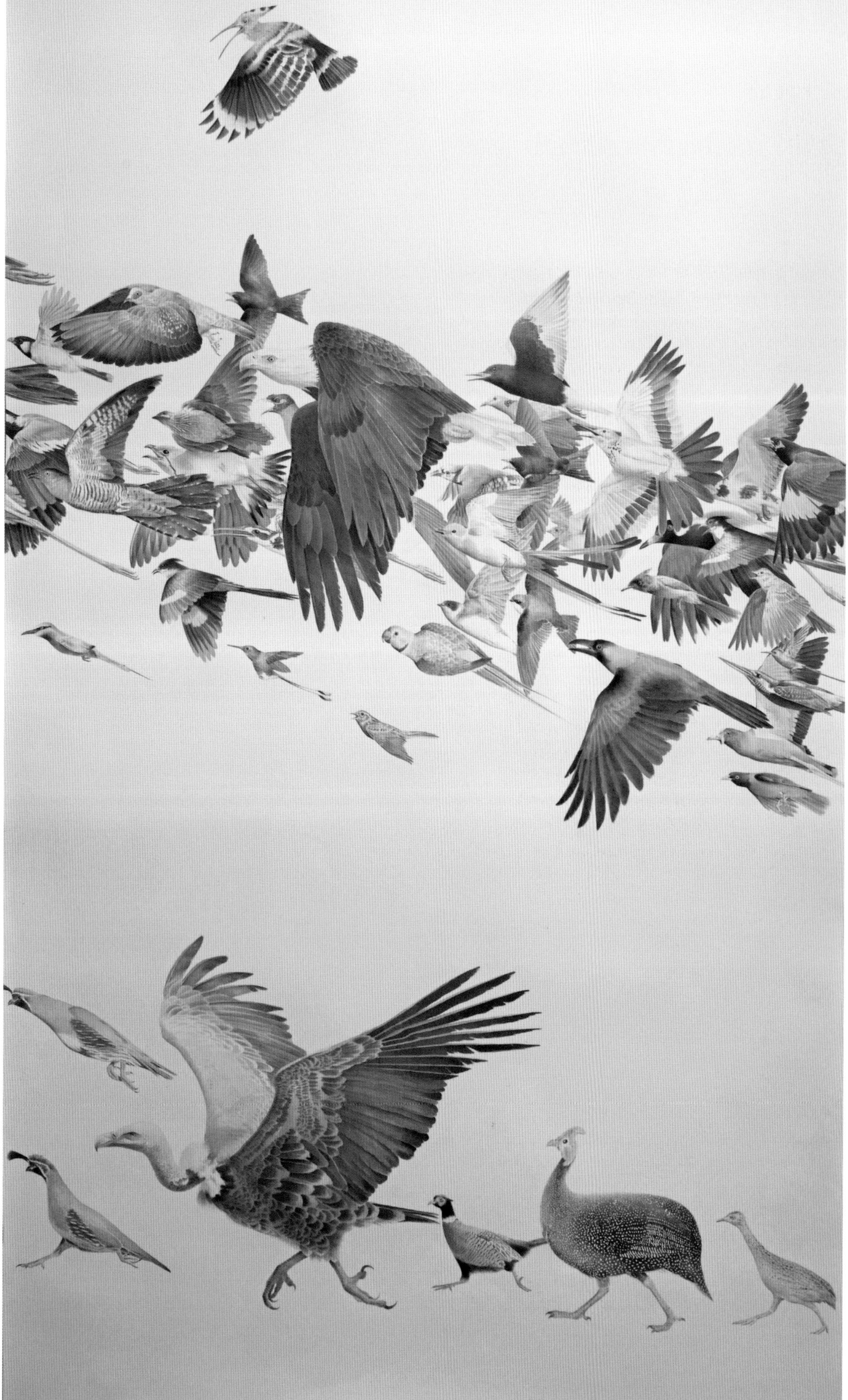

ALI KAZIM

149 Untitled (Children of Faith series)

2023 | watercolour pigments on paper | 16 portraits each 31 × 35 cm | courtesy of the artist and Jhaveri Contemporary

Untitled (Children of Faith series) (2023) is a grid of portraits of children and men dressed in ways that distinguish their faith. Kazim depicts each solitary figure against a plain background. Free of any external context, the images suspend the sitters in time and, with Kazim's attention to fine detail, capture the essence of each individual. Kazim was inspired to create the work by the painting of forty-one portraits at the V&A (see cat. 27).

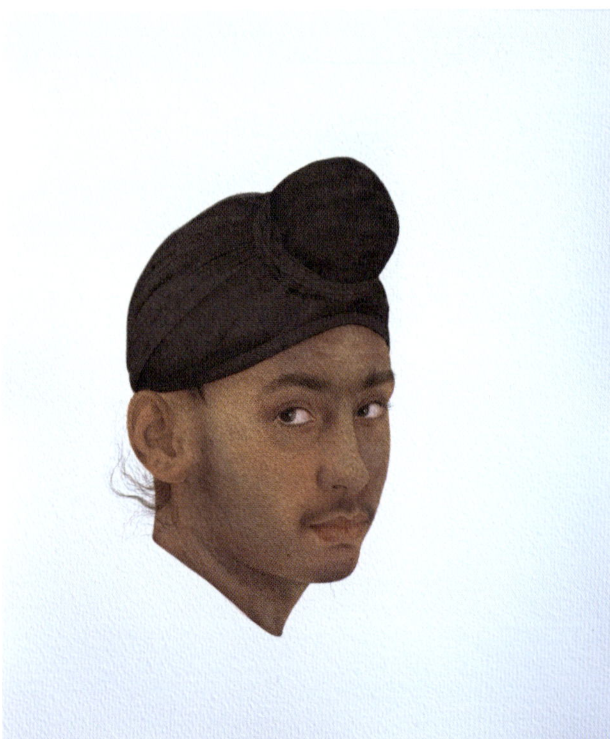

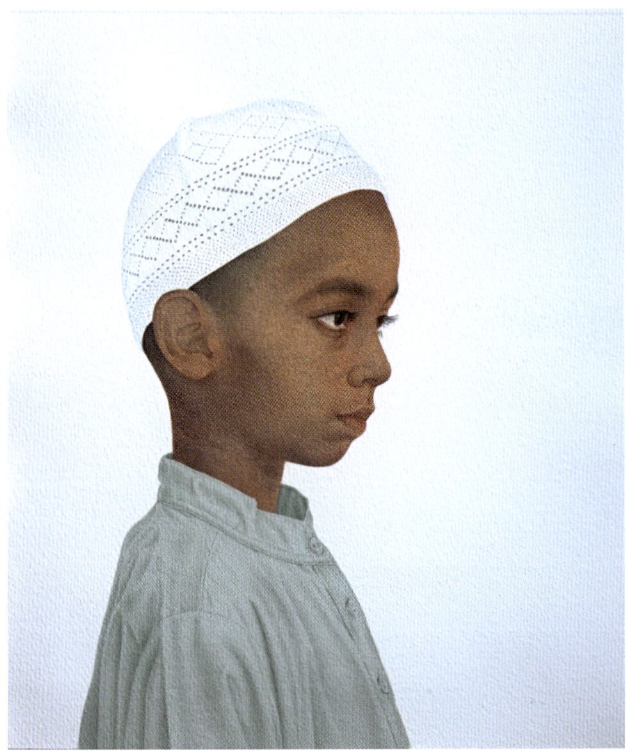

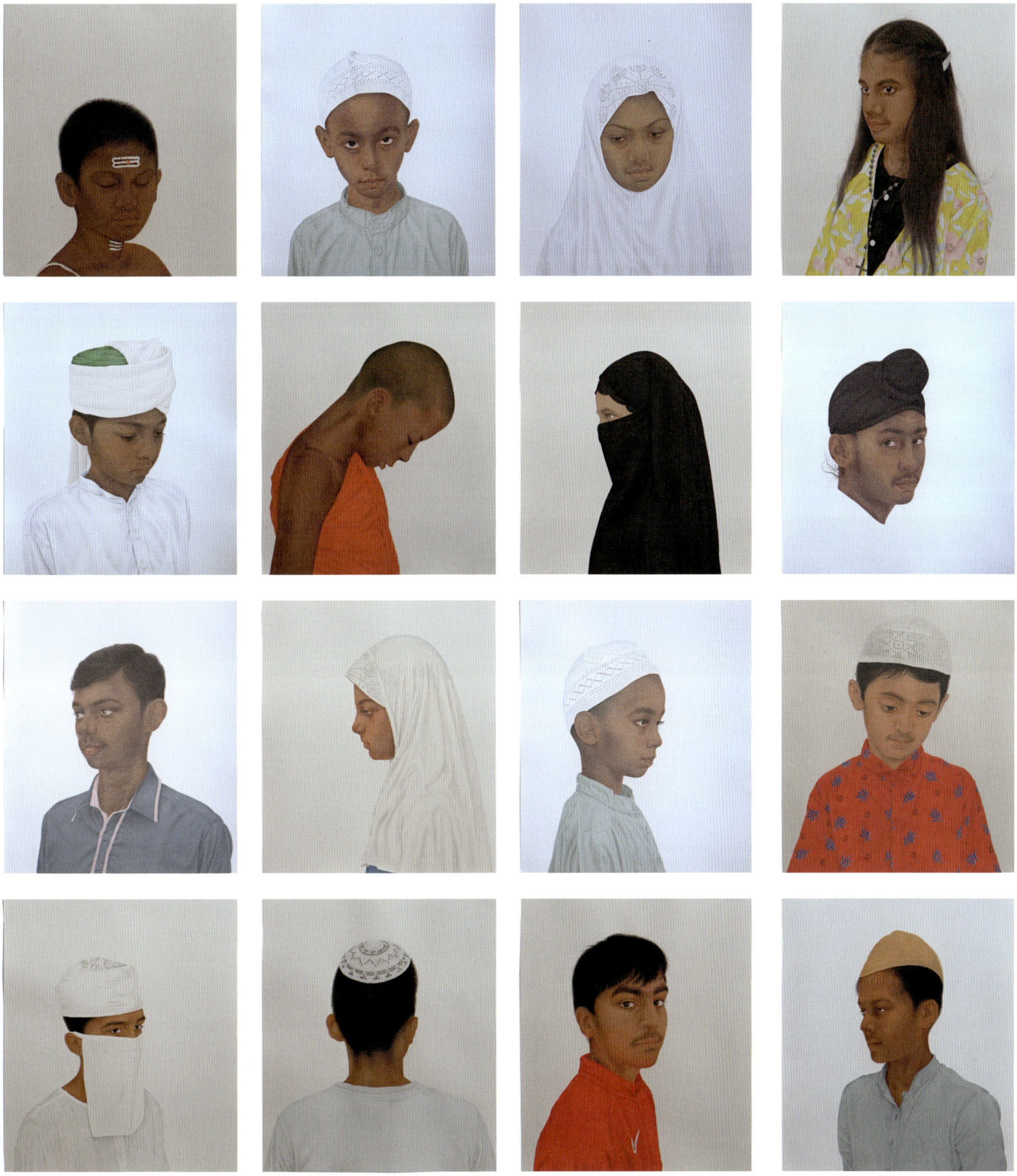

DAVID ALESWORTH & SHAKILA HAIDER

150 The Gardens of England, Plumbers Hill, Bristol

2017 | watercolour and ink on wasli paper | 26.5 × 33.5 cm | courtesy of the artist

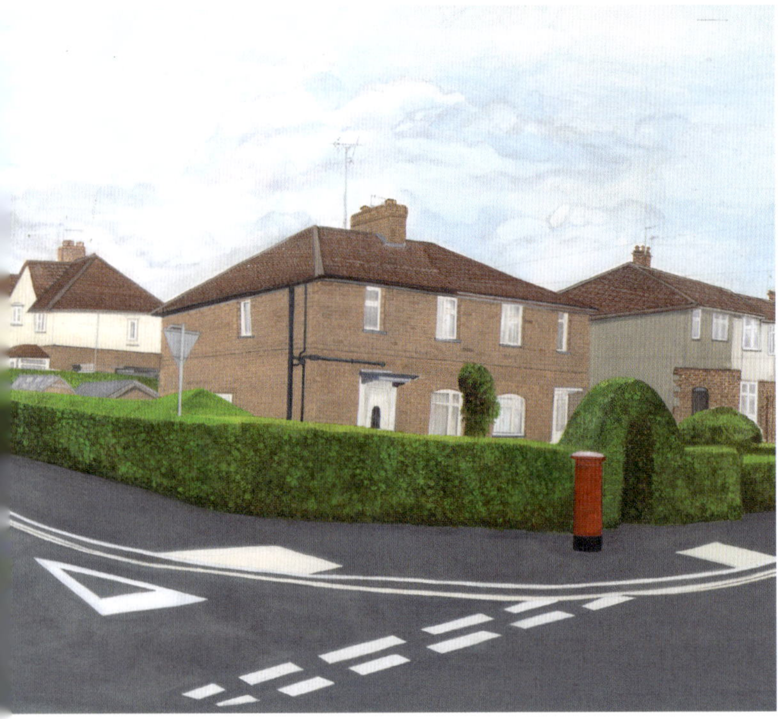

DAVID ALESWORTH & SHAKILA HAIDER

151 The Gardens of England, Bryants Hill, Bristol

2017 | watercolour and ink on wasli paper | 34 × 30.5 cm | courtesy of the artist

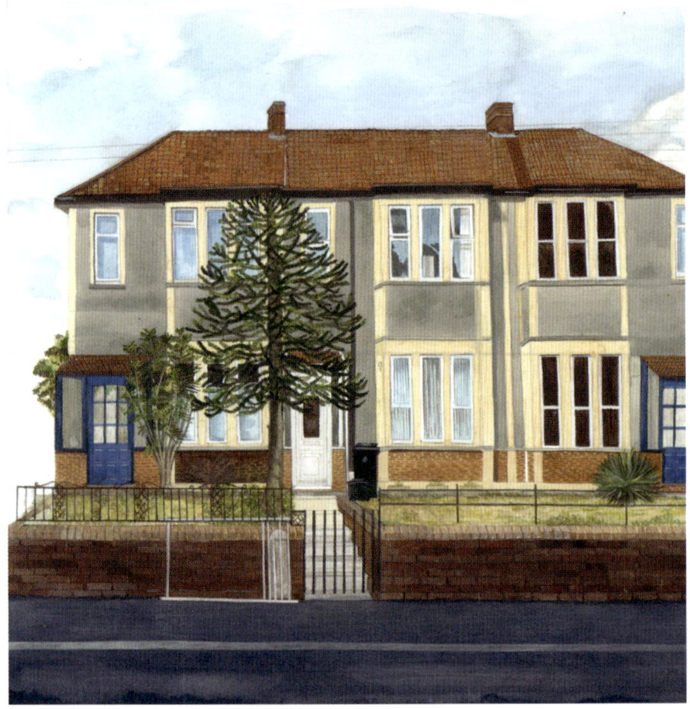

David Alesworth (b.1957, Surrey, UK) is a British artist who holds Pakistani nationality, a teacher and gardener who lived in Pakistan (Lahore and Karachi) for three decades between 1985 and 2015. His *Gardens of England* series, created in collaboration with Lahore-based artist Shakila Haider (b.1986, Quetta, Pakistan), can be read as a reverse Company School body of work, recalling the botanical paintings commissioned by East India Company natural historians in the late eighteenth and early nineteenth centuries (see cat. 32–36).[66] Alesworth took photographs of 'exotic' trees and plants across Bristol (a city enriched by East India Company merchants and British slave traders) and Milton Keynes, which Haider then translated into miniatures.

Alesworth has said of the series:

> I am really thinking of Dr Roxburgh and his *Flora indica*, which controversially documented the flora of India for the East India Company by commissioning two miniature painters in 1790. The folios received a mixed response when the Company gifted a set to Kew, the miniature technique producing a somewhat flattened or even 'pressed' look to the specimens. But while this reference to Roxburgh was a conscious one, I think that the relationship of Roxburgh and his two miniaturists is very different from my commissioning Haider, with whom I have collaborated closely on other projects, including *The Trees of Pakistan* (2012–13) and *The Heterotoparies* (2014).[67]

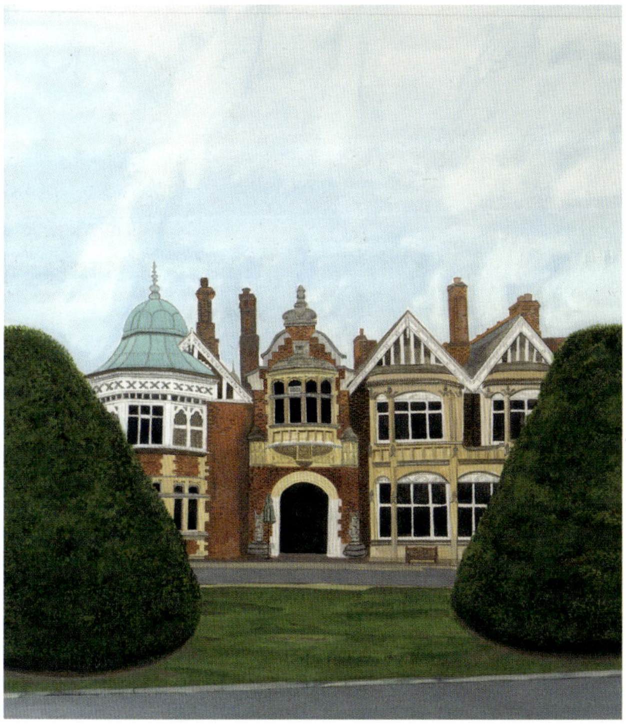

DAVID ALESWORTH & SHAKILA HAIDER

152 The Gardens of England, Bletchley Park, Milton Keynes

2023 | watercolour and ink on wasli paper | 33.5 × 26.5 cm | courtesy of the artist

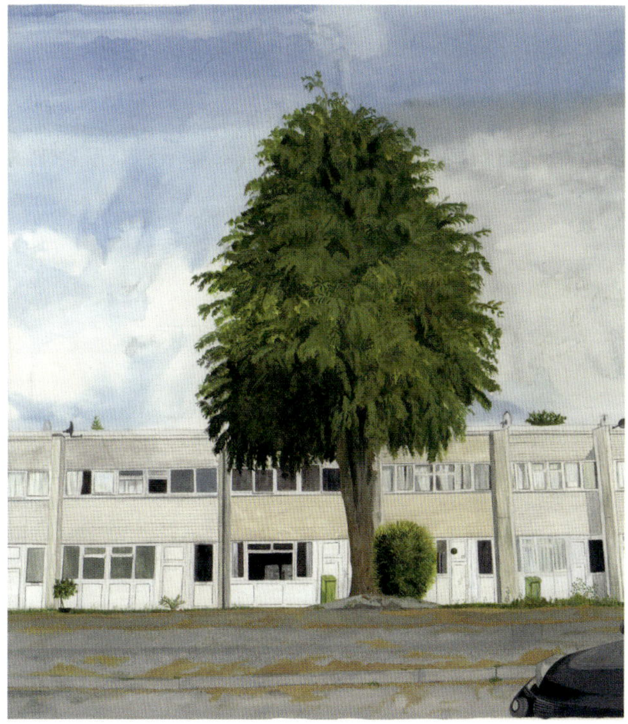

DAVID ALESWORTH & SHAKILA HAIDER

153 The Gardens of England, The Hide, Milton Keynes

2023 | watercolour and ink on wasli paper | 34.3 × 33 cm | courtesy of the artist

NOTES

INTRODUCTION

1. Virginia Whiles, 'Social, Political and Historical Formations Relating to Miniature Practice', *Art and Polemic in Pakistan: Cultural Politics and Tradition in Contemporary Miniature Painting* (London, 2010).
2. The idea of miniature as an attitude was explored in two earlier exhibitions – *Beyond the Page: Contemporary Art From Pakistan* (curated by Hammad Nasar) at Asia House, London and Manchester Art Gallery in 2006–7; and *Beyond the Page: Miniature as Attitude in Contemporary Art from Pakistan* (curated by Hammad Nasar with Anna Sloan and Bridget Bray) at the Pacific Asia Museum in 2010 – from which this book and exhibition borrow their title.

HISTORIC WORKS

1. South Asian paintings were introduced to the Pearson A-Level Art History curriculum for the first time in 2018 and, at the time of writing, I am aware of only one permanent academic position for a South Asian paintings specialist in the UK, at the University of Edinburgh.
2. See Margaret Makepeace, 'New Year's Gift', British Library *Untold Lives* blog, 31 December 2020. These English oil paintings arrived on an East India Company boat specifically named *New Year's Gifts*. The Company had instructed Edward Gall, the painter on board, on how to carry out any necessary repairs to the portraits on arrival and how to make their frames. See 'Commission from the EIC in London ... and a note, from the instructions of Rowland Buckett, on taking care of oil paintings carried in the New Year's Gift, 22 Feb 1614', in British Library IOR/G/40/25, pp. 15–44. Two large European oil paintings are depicted in a Mughal painting illustrating one of Jahangir's New Year celebrations, attributed to Manohar c.1617. The European paintings are displayed prominently on either side of the balcony where the emperor would appear on ceremonial occasions. See *Nauroz Durbar of Jahangir* (The St Petersburg Album, Russian Academy of Sciences, Institute of Oriental Manuscripts, E-44, f.22a) published in Milo C. Beach, Eberhard Fischer and B.N. Goswamy (eds), *Masters of Indian Painting 1100–1650*, vol. 1 (Zurich, 2011), p. 146.
3. 'Noch een boexken met eenige Oostindise tekeningen', transcribed in S.A.C. Dudok van Heel, 'Een Holbein uit de collectie Six', in *Maandblad Amstelodamum* 79 (1992), p. 55, quoted in Martin Royalton-Kisch, *Catalogue of Drawings by Rembrandt and His School* (London, 2010), Rembrandt, cat. no. 56, note 9, and Gary Schwartz, *Rembrandt's Orient: West Meets East in Dutch Art of the Seventeenth Century* (London, 2020), pp. 67–8 and n32.
4. S.A.C. Dudok van Heel noted that the heirs of the Countess of Arundel pawned 'A small book with East Indies drawings' with the tax collector and long-standing acquaintance of Rembrandt, Johannes Wtenbogaert (1557–1644). This was probably the same 'beautiful book with illustrations of the Mughals' presented by Wtenbogaert to Cosimo de Medici, the future grand duke of Tuscany (1642–1723) in Amsterdam on 5 January 1668. For this, see Schwartz, *Rembrandt's Orient*, p. 68 and n. 35. Francis I, Duke of Lorraine, husband of the future Habsburg empress Maria Teresa (r.1740–80), inherited the Medici Grand Duchy and its collections in 1737. The couple visited Florence in 1739 and Francis combined his library with that of the Medici, opening it to the public in 1765. The Mughal album would have been removed from Florence before this time and taken to the Schönbrunn Palace in Vienna where *c.*1760 Francis I and other members of their family were involved in cutting up a large quantity of Indian paintings to assemble them as collages on the walls of Maria Teresa's audience chamber, now known as the Millionenzimmer. For the decoration of this room, see Aaron M. Hyman, 'The Habsburg Re-making of the East at Schloss Schönbrunn, "or Things Equally Absurd"', *The Art Bulletin*, vol. 101, no. 4 (2019), pp. 39–69. For the connection between these

paintings and those copied by Rembrandt and Schellinks, see Emily Hannam, *Rembrandt, Schellinks and Schonbrunn: Further Evidence for a Mughal Album's Journey across Europe* (forthcoming).

5. *Calendar of State Papers, Colonial Series, East Indies and Persia*, Volume 8, *1630–1634* (London, 1892), p. 452, quoted in Jean McInyre 'The Eastern Journey of William Feilding, Earl of Denbigh (1631–33)', *Quidditas*, vol. 22, no. 1 (2001), p. 32. One of the items brought back from India by Denbigh was a Hindu statue presented to Charles I, described in van der Doort's catalogue of the king's collection as 'an East Indian Idoll of black brass which was sent by my Lord Denby taken out of there churches from there altar'. See Bodleian Library MS. Ashmole 1514, transcribed in Oliver Millar, 'Abraham van der Doort's catalogue of the collection of Charles I', *The Walpole Society* 37 (1958–60), p. 94. Another Indian object which Denbigh may have brought back with him is a silver rosewater sprinkler engraved with the arms of William, 3rd Earl of Denbigh (1640–1685), V&A IS.46-1988.
6. Denbigh arrived in Burhanpur in January 1632. The king recommended him to Shah Jahan as 'our trusty and well beloved cousin, servant, and subject ... a prince of our kingdom ... [who] being now transported with the fame and glory of your empire hath desired to see that Prince and Court so renowned in the remotest part of the world. We shall therefore desire you to receive and entertain him according to his quality and our friendship.' See Cecilia Feilding, Countess of Denbigh, *Royalist Father and Roundhead Son: Being the Memoirs of the First and Second Earls of Denbigh 1600–1675* (London, 1915), pp. 75–6, quoted in McIntyre 'The Eastern Journey of William Feilding, Earl of Denbigh (1631–33)', p. 27. The imperial Mughal album copied by Rembrandt was of far too high quality for a European merchant to have obtained in India.
7. *Calendar of State Papers, Domestic Series, of the Reign of Charles I, 1633–1634*, ed. John Bruce (London, 1863), pp. 476–7.
8. BM 1974,0617,0.2 (previously MS Sloane 5254). The album may have been bought by Sloane in the 1720s from the family of the German physician and traveller Engelbert Kaempher (1651–1716). In 1737 the English poet Alexander Pope (1688–1744) donated a similar album, of 178 portraits, to the Bodleian Library, bought by his friend, the East India Company employee and novelist John Cleland (1709–1789), in Surat: Bodleian MS. Ind. Misc. d.3. The dealer he bought it from made more grandiose claims, however, suggesting the portraits were copied directly from originals in the Mughal imperial library: 'The accompanying Collection of Portraits was procured by a Banyan Merchant broker to the Dutch at Surat upon his going up to Dehly, the present residence of the great Mogull. By making great Interest, he got permission to have copys taken from the Collection of Originall paintings, as they are Preserved at that Court. The sketches of the Line of Mogulls from Tamerlane down to Aurengzeb, the Last in this Collection, are in all Probability just and true, as they have been Compared severally with other loose Detatched Copys of the same Originalls.' A later inscription states: 'This Book, Containing one hundred and seventy eight Portraits of the Indian Rajahs, continued to Tamerlane and the Great Mogols his Successors as far as Aurnegzebe, was procured at Surat by Mr. John Cleland, and given to the Bodley Library, as a Token of Respect, by Alex. Pope. 1737.' See Theodor Aufrecht, *Catalogi Codicum Manuscriptorum Bibliothecae Bodleianae Pars Octava, Codices Sanscriticos* (Oxford, 1864), p. 358.
9. 'A list of Things sent under the care of Mr. and Mrs. Amyatt to the right honble Lady Clive. all received in 1766': British Library MSS Eur G37/18/8 ff.7–8.
10. For this painting, see Natasha Eaton, *Mimesis across Empires: Artworks and Networks in India, 1765–1860* (London, 2013), pp. 37–43.
11. Letter from William Palmer to Warren Hastings, 21 November 1790, Agra, British Library, Add. MS 29172, vol. XLI, 1790, p. 184. For the collection of Asaf ud-Dawla, see Emily Hannam, 'Two Late Mughal Albums in the Royal Library at Windsor Castle: Further Evidence for the Collections of Nawab Asaf al-Dawla', in Friederike Weis (ed.), *Eighteenth-Century Persianate Albums Made in India: Audiences, Artists, Patrons and Collectors* (Leiden, forthcoming).
12. These included contemporary paintings and copies that Tod commissioned from historic paintings and manuscripts in the Royal Library of Udaipur. Tod later bequeathed most of his Indian paintings to the Royal Asiatic Society's library. See Andrew Topsfield, 'Tod's Collection of Rajasthani Paintings', in Giles Tillotson (ed.), *James Tod's Rajasthan: The Historian and His Collections* (Mumbai, 2008), pp. 18–35. Tod also commissioned a local artist to make topographical drawings and plans; now held in the Royal Asiatic Society and British Library.
13. Literally 'Delhi pen/brush'.
14. Mildred Archer discovered the term *Kampani qalam* being used in Patna in the 1930s. The largest group of Company paintings in Britain are found in the India Office Additional Oriental (I.O. Add. Or.) collections of the British Library. These are the volumes and paintings donated to or purchased by the East India Company (later India Office) Library, in addition to the volumes and paintings in the Johnson collection. The majority of these (over 2,000) are Company paintings. See Toby Falk and Mildred Archer, *Company Drawings in the India Office Library* (London, 1981).
15. James Skinner was the son of a Scottish East India Company soldier and young Rajput woman who had been captured at the age of 14 during the war against the Maharaja of Benares. For James Skinner and his patronage, see Mildred Archer, 'The Two Worlds of James Skinner (1778–1841)', *History Today*, September 1960; and J.P. Losty and Malini Roy, *Mughal India: Art, Culture and Empire* (London, 2012), pp. 222–8.
16. British Library Add.Or. 1243–1283.
17. A considerable part of Swinton's collection was dispersed after his death in 1804. His library of Persian and Arabic manuscripts was put up for sale at Christie's in 1810 in 120 lots, including 8 illustrated manuscripts and 8 large folio volumes bound in red morocco of '*Tuzweerat o Khuttootat* [pictures and calligraphy], being a collection of the most elegant paintings and fine specimens of beautiful penmanship, in large and small hands, by the best masters'.
18. Polier sold his albums to Beckford through a mutual friend before leaving India. Much of the contents of Beckford's library at Fonthill Abbey was disposed of at auction between the years 1807 and 1823. Some of these volumes are now in the British Museum, British Library, John Rylands Library and the National Art Library. Beckford retained the finest albums that he acquired from Polier and after his death, and left them to his daughter Susan, the Duchess of Hamilton. In 1882 the twelfth Duke of Hamilton sold twenty albums of Indian miniatures, along with other volumes from his family library, to the Kupferstichkabinett in Berlin, now in the collection of the city's Museum for Islamic Art. Edward Ephraim Pote (d.1832), an East India Company civil servant in Patna, acquired 550 of Polier's other Indian manuscripts (eight chests' worth) in 1788. He sent the collection to England to be divided between Eton and King's College, Cambridge, and today both halves of the collection are now on permanent loan to Cambridge University Library. Polier retained many other volumes, including 42 now in the Bibliothèque

Nationale, Paris, and a copy of the Vedas acquired from the Maharaja of Jaipur, which he presented to the British Museum in 1789 through Sir Joseph Banks. For this, see Polier to Banks, 20 May 1789, BL Add. MS. 5346, fols 1-4, and BM Minutes of the Trustees' Standing Committee, 22 May 1789, pp. 200-205. See also Muzaffar Alam and Seema Alavi, *A European Experience of the Orient: The Ijaz-I Arsalani (Persian Letters, 1773-1779) of Antoine-Louis Henri Polier* (Oxford, 2001), introduction.

19. British Library IOR: Despatches to Bengal, E/4/647, 25 May 1798, ff. 430-39, quoted in Falk and Archer, *Indian Miniatures in the India Office Library*, p. 13.
20. Ibid., p. 14. For the Library of Tipu Sultan, see Ursula Sims-Williams, 'Collections Within Collections: An Analysis of Tipu Sultan's Library', *Journal of the British Institute of Persian Studies* 59 (2021).
21. Richard Johnson's paintings were later bound into 64 albums. For his collection, see Falk and Archer, *Indian Miniatures in the India Office Library*, pp. 14-29.
22. Quoted in ibid., Appendix 1: Arrangement and Cataloguing of the Collection, p. 307.
23. Papers of Henry Thomas Colebrooke, Royal Asiatic Society Archives GB 891 HTC.
24. 'Her Majesty's East India House', *East India and Colonial Magazine*, 28 February 1841, p. 221. See also Peter Gordon, *The Oriental Repository at the India House* (London, 1835).
25. The volumes remained in storage in Calcutta for 11 years and were not actually shipped to London until 1876. For the Delhi Collection now in the British Library, see Nur Sobers-Khan, 'Muslim Scribal Culture in India around 1800: Towards a Disentangling of the Mughal Library and Delhi Collection', in C.D. Bahl and S. Hanß (eds), *Scribal Practice and the Global Cultures of Colophons, 1400-1800* (London, 2022).
26. Arundell Esdaile, *Library of the British Museum: A Short History and Survey* (London, 1946), p. 306. See also Charles Rieu, *Catalogue of The Persian Manuscripts in the British Museum*, vol. 3 (London, 1883), p. xxi. Alexander Lindsay, 25th Earl of Crawford (1812-1880), purchased the remainder of Hamilton's collection in 1868, which were bought by Enriqueta Rylands (1843-1908) from James Ludovic Lindsay, 26th Earl of Crawford (1847-1913) in 1901 and are now in the John Rylands Library at the University of Manchester.
27. In 1891 this became the Department of Oriental Printed Books and Manuscripts when the Oriental printed books also transferred from the General Library. During the nineteenth century the number of Persian volumes in the British Museum grew from 150 to more than 2,500, most of them from India.
28. Hanna's collection is now part of the National Museum of Asian Art in Washington DC. See Milo Cleveland Beach, 'Colonel Hanna's Indian Paintings', *Apollo*, vol. 118, no. 258 (1983), pp. 154-9.
29. Morgan purchased 30 folios from Read's Mughal album, now in the Morgan Library and Museum in New York, but Read owned at least 48 others, now dispersed.
30. Michael Wheeler, 'The Conservation and Display of Mughal & Islamic Manuscripts and the Victoria & Albert Museum', *Contributions to the Symposium on the Care and Conservation of Middle Eastern Manuscripts, University of Melbourne, 26-28 November 2007* (Melbourne, 2008), pp. 22-9.
31. Henry Baden-Powell, *Hand-book of the Manufactures and Arts of the Punjab* (Lahore, 1872), quoted by Nadhara Shahbaz Khan, 'Industrial Art Education in Colonial Punjab', in Julius Bryant and Susan Weber (eds), *John Lockwood Kipling: Arts & Crafts in the Punjab and London* (New York, 2017), p. 474.
32. Established in 1850 (Madras), 1854 (Calcutta) and 1856 (Bombay).
33. See V&A IS.2491-1883 - I.S. 2500-1883 by Amir Bakhsh and Muhammad Din.
34. E.B. Havell, Memorandum on the present working of the Calcutta School of Art, West Bengal State Archives, Calcutta: Bengal Government (General Department) Educational Proceedings, June 1904, pp. 24-7, quoted in Tapati Guha-Thakurta, *The Making of a New 'Indian' Art: Artists, Aesthetics and Nationalism in Bengal, c.1850-1920* (Cambridge, 1992), p. 149.
35. Ibid., pp. 150-53.
36. For Havell and Tagore, see Partha Mitter, *Art and Nationalism in Colonial India: 1850-1922* (Cambridge, 1994), and Guha-Thakurta, *The Making of a New 'Indian' Art.*
37. 'Exhibition of Oriental Paintings', *The Englishman*, 30 January 1908.
38. Percy Brown, *Indian Painting* (Calcutta, 1918), and *Indian Painting under the Mughals, A.D. 1550 to A.D. 1750* (Oxford, 1924).
39. See E.B. Havell, 'Art Administration in India', *Journal of the Royal Society of Arts*, vol. 58, no. 2985 (4 February 1910), p. 285.
40. India Society Minute Book, 29/9/1910 MSS Eur F147/65A, quoted in Mitter, *Art and Nationalism in Colonial India*. The India Society published a journal, *Indian Art and Letters*, twice a year from 1925 into the 1960s. The Society also published pioneering books on Indian painting, including A.K. Coomaraswamy, *Indian Drawings* (London, 1911-12); E.B. Havell, *Handbook of Indian Art* (London, 1920) and Stella Kramrisch, *A Survey of Painting in the Deccan* (London, 1937). For the records of the India Society, see 'Royal Society for India, Pakistan and Ceylon papers', British Library MSS Eur F147.
41. W.G. Archer, *Indian Paintings from the Punjab Hills: A Survey and History of Pahari Miniature Painting* (London, 1973), p. xxvi. Pahari painting was largely unknown by Europeans in the nineteenth century. Writing in 1887, Lockwood Kipling noted that 'among native limners [miniature painters], Kangra ki Qalam [the Kangra style] is a phrase constantly heard and meant to distinguish the style of touch of a school of illumination and mythological painting that is supposed to have flourished there.' John Lockwood Kipling, *Journal of Indian Art and Industry*, 1887, quoted in ibid.
42. Quoted in Archer, *Indian Painting from the Punjab Hills*, p. xxvi.
43. See British Museum 1913,0415,0.5; 1913,0617,0.1-0.4; 1914,0217,0.9-0.16; 1914,0319,0.3-0.4; 1914,0512,0.1-0.6; and 1915,0217,0.1-0.6.
44. The exhibition also included works by contemporary artists, including Abanindranath Tagore and Nandalal Bose, although these received no attention from British art critics. See Mitter, *Art and Nationalism in Colonial India*, pp. 321-4.
45. Ernest Havell to William Rothenstein, 15 February 1910, University of Manchester: ML B.27.F.38, quoted in Michaela Jean Kathleen Jones, 'Christiana Herringham and the Art Collection of Royal Holloway and Bedford New College', PhD dissertation, University of London, 2019, p. 143.
46. See *Indian Art at the British Empire Exhibition*, with introduction by Lionel Heath (London, 1924). The Bengali artist Mukul Day also painted a room full of murals at the exhibition site.
47. O.C. Gangoly, *The Studio* LXXXIX (January-June 1925), p. 138, quoted in Partha Mitter, *The Triumph of Modernism: India's Artists and the Avant-Garde 1922-1947* (London, 2007), p. 194.
48. See Brinda Kumar, 'Exciting a Wider Interest in the Art of India: The 1931 Burlington Fine Arts Club Exhibition', *British Art Studies* 13 (2019).
49. For this exhibition, see the Indian Society's journal, *Indian Art and Letters*, vol. VIII, no. 2 (London, 1935), pp. 85-100.
50. Ibid., p. 96.

51. See Leigh Ashton (ed.), *The Art of India and Pakistan: A Commemorative Catalogue of the Exhibition Held at the Royal Academy of Arts, 1947–8* (London, 1950).
52. Bernard Denvir, 'Anon was India's Greatest Artist', *Daily Herald*, 10 December 1947. The article continues: 'These were the works of men whose attitude towards the profession of artist was very different from ours. To them time meant nothing, nor did personal fame. They could spend a lifetime carving one panel of an ivory door, and die knowing that no one would remember their names.' This Orientalist perception of South Asian artists is erroneous, particularly in relation to Indian miniature painters.
53. Ibid.
54. The original source of many of these was the famous Indian dealer Radha Krishna Bharanay based in Amritsar. For Bharanay, see Giles Tillotson (ed.), *A Passionate Eye: Textiles, Painting and Sculpture from the Bharany Collections* (Mumbai, 2014).
55. After the couple died, two months apart in Dehra Dun, their executors loaned works to the 1947 exhibition before the collection transferred to the NCAF, which offered the first right of refusal to the Fitzwilliam Museum at the University of Cambridge (Manuk's alma mater), followed by the British Museum, the Victoria and Albert Museum, and Bristol Museum and Art Gallery. The remainder was sold at Christie's, raising £5,326 for the art charity. For Manuk and Coles, see Mildred and W.G. Archer, *India Served and Observed* (London, 1994), p. 99. Mildred Archer recorded that the Europeans in Patna completely cut Gertrude Coles socially because she had originally been employed as a companion to look after Manuk's wife, Nellie, who had suffered from mental illness after their son's death in World War I and was eventually sent to an asylum in England. Coles stayed on with Manuk and they lived as a couple. In 2007 Richard Blurton curated a display of some of the British Museum's paintings from the Manuk and Coles collection entitled *A Loving Gift*.
56. For this, see Kajal Meghani, 'The Global and the Local: South Asian Collectors at the British Museum', PhD dissertation, University of Brighton, forthcoming.
57. Basil Grey had travelled to India to select the paintings for the 1947 exhibition and wrote the essay on Indian painting in the accompanying catalogue. He later published *Rajput Painting* (London, 1949), *Persian Painting* (London, 1961) and a contribution on Mughal painting and the painting schools of the Deccan in Douglas Barrett (ed.), *Painting in India* (London, 1963). He also wrote the accompanying essay for an exhibition catalogue of the Bikaner royal collection, *Treasures of Indian Miniatures in the Bikaner Palace Collection* (London, 1951), before the collection was sold on the London market in the following decades.
58. W.G. Archer took over from Kenneth de Burgh Codrington (1899–1986) after he was appointed the first Professor of Indian Art and Archaeology at the University of London. Archer had worked for the Indian Civil Service in the 1930s and 1940s, during which time he served alongside P.C. Manuk as a member of the managing committee of Patna Museum and was introduced through him to miniature painting.
59. W.G. Archer, *Visions of Courtly India: The Archer Collection of Pahari Miniatures* (Washington DC, 1976–78), p. ix.
60. Ibid., p. x.
61. See Kavita Singh, 'Museums and the Making of an Indian Art Historical Canon', in Shivaji K. Panikkar, Parul Dave Mukherji and Deeptha Achar (eds), *Towards a New Art History: Studies in Indian Art: Essays Presented in Honour of Prof. Ratan Parimoo* (New Delhi, 2003), pp. 332–57, p. 350.
62. See W.G. Archer, *Indian Painting in the Punjab Hills* (1952) and the follow-up 2-volume *Indian Paintings from the Punjab Hills* (1973).
63. W.G. Archer, *India and Modern Art* (London, 1959). He also wrote the exhibition catalogue for Anwar Jalal Shemza's 1960 London exhibition at Gallery One. See W.B. Archer, *Shemza: Paintings* (London, 1960).
64. Mildred and W.G. Archer, *India Served and Observed*, pp. 137–9.
65. Ibid.
66. Mildred Archer, *Indian Painting for the British* (1955); *Natural History Drawings in the India Office Library* (1962); *Indian Architecture and the British: 1780–1830* (1968); *British Drawings in the India Office Library* (1969); *Company Drawings in the India Office Library* (1972); *Indian Popular Painting in the India Office Library* (1977); *India and British Portraiture 1770–1825* (1979); *Early Views of India: Picturesque Journeys of Thomas and William Daniell, 1786–94* (1980); *Indian Miniatures In the India Office Library* (1981); *India Observed: British Artists in India* (1982); *The Marquis Wellesley Collection: Indian Artists under British Patronage* (1983); *Visions of India: The Sketchbooks of William Simpson, 1859–62* (1986); *India Revealed: Art and Adventures of James and William Fraser, 1815–26* (1989); *Catalogue of Paintings, Drawings, Engravings and Busts Catalogue in the Collection of the Royal Asiatic Society* (1991). Her final book was an autobiography: *India Served and Observed* (1994). After the Archers' retirement, they donated many paintings from their own collection to the India Office and the V&A: See Mildred and W.G. Archer, *Indian Miniatures from the Collection of Mildred and W.G. Archer* (London, 1963); Archer, *Visions of Courtly India*; British Library MSS Eur. F. 236.
67. In 2010 all 99 paintings from the James Ivory collection were bought by the Louvre, Abu Dhabi.
68. See Howard Hodgkin, 'Notes on the Collection', in Andrew Topsfield and Milo Cleveland Beach, *Indian Paintings and Drawings from the Collection of Howard Hodgkin* (New York, 1991), republished in Andrew Topsfield, *Visions of Mughal India: The Collection of Howard Hodgkin* (Oxford, 2012), p. 10.
69. The Fraser Album paintings were sold in 1979 and 1980. The Clive albums were accepted by HM Government in lieu of inheritance tax and allocated to the V&A in 1964; the Swinton paintings in 2021 and allocated to the National Museum of Scotland (see cat. 7).
70. Robert Skelton (ed.), *The Indian Heritage: Court Life and Arts under Mughal Rule* (London, 1982).
71. J.P. Losty, *The Art of the Book in India* (London, 1982).
72. These exhibitions include *King of the World: The Padshahnama* at the Queen's Gallery, Buckingham Palace (1997), curated by Milo Cleveland Beach and Ebba Koch; *Faith, Narrative and Desire: Masterpieces of Indian Painting in the British Museum* (2007), curated by Richard Blurton; *Maharaja: The Splendour of India's Royal Courts* at the V&A (2009), curated by Anna Jackson and Amin Jaffer; *The Indian Portrait* at the National Portrait Gallery (2010), curated by Rosemary Crill and Kapil Jariwala; *Mughal India: Art, Culture and Empire* at the British Library (2012), curated by J.P. Losty and Malini Roy; *Ragamala Paintings from India* at the Dulwich Picture Gallery (2012), curated by Lizzie Watson; *Splendours of the Subcontinent* at the Queen's Gallery, Buckingham Palace (2018), curated by Emily Hannam; and *Forgotten Masters* at the Wallace Collection (2010), curated by William Dalrymple.
73. Andrew Graham Dixon, review of *Faith Narrative and Desire: Masterpieces of Indian Painting in the British Museum*, *Sunday Telegraph*, 9 September 2007. Exhibitions and displays of Indian paintings in the British Museum since 1947 included: *Indian Paintings Received through the National Art Collections Fund from the P.C. Manuk and Coles Collections* (1953); *Indian Paintings and Drawings from the J.C. French Collection* (1955); *Books from the East* (1960); *Islamic Art in India of the 16th and 17th Centuries* (1961); *The Lion in Asia* (1965); *History and Romance in Mughal*

India (1966); *Polo Miniatures from Persian and Mughal Manuscripts* (1972); *Oriental Manuscripts* (1973); *Paintings from the Muslim Courts of India*, part of the World of Islam Festival (1976); *Animals in Art* (1977); *Painting of Rajasthan* (1978); *Myth and Ceremony in Islamic Painting* (1978); *Flowers in Art from East and West* (1979); *Princely Paintings from Mughal India*, a travelling exhibition (1981); *Deities and Devotion: The Arts of Hinduism* (1993); *Indian Paintings and Drawings from the Collection of Howard Hodgkin* (1994); *Persian Paintings from India on Loan from the British Library* (1996); *'Like a Stream of Gold': Painting and Sculpture from South India* (1996); *Women in Islamic Painting* (1996); *Princes, Poets and Paladins: Islamic and Indian Paintings from the Collection of Prince and Princess Sadruddin Aga Khan* (1998); *Princes, Poets and Paladins: Related Works from the British Museum* (1998); *Persian and Indian Manuscripts and Paintings: From the Collection of the Royal Asiatic Society* (1998); *Painted Poetry: Illustrations from the Works of Nizami and Jami* (1999); *Botanical Watercolours from the Pearson Album* (2000); *Mughals Adorned* (2001); *Birds in Persian and Indian Painting* (2002); *Islamic Paintings of the Hunt* (2002); *War in Islamic Painting* (2003). See Joanna Bowring, *Chronology of Temporary Exhibitions at the British Museum*, British Museum Research Publication no. 189 (London, 2012).

74. The album, formerly British Museum Add.23610, has the Persian stamp of Major Polier dated 1181 (1766–7) embossed on its leather cover.
75. For this album, see Molly Aitkin, 'The Laud Ragamala Album, Bikaner, and the Sociability of Subimperial Painting', *Archives of Asian Art*, vol. 63, no. 1 (2013), pp. 27–58; John Seyller, 'Workshop and Patron in Mughal India: The Freer Ramayana and Other Illustrated Manuscripts of 'Abd al-Rahim', *Artibus Asiae Supplementum* 42 (Zurich, 1999) p. 11; Herbert J. Stooke and Karl Khandalavala, *The Laud Ragamala Miniatures: A Study in Indian Painting and Music* (Oxford, 1953); Hermann Goetz, 'The Laud Album and Early Rajput Painting', *Journal of the Royal Asiatic Society of Great Britain and Ireland* 1/2 (April 1954) pp. 63–74; Karl Khandalavala, 'The Laud Ragamala Miniatures', *Marg*, vol. 6, no. 4 (1953), pp. 26–9.
76. A tracing of this painting can be found in the Edward Moor collection of the British Library: BM 1940,0713,0.250 For the *Nava Nari Kunjara* motif, see Kanu Priya, 'Representation of Navanarikunjara: The Nine Women Elephant Depicted in Various Type of Indian Art', *Proceedings of Indian Art History Congress 23rd Session* (New Delhi, 2014), pp. 187–91.
77. Many thanks to Alastair Watson for suggesting the relationship between the painting and the calligraphy.
78. For Schellinks' poem, see Jos Gommans and Jan de Hond, 'The Unseen World of Willem Schellinks: Local Milieu and Global Circulation in the Visualization of Mughal India', in J.G. Singh, ed., *A Companion to the Global Renaissance: English Literature and Culture in the Era of Expansion, 1500–1700*, 2nd edn, (Chichester, 2021), pp. 237–8, and Jos Gommans, *The Unseen World: The Netherlands and India from 1550* (Amsterdam, 2018), pp. 218–19.
79. Victoria and Albert Museum IS.30-1892, Musée Guimet Inv. No. MA1909/J3673; Royal Collection RCIN 406161; Orientalist Museum, Doha, OM.672; National Trust NT 530882; private collection ('A Turkish Sultan and His Court' sold at Sotheby's, 4 July 1984).
80. The sketches attributed to Rembrandt after paintings from this royal Mughal album are: Albertina Museum 24471; British Museum 1895,09.1275; British Museum 1895,0915.1280; British Museum 1895,0915.1281; British Museum 1910,0212.182; Cleveland Museum 1978.38; Fine Arts Museum of San Francisco 2000.70; J. Paul Getty Museum 85.GA.44; Morgan Library and Museum 1909, I, 207; Morgan Library and Museum 1909, I, 208; Museum Boijmans Van Beuningen R 35 (PK); Museum Boijmans Van Beuningen R 36 (PK); Musée du Louvre RF 693; private collection; Rijksmuseum RP-T-1897-A-3203; Rijksmuseum RP-T-1930-41; Rijksmuseum RP-T-1961-82; Rijksmuseum RP-T-1961-83.
81. For this painting, see Gommans and De Hond, 'The Unseen World of Willem Schellinks'; Gommans, *The Unseen World: The Netherlands and India from 1550*, p. 218; Sanjay Subrahmanyam, *Courtly Encounters: Translating Courtliness and Violence in Early Modern Eurasia*, (Cambridge MA, 2012) pp. 184–98.
82. See note 4 above.
83. For these portraits by Gujarati artists, see Hannam (forthcoming). Some of this series survives in Vienna, one of which has an inscription written in Gujarati (Schloss Schonbrunn, Vienna SKB002605).
84. The sketches attributed to Rembrandt after portraits by Gujarati artists are British Museum PD Gg,2.262 and Gg,2.263, Fogg Art Museum, Harvard 1932.366; Musée du Louvre RF 4733; Fondation Custodia, Collection Frits Lugt 592. The sketches attributed to another artist are Plymouth, Cottonian Collection CD 282 and CD283.
85. Persian numerals on the pages indicate the album originally contained at least 76 folios and 44 paintings. For this album, see Emily Hannam, *Eastern Encounters: Four Centuries of Paintings and Manuscripts from the Indian Subcontinent* (London, 2018), cat. nos 3–12. A second similar album of 73 folios exists with calligraphy by Muhammad Husayn Kashmiri and other Mughal and Timurid calligraphers, and with slightly differing border colours and styles of illumination, and a different numerical system. The folios of this album were rebound into new covers in Qajar Iran, suggesting the album left India in the 1730s with Nadir Shah's invasion: 37 bound folios (Sotheby's, 18 October 1995, lot 68); 29 folios, bound into two albums (Sotheby's, 27 October 2020, lot 425); 2 loose folios (Sotheby's, 18 October 1995, lots 90 and 91); 5 loose folios (Christie's, 17 April 2007, lots 211–15, 218). Many of these are now in the Museum of Islamic Art, Doha.
86. For the inscription referring to 'Thomas Sahib', see RCIN 1005042. A seal on RCIN 1005041 gives the date 1132 AH (1721). The eighteenth-century folder in which these folios were originally housed may be the 'Book with some Indian Pictures' recorded among several albums of prints and drawings kept in a bureau at Kensington House with a note that they were 'deliver'd for her Majtys [Queen Caroline's] use in ye year 1728' (BL Add. MS 20101, f. 28r).
87. Nizami, Makhzan al-Asrar (The Treasury of Mysteries), the first prayer:
تسارت سب اقب و ىناف همه ام
تسارت سدقت و ىلاعت كلم
دنز قلبا رب گناب مدع هكنوچ
88. Abu-Said Abul-Khayr, rubai 397:
لپ رس ناتسود دهع وت دهع يا
لذ وت رهق زا و دزيخ نيک وت رهم زا
لهد وچمه يهت نايم و هلغشم رپ
لگ وچ هزور کي و عمش وچمه هبش کي يا
89. Thanks to paper conservator Rachael Smith for sharing her research on these album pages.
90. Letter from Polier to Mihr Chand dated 14 Safar 1189 AH. f 256b', in Alam and Alavi, *A European Experience of the Mughal Orient*, and quoted in Malini Roy, 'Idiosyncrasies in the Late Mughal Painting Tradition: The Artist Mihr Chand, Son of Ganga Ram, Fl. 1759–86', PhD dissertation, University of London, 2009, p. 119.
91. The folio is from an album discovered in a Scottish antique shop in 1929 by a Mr and Mrs Jack S. Rofe, who bought it for £100. They sold it at Sotheby's the same year for £10,500 to the New York-based Armenian dealer Hagop Kervorkian. Kervorkian later sold its pages in instalments to the Freer Gallery (in 1939 and

1948) and the Metropolitan Museum (in 1955). For the so-called Kervorkian Album, see Stuart Carey Welsh et al., *The Emperors' Album: Images of Mughal India* (New York, 1987).

92. For Archibald Swinton's collection, see Lucian Harris, 'Archibald Swinton: A New Source for Albums of Indian Miniatures in William Beckford's Collection', *Burlington Magazine*, vol. 143, no. 1179 (June 2001), pp. 360–66, and J.P. Losty, 'Eighteenth Century Mughal Paintings from the Swinton Collection', *Burlington Magazine*, vol. 159, no. 1375 (October 2017), pp. 789–99.
93. For Ghulam Husayn Khan, see A.S. Bazmee Ansari, 'Sayyid Ghulām Husayn Khān Tabātabā'ī', in P. Beraman et al. (eds), *Encyclopaedia of Islam*, 2nd edn (Leiden, 1960–2007). Ghulam Husan Khan owned an album later in the collection of Lord Berwick and bought by Sir John Soane in 1827. *Sir John Soane's Museum*, vol. 144.
94. Harris, 'Archibald Swinton', pp. 360–66, p. 365 and n. 49.
95. For these, see the handlists compiled for the National Museum of Scotland by J.P. Losty.
96. The acceptance of this collection settled £2,267,370 of tax. See National Museums Scotland Press Office, *Archibald Swinton Collection of Eighteenth Century Paintings and Lacquer Work Saved for the Nation*, 24 June 2021.
97. The *Baharistan* is one of five Persian classics on the subject of moral cultivation, written, illumined, illustrated and bound to a consistent level of quality in the Mughal imperial atelier between 1595 and 1598: the *Gulistan* of Sadi (now dispersed, with folios in the Cincinnati Art Museum and Walters Art Museum W.668); the Baharistan of Jami (Bodelian MS. Elliot 254), the *Khamsa* of Nizami (BL MS Or. 12208 and five folios in Walters Art Museum MS W.613); the *Khamsa* of Amir Khusrow (Walters Art Museum MS W.624); and the *Anwar-i Suhayli* (Bharat Kala Bhavan Museum, Varanasi, MS1). See Emily Hannam, 'The Bodleian Baharistan (MS. Elliott 254): A Major Mughal Manuscript of 1595', M.Phil. dissertation, University of Oxford, 2014. For this painting, see also Andrew Topsfield, *Indian Paintings: From Oxford Collections* (Oxford, 1982), no. 16.
98. Adapted from Edward Rehatsek (trans.), *The Behâristân (Abode of Spring): A Literal Translation from the Persian* (Benares, 1887), pp. 78–80.
99. Ouseley's introductory notes in Bodleian Library MS. Elliot 254 ff. iv–vii are dated November 1817.
100. The poet Edward Fitzgerald quoted from Ouseley's note in his 1887 analysis of Jami and claimed his *Baharistan* manuscript was 'said to have cost some thousands of pounds ... [and is] now reposited away from "the Drums and Tramplings" of Oriental Conquest in the tranquil seclusion of an English library'. E. Fitzgerald, *Works of Edward FitzGerald*, vol. 1 (1873), p. 105.
101. For Aqa Riza, see Milo C. Beach, 'Aqa Riza and Abu'l Hasan', in Beach et al. (eds), *Masters of Indian Painting*, pp. 211–30.
102. For the artist Govardhan, see John Seyller, 'Govardhan', in Beach et al. (eds), *Masters of Indian Painting*, vol. 1, pp. 357–74.
103. For this manuscript (RCIN 1005032), see Hannam, *Eastern Encounters*, pp. 98–107. The illustration on folio 35 of this manuscript is the only one that survives on the original paper. For the others, the pages were split to remove the earlier paintings, as evident from the tears and wrinkling on the text sides of those folios. New (thicker) paper borders were pasted on top and the new Mughal paintings dating to *c.*1605–10 inserted into these.
104. 'Description of Persian Manuscripts designed by Lord Teignmouth as a present to His Majesty's Royal Collection RCIN 1005091.b. For this manuscript, see Hannam, *Eastern Encounters*, pp. 108–131; Saqib Baburi, 'Beyond the Akbarnama: Padshahnamahs and Official Regnal Chronography for Shah-Jahan Padshah (r.1037/1628–1068/1658)', PhD dissertation, University of London, 2010; Milo Beach and Ebba Koch, *King of the World: The Padshahnama, an Imperial Mughal Manuscript from the Royal Library, Windsor Castle* (London, 1997).
105. For Balchand, see John Seyller, 'Balchand', in Beach et al. (eds), *Masters of Indian Painting*, vol. 1, pp. 337–56.
106. The artist Balchand signed the shield in the lower right corner of the painting 'God is great. The work of Balchand, the aged servant.' A drawing of the same scene exists in the Harvard Art Museum (no. 1999.301).
107. For Abid, see Milo C. Beach, 'Abid' in Beach et al. (eds), *Masters of Indian Painting*, vol. 1, pp. 231–42.
108. See J.W. Redhouse (trans.), *Diary of H.M. the Shah of Persia during his tour through Europe in A.D. 1873* (London, 1874), pp. 201–2, and Naser ud-din Shah, *Ruznamaj-i safari-i Farangistan* (Tehran, 1873), p. 97. Other admirers included Mirza Abu Taleb Khan, a Persian raised in Lucknow who visited England from 1799 to 1803, and recorded that he viewed the manuscript in the King's Library at Buckingham House (see Charles Stewart, trans., *The Travels of Mirza Abu Taleb Khan in Asia, Africa and Europe*, London, 1810). By 1830 the manuscript had moved to the new Royal Library established by William IV at Windsor Castle. On 22 August 1847 Sir Frederic Madden (1801–1873; Keeper of Manuscripts at the British Museum) visited the Royal Library at Windsor with his family and recorded: 'Lastly we were shewn the MS of the Shah Jehan Nameh, a large folio, in the original oriental gilded binding. This is a Book of Books. Of all the volumes I ever saw, none comes near in it in point [*sic*] of beauty of ornament and delicacy of painting. It is a real treasure, and better worth seeing than all the castle possessions besides. This volume was offered as a present to Sir John Shore, when Governor Genl. of India, but refused by him, as too costly for a subject to accept. It was then presented to George the Third... It deserves a case of gold, instead of being consigned to the drawer of a cabinet!' (see Bodleian Library MSS. Eng. Hist. c.160, pp. 273–81).
109. 'Prince Henry the Navigator' (1960); 'Paintings from the Muslim Courts of India' (1976); 'The Art of the Book in India (1982).
110. National Museum, New Delhi; Queen's Gallery, London; The Sackler Gallery, Washington; The Metropolitan Museum, New York; The Los Angeles County Museum of Art, California; The Kimbell Art Museum, Texas; Indianapolis Museum of Art, Indiana.
111. For this drawing, see Losty and Roy, *Mughal India*, pp. 137–9, in which the authors suggest the drawing may have been a preparatory work made earlier than Murar's painting.
112. In the 1960s the American collector Edwin Binney (1925–1986) purchased another unfinished painting related to Murar's work from the son of art historian Ananda Coomaraswamy (see p. 21): San Diego Museum of Art 1990.351. Edwin Binney, 28 August 1970: 'This is one of the group that I purchased from Dr. [Rama] Coomaraswamy from the estate of his mother, Dona Luisa [wife of Ananda Coomaraswamy]. She had mentioned it at one point when I went to see her ... 1960s ... as being something she wanted me to have.' The drawing is probably also an artistic exercise by an eighteenth-century Mughal artist.
113. Quoted in Beach and Koch, *King of the World*, p. 60.
114. See Ibid.
115. It was the celebrated Oriental scholar Thomas Arnold (1864–1930), then Assistant Librarian of the India Office Library, who encouraged the library to purchase this and other high-quality Mughal works, including a scene of Shah Jahan in Durbar (see fig. 20).
116. Hodgson & Co., *A Catalogue of Valuable Miscellaneous Books... Thursday June 17th, 1908* (London, 1908) p. 27. The British Library's copy includes a handwritten note of the purchase prices.

117. The inscription reads: 'This precious volume was given to his dearest intimate friend Nadira Banu Begam by Muhammad Dara Shikoh son of Shah Jahan emperor and victor, year 1056 ah/ad 1646–47'. See Losty and Roy, *Mughal India*, p. 125. See also J.P. Losty, 'The Dara Shikoh Album: A Reinterpretation', in Ebba Koch and Ali Anooshahr (eds), *The Mughal Empire under Shah Jahan (1628–58) – New Trends of research* (Vienna, 2014), and Falk and Archer, *Indian Miniatures in the India Office Library*, pp. 72–81.
118. Folios 1 and 78 also have the seal impression of Sayyid Ali al-Husayni, a servant of Alamgir, dated 1069 (1658–9). Another entry records it being handed over to Muhammad Muzzafar in the fifteenth year of the reign and gives a collation of its contexts.
119. See RCIN 1005069.z and 1005069.ak and V&A IS.48:25/B-1956.
120. See letter and bookplate in the album and A.J. Arberry's description in BL MSS. Eur. D. 542.
121. For this album, see Saqib Baburi, 'Beyond the Akbarnama: Padshahnamahs and Official Regnal Chronography for Shah-Jahan Padshah (r.1037/1628–1068/1658)', PhD dissertation, University of London, 2010, pp. 396–401.
122. John Nichols, *Literary Anecdotes of the Eighteenth Century*, vol. 9 (London, 1812–15), p. 636.
123. See Leigh & Sotheby, *A Catalogue of the elegant and valuable Libraries of Charles Chauncy ... and of his brother Nathaniel Chauncy ... which ... will be sold by auction, by Leigh & Sotheby ... on Thursday, April 15, 1790, etc* (London, 1790), p. 116, no. 3153, the second of two Indian albums: 'with several Rules for Beautiful Writing, and many very beautiful paintings, containing several portraits and illuminations'. The 'Rules for Beautiful Writing' refers to the album's preface, a famous introduction for a treatise on calligraphy written by the Mir Ali. The first album listed (cat. no. 3152) is Bodleian Library MS. Douce Or. b.1.
124. Apart from the three signed and one attributed paintings in this album, Muhammad Panah is known only by three other works: Bodleian MS. Douce Or. a3, fol. 23r dated 1139 AH/AD 1726 and two portraits of Nadir Shah (Bodleian MS. Ouseley Add. 173, fol. 29v, dated 1741 and a later copy of the same image, V&A IM.237-1921). Two further paintings of Nadir Shah in the Israel Museum are attributed to Muhammad Panah: O.S. 3975.10.77 and 4356.11.77. For a discussion of Muhammad Panah and the possibility of his later career in Iran, see Marcus Fraser, 'Muhammad Riza-i Hindi. An Important Indo-Persian Artist of the Mid-Eighteenth Century', *Journal of the David Collection* 5 (2021), pp. 179–229.
125. For this album, see Hannam, *Eastern Encounters*, pp. 136–51.
126. Translation by Michael Barry from the *Haft Piakar*, published in Michael Barry, 'Diabolic Fancies and Composite Animals: Persian Poetry and the Grotesques of Deccani and Mughal Painting', in Navina Najat Haidar and Marika Sardar (eds), *Sultans of the South: Arts of India's Deccan Courts, 1323–1687* (New York, 2011), p. 102. See also Princeton Museum and Art Gallery, Composite Elephant x1979-56, gift of Harold H. Hochschild, British Museum 1880,0.2403, and National Gallery of Victoria, Melbourne AS286-1980.
127. British Library Add.15296 and Add.15297. For this manuscript, see J.P. Losty, 'Curator's Perspective: Accessing the Mewar Ramayana', *British Library Asian and African Studies* blog, 1 April 2014. The other paintings from the series, which remained in India, are now in three separate institutions and one private collection.
128. The inscription on the reverse reads 'portrait of Mubariz Khan, subedar of the Deccan during the reign of Aurangzeb'.
129. Formerly known as 'the Johnson Painter'. See John Seyller, *Deccani Paintings, Drawings, and Manuscripts in the Jagdish and Kamla Mittal Museum of Indian Art* (Delhi, 2018), vol. 1, cat. no. 104 and pp. 208–12.
130. British Library Johnson Album 37; see Falk and Archer, *Indian Miniatures in the India Office Library*, no. 426.
131. Writing from Madras in 1751, East India Company officer John Andrews informed his superiors that Raja Vijayaram Raz of Vizanagarum is 'very desirous of a Gold watch, a Perspective and Pictures ... things if your Honour think proper to send me by land soon, I shall present them to him, and I believe we may get what we want from him.' IOR/G/18/16, Letters to Fort St David (vol. 5) 1750–1751, p. 214.
132. For this painting, see Andrew Topsfield, *Indian Paintings in Oxford Collections* (Oxford, 1994), pp. 68–9, and Seyller, *Deccani Paintings, Drawings, and Manuscripts* , vol. 1, pp. 209–12. Seyller suggests the figure depicted is Charles Joseph Patissier, Marquis de Bussy-Castlenau (1718–1785), a French ally of Nizam Salabat Jang until 1759. Another version of the subject by the same painter is in the Fondation Custodia, Paris.
133. Douce's collection also included several paintings from the collection of Elijah Impey. The London firm of Harry Phillips sold Elijah Impey's miniature collection after his death as part of his library sale on 21 May 1810. Many of the folios in Bodleian Library MS. Douce Or. a. 3 are stamped with Elijah Impey's seal dated 1775. Other paintings from the Impey collection include a series of Ragamala paintings c.1760 now in the British Library (Add Or. 3–7, 27, 28, 30, 31) and the Victoria and Albert Museum (I.S. 71–1954); a *Ramayana* series, now dispersed; an album of 23 paintings in the British Museum (former Add 11747: 1920,0917,0.154–182) and single folios (including 1974,0617,0.19.1–5); folios in Sir John Soane's Mughal album; in the Victoria and Albert Museum (IS-156-1952) and other folios now in the John Rylands Library (including Persian MS 51, f.3 and folios in Indian Drawings 7, Indian Drawings 21) the Chester Beatty Library.
134. Fullerton was tasked with translating correspondence and charged with misconduct by the Calcutta Council for misrepresenting one of Nand Kumar's letters.
135. M. Raymond (trans.), *The Seir Mutaqherin or Review of Modern Times. Being a history of India containing in general the reigns of the seven last Emperors of Hindostan* (Delhi, 1990), quoted in K.K. Sinha, 'Dr William Fullerton and the Patna Massacre of 1763', *Proceedings of the Royal College of Physicians of Edinburgh*, vol. 25, no. 2 (1995), pp. 279–93, p. 292.
136. Signed below: *work of Dip Chand the artist*. Evidence suggests that he initially moved to Patna in the employ of Mir Qasim Ali Khan, the Nawab of Bengal (r.1760–63) but accepted commissions from members of the nobility and Fullerton as well. For Dip Chand, see Losty and Roy, *Mughal India*, pp. 171–3; J.P. Losty, 'Towards a New Naturalism: Portraiture in Murshidabad and Avadh', in Schmitz (ed.), *After the Great Mughals* (Mumbai, 2002), pp. 35–55, and Robert Skelton, 'Murshidabad Painting', *Marg*, vol. X, no. 1 (December 1956), pp. 10–22.
137. See V&A D.1181 to 1183-1903 and D.1187-1903, D.1193 to 1195-1903, and others purchased in 1903 from Martinus Nijhoff.
138. British Library MS Add Or 735–738.
139. See Mildred Archer, *Company Paintings: Indian Paintings of the British Period* (London, 1992), cat. no. 45.
140. Zayn ud-Din later worked for Sir William Jones and his wife Anna Maria, whose collection of botanical studies are now held in the Royal Asiatic Society. See Andrew Topsfield, 'The Natural History Paintings of Shaikh Zain ud-Din, Bhawani Das and Ram Das', in William Dalrymple (ed.), *Forgotten Masters: Indian Painting for the East India Company* (London, 2019), pp. 40–47.
141. John Latham, *A General History of Birds*, vol. 3 (Winchester, 1822), p. 213.

142. Sold at Sotheby's, London, on 19 June 1963, pages can now be found in the Wellcome Institute, London; Bodleian Library, Oxford; Radcliffe Science Library, Oxford; Victoria & Albert Museum, London; Metropolitan Museum of Art, New York; Minneapolis Institute of Arts; and San Diego Museum of Art.
143. H.J. Noltie, 'Indian Export Art? The Botanical Drawings', in Dalrymple (ed.), *Forgotten Masters*, pp. 79–80.
144. For the Wellesley and Buchanan-Hamilton collections, see ibid. A less-well-known collection is that of Claude Martin: 600 watercolours of flora and fauna by Indian artists, which are now housed in the library of the Royal Botanic Gardens, Kew. For this, see Rosie Llewellyn-Jones, 'Painting in Lucknow, 1775–1800', in Dalrymple (ed.), *Forgotten Masters*, p. 30.
145. See Mildred Archer, *The Marquis Wellesley Collection: Indian Artists under British Patronage* (London, 1983).
146. For Tipu's cheetahs, see 'Lists of the Spoils of Tippu Sultan' sold at Sotheby's, London, 10 July 2012, lot 17.
147. See Mildred Archer, *Natural History Drawings in the India Office Library* (London, 1962), pp. 6–7.
148. For Roxburgh and his artists, see H.J. Noltie, 'Indian Export Art? The Botanical Drawings', in Dalrymple (ed.), *Forgotten Masters*, p. 80.
149. Preserved in the Central National Herbarium, Botanical Survey of India, Howrah.
150. See J.R. Sealy, 'The Roxburgh Flora Indica Drawings at Kew', *Kew Bulletin*, vol. 11, no. 2 (1956), pp. 297–348.
151. For Chunni Lal, see H.J. Noltie, 'Indian Export Art? The Botanical Drawings', in Dalrymple (ed.), *Forgotten Masters*, pp. 82, 99.
152. Ibid., p. 99.
153. Ibid., p. 80.
154. Letter from James Baillie Fraser to his father, 26 August 1815, quoted in Mildred Archer and Toby Falk, *India Revealed: The Art and Adventures of James and William Fraser 1801–35* (London, 1989), p. 37. James wrote again the week after, saying 'I have had Malaguire the Nautch woman here today to sit for her picture and am to get Lalljee to take it.' Lalji's son, Hulas Lal, may have also worked for the Fraser brothers, but their letters refer only to 'the native artist' or 'the painter'. Five years later, in 1821, William wrote that 'I have got a good painter of figures, portraits and groups', thought to be a family member of Delhi artist Ghulam Ali Khan, although he does not explicitly name him. For Ghulam Ali Khan, see Yuthika Sharma, 'Ghulam Ali Khan and the Delhi School of Painting', in Dalrymple (ed.), *Forgotten Masters*, pp. 140–47.
155. Quoted in Archer and Falk, *India Revealed*, p. 39.
156. Ibid., p. 40.
157. In a related painting the nurse Munni Banu is labelled 'Sanu Dai' and the child in her care identified as 'Osman Khan Kudak'. See 'A group of Afghan figures beneath trees', attributable to Ghulam Ali Khan, Delhi, c.1815–20, The Sven Gahlin Collection, Sotheby's, 6 October 2015, lot 39.
158. The loose pictures were sold at Sotheby's, London, on 7 July 1980 (lots 1–45) and the pictures that had been mounted into an album were sold with the binding at Sotheby's, New York, on 9 December 1980 (lots 130–187). Other Company School paintings had also been pasted into that album and were sold at the New York sale.
159. Letter from James Baillie Fraser to his father, 20 October 1820, quoted in Archer and Falk, *India Revealed*, p. 43.
160. Mawlavi Salamat Ullah is also depicted in an album compiled by James Skinner (British Library Add. Or. 1250); however, the accompanying inscription identifies him as living in 'Cawnpore' (Kanpur).
161. See British Library Add MS 27255 , f.451b, and Library of Congress Rosenwald MS. no. 34, f. 285.
162. Fraser papers B292, quoted in Archer and Falk, *India Revealed*, p. 43.
163. Quoted in Mildred Archer, 'The Two Worlds of James Skinner (1778–1841)', *History Today*, September 1960, pp. 612–13.
164. For this manuscript, see Charles Rieu, *Catalogue of the Persian Manuscripts in the British Museum*, vol. 1 (London, 1879), pp. 302–3, and J.P. Losty, 'James Skinner's Tazkirat al-Umara now digitised', *British Library Asian and African Studies* blog, 7 August 2014.
165. In addition to the royal Mughal calligraphy in this album, several specimens in the hands of Emperor Shah Jahan and his son Dara Shikoh are found in British collections: see Bodleian Library MS. Per b1; MS Ouseley 173, f. 29r; Victoria and Albert Museum IS. 37–1972 and IS. 37:2–1972; British Museum 1921,1011,0.4.b. The India Office collection in the British Library also holds an illuminated Quran copied by Mughal emperor Shah Alam II: British Library IO Islamic 3113A.
166. BL Add Or 21474. For this manuscript, see Charles Rieu, *Supplement to the Catalogue of the Persian Manuscripts in the British Museum* (London, 1895), p. 787. Lewin Bowring later became secretary to Charles Canning (1812–1862), the last governor general and first viceroy of India. He oversaw the translation into the principal Indian vernacular languages of Queen Victoria's Proclamation to the People of India, published on 1 November 1858 after the suppression of the Indian Mutiny, which was read out loud in formal ceremonies across India and wider South and South East Asia. See Miles Taylor, *Empress: Queen Victoria and India* (London, 2018), p. 86.
167. For this manuscript, see Hannam, *Eastern Encounters*, pp. 218–27; Natalia di Di Pietrantonio, 'Erotic Visions: Poetry, Literature, and Book Arts from Avadh, 1754–1857', PhD dissertation, Cornell University, 2018; and Tushara Bindu Gude, 'Hybrid Visions: The Cultural Landscape of Awadh', in Stephen Markel, Tushara Bindu Gude and Muzaffar Alam (eds), *India's Fabled City: The Art of Courtly Lucknow* (Los Angeles, 2010) pp. 98–9.
168. For Ahmad Ali Khan, see Sophie Gordon, 'A City of Mourning: The Representation of Lucknow, India in Nineteenth-century Photography', *History of Photography*, vol. 30, no. 1 (2006) pp. 80–91.
169. In June 1859 he wrote to Lady Elizabeth Gomm (1807–1877), wife of General Gomm, recently retired as commander-in-chief of the British Army in India: 'My Dear Lady Gomm, I send you the illustrated manuscript work of which I formerly spoke. It only came from the bookbinders a few days ago. He preferred to restore the old binding as in keeping with the work, to rebinding it in the English fashion. This book is curious & interesting from two circumstances. It was prepared in the Palace of Lucknow under the direction of the King of Oude, & is of course a faithful illustration of the life and dress of the highest Mahomedan families in India. Secondly, it was taken by some Seikhs [Sikhs] of one of the Punjabee Regiments at the time the Palace of Lucknow was stormed – they gave it to their commanding officer, who was good enough to present it to me, as the Corps was raised under my orders. If you consider that it would be a suitable offering to Her Majesty & could ascertain whether it would be acceptable, I shall feel much obliged to you. Yours very sincerely, John Lawrence.' John Lawrence to Lady Gomm, 26 June 1859: RCIN 1005035.da.
170. For the *Darabnama*, see William L. Hanaway, 'Dārāb-Nāma', in *Encyclopædia Iranica*, vol. 7 (1994), pp. 8–9. For this manuscript, see Losty and Roy, *Mughal India*), pp. 32–7; J.P. Losty, *The Arts of the Book in India* (London, 1982), p. 88; Norah M. Titley, *Miniatures from Persian Manuscripts: A Catalogue and Subject Index of Paintings from Persia, India and Turkey in the British Library and the British Museum* (London, 1977), pp. 8–11; Rieu, *Supplement to*

the Catalogue of the Persian Manuscripts in the British Museum, no. 385.

171. Wilhelm Staude, 'Miskine', *Revue des Arts Asiatiques* 5 (1928), pp. 169–82, mentioned in Michael Brand, 'Miskin', in Beach et al. (eds), *Masters of Indian Painting*, vol. 1, p. 171.
172. One of these paintings was acquired by the collector Richard Johnson and is now in the British Library; see Johnson Album 8, f.4.
173. Susan Stronge, *Painting for the Mughal Emperor: The Art of the Book 1560–1660* (London, 2002), p. 36.
174. H. Blochmann (trans.), *The Ain-i Akbari*, vol. 1 (New Delhi, 1977), p. 115, quoted in ibid., p. 17.
175. Howard Hodgkin, 'On Collecting Indian Paintings', *The Ashmolean* 23 (Christmas 1992).
176. Stronge, *Painting for the Mughal Emperor*, p. 21.
177. Ibid.
178. The original oil painting on board painted in 1902 is now in the Victoria Memorial Hall, Kolkata.
179. The painting was exhibited soon after at the Congress Industrial Exhibition (1903), where it won a gold medal.
180. Abananindranath Tagore, *Jarasankar Dhore*, pp. 157–8, quoted in Mitter, *Art and Nationalism in Colonial India*, p. 226.
181. For Ishwari Prasad and Shiva Lal, see Mildred Archer, *Patna Painting* (London, 1948), and *India Served and Observed*. Ishwari Prasad and his son later worked for P.C. Manuk, restoring and mounting his miniatures. Paintings by the artists can also be found in the Victoria and Albert Museum, from the collection of P.C. Manuk, and in the Ashmolean Museum: EAX.2030. Works from Ishwari Prasad's family collection are also now in the British Library and Victoria and Albert Museum, having been purchased in 1947 by W.G. Archer.
182. British Library Photo 273.
183. Guha-Thakurta, *The Making of a New 'Indian' Art*, p. 155.
184. Abanindranath Tagore, *Gharoya* (1941), p. 74, quoted in Guha-Thakurta, *The Making of a New 'Indian' Art*, p. 242.
185. See Partha Mitter, 'The Raj, Indian Artists and Western Art', in Joachim K. Bautze (ed.), *Interaction of Cultures: Indian and Western Painting, 1780–1910: The Ehrenfeld Collection* (Alexandria VA, 1998), pp. 33–7.
186. V&A Registered file 1191/4456M.
187. For this painting, see Rita Banerjee, *India and the Traveller: Aspects of Travelling Identity* (London, 2022), pp. 64–9.
188. The pageant was organized by Frank Lascelles, who also curated the Coronation Durbar later that year in Delhi.
189. See William Foster, *A Descriptive Catalogue of the Paintings, Statues, etc. in the India Office* (London, 1924), Room 181 (Secretary of State).
190. Atiya later recalled, 'It was in a tiny fishing village near the seaside, Bombay, in 1913 ... I sang the eternal limpid melodies. Rahamin immortalized them in a series of beautiful paintings, the Ragas and Raginis (the male and female melodies). I dashed off a few lines in explanation. We soon left for Europe, where the written text was brought out in book form, and helped to explain the symbolic significance of he Ragas and Raginis.' Atiya Begum Fyzee-Rahamin, *The Music of India* (London, 1925), Foreword, p. 5.
191. In 1930 Samuel Fyzee-Rahamin had a retrospective exhibition at Manchester Art Gallery. Although titled *Exhibition of Decorations for Delhi*, it included his early portraits and his miniature paintings, as well as sketches and drawings for his murals in Delhi. In 1939 he had another solo London exhibition at the Arlington Galleries.
192. Anon., 'Indian Art at Wembley', *Malaya Tribune*, 1 October 1925, p. 2.
193. Anon., 'Mr Fyzee-Rahamin's Paintings', *Apollo* 2 (1925), p. 93, with the painting reproduced in colour on p. 94.
194. Letter of 24 February 1960, quoted in Ronald Alley, *Catalogue of the Tate Gallery's Collection of Modern Art other than Works by British Artists* (London, 1981), pp. 230–31.
195. Sotheby's, 6 April 1925, lot 480. See Stronge, *Painting for the Mughal Emperor*, pp. 145–6.
196. V&A I.M 108-1921 to 139-1921.
197. Bodleian Library MS. Douce.Or.a.1 folio 24b.
198. Guha-Thakurta, *The Making of a New 'Indian' Art*, pp. 299–301.
199. Nadeem Aslam, quoted in an interview with Anita Sethi, *Independent*, 31 August 2008.
200. For Dr Paira Mall and the South Asian collections of the Wellcome Institute, see Bárbara Rodríguez Muñoz, *Ayurvedic Man: Encounters with Indian Medicine* (London, 2017), and Dominik Wujasty, *The South Asian collections of the Wellcome Institute for the History of Medicine* (London, 1984).
201. Rodríguez Muñoz, *Ayurvedic Man*.
202. The three paintings in the V&A are I.M.87-1930, IM.88-1930 and IM.89-1930. The Victoria and Albert Museum had already acquired worked from Maulvi Muhammad Hussain's collection, which he had sold to Sir Robert Nathan, then permanent secretary to the viceroy, in 1904–5. Nathan gave them to the museum in 1921. See V&A 1921/4451.
203. For this series, see B.N. Goswamy and Eberhard Fischer, *Pahari Masters: Court Painters of Northern India* (Zurich, 1992), pp. 239–66; Archer, *Indian Paintings from the Punjab Hills*, pp. 46–8; F.S. Aijazuddin, *Pahari Paintings and Sikh Portraits in the Lahore Museum* (London, 1977), pp. 6–11.
204. For the debate as to reading of the manuscript's colophon, see Goswamy and Fischer, *Pahari Masters*, pp. 241–3.
205. Translation adapted from Barbara Stoller Miller, *Gitagovinda of Jayadeva: Love Song of the Dark Lord* (New York, 1977).
206. For this series, see Imma Ramos, '"Private Pleasures" of the Mughal Empire', *Art History*, vol. 37, no. 3 (2014), pp. 409–27. The British Museum acquired a related series before 1880: BM 1880,0.412-435.
207. For Ruknuddin, see Molly Emma Aitken, Shanane Davis and Yana Van Dyke, 'Old Methods in a New Era: What Can Connoisseurship Tell Us about Rukn-ud-din?', in Rebecca Brown and Deborah Hutton (eds), *A Companion to Asian Art and Architecture* (Oxford, 2011), p. 233.
208. Ramos, '"Private Pleasures" of the Mughal Empire'.
209. For an English translation, see Sir Richard Francis Burton, *Ananga-Ranga (Stage of the Bodiless One) or, The Hindu Art of Love* (London and Benares, 1885).
210. Ramos, '"Private Pleasures" of the Mughal Empire', pp. 417–19.
211. Ibid., p. 417.
212. Sonya Rhie Quintanilla, *Rhythms of India: The Art of Nandalal Bose* (San Diego, 2008) pp. 27–8.
213. See also V&A 159-1951.
214. For this painting, see Archer, *Indian Paintings from the Punjab Hills*, vol. 1, p.118.
215. See Anon., 'The India Society Again', *Times of India*, 1 April 1931, p. 5, quoted in Brinda Kumar, 'Exciting a Wider Interest in the Art of India: The 1931 Burlington Fine Arts Club Exhibition', in *British Art Studies* 13, 30 September 2019. After Rothenstein's death, Kenneth de Burgh Codrington, then Keeper of the Indian Section of the Victoria and Albert Museum, selected 80 works for an Arts Council touring exhibition, *Indian Paintings and Drawings from Sir William Rothenstein's Collection*, and laid the groundwork for the V&A's acquisition. See K. de B. Codrington, *Indian Paintings and Drawings from Sir William Rothenstein's Collection* (London, 1947).

216. The V&A bought these paintings from Ananda Coomaraswarmy (Victoria and Albert Museum I.M. 74-1912); the Bombay-born dealer Nasli M. Heeramaneck (I.M. 156-1914 and 157-1914); and the estate of Manuk and Coles; (I.S 43-194 up to I.S 52-194 and I.S 138-1949). For this series, see Archer, *Indian Paintings from the Punjab Hills*, vol. 1, pp. 305–6, cat. no. 66, and Falk and Archer, *Indian Miniatures in the India Office Library*, no. 548.
217. Harsha V. Dehejia, *Rasikapriya: Ritikavya of Keshavdas in Ateliers of Love* (New Delhi, 2013), quoted in J.P. Losty, 'Pahari Paintings at the British Library', *British Library Asian and African Studies* blog, 22 January 2014.
218. British Library MSS Eur D241, f. 67, quoted in Archer, *Indian Paintings from the Punjab Hills*, vol. 1, pp. 262–3.
219. V&A Registered file 1956/937 states the painting was purchased from a D.G. Wells.
220. See Aijazuddin, *Pahari Paintings and Sikh Portraits in the Lahore Museum*, p. 37, no. 55.
221. See also Ashmolean Museum EA1995.34 and EA2013.30.
222. Howard Hodgkin, 'About My Collection', *Asian Art*, 1991, howard-hodgkin.com/indian-collection/resource/about-my-collection.
223. For this painting, see Andrew Topsfield, *Visions of Mughal India: The Collection of Howard Hodgkin* (Oxford, 2012), pp. 196–7.
224. Gabriella Angeleti, 'The Metropolitan Museum of Art acquires rejected Howard Hodgkin collection of Indian Art', *Art Newspaper*, 21 July 2022.
225. Henry Brownrigg also sold South Asian art to the British Museum.
226. See A.L. Dallapiccola, *South Indian Paintings: A Catalogue of the British Museum Collections* (London, 2010), pp. 278–95.

CONTEMPORARY WORKS

1. Gulammohammed Sheikh, artist statement in catalogue for the exhibition *Place for People*, Jehangir Art Gallery (Bombay, 1981), unpaginated.
2. 'Vishakha N. Desai interviews Nilima Sheikh and Shahzia Sikander', *Conversations with Traditions* (New York, 2001), p. 68.
3. For an explanation on the nomenclature of 'miniature', see the Introduction to this catalogue.
4. The Gulammohammed Sheikh Archive is part of the Baroda Archives at Asia Art Archive, accessible at aaa.org.hk/en/collections/search/archive/gulammohammed-sheikh-archive.
5. John Clark, 'Gulammohammed Sheikh and Multidiversity', in *The Asian Modern*, vol. 2 (Singapore, 2020).
6. Gulammohammed Sheikh, 'A Great Friend of India: Robert Skelton (1929–2022)', in the online platform *Critical Collective*, 25 October 2022.
7. See Anna Sloan, 'Embodied Space: The Miniature as Attitude', in Anita Dawood and Hammad Nasar (eds), *Beyond the Page: Contemporary Art from Pakistan* (London and Manchester, 2006), pp. 26–45.
8. Gulammohammed Sheikh, 'Mobile Vision: Some Synoptic Comments', *Journal of Arts & Ideas* 5 (October–December 1983), p. 52, cdn.aaa.org.hk/_source/1983-oct-dec-journal-of-arts-and-ideas-mobile-vision.pdf.
9. Chaitanya Sambrani, 'At Home in the World', in Chaitanya Sambrani (ed.), *At Home in the World: The Art and Life of Gulamohammed Sheikh* (New Delhi, 2019), pp. 132–3.
10. Suman Gopinath, 'In Conversation with Gulammohammed Sheikh', in Kunstmuseum Bern (ed.), *Horn Please: Narratives in Contemporary Indian Art* (Ostfildern, 2007), p. 47.
11. Nilima Sheikh, 'A Post-Independence Initiative in Art', in G. Sheikh (ed.), *Contemporary Art in Baroda* (New Delhi, 1997), p. 60.
12. Ajay Sinha, 'Envisioning the Seventies and the Eighties', in Sheikh (ed.), *Contemporary Art in Baroda*, p. 192.
13. Geeta Kapur, 'The Uncommon Universe of Bhupen Khakhar', in Kobena Mercer (ed.), *Pop Art and Vernacular Cultures* (Cambridge MA and London, 2007), pp. 110–35.
14. G. Sheikh submitted the unsuccessful proposal for an MA course on 'The Living Traditions of Indian Art, including miniature painting', on 12 August 1987. Digital copy accessed in G. Sheikh's archives at Asia Art Archive, Hong Kong.
15. Geeta Kapur, 'Partisan Views about the Human Figure', in the catalogue for *Place for People* (Bombay and New Delhi, 1981). Timothy Hyman curated *Narrative Paintings: Figurative Art of Two Generations at the Arnolfini* in Bristol (1980), with Bhupen Khakar as the sole Indian artist.
16. Simone Wille, *Modern Art in Pakistan* (New Delhi, 2015) pp. 81–2. Wille's chapter on Zahoor ul Akhlaq (pp. 40–82) in the volume is one of the most significant art-historical accounts of the artist's practice to date.
17. Salima Hashmi, *The Painter between Tradition and Contemporaneity*, in the Salima Hashmi Archive at Asia Art Archive, accessible at aaa.org.hk/en/collections/search/archive/salima-hashmi-archive-manuscripts-and-notes/object/zahoorul-akhlaq-the-painter-between-tradition-and-contemporary.
18. See Virginia Whiles, 'Deconstructing the Miniature', in Dawood and Nasar (eds), *Beyond the Page*, pp. 55–6.
19. Zahoor ul Akhlaq, quoted in an interview with Gregory Minissale, 'Black is the Beginning', *The Herald* (Karachi), May 1991, p. 151.
20. For Akhlaq's engagement with miniature practice, see Wille, *Modern Art in Pakistan*. For his pedagogic intervention, see Virginia Whiles, 'Revival or Re-Invention', in Hammad Nasar with Anita Dawood (eds), *Karkhana: A Contemporary Collaboration* (London and Ridgefield CT, 2005), pp. 26–33.
21. The idea of miniature as an attitude was explored in the exhibition *Beyond the Page: Miniature as Attitude in Contemporary Art from Pakistan* (curated by Hammad Nasar with Anna Sloan and Bridget Bray) at the Pacific Asia Museum in 2010. An earlier version of the exhibition (curated by Hammad Nasar) was realized in two parts at Manchester Art Gallery and Asia House, London, in 2006, and accompanied by a catalogue edited by Anita Dawood and Hammad Nasar.
22. See Salima Hashmi, 'Studies in Excellence', *Newsline*, March/April 1992, p. 112.
23. *Karkhana: A Contemporary Collaboration*, at the Aldrich Contemporary Art Museum in Ridgefield, Connecticut, and the Asian Art Museum, San Francisco (2005–6), was curated by Jessica Hough, Hammad Nasar and Anna Sloan, and accompanied by an ambitious publication of the same name edited by Hammad Nasar with Anita Dawood, with multiple scholarly essays introducing the project in the context of the wider development of the contemporary miniature.
24. See Hough, Nasar and Sloan, 'Introduction', in *Karkhana*, p. 8. Examples of its favourable reception included: the veteran *New York Times* (NYT) critic Holland Cotter penning an admiring review of the exhibition on the front page of the *NYT Arts & Leisure* section; Yale University (CT) and the New School (NY) organizing significant public programmes in response to the exhibition; and the Hong Kong-based arts magazine *Art Asia*

Pacific picking the *Karkhana* publication as one of their 'Books of the Year' for 2005.

25. In conversation with Hammad Nasar in 'Same Planet, Different Worlds', *The Herald* (Karachi), February 2004, p. 97.
26. While there are too many exhibitions to list, the following public exhibitions were notable in being accompanied by significant scholarly catalogues: *Contemporary Miniature Paintings from Pakistan* at the Fukuoka Asian Art Museum, 2004 (curated by Virginia Whiles); *Karkhana: A Contemporary Collaboration* at the Aldrich Contemporary Art Museum, Ridgefield CT, and the Asian Art Museum, San Francisco CA, 2005–6 (curated by Jessica Hough, Hammad Nasar and Anna Sloan); *Beyond the Page: Contemporary Art from Pakistan* at Manchester Art Gallery and Asia House, London, 2006 (curated by Hammad Nasar); and *Living Traditions: Contemporary Art from Afghanistan, Iran and Pakistan*, at Bagh-e-Babur, Kabul & National Art Gallery, Islamabad, 2009 (curated by Jemima Montagu).
27. Sloan, 'Embodied Space'.
28. Rachel Spence, in conversation with Hammad Nasar, 'What if all Turner's best paintings were in Lahore?', *Financial Times Weekend*, 11–12 February 2023, www.ft.com/content/4f9a1aba-a3b2-4da0-8463-e62d6d604628.
29. Arindam Dutta, *The Bureaucracy of Beauty: Design in the Age of Its Global Reproducibility* (London and New York, 2007), p. 73.
30. indianexpress.com/article/express-sunday-eye/an-artist-of-the-changing-world-5647256.
31. aaa.org.hk/en/collections/search/archive/gulammohammed-sheikh-archive-manuscripts-of-essays-and-articles-on-art/object/in-many-worlds; copyright Gulammohammed Sheikh.
32. B. Khakhar, *Truth is Beauty and Beauty is God*, Gallery Chemould (Mumbai, 1972), unpaginated.
33. U. Beier and B. Khakhar, *Courtesy Aspect Magazine* 23 (January 1982), unpaginated.
34. scroll.in/magazine/850531/a-brief-history-of-pakistani-art-and-the-people-who-shaped-it.
35. www.tate.org.uk/art/artworks/akhlaq-untitled-t14309.
36. Howard Hodgkin, 'Notes on the Collection', in Andrew Topsfield and Milo Cleveland Beach, *Indian Paintings and Drawings from the Collection of Howard Hodgkin* (New York, 1991); republished in Topsfield, *Visions of Mughal India*, p. 11.
37. Andrew Graham Dixon, *Howard Hodgkin*, rev. edn (London, 2001), p. 118, quoted in Topsfield, *Visions of Mughal India*, p. 17.
38. Alan Davie, 'Notes by the Artists', in *Catalogue of an Exhibition of Paintings and Drawings From 1936–1958*, Whitechapel Art Gallery (London, 1958). See Carl Jung, *The Archetypes and the Collective Unconscious* (1959).
39. Alan Davie in *Alan Davie* (London, 1992), p. 82.
40. Ian McKeever, 'Strange Business', in *Alan Davie: The Quest for the Miraculous* (Brighton and London, 1993), p. 77.
41. Artist statement, *Arpita Singh* (Kolkata, 1995), unpaginated.
42. Gayatri Sinha, *Arpita Singh Works on Paper* (New Delhi, 2015).
43. www.themorgan.org/exhibitions/online/shahzia-sikander/scroll.
44. www.themorgan.org/exhibitions/online/shahzia-sikander/riding-written.
45. Sent via email to Anthony Spira, 21 April 2023.
46. www.themorgan.org/exhibitions/online/shahzia-sikander/many-faces-islam.
47. Olivia Fraser in an interview with *Platform Magazine*, New Delhi, November 2019; www.platform-mag.com/art/olivia-fraser.html.
48. Email from Olivia Frase Fraser to Anthony Spira, 14 March 2023.
49. Virginia Whiles, *Olivia Fraser: A Passionate Quest* (London, 2012).
50. Ibid.
51. Rashid Rana, from correspondence with the Artist's Studio, September 2020, www.sothebys.com/en/buy/auction/2020/modern-contemporary-south-asian-art-2/rashid-rana-i-love-miniatures.
52. From Virginia Whiles, 'The Role of Portraiture in Pakistani Contemporary Miniature Painting', in Crispin Branfoot (ed.), *Portraiture in South Asia Since the Mughals: Art, Representation and History* (London, 2019).
53. hblog.saffronart.com/2012/11/06/karkhana-a-contemporary-collaboration.
54. asiasociety.org/triennial/updates/dreaming-hamra-abbas.
55. Virginia Whiles, 'Rough and Abrasive: A Critique of the Miniature', in Muhammad Zeeshan, *Dying Miniature* (London, 2008), p. 8.
56. Raqib Shaw, quoted in Maria Balshaw, Foreword (i) in *Raqib Shaw* (Manchester, 2013), p. 9.
57. Petr Nedoma, Foreword (ii) in *Raqib Shaw*, pp. 15, 18.
58. smarthistory.org/noor-ali.
59. articulate.org.in/bagh-e-hind-a-curatorial-stroll-through-mughal-and-rajput-garden-paintings.
60. The Singh Twins in an interview with *Platform* magazine (the Film Issue), New Delhi, 2013, www.platform-mag.com/art/the-singh-twins.html.
61. Alexander Gorlizki, interview with Susie Pentelow, *Traction Magazine*, 7 January 2015.
62. Alexander Gorlizki, Interview with Suryasarathi Bhattacharya, *Firstpost*, 5 March 2020.
63. Emily King in conversation with Lubna Chowdhary', *Lubna Chowdhary* (London, 2017), p. 13.
64. Lubna Chowdhary, interview, *Studio International*, 12 August 2022.
65. Chowdhary created drawings and designs for the sculptures, which were carved with Computer Numerical Control (CNC), then assembled and hand-finished.
66. See www.britishartstudies.ac.uk/issues/issue-index/issue-10/gardening-archive.
67. Ibid.

IMAGE CREDITS

ii detail of p. 43
iv detail of p. 187
vi detail of p. 45
5 detail of p. 132
6 Courtesy Milton Keynes City Council MK9_JR_5018
8 detail of p. 46
10 detail of p. 44
12 Library of Congress G159.P98
13 © The British Library Board, Foster 91
14 Royal Collection Trust/© His Majesty King Charles III 2023 RCIN 1005032
16 The Picture Art Collection/Alamy Stock Photo/Victoria Memorial Hall, Calcutta
18 © The British Library Board, Or.4615, f 129v
19 © Victoria and Albert Museum, London
22 Sueddeutsche Zeitung Photo/Alamy Stock Photo
26 detail of pp. 48–9
28 (*left*) Photo: National Portrait Gallery, London D42343
28 (*right*) © The Trustees of the British Museum. All rights reserved BM 1920,0917,0.110
29 Photo: © Bodleian Libraries, University of Oxford MS. Laud Or. 149 f. 13b
30 © Victoria and Albert Museum, London IS.30-1892
31 Collection Museum Boijmans Van Beuningen, Rotterdam R36 (PK). Loan: Stichting Museum Boijmans Van Beuningen 1940 (former collection Koenigs)/photographer: Studio Tromp
32 © The Trustees of the British Museum. All rights reserved BM 1923,0113.20
33 (*top and detail left*) Photo: OM.672, Qatar Museums/Lusail Museum, Doha - Qatar OM.672
33 (*detail centre*) Photo: Fondation Custodia, Collection Frits Lugt, Paris inv. no. 592
33 (*top right*) © Schloss Schönbrunn Kultur und Betriebsges.m.b.H./ Digitalisat: Salon Iris SKB002632
33 (*detail right*) © Schloss Schönbrunn Kultur und Betriebsges.m.b.H./ Digitalisat: Salon Iris
34 Royal Collection Trust/© His Majesty King Charles III 2023 RCIN 1005047 verso
35 (*left*) Image © The Metropolitan Museum of Art/Art Resource/ Scala, Florence
35 (*right*) © The Trustees of the British Museum. All rights reserved BM 1936,0111,0.6
36 Image © National Museums Scotland V.2021.38 and V.2021.39
38 Photo: © Bodleian Libraries, University of Oxford MS. Elliott 254, fol. 35b
39 Photo: © Bodleian Libraries, University of Oxford MS. Ouseley Add. 170, fol. 5b
40 Royal Collection Trust/© His Majesty King Charles III 2023 RCIN 1005032.g
41 Royal Collection Trust/© His Majesty King Charles III 2023 RCIN 1005025.ae
42 (and detail p. 43) Royal Collection Trust/© His Majesty King Charles III 2023 RCIN 1005025.al
43 The Morgan Library and Museum MS.M659
44 Royal Collection Trust/© His Majesty King Charles III 2023 RCIN 1005025.j
45 Courtesy of the British Library Board Johnson Album 4, 2
46 Royal Collection Trust/© His Majesty King Charles III 2023 RCIN 1005025.v
47 Courtesy of the British Library Board Add. Or. MS 3129, f. 57v
48 Photo: © Bodleian Libraries, University of Oxford Or a.1- ff.55b and 56a
50 Royal Collection Trust/© His Majesty King Charles III 2023 RCIN 1005068.n-o
51 Royal Collection Trust/© His Majesty King Charles III 2023 RCIN 1005068.n-o
52 © Victoria and Albert Museum, London D.1186-1903
53 Photo: © Bodleian Libraries, University of Oxford MS. Ouseley Add. 171 folio 9v
54 Courtesy of the British Library Board Add. Or. MS 3129, f. 57v Add 15297 (2), f.70
55 Photo: The Box, Plymouth /Cottonian Collection CD280
56 Photo: © Bodleian Libraries, University of Oxford MS. Douce Or. b. 3 f.31a
57 (top) Photo: © Bodleian Libraries, University of Oxford MS Douce Or. b. 3 f.25a
57 (*bottom left*) © The Trustees of the British Museum Ee,8.70
57 (*bottom right*) © The Trustees of the British Museum 1880,113.2257
58 © Victoria and Albert Museum, London IM.33-1912
59 (*left*) Photography by John McKenzie for L&T by kind permission National Museums Scotland v.2021.30
59 (*right*) © Victoria and Albert Museum, London. D.1181-1903
60 © Victoria and Albert Museum, London. IS.11:48-1887
61 Private collection, London/Karachi
62 (*left*) Wellcome Collection, London 566384i
62 (*right*) Courtesy of the British Library Board NHD 3/498
63 Courtesy of the British Library Board NHD 32/3
64 © Board of Trustees, Royal Botanic Gardens, Kew
65 © Board of Trustees, Royal Botanic Gardens, Kew
66 © Board of Trustees, Royal Botanic Gardens, Kew
67 Private collection, London/Karachi

68 Private collection, London/Karachi
69 Private collection, London/Karachi © Photo courtesy Sotheby's, 2023
70 Courtesy of the British Library Board Add MS 27254, ff. 227v–228r
71 Courtesy of the British Library Board Add Add.21474, f. 4
72 (*left*) Courtesy of the British Library Board Photo 500(3)
72 (*right*) Royal Collection Trust/© His Majesty King Charles III 2023 RCIN 1005035.a
73 Courtesy of the British Library Board Or.4615, f 44r
75 © Victoria and Albert Museum, London. IS.2:100-1896
77 © Victoria and Albert Museum, London. IS.2509-1883
78 Wellcome Collection, London 582929i
79 Courtesy of the British Library Board Add Or 2537
80 © Victoria and Albert Museum, London. IS.305-1951
81 © Victoria and Albert Museum, London. IM.117-1911
82 © Bradford Museums & Galleries/Bridgeman Images 2005-015
83 (*left*) Courtesy of the British Library Board BL Add.Or.2853
83 (*right*) © The Trustees of the British Museum BM 1933,0610,0.1
84 © Tate: Presented by Sir Victor Sassoon 1925 N04095
85 © Tate: Presented by the State of Bhavnagar 1925 N04096
86 © Victoria and Albert Museum, London. IM.13-1925
87 Property of a collector, photo: Prudence Cuming
88 © Arif Rahman Chughtai and the Chughtai Museum
89 © Arif Rahman Chughtai and the Chughtai Museum
90 Wellcome Collection, London MS Indic Gamma 453
91 © Victoria and Albert Museum, London IM.89-1930
92 © The Fitzwilliam Museum, Cambridge PD.205-1948.14
93 (*left*) © The Fitzwilliam Museum, Cambridge PD.205-1948.16
93 (*right*) © The Fitzwilliam Museum, Cambridge PD.205-1948.12
94 Private collection, London/Karachi, © Estate of Nandalal Bose
95 © Victoria and Albert Museum, London IS.160-1951
96 Courtesy of the British Library Board Add.Or.26
97 © Victoria and Albert Museum, London IS.15-1956
98 © Victoria and Albert Museum, London IS.42-1956
99 © Ashmolean Museum EA2016.23
100 © Victoria and Albert Museum, London IS.18-1991
102 detail of p. 168
104 detail of p. 125
106 © The artist/Courtesy of the artist and Vadehra Art Gallery
107 detail of p. 122
108 © The artist/Gallery Chemould
110 © Estate of Zahoor ul Akhlaq/AAN Collection
112 Photograph by Ka-Man Tse for Times Square Arts
113 © The artist/Courtesy of the artist
116 © The artist/Courtesy of the artist
118 detail of p. 154
120 © Courtesy the artist/Vadehra Art Gallery
121 © Courtesy the artist/Kiran Nadar Museum of Art
122 © Courtesy the artist/Vadehra Art Gallery/Victoria and Albert Museum IS.15-1986
125 © Estate of Bhupen Khakhar/Courtesy of Sotheby's
126 © Estate of Bhupen Khakhar/Private collection
127 (*both*) © Estate of Bhupen Khakhar/Private collection, London/Karachi
128 (*left*) © Estate of Zahoor ul Akhlaq/Private collection, London/Karachi
128 (*right*) © Estate of Zahoor ul Akhlaq/private collection
129 © Estate of Zahoor ul Akhlaq/Private collection, London/Karachi
130 © Estate of Zahoor ul Akhlaq/Tate. Purchased with funds provided by the South Asia Acquisitions Committee 2015 T14311
131 (*left*) © Estate of Zahoor ul Akhlaq/Tate. Purchased with funds provided by the South Asia Acquisitions Committee 2015 T14312
131 (*right*) © Estate of Zahoor ul Akhlaq/Tate. Purchased with funds provided by the South Asia Acquisitions Committee 2015 T14310
132 © Estate of Zahoor ul Akhlaq/Private collection, London/Karachi
133 © The Estate of Howard Hodgkin. All rights reserved, DACS 2023/Private collection, London/Karachi. © 2022 Phillips Auctioneers LLC. All Rights Reserved
134 © The Estate of Howard Hodgkin. All rights reserved, DACS 2023/Private collection, London/Karachi
136 © Estate of Mohan Samant/Courtesy Jhaveri Contemporary/Presented by Jillian Samant (Tate Americas Foundation 2020) L04294
137 © Estate of Mohan Samant/Courtesy the estate of Mohan Samant
138 (*left*) © Estate of Mohan Samant/Courtesy Jhaveri Contemporary/Presented by Jillian Samant (Tate Americas Foundation) 2020 L04295
138 (*right*) © Estate of Mohan Samant/Courtesy the Estate of Mohan Samant
139 © The Estate of Alan Davie. All rights reserved, DACS 2023/National Galleries of Scotland
140 © The artist/Gallery Chemould/Leicester Museums and Galleries L.F35.1990.1-12.0
142 © The artist/Vadehra Art Gallery/Private collection
143 © The artist/Vadehra Art Gallery/Private collection, London/Karachi
144 © The artist/Vadehra Art Gallery/Private collection
145 (*left*) The artist/Vadehra Art Gallery/Private collection
145 (*right*) The artist/Vadehra Art Gallery/Private collection
146 © The artist/Pilar Corrias/Courtesy of the artist
147 (*top*) © The artist/Pilar Corrias/Private collection, London/Karachi
149 (*top*) © The artist/Pilar Corrias/Courtesy of the artist
149 (*bottom*) © The artist/Pilar Corrias/Private collection, London/Karachi
151 © The artist/Private collection
152 © The artist/Private collection, London/Karachi
153 (*both*) © The artist/Deutsche Bank Collection
154 © The artist/Private collection. Photo: Balthazar Serreau
155 (*both*) © The artist/Private collection. Photo: Balthazar Serreau
156 Photo courtesy of Grosvenor Gallery © Olivia Fraser/Private collection
157 Photo courtesy of Grosvenor Gallery © Olivia Fraser/Private collection
159 (and detail p. 158) © The artist/Courtesy Studio RR/Private collection
160 (*left*) © The artist/Courtesy Joost van den Bergh, London
160 (*right*) © The artist, Payal and Anurag Khanna collection, India/Courtesy Joost van den Bergh, London
161 © The artist, Private collection/Courtesy Joost van den Bergh, London
162 (all) © The artist, Payal and Anurag Khanna collection, India/Courtesy Joost van den Bergh, London
163 (top) © The artist, private collection UK/Courtesy Joost van den Bergh, London
163 (*bottom*) © The artist, Payal and Anurag Khanna collection, India/Courtesy Joost van den Bergh, London
164 (through p. 166) © The artists/Guggenheim, Abu Dhabi
167 © The artist/Private collection. Photo: Balthazar Serreau
168 © The artist/collection of Kamran M. Anwar
170 (*left*) © The artist/Private collection
170 (*right*) © The artist/Vanhaerents art collection. Image/Photo: © 2021 Christie's Images Limited
171 © The artist/Courtesy the artist and Lawrie Shabibi
172 © The artist/Courtesy the artist and Kristin Hjellegjerde Gallery/Private collection
173 © The artist/Courtesy the artist and Kristin Hjellegjerde Gallery
174 © The artist/Courtesy the artist
175 © The artist/Courtesy the artist
176 © Raqib Shaw. Photo © Prudence Cuming Associates Ltd. Courtesy of Raqib Shaw and White Cube
179 © N.S. Harsha. Courtesy the artist and Victoria Miro
180 © N.S. Harsha. Courtesy the artist and Victoria Miro
181 © N.S. Harsha. Courtesy the artist and Victoria Miro
182 © The artist/Joost van den Bergh, London
183 © and courtesy Bharti Lalwani and Nicolas Roth
185 © The Singh Twins: www.singhtwins.co.uk
186 © The artist/Joost van den Bergh, London
187 (*both*) © The artist/Joost van den Bergh, London
188 (*left*) © The artist. Photo: Peter Mallet/Private collection, Kent
188 (*right*) © The artist. Photo: Peter Mallet/Private collection
189 (*left*) © The artist. Photo: Peter Mallet/Private collection
189 (*right*) © the artist. Photo: Peter Mallet/Gordon Watson Ltd
191 (*all*) © The artist/Courtesy the artist and Jhaveri Contemporary
192 © The artist/Courtesy the artist and Jhaveri Contemporary
195 © The artist/Courtesy the artist and Jhaveri Contemporary
196 © The artist/Courtesy the artist and Jhaveri Contemporary
198 © The artist/Courtesy the artist
200 detail of p. 128

INDEX OF WORKS

ACKNOWLEDGEMENTS

This publication accompanies the exhibition
Beyond the Page: South Asian Miniature Painting and Britain, 1600 to Now
at MK Gallery, Milton Keynes, from 7 October 2023 to 28 January 2024
and The Box, Plymouth, from 17 February to 2 June 2024.

The exhibition is curated by Hammad Nasar and Anthony Spira with advice from Emily Hannam.
Catalogue entries by Emily Hannam and Cleo Roberts-Komireddi with Elizabeth Brown.

The exhibition and publication would not have been possible without generous support from:

The Bagri Foundation

The Australia Council

and the Circle of Friends, chaired by Tarana Sawhney:

PLATINUM Tarun & Tarana Sawhney; Kirsty and George Anson; Krishna Choudhary; Lady Ghazala Hameed; Taimur Hassan; Jhaveri Contemporary; Vadehra Art Gallery, New Delhi

GOLD Francesca Galloway; The Rangoonwala Foundation; Lawrie Shabibi, Dubai; Pooja Singhal

SILVER Joost van den Bergh; Grosvenor Gallery; Kristin Hjellegjerde; Victoria Miro Gallery

and those who wish to remain anonymous.

This exhibition has been made possible as a result of the Government Indemnity Scheme.
MK Gallery would like to thank HM Government for providing Government Indemnity and the Department for Digital, Culture, Media and Sport and Arts Council England for arranging the indemnity.

MK GALLERY

900 Midsummer Boulevard
Central Milton Keynes MK9 3QA
www.mkgallery.org

MK Gallery brings world-class exhibitions and events
together with pioneering learning and community programmes to Milton Keynes.

MK Gallery gratefully acknowledges regular support form Arts Council England
and Milton Keynes Council.

Registered charity No. 1059678

MK GALLERY TRUSTEES

MK GALLERY

DIRECTOR Anthony Spira

Jamie Aylard, Charlotte Baker, Sophie Bennett, Fay Blanchard, Niki Braithwaite, Roisin Callaghan, Ben Charter, Cherelle Cunningham, Pallavi Ghosh, Madeleine Jordan, Judy Kendrick-Simonsen, Sam Lennon, Monika Lorincova, Rosie May, Leila Matthews, Ben Montgomery, Francis Nielsen, Angus Norton, Andrew Papworth, Annette Parmar, Patrick Phillips, Julia Roach, Tony Thorne, Sonia Tsesarsky, Diana Volokha, Xander Webster, Linda Wright and with thanks to our dedicated team of volunteers.

EXHIBITION TECHNICIANS Philip Amy, Anna Bird, Adam Darby, Nick Duxbury, Lee Farmer, Sam Foley, Suzi Osborn, Thom Rees, Steve Rubacki, Larissa Shaw, Emma Wilde.

Philip Wilson Publishers
Bloomsbury Publishing Plc
50 Bedford Square, London, WC1B 3DP, UK
29 Earlsfort Terrace, Dublin 2, Ireland

Bloomsbury, Philip Wilson Publishers and the Philip Wilson logo are trademarks of Bloomsbury Publishing Plc

Published on the occasion of the exhibition:
Beyond the Page: South Asian Miniature Painting and Britain, 1600 to Now
MK Gallery, 7 October 2023 to 28 January 2024 and The Box, 17 February to 2 June 2024

First published in Great Britain in 2023

A catalogue record for this book is available from the British Library
Library of Congress Cataloguing-in-Publication data has been applied for

ISBN 978-1-7813-0125-8

2 4 6 8 10 9 7 5 3 1

Designed and typeset in Walbaum by illuminati, Grosmont
Printed and bound in Slovenia by DZS Grafik

FSC www.fsc.org MIX Paper | Supporting responsible forestry FSC® C106600